Transcultural Justice at the Tokyo Tribunal

History of Warfare

Editors

Kelly DeVries (*Loyola University Maryland*)
John France (*University of Wales, Swansea*)
Michael S. Neiberg (*United States Army War College, Pennsylvania*)
Frederick Schneid (*High Point University, North Carolina*)

VOLUME 117

The titles published in this series are listed at *brill.com/hw*

Contents

Acknowledgements

The idea for this volume came out of despair: when starting the research group 'Transcultural Justice' at Heidelberg University about war crimes trials in Asia in 2013, surprisingly little was known about the individual national teams which contributed to the Tokyo International Military Tribunal, especially from the 'smaller' nations. It quickly turned out that only a joint scholarly effort, pooling not only expertise but language skills, would be able to close this gap. This book is our modest contribution, and we hope it will inspire many other scholars all over the world to refine its findings.

We are grateful for the generous funding by the German Research Council (DFG), which enabled a workshop at Heidelberg to bring contributors together and discuss first drafts of all chapters in December 2015. The DFG is also to be lauded for funding my own Research Group (see website at www.transcultural-justice.uni-hd.de) at Heidelberg University over the last five years within the framework of the Cluster of Excellence 'Asia and Europe in a Global Context'.

This volume would have been largely impossible without the commitment not only of the contributors, who assembled for this project and devoted all their energy and academic spirit, but also much needed technical support. The manuscript has been put together by Heidelberg-based student assistants Raffaela Graf and Michael Dunn. It received a warm professional welcome from the team at BRILL publishers, was taken good care of by Marcella Mulder, and benefited greatly from the copyediting of Marianne Noble. We would further like to thank the Stillpix section of NARA, College Park, in helping us with the photo section and for their overall generous support, and thank Narrelle Morris and Yuki Takatori for their valuable advice in selecting the photo sample.

There would be no story to tell about the Tokyo tribunal if not for the indefatigable work of hundreds of men and women in 1946-48, in front of and behind the scenes of a remarkable court in Japan, who have been unjustly forgotten. In the year of the judgment's seventieth anniversary, we feel it is high time to remember them, and honour their service in the pursuit of justice, paving the way for international criminal courts as we know them today.

Kerstin von Lingen
Heidelberg, October 2017

List of Illustrations

Notes for Readers

For the sake of consistency for the Index, Japanese names in the notes and bibliography appear in Western style, that is personal names first, followed by surname.

List of Contributors

Milinda Banerjee

is a research fellow at Ludwig-Maximilians-Universität, Munich and an assistant professor, Department of History, Presidency University, Kolkata. From 2013-2016 he was a post-doctoral fellow in the research group 'Transcultural Justice' in the Cluster of Excellence 'Asia and Europe in a Global Context' at Heidelberg University, where he conducted research into the Indian involvement with the Tokyo trial, focusing especially on the judge Radhabinod Pal. His doctoral dissertation (from Heidelberg University), on concepts of rulership and sovereignty in colonial India (ca. 1858-1947), is now forthcoming as a book with Cambridge University Press. He is also co-editor of *Transnational Histories of the 'Royal Nation'* (Cham: Palgrave Macmillan 2017), and author of two published books and several essays at the intersections of South Asian and transregional intellectual history. He published the chapter 'Decolonization, Rule of Law, and Subaltern Sovereignty: India and the Tokyo Trial' in Kerstin von Lingen (ed.), *War Crimes Trials in the Wake of Decolonization and Cold War in Asia, 1945-1956: Justice in Time of Turmoil* (Basingstoke: Palgrave, 2016), pp. 69-91. His current project in Munich relates to a global intellectual history of the Tokyo trial, focusing especially on debates about legal philosophy in the contexts of Cold War and decolonization.

Anja Bihler

is completing her PhD in Chinese studies at the Cluster of Excellence 'Asia and Europe in a Global Context' at Heidelberg University. For her doctoral research, she focuses on war crimes trials under the Chinese Nationalist government between 1946 and 1948. She holds a Magister Artium degree in Chinese studies, economics and law from Ludwig-Maximilians-Universität, Munich and is author of 'Late Republican China and the Development of International Criminal Law: China's Role in the United Nations War Crimes Commission in London and Chungking', in Morten Bergsmo, Cheah Wui Ling and Yi Ping (eds.), *Historical Origins of International Criminal Law*, vol. 1 (Brussels: Torkel Opsahl, 2014), pp. 507-40; as well as of 'The Trial of Japanese War Criminals and the Legacy of Foreign Extraterritoriality in the Republic of China' in Kerstin von Lingen (ed.), *War Crimes Trials in the Wake of Decolonization and Cold War in Asia, 1945-1956: Justice in Time of Turmoil* (Basingstoke: Palgrave, 2016), pp. 93-116.

Neil Boister

professor of law at the University of Canterbury, New Zealand, is the author of a number of texts on the Tokyo war crimes tribunal, including (with Professor Robert Cryer), *The Tokyo International Military Tribunal: A Reappraisal* (Oxford University Press, 2008), described in the *Journal of Japanese Studies* as 'the most complete and objective account of the Tokyo Trials to date'. He also (together with Professor Cryer) edited *Documents on the Tokyo War Crimes Tribunal: Charter, Indictment and Judgments* (Oxford University Press, 2008), 1568 pp., and has published a number of journal articles on the Tokyo war crimes tribunal.

David M. Crowe

is a Presidential Fellow at Chapman University and Professor Emeritus of History at Elon University. He has been a visiting scholar at Columbia University's Harriman Institute and a fellow at the Center for Slavic, Eurasian, and East European Studies at the University of North Carolina, Chapel Hill. His most recent works include *Soviet Criminal Justice under Stalin: 'Show' Trials, War Crimes Trials, and Nuremberg* (Bloomsbury 2018); 'The Allied Occupation of Germany and Japan: A Comparative Study' in Joanne Cho, *Transnational Encounters between Germany and East Asia since 1900* (London: Taylor and Francis, 2017); 'The German Plunder and Theft of Jewish Property in the General Government' in John Michalczyk, *Nazi Law: From Nuremberg to Nuremberg* (London: Bloomsbury, 2017); *Da tu-sha gen-yuan li-shi yu yubo* [The Holocaust: roots, history and aftermath] (Shanghai People's Publishing House, 2015); *Oskar Schindler: Prawdziwa historia* [Oskar Schindler: The true history] (Warsaw: Proswzynski I S-ka, 2015); co-editor, *Germany and China: Transnational Encounters since the 18th Century* (New York: Palgrave Macmillan, 2014); 'Sino-German Relations, 1918-1945' in *Germany and China* (2014) and *War Crimes, Genocide, and Justice: A Global History* (New York: Palgrave Macmillan, 2013). He is currently writing *Raphael Lemkin: The Life of a Visionary* and doing preliminary research for a biography of Pearl S. Buck.

Kerstin von Lingen

is a historian and researcher/lecturer at Heidelberg University at the Cluster of Excellence 'Asia and Europe in a Global Context' and currently a guest professor at the University of Vienna. Since 2013, she has led an independent research project at Heidelberg entitled 'Transcultural Justice: Legal Flows and the Emergence of International Justice within the East Asian War Crimes Trials, 1946-1954', supervising four doctoral dissertations on the Soviet, Chinese, Dutch and French war crimes trial policies in Asia, respectively. Her many publications include two monographs in English, *Kesselring's Last Battle: War*

Crimes Trials and Cold War Politics, 1945-1960 (Lawrence: University of Kansas Press, 2009) and *Allen Dulles, the OSS and Nazi War Criminals: The Dynamics of Selective Prosecution* (Cambridge: Cambridge University Press, 2013), as well as the (co-)edited volumes *War Crimes Trials in the Wake of Decolonization and Cold War in Asia, 1945-1956: Justice in Time of Turmoil* (Basingstoke: Palgrave, 2016) and *War Crimes Trials in Asia: Debating Collaboration and Complicity in the Aftermath of War* (Basingstoke: Palgrave, 2017). In German, she has edited the volumes *Kriegserfahrung und nationale Identität in Europa nach 1945* [War experience and national identity in Europe after 1945] (Paderborn: Schoeningh, 2009), and with Klaus Gestwa, *Zwangsarbeit als Kriegsressource in Europa und Asien* [Forced labour as a resource of war in Europe and Asia] (Paderborn: Schoeningh, 2014).

Narrelle Morris
is a senior lecturer at the Curtin Law School, Curtin University, Western Australia and an honorary research fellow in the Asia Pacific Centre for Military Law at the University of Melbourne. She obtained her PhD in Japanese studies from Murdoch University in 2007 and also holds degrees in Asian studies and law. She is the principal legal researcher on the Australia Research Council (ARC)-funded project 'Australia's Post-World War II War Crimes Trials of the Japanese: A Systematic and Comprehensive Law Reports Series'. She holds an ARC grant for 2014-2017 to research the Australian war crimes investigator and jurist Sir William Flood Webb. Her book *Japan-bashing: Anti-Japanism since the 1980s* was published by Routledge in 2010. She is co-editor of and contributor to *Australia's War Crimes Trials 1945-51* (Leiden: Brill | Nijhoff, 2016), which was shortlisted for the New South Wales Premier's Prize for Australian History in 2017. She is also the author of a number of journal articles on war crimes, which have been published in the *Journal of International Criminal Justice*; *Journal of Pacific History, Intelligence & National Security*; and *European Journal of International Law*.

Hitoshi Nagai
is a professor at the Hiroshima Peace Institute of Hiroshima City University. He majors in modern Japanese history mainly focusing on Japan-Philippines relations, and was a visiting fellow at Ateneo Center for Asian Studies (ACAS) of Ateneo de Manila University from June 2016 to March 2017. He is the author of *Firipin to Tainichi Senpan Saiban, 1945-1953* [The War Crimes Trials and Japan-Philippines Relations, 1945-1953] (Tokyo: Iwanami Shoten, 2010), *Firipin BC-kyū Senpan Saiban* [The BC Class War Crimes Trials in the Philippines] (Tokyo:

Kodansha, 2013) and *Philippines-Japan Relations* (co-authored) (Quezon City: Ateneo de Manila University Press, 2003).

Valentyna Polunina

is a researcher in Russian-Asian studies at Ludwigs-Maximilians-Universität in Munich. She completed her PhD in history at the Cluster of Excellence 'Asia and Europe in a Global Context' at Heidelberg University with her project 'Soviet War Crimes trials policy in the Far East: the bacteriological warfare trial at Khabarovsk (1949)'. She holds a magister in international relations from Kiev State University and a Masters in peace and conflict studies from Marburg University, and has gained experience as a student research assistant in the International Centre for the Research and Documentation of War Crimes Trials. She is the author of 'Soviet War Crimes Policy in the Far East: The Bacteriological Warfare Trial at Khabarovsk, 1949' in Morten Bergsmo, Cheah Wui Ling and Yi Ping (eds.), *Historical Origins of International Criminal Law*, vol. 2 (Brussels: Torkel Opsahl, 2014), pp. 539-62; and 'The Khabarovsk Trial: The Soviet Riposte to the Tokyo Tribunal' in Kirsten Sellars (ed.), *Trials for International Crimes in Asia* (Cambridge University Press, 2015), pp. 121-44; and 'From Tokyo to Khabarovsk – Soviet War Crimes Trials in Asia as Cold War Battlefields', in Kerstin von Lingen (ed.), *War Crimes Trials in the Wake of Decolonization and Cold War in Asia, 1945-1956: Justice in Time of Turmoil* (Basingstoke: Palgrave, 2016), pp. 239-60.

Ann-Sophie Schoepfel

completed her doctoral thesis on French war crimes trials policy in Japan and in Indochina in the wake of decolonization within the Cluster of Excellence 'Asia and Europe in a Global Context' at Heidelberg University. She holds an MA in history (Tübingen University and Aix-en-Provence University) and in legal anthropology (Strasbourg University). She is the author of 'War Court as a Form of State Building: The French Prosecution of Japanese War Crimes at the Saigon and Tokyo Trials', in Morten Bergsmo, Cheah Wui Ling and Yi Ping (eds.), *Historical Origins of International Criminal Law*, vol. 2 (Brussels: Torkel Opsahl, 2014), pp. 119-42 and 'La voix des juges français dans les procès de Nuremberg et de Tokyo, Défense d'une idée de justice universelle', *Guerres Mondiales et Conflits Contemporains*, 249 (2013), 101-14; as well as 'Defending French National Interests? The Quai d'Orsay, Ambassador Zinovy Peshkoff, Justice Henri Bernard and the Tokyo Trial' in Kerstin von Lingen (ed.), *War Crimes Trials in the Wake of Decolonization and Cold War in Asia, 1945-1956: Justice in Time of Turmoil* (Basingstoke: Palgrave, 2016), p. 167-94.

Lisette Schouten

completed her PhD in history in the Cluster of Excellence 'Asia and Europe in a Global Context' at Heidelberg University. Her research focuses on Dutch war crimes trial policy in the Netherlands East Indies and Japan, 1945-1955. She also holds an MA from Leiden University and is the author of 'From Tokyo to the United Nations: B.V.A. Röling, International Criminal Jurisdiction and the Debate on Establishing an International Criminal Court, 1949-1957' in Morten Bergsmo, Cheah Wui Ling and Yi Ping (eds.), *Historical Origins of International Criminal Law*, vol. 2 (Brussels: Torkel Opsahl, 2014), pp. 170-210; 'Colonial justice at the Netherlands Indies war crimes trials' in Kirsten Sellars (ed.), *Trials for International Crimes in Asia* (Cambridge University Press, 2016), pp. 75-99; and 'Netherlands East Indies' War Crime Trials in the Face of Decolonization' in Kerstin von Lingen (ed.), *War Crimes Trials in the Wake of Decolonization and Cold War in Asia, 1945-1956: Justice in Time of Turmoil* (Basingstoke: Palgrave 2016), pp. 195-220.

James Burnham Sedgwick

is an assistant professor and a Harrison McCain Emerging Scholar at Acadia University in Nova Scotia, Canada. He holds a PhD in history from the University of British Columbia, an MA in history from the University of Canterbury (New Zealand), and served as a visiting scholar at the Strassler Center for Holocaust and Genocide Studies at Clark University in Worcester, Massachusetts. An international historian of global governance, human rights, mass violence, and justice, he has published articles and reviews in multiple fields, including law, international relations, history and Asian studies. He is the author of 'A People's Court: Emotion, Participant Experiences, and the Shaping of Postwar Justice at the International Military Tribunal for the Far East, 1946-1948', *Diplomacy & Statecraft*, 22 (2011), 480-99; 'Memory on Trial: Constructing and Contesting the "Rape of Nanking" at the International Military Tribunal for the Far East, 1946-1948', *Modern Asian Studies*, 43, 1229-54; 'Brother, Black Sheep, or Bastard? Situating the Tokyo Trial in the Nuremberg Legacy, 1946-1948' in Beth Griech-Polelle (ed.), *The Nuremberg Trials and Their Policy Consequences Today* (Baden-Baden: Nomos Verlag, 2008), pp. 63-76 and *The Justice E.H. Northcroft Tokyo War Crimes Trial Collection: A Working Inventory* (Christchurch: University of Canterbury Library, 2004). He is currently completing a manuscript entitled 'Inside Justice: Being International in Postwar Tokyo, 1946-1948'.

Yuki Takatori

is an associate professor of Japanese at Georgia State University (Atlanta, USA). She is the author of 'America's War Crimes Trial? Commonwealth leadership at the International Military Tribunal for the Far East (1946-48)', *Journal of Imperial and Commonwealth History*, 35:4 (2007), 548-68; and the translator of *The Tokyo Trial: A Bibliographic Guide to English-Language Sources* (Tokyo: Gendai Shiryō Shuppan, 2001). During 2012-15, she was involved in the production and translation of a four-part TV series, *Tokyo Trial*, directed by Pieter Verhoeff and Rob King, and aired on NHK, the national public broadcaster in Japan, from 12-15 December 2016.

Urs Matthias Zachmann
is Professor for Culture and History of Modern Japan at Freie Universität (FU) Berlin. Before that, he was the Handa Professor of Japanese-Chinese Relations at the University of Edinburgh, Scotland. He is a graduate from Heidelberg Law School (1998) and obtained a PhD (Heidelberg 2006) and Habilitation (LMU Munich 2010) in Japanese studies. His fields of specialization are the history of North-east Asia's international and transcultural relations, the history of political ideas and the history of law (particularly international law) in this region. In 2013, he published a monograph (in German) on the development of international legal thought in Japan, 1919-60. He is currently preparing a revised and expanded study of Japan's engagement with international law for English-speaking audiences.

Introduction

Kerstin von Lingen

War crimes trials after the Second World War, in particular the first two International Military Tribunals at Nuremberg (IMT) and at Tokyo (IMTFE), claimed to be enforcing 'justice', but nevertheless proved to be battlegrounds for intense political and ideological struggle within the new post-war world order.[1] They have contributed to the development of international criminal law, the formation of transcultural norms of legality and legitimacy, as well as transnationally debated (and contested) notions of justice. While this certainly holds true for the tribunal at Nuremberg, which is often cited as the legal forerunner to key institutions of international justice, such as, for example, the International Criminal Court, active since 2002, or the Yugoslavia and Rwanda tribunals, the legacy of the Tokyo tribunal had practically fallen into oblivion in the West until its scholarly awakening with R. John Pritchard's laudable publication of the trial transcripts in 1981.[2] This is all the more surprising as the tribunal started with high hopes on the part of the Western Allies and all convening parties at the judge's bench for achieving a second 'Nuremberg'.

The present volume aims at reassessing the Tokyo tribunal by foregrounding its members and thereby emphasizing its transcultural nature and the 'legal flows' emanating from it. The Tokyo IMT was not only one of the first international tribunals in history, but was at the same time the first 'interracial and multilingual criminal trial'.[3] Its eleven judges and prosecution teams, as well as a team of Western and Japanese defence attorneys, brought together not only different national backgrounds, languages and ideologies, but at the same time different perceptions of justice, deriving from very different legal traditions, personal training and different experience with courts and – as this was a new thing – international military trials. War crimes trials like the Tokyo tribunal are thus to be studied not only as the scene of battles for justice between defence and prosecution, or as arenas for abstract struggles amongst political interests and ideological principles, but as arenas of constant negotiation. The

---

1   The author wishes to thank Neil Boister, David Crowe, Yuki Takatori and Milinda Banerjee for commenting on the draft.

2   R.J. Pritchard, S.M. Zaide and D.C. Watt, *The Tokyo War Crimes Trial. Transcripts and Index*, 22 vols. (New York: Garland 1981).

3   This was noted for the first time by G. Ireland, 'Uncommon Law in Martial Tokyo', *The Yearbook of World Affairs*, 4 (1950), 54-104, 66.

© KONINKLIJKE BRILL NV, LEIDEN, 2018 | DOI 10.1163/9789004361058_002

courtroom assembled in a small space dozens, sometimes even hundreds, of individuals, each of them bringing strengths and weaknesses to their role in the courtroom drama. It is thus important that research takes a closer look at the impact of the different cultural, linguistic, political and legal traditions of the various participants on the tribunal's planning and operation. This volume aims at restoring agency to all eleven national teams, judges and prosecutors, thus better situating the significance of individual contributions to verdicts, and thus bringing back to the centre the national positions of countries which have been sidelined as 'minor' players in the Tokyo trial. It also needs to be contextualized whether all actors involved were serving a national agenda or, on the contrary, used this occasion to display forcefully their personal opinion even against the instructions received from their home capital, as the French, Dutch and Indian examples will show.

Furthermore, the volume contextualizes these legal agents as products of transnational forces, constituted through dialogues about legal concepts, frameworks of international legal institutions, and processes of faction-making. It brings together recent scholarship on the global interconnectedness of war crimes policy in East Asia, foregrounding the Allied powers which sent judges to sit on the Tokyo Military Tribunal and the Japanese legal community's perception of the trial, which is framed under the provocative heading of 'loser's justice'. The method adopted combines historical and legal research with intellectual history, network and actor-centred analysis and biographical sources, using trial papers, public and private archives, and minutes of international bodies like the *United Nations War Crimes Commission* (UNWCC), adding also elements from political science perspectives (especially, the theory of transitional justice).

The authors draw attention to judges from the United States, the United Kingdom, Australia, France, the Netherlands, China, the Philippines, New Zealand, Canada, India and the USSR, as well as offering a comprehensive analysis of the building of majorities and alliances at Tokyo. This analysis is complemented by a study of the Japanese defence lawyers' team, which grappled with Allied strategic considerations and Anglo-American juridical principles, but who also subverted them by bringing their own juridical, political and moral viewpoints into play.

The Tokyo Tribunal

The Tokyo tribunal was held from May 1946 until November 1948 under its official heading 'International Military Tribunal for the Far East' (IMTFE). The name, as Boister and Cryer have noted, echoes an orientalist approach and would therefore be better replaced by either 'Tokyo tribunal' or 'Tokyo IMT'.[4] In total, the tribunal consisted of eleven judges and national prosecution teams, and a mixed Japanese-US team of defence lawyers. It indicted twenty-eight defendants, amongst them former prime ministers, cabinet ministers, military leaders and diplomats, and displayed an impressive list of fifty-five charges. The judgment was not unanimous: besides a majority judgment, there were two concurring opinions and three dissenting opinions.

The idea of holding an international trial in Tokyo goes back to the Potsdam Declaration by the Western Allies, which proclaimed on 26 July 1945 with respect to Japan in Article 10 that 'stern justice shall be meted out to all war criminals, including those who have visited cruelties upon our prisoners'.[5] After the US had dropped atomic bombs on Hiroshima and Nagasaki, Japan formally surrendered on 2 September 1945; thereby, the Potsdam Declaration was also accepted.[6] The US State, War and Navy Department Coordinating Committee (SWNCC) which had been entrusted with coordinating US Foreign Policy with a view to Japan became the driving force behind planning the tribunal. Together with the US Supreme Commander for the Allied Powers (SCAP), Douglas MacArthur, SWNCC invited on 26 August 1945 the UK, China, Australia, Canada, the Netherlands, New Zealand and France to join the Far Eastern Advisory Committee (FEAC), to coordinate steps concerning the Japanese surrender with the main Allies from the Pacific War. On 7 October 1945, India and the Philippines joined the FEAC out of political considerations. Several drafts by SWNCC about the international court to be set up were debated and the initial FEAC members already invited to search for suitable candidates, but only after a Moscow conference of 26 December 1945 did the Soviet Union also agree to join and thus complete the circle of Allies. Subsequently, the FEAC was renamed the Far Eastern Commission (FEC).[7]

On 19 January 1946, SCAP proclaimed the Tokyo Charter, modelled after the Nuremberg Charter,[8] in which Article 2 defined that the court would consist of

---

4   N. Boister and R. Cryer, *The Tokyo International Military Tribunal: A Reappraisal* (Oxford University Press, 2008), p. 3.

5   Proclamation Defining Terms for Japanese Surrender, Issued at Potsdam, July 26, 1945, in The Ministry of Foreign Affairs 'Nihon Gaikō Nenpyō Narabini Shuyō Bunsho: 1840-1945', vol. 2, 1966. Online at <http://www.ndl.go.jp/constitution/e/etc/co6.html> (accessed 27 July 2016).

6   Boister and Cryer, *Tokyo IMT*, p. 21.

7   Ibid., p. 24.

8   There is evidence that Joseph Keenan led the drafting of the Charter, see P.R. Piccigallo, *The Japanese on Trial: Allied War Crimes Operations in the East, 1945-1951* (Austin:

no more than nine judges, which would represent the powers that had signed the instrument of surrender. As already in Nuremberg, the Tokyo Charter also centred on the charge of 'crimes against peace', whilst 'crimes against humanity' became bound to 'aggression' and 'war crimes'.[9] The Tokyo tribunal focused on the so-called 'class A' war criminals, who were charged with crimes against peace.[10] While the selection of judges for Tokyo was in process, the US held two military trials, one against General Tomoyuki Yamashita and one against General Masaharu Homma in Manila; both commanders were found guilty and sentenced to death before the Tokyo trial even started. The trials later became the object of much criticism for their haste and legal flaws, and many journalists sensed a personal revenge on the part of MacArthur in conducting them.[11]

On 15 February 1946, MacArthur appointed the nine judges who had been put forward by the nine signatory states of the Japanese surrender.[12] The US, in particular, hoped that by holding the trial it would be possible to criminalize 'the Germans and Japanese for starting the war in order to justify, respectively, breaching their own neutrality against Germany, and succumbing to military defeats at the hands of Japan'.[13] They hoped the Tokyo judgment would 'confirm Nuremberg's determinations on aggressive warfare'.[14]

The limitation on the surrender signatories prompted some criticism in the FEC, where India as well as the Philippines held a seat, and in view of their wartime services rendered they successfully claimed a seat on the bench. The Charter was amended to eleven judges on 26 April 1946 and India and the Philippines were invited to also nominate a judge.[15] The new Charter provided

---

University of Texas Press, 1979), p. 11. In contrast, R.J. Pritchard (ed.), *The Tokyo Major War Crimes Trial: The Records for the International Military Tribunal for the Far East with an Authoritative Commentary and Comprehensive Guide*, 124 vols. (Lewinston: Edwin Mellen Press, 1998-2005), p. xix argues against Keenan's role.

9   C.M. Bassiouni, '"Crimes against Humanity". The Need for a Specialized Convention', *Columbia Journal of Transnational Law*, 31 (1993-1994), 457-94, 463.

10   Boister and Cryer, *Tokyo IMT*, p. 49.

11   On the controversy, see D. Crowe, *War Crimes, Genocide and Justice* (New York: Palgrave MacMillan, 2014), p. 199.

12   Boister and Cryer, *Tokyo IMT*, p. 26.

13   K. Sellars, 'William Patrick and "Crimes Against Peace" at the Tokyo Tribunal, 1946-1948', *The Edinburgh Law Review*, 15(2) (2011), 166-96, 168.

14   Ibid., 169.

15   *Foreign Relations of the United States* (hereafter *FRUS*), *1946*, 'Far Eastern Commission policy decision FEC 007/3,' 3 April 1946, United States, Department of State, vol. 8 (Washington DC: USGPO, 1971), p. 424-27.

that six members were enough to convene the tribunal, and a majority of all members constituted a quorum.[16] Thus Tokyo was soon also to become the largest war crimes tribunal in history, consisting of eleven judges. Due to this late decision, however, when the IMTFE opened on 3 May 1946 in Tokyo, only the initially nominated nine judges had so far arrived in Japan.

The judges selected were Sir William Flood Webb for Australia as president of the court, Lord William Patrick for the United Kingdom, Edward Stuart McDougall for Canada, Erima Harvey Northcroft for New Zealand, Mei Ru'ao for China, Ivan Zaryanov on behalf of the Soviet Union, Bernard Röling for the Netherlands, Henri Bernard representing Free France, Radhabinod Pal as the Indian judge, and Delfin Jaranilla for the Philippines. The US had first sent J.P. Higgins, who was, however, replaced after six weeks by Myron C. Cramer as US judge. None of them spoke Japanese. The fact that six of the eleven judges were familiar with Anglo-American common law influenced the tribunal quite heavily, and was seen as a disadvantage by those affected.[17]

Also, the prosecution was organized under US leadership, as Joseph Keenan headed the International Prosecution Section (IPS), and all national teams sent in their 'associate prosecutors'. There was also a mixed defence team: because of the problem that Japanese attorneys were acquainted neither with English nor with the legal procedure, a US team was sent to enforce the defence.[18] Every nation was responsible for a certain period within the trial, which was connected to several charges which were of special importance to the nation in charge. However, the lack of an overall and joint strategy resulted in an unbalanced trial conduct, as well as a distorted space to manoeuvre its outcome, which in the end threatened the overall mission to bring about 'justice'.

It has been an often heard complaint that the trial was not planned as a joint effort of the eleven nations involved, but was imposed on many of the participating nations on arrival. This view emphasizes the US dominance of the trial and the internal dynamics, where not all were considered to be in the front row of preparations. On the other hand, Tokyo also gave the smaller Allied nations a voice in the trial – unlike at Nuremberg, where only four of the victorious powers took a seat. Thus it is maybe be fair to state that Tokyo produced a broader variety of meanings of justice than Nuremberg.

---

16   Boister and Cryer, *Tokyo IMT*, p. 27.

17   Crowe, *War Crimes, Genocide and Justice*, p. 209; Boister and Cryer, *Tokyo IMT*, p. 82.

18   R. Minear, *Victors' Justice: The Tokyo War Crimes Trial* (Princeton University Press, 1971), p. 23.

Scholarship

While scholarship on the Tokyo trial in Japan is very comprehensive and there is a huge field of research, decades old, started off by the seminal studies of Kentarō Awaya and Yoshinobu Higurashi,[19] few studies by Japanese scholars have also been published in English or were completely written in English.[20] Thus English scholarship started comparatively late, and was for a long time dominated by the debate on whether it represented a sort of 'victors' justice' (to cite the famous, but often misunderstood book title of political scientist Richard Minear[21]) on the part of the Allied powers. Piccigallo[22] published a seminal study in 1979 of war crimes trials in Asia, which provided a solid basis for future research. The concentration of scholarship on the US influence within the tribunal, and the critique of the trial as an 'American show', obscures the role of the ten other delegations, and does not explain the dissenting opinions – which needs to be contextualized within the domestic politics of the involved nations, and linked to the foreign policy ambitions of ascending or declining colonial powers in regard to the leading US view.

---

19   K. Awaya, 粟屋憲太郎. *Tōkyō Saiban ron* 東京裁判論 [Views on the Tokyo Trial] (Tokyo: Ōtsuki Shoten, 1989); K. Awaya, 粟屋憲太郎. *Tōkyō Saiban e no michi* 東京裁判への道 [Road to the Tokyo Trial], 2 vols. (Tokyo: Kōdansha, 2006); Y. Higurashi, 日暮吉延. *Tōkyō Saiban no kokusai kankei: kokusai seiji ni okeru kenryoku to kihan* 東京裁判の国際関係: 国際政治における権力と規範 [International relations at the Tokyo Trial: Power and norms in foreign policy] (Tokyo: Bokutakusha, 2002); N. Kojima 児島襄. *Tōkyō Saiban* 東京裁判 [The Tokyo Trial], 2 vols. (Tokyo: Chūō Kōronsha, 1971); Y. Ōnuma, 大沼保昭. *Tōkyō Saiban kara sengo sekinin no shisō e* 東京裁判から戦後責任への思想へ [From the Tokyo Trial to the doctrine of post-war responsibility] (Tokyo: Yūshindō, 1985); K. Takeda, 武田珂代子. *Tōkyō Saiban ni okeru tsūyaku* 東京裁判における通訳 [Interpreting at the Tokyo Trial] (Tokyo: Misuzu Shobō, 2008). The author wishes to thank Yuki Takatori for a rough translation of the titles.

20   Y. Totani, *The Tokyo War Crimes Trial: The Pursuit of Justice in the Wake of World War II* (Cambridge, Mass.: Harvard University Asia Centre, 2008); H. Hayashi, 'British War Crimes Trials of Japanese', *Nature-People-Society: Science and the Humanities*, No. 31, July 2001, online journal at <http://www.geocities.jp/hhhirofumi/engo8.htm> (last accessed August 4, 2016); M. Futamura, *War Crimes Tribunals and Transitional Justice* (New York: Routledge, 2008); K. Takeda, *Interpreting the Tokyo War Crimes Tribunal* (Tokyo: Misuzu Shobō, 2010); N. Nakazato, *Neonationalist Mythology in Postwar Japan: Pal's Dissenting Judgment at the Tokyo War Crimes Tribunal* (Lanham: Lexington Books, 2016).

21   Minear, *Victors' Justice*.

22   Piccigallo, *The Japanese on Trial*.

English-language scholarship on the Tokyo trial started comparatively recently (one early article from 1950 by Horwitz,[23] a member of the US staff who gave an overview, being the exception), and can be contrasted with the vast and early scholarship on the Nuremberg trial. The delay in research was partly due to the trial's much more complex nature and duration, but also on the unavailability of primary sources, as the huge amount of trial transcripts was published in twenty-two volumes and given an index only decades after the event (Pritchard with Zaide (1981) republished in 1998 a larger edition, selected parts including indictment, sentence and dissenting votes edited anew by Boister and Cryer in 2008[24]). The late publication of transcripts allowed, however, the inclusion of introductory essays, as in Pritchard's first edition (1981). Pritchard was also the author of the five-volume companion *Comprehensive Index and Guide.*[25] Wells published a collection focusing on the exhibits of the trial.[26] The Japanese newspaper *Asahi Shinbun* published a collection of news reports from 1947-49 on the Tokyo tribunal in nine volumes, which were in 1995 abridged to a two-volume paperback study edition.[27] The editions complement each other, but require scholarly access to trial transcripts. Not all significant documents are published – personal witness accounts, memoirs, newspaper articles, and the like have largely been ignored in this corpus, or have just been referred to in passing. Some scholarship is available on the impact of the Tokyo trial on Japanese criminal law.[28]

Since 2008, the studies of the IMTFE written by the historian Yuma Totani,[29] and the legal scholars Neil Boister and Robert Cryer (working together)[30] and Kirsten Sellars[31] have enhanced historical and legal scholarship substantially.

---

23   S. Horwitz, 'The Tokyo trial', *International Conciliation* 28 (1950), 475-588.

24   N. Boister and R. Cryer (eds.), *Documents on the Tokyo International Military Tribunal: Charter, Indictments and Judgments* (Oxford University Press, 2008).

25   R.J. Pritchard and S.M. Zaide, *The Tokyo War Crimes Trial: Comprehensive Index and Guide to the Proceedings of the International Military Tribunal for the Far East* (New York: Garland, 1987).

26   K.M. Wells, *Index to the Records of the International Military Tribunal for the Far East* (Christchurch: University of Canterbury Press, 1983).

27   Asahi Shinbun, Tōkyō Saiban Kishadan. 朝日新聞東京裁判記者団. *Tōkyō Saiban* 東京裁判 [*The Tokyo Trial*] (Tokyo: Asahi Shinbunsha, 1995).

28   P. Osten, *Der Tokioter Kriegsverbrecherprozeß und die japanische Rechtswissenschaft* (Berliner Wissenschaftsverlag, 2003); U.M. Zachmann, *Völkerrechtsdenken und Außenpolitik in Japan, 1919-1960* (Baden-Baden: Nomos, 2013).

29   Totani, *Tokyo War Crimes Trial.*

30   Boister and Cryer, *Tokyo IMT.*

31   K. Sellars, *'Crimes Against Peace' and International Law* (Cambridge University Press, 2013).

The present volume goes beyond recent scholarship on the IMTFE, such as is embodied in English by Tanaka, McCormack and Simpson, entitled *Beyond Victor's Justice?*,[32] which offers five select biographies of the eleven judges but without raising any broader reflection on the role of judicial biographies in legal-historical research. Kushner offered a first comprehensive study on the Chinese perception of Justice in Asia.[33] In 2016, the Melbourne-based project group around Tim McCormack, Georgina Fitzpatrick and Narrelle Morris published a volume on the Australian trials in Asia, which also takes the Tokyo IMTFE into consideration.[34] Recently, the volume of Wilson, Cribb, Trefalt and Aszkielowicz has added substantially towards the question of dealing with Japanese War Criminals, and its chapter on Tokyo is a substantial part thereof.[35]

The developing scholarship on the Tokyo trial grew in parallel with research on the topic of war crimes trials policy in East Asia, which had long been marginalized in scholarship. For decades, Piccigallo[36] (1979) was the major reference work. Following research on Japanese war crimes in the Pacific by Tanaka[37] (1996), interest shifted subsequently from the nature of crimes to their punishment, and British (Pritchard 1996[38]) or US war crimes policy were among the first research fields (Maguire 2000).[39] Gong linked the East Asian retribution and war crime trials issue with transitional judicial concepts and the impact of the trials on memory (2002),[40] which has since received further elaboration on the question of memory and guilt (see for example Jager and

---

32   Y. Tanaka, T. McCormack and G. Simpson (eds.), *Beyond Victor's Justice? The Tokyo War Crimes Trial Revisited* (Leiden: Martinus Nijhoff, 2011).

33   B. Kushner, *Men to Devils, Devils to Men: Japanese War Crimes and Chinese Justice* (Harvard University Press, 2015).

34   Tim McCormack, Georgina Fitzpatrick, and Narrelle Morris, eds., *Australia's War Crimes Trials, 1945-1951*. (Leiden: Brill, 2016).

35   Sandra Wilson, Robert Cribb, Beatrice Trefalt and Dean Aszkielowicz, *Japanese War Criminals: The Politics of Justice after the Second World War* (New York: Columbia University Press, 2017).

36   Piccigallo, *The Japanese on Trial*.

37   Y. Tanaka, *Hidden Horrors. Japanese War Crimes in World War II* (Westview: Boulder 1996).

38   R.J. Pritchard, 'The Gift of Clemency Following British War Crimes Trials in the Far East, 1946-1948,' *Criminal Law Forum*, 7:1 (1996), 15-50.

39   Peter Maguire, *Law and War: An American Story* (New York: University of Columbia, 2000).

40   G.W. Gong (ed.), *Memory and History in East and South East Asia: Issues of Identity in International Relations* (Washington: Center for Strategic and International Studies, 2002).

Mitter;[41] Gallicchio;[42] Hasegawa and Tōgō;[43] Kushner;[44] Trefalt, Brawley and Dixon[45]).

Of course, the Tokyo tribunal is also mentioned in passing in general studies on post-war Japan: historians such as Richard Frank have examined the process of the end of empire, Lori Watt has looked at repatriation of war criminals; Herbert Bix scrutinized the larger role of the emperor; and John Dower examined the occupation within Japan.[46]

Historical studies following biographical approaches have for a long time avoided the trials as a field of research, and apart from personal recollections and the vast memoir literature of Japanese defendants,[47] or written by defence lawyers available only in Japanese,[48] or more journalistic accounts of the trial,[49] have not focused on legal staff. If attention was given, then the focus lay exclusively on the authors of dissenting opinions, such as the Dutch judge Bernard

41   S.M. Jager and R. Mitter, *Ruptured Histories: War, Memory and Post-Cold War in Asia* (Harvard University Press, 2007).

42   M. Gallicchio, *The Unpredictability of the Past: Memories of the Asia-Pacific War in US-East Asian Relations* (Durham: Duke University Press, 2007).

43   T. Hasegawa and K. Tōgō, *East-Asia's Haunted Present: Historical Memories and the Resurgence of Nationalism* (Westport: Praeger Security International, 2008).

44   B. Kushner, 'Pawns of Empire: Postwar Taiwan, Japan and the Dilemma of War Crimes', *Japanese Studies*, (Special issue on Japan and Taiwan), vol. 30, no. 1 (May 2010), 111-33.

45   B. Trefalt, S. Brawley and C. Dixon (eds.), *Competing Voices From The Pacific War* (Berkeley University Press, 2009).

46   R. Frank, *Downfall: The End of the Imperial Japanese Empire* (New York: Random House, 1999); L. Watt, *When Empire Comes Home: Repatriation and Reintegration in Postwar Japan* (Harvard University Press, 2009); H. Bix, *Hirohito and the Making of Modern Japan* (Hamburg: HarperCollins Publishers, 2000); J. Dower, *Embracing Defeat: Japan in the Wake of World War II* (New York: W.W. Norton & Co.1999).

47   K. Kobori, *The Tokyo Trials: The Unheard Defense* (Rockport, Maine: New England History Press, 2003); C. Hosoya, N. Andō, Y. Ōnuma, and R. Minear, *The Tokyo War Crimes Trial: An International Symposium* (Tokyo: Kodansha, 1986), for more on the Japanese perspective.

48   I. Kiyose 清瀬一郎, *Hiroku Tōkyō Saiban* 秘録東京裁判 [A secret history of the Tokyo Trial] (Tokyo: Yomiuri Shinbunsha, 1967); Y. Sugawara 菅原裕, *Tōkyō Saiban no shōtai* 東京裁判の正体 [The truth about the Tokyo Trial] (Tokyo: Kokusho Kankōkai, 2002); K. Takayanagi 高柳賢三, *Kyokutō saiban to kokusaihō: Kyokutō Kokusai Gunji Saibansho ni okeru benron* 極東裁判と国際法: 極東国際軍事裁判所における弁論 [The Far East Trial and international law: The arguments presented at the International Military Tribunal for the Far East] (Tokyo: Yūhikaku, 1948); M. Takigawa 滝川政次郎, *Tōkyō Saiban o sabaku* 東京裁判をさばく [A judgment of the Tokyo Trial], 2 vols. (Tokyo: Tōwasha, 1962).

49   A.C. Brackman, *The Other Nuremberg: The Untold Story of the Tokyo War Crimes Trials* (New York: William Morrow and Company, 1987).

V.A. Röling[50] and the Indian judge Radhabinod Pal,[51] as well as on a much smaller scale on the French judge Henri Bernard, who had tried his utmost to obscure his tracks and destroyed most of his private papers.[52] Pal, in particular, has developed over the years into a kind of heroic figure amongst right-wing Japanese nationalists (Nakajima;[53] English language analysis available with Ushimura;[54] Nakazato[55]). Among the judges, only Röling has given biographic accounts and drawn a line of continuity between post-war justice and today's international legal challenges (Cassese and Röling 1993), although this volume, considering its style, seems more a personal narrative than a historical or legal analysis.

In the last decade, research into the Tokyo tribunal has regained momentum. New studies on the Tokyo trial show the entanglement of Allied policy considerations and the rule of law, as visible in Ushimura,[56] and Futamura,[57]

---

50   R. Cryer, 'Röling in Tokyo. A Dignified Dissenter', *Journal of International Criminal Justice*, 8 (2010), 1109-26; R. Cryer, 'Röling (The Netherlands)' in Tanaka, McCormack and Simpson, *Beyond Victor's justice? The Tokyo War Crimes Trial Revisited* (Leiden: Martinus Nijhoff, 2011), pp. 109-26.

51   A. Nandy, 'The Other Within: The Strange Case of Radhabinod Pal's Judgment on Culpability', *New Literary History*, 23, 1, (1992), 45-67; E.S. Kopelman, 'Ideology and International Law: The Dissent of the Indian Justice at the Tokyo War Crimes Trial', *New York University Journal of International Law and Politics*, 23 (1991), 373-444; T. Brook, 'Radhabinod Pal on the Rape of Nanking: The Tokyo Judgment and the Guilt of History' in B.T. Wakabayashi (ed.), *The Nanking Atrocity 1937-38: Complicating the Picture* (New York: Berghahn 2007), pp. 149-78; Shamsur Rahman, 'Judgment of Justice Radhabinod Pal at the Tokyo War Crimes Trial, 1946-48', *Journal of the Asiatic Society of Bangladesh*, 55, 1 (2010); T. Nakajima, 'Justice Pal (India)' in Tanaka, McCormack and Simpson, *Beyond Victor's justice?*, pp. 127-44 ; L. Varadarajan, 'The Trials of Imperialism: Radhabinot Pal's Dissent at the Tokyo Tribunal', *European Journal of International Relations* (Dec. 2014), 1-24.

52   J. Esmein, 'Le Juge Henri Bernard au Procès de Tokyo', *Vingtième Siècle. Revue d'histoire*, 59 (1998), 3-14; M. Ho Foui Sang, 'Justice Bernard (France)' in Tanaka, McCormack and Simpson, *Beyond Victor's Justice?*, pp. 93-102.

53   T. Nakajima 中島岳志, Pâru hanji Tōkyō saiban hihan to zettai heiwa-shugi パール判事 – 東京裁判批判と絶対平和主義 [Justice Pal: Criticisms of the Tokyo trial and absolute pacifism] (Tokyo: Hakusuisha, 2007).

54   K. Ushimura, 'Pal's "Dissentient" Judgment Reconsidered: Some Notes on Postwar Japan's Responses to the Opinion', *Japan Review*, 19 (2007), 215-24.

55   N. Nakazato, *Neonationalist Mythology in Postwar Japan: Pal's Dissenting Judgment at the Tokyo War Crimes Tribunal* (Lanham: Lexington Books, 2016).

56   K. Ushimura, *Beyond the 'Judgment of Civilization'* (LTCB International Library Section no. 14 and published by the International House of Japan in 2003); Original title: 'Bunmei no sabaki' o koete – Tainichi senpan saiban dokkai no kokoromi「文明の裁き」をこえて – 対日戦犯裁判読解の試み (Chūō kōron shinsha, 2001).

57   M. Futamura, *War Crimes Tribunals and Transitional Justice*.

as well as Higurashi[58] and Hayashi[59] (the latter two only in Japanese). The multi-authored volume in French edited by Annette Wieviorka[60] followed a more global approach and has addressed the legal aspects of both international trials and compared their legacies.

The present volume brings together fresh research by historians and legal scholars alike on the political contexts in which new norms and practices of international criminal law emerged after 1945 in Asia, studying how the Tokyo tribunal operated under the impact of external political and legal pressures, while also evolving new standards and debates that left a global impact beyond Japan. Some of the contributors to this volume have previously worked on biographical approaches to the judges of the Tokyo tribunal (Takatori on the dismissed US judge Higgins,[61] Schoepfel on Bernard,[62] Banerjee on Pal,[63] Nagai on Jaranilla[64]). Boister, as cited, has issued a legal analysis together with Robert Cryer, and Crowe has given a comprehensive overview of the trial in his study on genocide.[65]

Critiquing the Tokyo Tribunal

From the outset, the tribunal suffered from several flaws. This volume builds on existing scholarship and thus does not comprehensively discuss its many jurisdictional challenges, ranging from 'victor's justice' to challenges to the crimes,[66] and is mainly concerned with summarizing the national positions

---

58   Y. Higurashi 日暮吉延, *Tōkyō saiban* [The Tokyo trial] (Tokyo: Kōdansha, 2008).

59   United Nations War Crimes Commission (selected documents in Japanese), with a Commentary by H. Hayashi (ed.), Tokyo 2008, 15 vols.

60   A. Wieviorka (ed.), *Les procès de Nuremberg et de Tokyo* (Brussels: A. Versailles, 1999, 2010).

61   Y. Takatori, 'The Forgotten Judge at the Tokyo War Crimes Trial', *Massachusetts Historical Review*, 10 (2008), 115-141.

62   A.-S. Schoepfel, 'La voix des juges français dans les procès de Nuremberg et de Tokyo, Défense d'une idée de justice universelle', *Guerres Mondiales et Conflits Contemporains*, 249 (2013), 101-14.

63   M. Banerjee, 'Does International Criminal Justice Require a Sovereign? Historicising Radhabinod Pal's Tokyo Judgment in Light of his "Indian" Legal Philosophy' in M. Bergsmo, W.L. Cheah and P. Yi (eds.), *Historical Origins of International Criminal Law*, vol. 2. (Brussels: Torkel Opsahl, 2014), pp. 67-118.

64   H. Nagai, 'Wasurerareta Tōkyō saiban Firipin hanji: Delfin Jaranilla hanji no shōgai' [The forgotten Filipino judge at the Tokyo trial: A biography of Justice Delfin Jaranilla] in Kentarō Awaya (ed.), *Kingendai Nihon no sensō to heiwa* [War and peace in modern Japanese history] (Tokyo: Gendai Shiryo Shuppan, 2010).

65   Crowe, *War Crimes, Genocide, and Justice*, pp. 195-242.

66   See, for details, Boister and Cryer, *Tokyo IMT*, pp. 28-48.

on, for example, the non-indictment of the emperor,[67] the dismissal of bacteriological warfare charges, the question of sexual slavery, or the 'more representative than comprehensive selection of defendants'.[68] It places a great deal of emphasis, however, on the selection process of its judges, national strategies and the preference for special charges, as well as on justified claims of the defence. The defence suffered from a lack of time to prepare, language difficulties, inferior translation facilities and logistical issues (such as the shortage of desks, typewriters, paper and money).[69] The most serious challenges came, however, from Webb's trial conduct, and the rejection of documents of evidence presented by the defence in court.[70]

When contextualizing the Tokyo trial, it is vital to reassess the national strategies behind the performance in court. What does the legal strategy adopted in court tell us about the national perceptions of the Pacific War, and which hopes were connected to a successful performance in this international court? What was the understanding of a 'successful outcome' of the trial, and how did that differ between the teams? What happened to Tokyo's legal actors once they left the trial? What was the impact of Tokyo on their subsequent legal careers, mental horizons and politics? Can we detect connections and 'legal flows' emanating from the lawyers at Tokyo? Can their biographies highlight broader social tensions and transformations?

Judges varied greatly in how they were affected by their different legal backgrounds, accommodation issues, postal delivery, the absence of their wives, the poor quality of translation of the trial, as well as questions of procedures, in particular the absence from duty and the sheer length of the trial. The language barrier on the bench, notably access to English, hampered smooth communication between the judges,[71] as at least two judges (Zaryanov and Bernard) did not speak English, and therefore Russian and French could be used in court as an exception, but only while the national prosecution period lasted. The drafting of indictment and judgment was contested, as were procedural questions of the trial, as will be shown in more detail in the chapters. The alleged bias of judges who had personal experiences in the war with Japan or had served in their national armies (such as Webb, Cramer, Zaryanov

---

67   Crowe, *War Crimes, Genocide and Justice*, pp. 202-5.

68   Quote from D.C. Watt, historical introduction, in Pritchard and Zaide (eds.), *Tokyo war Crimes Trial: Index and Guide*, p. xix.

69   See, for example, IMTFE transcript, p. 17215, p. 21825, p. 42491. Also M. Harries and S. Harries, *Sheathing the Sword: The Demilitarisation of Japan* (New York: Macmillan, 1987), p. 145. Crowe, *War Crimes, Genocide and Justice*, p. 209.

70   Crowe, *War Crimes, Genocide and Justice*, p. 235 and 241.

71   Ibid., p. 209.

and Jaranilla),[72] as well as the impact of political motivations on the trial's conduct[73] or even racism on the bench,[74] has been discussed in previous scholarship.

One element of the critique of the Tokyo trial has been that, compared to Nuremberg, Tokyo was seen a failure, first and foremost due to its sentence policy and legal discord, and secondly, because of the claim that the judges and legal staff involved were 'less experienced' when compared to the first choice personnel assembled at Nuremberg. This legacy needs contextualization to be readdressed, and, as the following chapters show, the criticism is unfounded. Some of the most eminent attorneys were assembled at Tokyo, representing 'legal excellence to lead the prosecution', as Harries and Harries underlined – among them Arthur Comyns-Carr from England, with Christmas Humphreys as one of his juniors; Govinda Menon from India, with Krishna Menon as his junior; Sergej Golunsky from the Soviet Union, a jurist and diplomat who had attended the conferences of Dumbarton Oaks, Yalta and Potsdam; and the US counsels Fihelly and Darsey.[75]

It is thus important for researchers to reassess the selection process of judges and staff, to understand the importance and legal background of candidates. It reveals a lot about political interests, national self-perception and the importance the trial was given in domestic politics. Often, instead of forming a national team, they formed competing bodies and interpreted the national role at Tokyo differently. As the French example shows, this problem was further aggravated by additional members of the national *équipe*, as, for example, diplomatic staff who claimed to be merely 'observing' but were indeed playing the role of 'supervising' the legal body. The Canadian example even shows how a Japanologist became an important member of the team, delivering priceless services because of his linguistic competence and his inside knowledge of Japanese politics.

When addressing the 'human element' of a trial, it is important to focus not only on the judges, but also on the chief prosecutors, and on the defence coun-

---

72   Boister and Cryer, *Tokyo IMT*, p. 83-84.

73   M. Cherif Bassiouni, 'From Versailles to Rwanda in Seventy-Five Years: The Need to Establish a Permanent International Court', *Harvard Human Rights Journal*, 19 (1997), 11-62, 33, FN 96.

74   Terry Hewton, 'Webb's Justice. The Role of Sir William Flood Webb in the Tokyo Trial, 1946-1948: An Examination of the Australian Judge in a Political Trial' (unpublished Honours thesis, University of Adelaide, 1976), p. 30, quoted in Boister and Cryer, *Tokyo IMT*, p. 94.

75   Harries and Harries, *Sheathing the Sword*, p. 115.

sel, and even to take a look systematically at translators and other staff, which remains a lacuna.

A special case in point for Tokyo is the employment of female attorneys in the prosecution and as legal aides in the defence team. Scholarship has not yet comprehensively addressed the gender dimension of Tokyo, as there were several female attorneys on duty at the IMTFE: Virginia Bowman, Lucille Brunner, Eleanor Jackson, Helen Grigware Lambert, Grace Kanode Llewellyn, Bettie Renner (all from the USA), and the Dutch attorney Coomee Strooker-Dantra. They all worked on various phases of the prosecution's case and presented to the court. It is still open to research to what degree the employment of female colleagues was a side effect of the shortage of personnel at Tokyo, or a purposeful experiment. The fact remains that Tokyo was a pioneer in this regard and thus more modern than, for example, the tribunal at Nuremberg, where women were in large part employed as stenotypists or secretaries only.

A recurring cause for complaint is the repeated absences of judges from the trial, especially in times when the defence presented the case, or requests came from their home courts for the protagonists to be sent on leave to fulfil their duties at home (Webb as well as Pal returned home for court duties). Defence attorney Owen Cunningham, in his critique of the trial,[76] calculated that out of 466 days of the Tokyo tribunal, Webb was absent for 53 days and Pal 109 days.[77] Sedgwick concludes: 'By skipping court time, judges elevated personal motives over national and judicial responsibilities. Absences also reveal a distinct prejudice against the defence case.... In practice, this policy amounted to clear bias when judges missed disproportionately large portions of the defence case. Of the 438 workdays missed by judges, 333 came during the defence phase'.[78] The trial was thus not balanced, as was also underlined by Minear,[79] Dower,[80] and Pritchard.[81]

A third point of friction at the Tokyo trial was the clash of legal cultures, not only between Western and 'non-Western' ones, but also within European traditions of law, such as between European civil law and Anglo-Saxon common

---

76   Owen Cunningham delivered a paper to the American Bar Association in 1948, entitled 'The Major Evils of the Tokyo War Crimes Trial'; Seattle 1948, cited in Boister and Cryer, *Tokyo IMT*, p. 60.

77   Harries and Harries, *Sheathing the Sword*, p. 149.

78   J. Sedgwick, 'A People's Court: Emotion, Participant Experiences, and the Shaping of Post-war Justice at the International Military Tribunal for the Far East, 1946-48', *Diplomacy & Statecraft*, vol. 22. no. 3, (2011), 480-99, 491.

79   Minear, *Victors' justice.*

80   Dower, *Embracing Defeat.*

81   R.J. Pritchard, 'The Historical Experience of British War Crimes Courts in the Far East, 1946-1948', *International Relations*, 6 (1978), 311-26.

law traditions. The legal strategy of the national teams differed markedly. Not only was the question of indicting the emperor highly controversial, but also the US strategy of focusing, as in Nuremberg, largely on the notion of 'crimes against peace' was challenged. As Crowe notes, the ample testimonies about atrocities were all 'filtered through the conspiratorial aggressive war theme', and thus lost the meaning they could have had (and had in Nuremberg).[82] The result was a lot of time wasted, on both the prosecutors' and defence attorney's sides, on irrelevant material.

Looking into the professional background of lawyers and judges reveals who was familiar with international law, and who derived approaches from other legal fields, when crafting a national strategy. Research also needs to pay attention to the impact of transnational legal institutions (the trial itself, but also the United Nations War Crimes Commission (UNWCC), International Law Commissions, student networks of law schools, etc) as well as of personal ties between the judges (reflected, for example, in the developing friendship between Pal and Röling).

A fourth point comes under the heading of management of the trial, and is connected to the person of the president, Judge William Webb from Australia. He turned out to be highly controversial, as he was unable to moderate the competing interests and legal approaches of the group of eleven judges. Patrick did not hold back in his opinion of Webb, who did nothing to calm the bench and hold the group together, but instead was, in Patrick's view, a 'turbulent, quick-tempered bully'.[83] Webb was also unhappy about the situation, as Narrelle Morris's chapter shows.

The trial was further hampered, and this is the fifth point, by technical issues and questions related to status: Webb being the possessor of the only microphone on the bench and thus the only of eleven judges able to intervene or pose questions; questions of lodging and car number plates; translation issues and the problem of sworn witness evidence; the difficulties of a lack of written material; and the linguistic problems within the team of eleven judges, of whom at least two spoke not a word of English, while others were not fluent. All of these factors hindered a smooth academic exchange of ideas and positions. This problem was perpetuated going down the ranks within the national teams, however, sometimes also in reverse order (as the lower ranks often proved more fluent in English than either judges or prosecutors, or even spoke Japanese).

---

82   Crowe, *War Crimes, Genocide and Justice*, p. 210.
83   TNA, LC02/2992: Patrick to Normand, probably January 1947.

Finally, individual problems overshadowed the trial, which had to do with the feeling of otherness and maybe even loneliness in a foreign environment for many months. Another interesting field of research is the formation of alliances behind the scenes, and the socializing aspect of the trial. As Brackman notes, 'Although the judges isolated themselves from the prosecutors and defence lawyers, in the close foreign community in occupied Tokyo it was inevitable that they socialized to some extent.'[84]

This volume takes a look at the consequences of the turbulent interaction of personalities for the legal character of the trial. Judges and lawyers in Tokyo were constrained to varying degrees by their respective national policies on one side and their legal training and experience on the other, but they also displayed powerful individual voices on basic questions of legal ethics.

As a caveat, it has, however, also to be noted that an actor-centred approach has its clear limitations. What happens when state pressure is too heavy, or individual action sparsely documented, can be understood in the chapters on the Soviet and Chinese case. The political context and Cold War realities are important and show the limitations of actor-centric approaches. They also show the limitations of Western-dominated historiography, as the bipolar world order tended to obscure important contributions made by either the Soviet or the Chinese team at Tokyo for Western scholars for many decades.

Whilst some judges underlined their national independence by voicing dissenting judgments, others were anxious to keep the bench as united as possible, so as to reinforce the legacy of international tribunals as a whole and of Tokyo in particular. When assessing the British team and its partner teams from the dominions of Canada and New Zealand, we see additionally something like an argumentation of professional honour, voicing standards of 'British justice' as the basis for the trial, and upholding duties despite deep personal frustrations and the wish to withdraw from Tokyo's lengthy proceedings. The chapter by Sedgwick will discuss this mentality of 'belonging and buying in' in more detail.

In December 1948, the sentences were handed down, and all Japanese leaders were found guilty. Seven of the accused were condemned to death, sixteen more were given life sentences. No defendant was acquitted. The split on the bench was also reflected in the judge's votes on death sentences: Sellars surmises that those who voted against capital punishments were Webb, Pal, Bernard and Zaryanov (the Soviet Union having temporarily abolished capital punishment).[85] In view of the Cold War realities, the Allies were looking to

---

84   Brackman, *The Other Nuremberg*.
85   Sellars, 'William Patrick and "Crimes Against Peace"', 192.

Japan as an ally. In February 1949, the Far Eastern Commission (FEC) ruled that no further Japanese leaders would be tried for aggression.[86]

Structure of Chapters

The structure of chapters in this volume follows the logic of the judge's bench, with Australian president Webb at the head, followed by the supporters of the majority judgment, and by the dissenters. The biographical analysis is framed by two overview chapters, one on the bench in general, and one on the position of the 'other', the Japanese defence lawyers. Biographical emphasis allows a focus on the transformation of juristic subjectivities, instead of regarding the judges as static instruments of the policy considerations of their respective nations. The dialogic relationships between the judges, the Asian theatres of war and politics, Euro-American institutions (including universities and courts) as well as global legal networks (such as the UNWCC or after Tokyo, a subsequent career in the UN International Law Commission) and 'legal flows' emanating from it are taken into consideration, thereby exploring the Tokyo trial in its broader resonances and legacies. As the different chapters will focus on judges and other legal personnel composing a national delegation as the 'transmitters of ideas and flows', the biographical reference forms an innovative and important level of investigation.

In the opening chapter, *James Burnham Sedgwick* offers an overview analysis of the process of 'manufacturing majorities' behind the scenes at Tokyo, thus in a way offering another introductory view to the tribunal. Social networks defined by personal sensibilities split its members. Judges either bought into the IMTFE's legal project and felt belonging, or defined themselves by difference. Internal critics formed a distinct community of dissent in which they fed off each other; interaction cemented opposition to the court. The manufactured 'majority' relied on a shared sense of purpose rather than actual legal consensus. International judgment in Tokyo meant building blocs amongst dissonant personalities – creating a law unto itself. Sedgwick also addresses the difficulties the various actors had in what he calls a 'community of dissent', for example, Mei and Zaryanov's arguments regarding the Charter and the pivotal issue of conspiracy charges, and how dissent 'poisoned the war's legacy'.

Narrelle Morris's chapter sheds light on the personality of William Webb and his team from Australia. In his appointment to the role of President of the International Military Tribunal for the Far East (IMTFE), the Australian judge Sir William Flood Webb brought the weight of his considerable wartime expe-

---

86   TNA LCO 2/2992, handwritten note (Feb. 1949).

rience investigating Japanese war crimes. He also carried (or was burdened) by the hopes and expectations of the Australian people, who had been reassured repeatedly by the Australian government that all Japanese war criminals would be brought to justice. Morris's chapter discusses William Webb and Australia's role at the centre of the trial and describes Webb's role as controversial president, and furthermore Alan Mansfield's appointment as associate prosecutor. Morris goes into great personal detail of Webb's at times grandiose and hyperbolic view of the trial, while at the same time withdrawing periodically from said trial. The chapter draws on many of Webb's private views on the trial, including letters to his wife, and his opinions surrounding, according to him, the 'slowest trial in history'. It discusses the extent to which Webb was able to bring them to bear upon the IMTFE given the competing policy considerations of the other nations and judges involved.

David Crowe opens the account of the judge's bench with his analysis of the American team and the notion of 'victor's justice', for which the United States has to bear a great deal of the responsibility because of the way the trial was organized by Douglas MacArthur as SCAP and Washington's SWNCC, which granted him immense authority to create tribunals to try major Japanese war criminals after the end of the conflict. In this role, for example, he, in league with the SWNCC, decided not to indict Emperor Hirohito for war crimes, a decision that weakened what had been Nuremberg's central charge – conspiracy. As SCAP, MacArthur felt he had unlimited power to control and direct the course of such trials, including the IMFTE. Fortunately, this authority was later successfully challenged by many of the IMTFE judges, and, once the trial began, MacArthur pretty much left its conduct to Keenan, the different allied prosecutors, and the eleven judges. Sadly, Keenan was not up to the task in Japan, and proved to be so incompetent that many on his staff complained constantly about his missteps. Fortunately, this allowed prosecutors from other countries, as well as members of Keenan's staff, to play a far stronger prosecutorial role in the trial. If there was a bright spot in the American role in the trial, it was the work of the junior US military JAG officers as attorneys for the Japanese defendants. In the end, these young officers and their Japanese counterparts mounted a strong defence that surprised many of the other prosecution teams and the court.

As *Anja Bihler*'s chapter shows, China's participation in the IMTFE was an event of great political importance for the Republic of China, which was vying for a place amongst the ranks of the major powers and had only recently achieved relinquishment of foreign extraterritorial rights. A wave of publications in the PRC mostly evaluates the Chinese participation in Tokyo favourably, stressing the contributions made by the Chinese judge as well as the Chinese members of the prosecution team. This chapter clarifies the Nationalist government's strategic interests in the Tokyo trial and re-evaluates its actual contributions to the trial based on personal writings of the members of the delegation and archive materials from the Chinese Ministry of Foreign Affairs, as well as historical newspapers and legal journals.

Kerstin von Lingen examines the role of the British team, by focusing on its judge, Lord William Patrick, and its prosecutor, Arthur Comyns-Carr, who drafted the indictment and left his mark as the 'secret manager' of the tribunal. The main focus is on the Scottish judge's selection, as well as on Lord Patrick's impact on the trial in bringing about a majority judgment and managing a split in the bench in 1947. Whitehall was surely on a mission to strengthen the Nuremberg principles, set down in the London Charter of August 1945, and Tokyo was envisioned as a 'second Nuremberg'. The British role in the trial mirrors London's effort to 'manage' the trial's outcome, while at the same time trying to balance the difficult equilibrium between the national teams coming from not only different cultural and political backgrounds, but also fundamentally different legal traditions.

Valentyna Polunina's study focuses on the role of the Soviet members of the delegation, specifically Major General Justice Ivan Zaryanov and Prosecutor Sergej Golunsky (whose previous work as Stalin's consultant and interpreter helped him gain experience for the trial). In general, the Soviet leadership had an ambivalent attitude towards the Tokyo trial. On the one hand, there was an interest in its successful outcome. They were less interested in the tribunal's many legal flaws, which set them apart from the dissenting judges from India, the Netherlands and France. The chapter is largely based on unpublished Russian archival materials, as well as publications and memoirs of the Soviet delegation members. It looks closely at their roles during the trial, the lack of language proficiency and the problems caused by translation difficulties, while at the same time shedding light on the groundbreaking legal achievements of the Soviets at Tokyo regarding counts 35 and 36 (war of aggression).

Yuki Takatori's chapter examines Canada's involvement in the Japanese war crimes trials. Despite Ottawa's reluctance to participate in this unprecedented judicial undertaking, F. Stuart McDougall (Canadian judge), and E.H. Norman (Canadian representative to the Supreme Commander of the Allied Powers and Japanologist) influenced the trial quite significantly. The chapter examines closely the concepts of autonomy and neutrality applied during the case, and McDougall's own judicial autonomy in a trial highly political in nature. The general patterns of Canadian involvement reveal how geopolitics forced Ottawa to rely heavily upon the initiatives taken by the United States with regard to pre-trial groundwork and post-trial parole and clemency policies; in contrast, realities experienced in Tokyo, including the incompetence of the US chief prosecutor and the controversy over the appointment of the second US judge, moved Ottawa's agents there to distance themselves from Washington's and to work closely with their Commonwealth counterparts.

Neil Boister focuses on New Zealand's approach to the Tokyo trial in a *longue durée* perspective, drawing a line from its involvement in international criminal law in the period from 1919 up to the Tokyo trial. He analyses the role of New Zealand at the Tokyo trial, by concentrating on Prosecutor Quilliam and Justice Northcroft. New Zealand played a small but important part at the Tokyo trial, and had an inordinate impact considering the size of the country. His chapter explores the poorly understood motivating factors for what appears to be an enthusiastic involvement in the developing international criminal law enterprise moderated by limited resources, geographical isolation, and deference to British influence. According to Boister, New Zealand began to align itself with other smaller powers against Britain in their approach to international affairs. His chapter offers a case study of how a small state positioned itself in the international criminal law discourse.

Hitoshi Nagai's chapter completes the analysis of the judges' bench by shedding light on the role of Justice Delfin Jaranilla, the Philippines representative, who in November 1948 submitted his 'Concurring Opinion'. Why did Justice Jaranilla decide to write his 'Concurring Opinion'? The reasons lay partly in political considerations, as the Philippines, like India, was an emerging nation that became independent after the commencement of the Tokyo trial, and partly in personal motivations. This chapter discusses these issues as they impacted on the selection, national strategy and personal commitment of a judge who had only just survived the so-called 'Bataan Death March' and was eager to prove his professionalism and impartiality. The chapter is based on Justice Jaranilla's private papers, interviews with his family, the Philippine Presidential papers and local newspapers.

Ann-Sophie Schoepfel's analysis sheds light on the role of the French government at the Tokyo trial, and highlights the triangular relationship between three main protagonists of the French legal commitment in East Asia: the French prosecutor, Robert Oneto, who was influenced by the Nuremberg trial; the French colonial judge, Henri Bernard, who protested against the legitimacy of the tribunal; and finally, the Chief of the French Mission to the occupation government in Japan, Brigadier Zinovy Peshkoff, who was concerned with the historical interpretation of France's invasion of Indochina. Although the Tokyo trial revealed the fragility of France as an emerging power after 1945, the French representatives nevertheless played a role in the emergence of modern international law by asserting their specific perceptions of justice and peace.

Lisette Schouten scrutinizes the Dutch involvement in the Tokyo trial, which is often overshadowed in scholarship by its outcome, the dissenting judgment by Judge Röling. Preoccupied with a de facto colonial war in the Netherlands Indies and facing an enormous loss of economic and political power, their presence at an international tribunal at Tokyo was at first not a priority for the Dutch authorities (unlike the smaller-scale national trials in Indonesia as well as in the Netherlands itself). Eventually, adherence to the long-standing Dutch tradition of the promotion of an international legal system and the newly required responsibilities as a Western ally prevailed, but all in all the decision to send a Dutch representation to Tokyo was more a political than a moral one. In this chapter, focus is placed on the small but dedicated Dutch prosecution section headed by Mr. W.G.F. Borgerhoff-Mulder, which, irrespective of and perhaps even due to the lack of interest and guidance from its government, was able to contribute to the proceedings, with several well received statements that fitted into the general framework of the indictment and strengthened the tribunal's main charge: the crime against peace. By doing so, this chapter transcends the usual approach of addressing solely the impact of Dutch justice Röling, who through his interactions with his fellow judges and several well-known Japanese, developed new ideas about international law and justice which culminated in a dissenting opinion that proved to be of lasting value both in the West and in the East.

Milinda Banerjee in his chapter shows how Indian involvement in the Tokyo trial was characterized by a remarkable diversity of voices. His chapter scrutinizes the role of the two main protagonists from India, by focusing not only on Judge Radhabinod Pal, who became famous for his dissenting opinion, but also on the Agent General for India in Washington and later Indian representative in the FEC, Girja Shankar Bajpai. The very ambiguity of India's decolonizing status allowed for certain actors to have a dominant, and individualized, influence, from enabling the country's very (late) entry into the trial (through a maelstrom of race-inflected debate) to challenging the fundamental premises of the trial itself, including on the vital questions of colonialism and state sovereignty. Perhaps in the case of no other participating country at Tokyo was the individualized nature of intervention so striking, and the lack of any effective 'national' policy so obvious.

The volume is concluded by *Urs Matthias Zachmann*'s analysis of the Japanese view of the trial, which is one of the most emblematic icons of Japan's early post-war history. However, it is also one of the sore points in revisionist narratives which until today (and increasingly so) singles out the fact that Japan was unilaterally subjected to a trial in which it had no part other than as a defendant, and therefore for political reasons was robbed of its autonomous agency, reducing the trial to 'victor's justice'. However, relatively little is known about what the Japanese who were most involved in a legal capacity in the trial actually *thought* about the justice administered, namely the lawyers who worked as counsel for the defendants in the trial, and the lawyers who stood outside, but were involved as public intellectuals commenting on the proceedings while they lasted and afterwards. Zachmann's chapter analyses these 'marginal' positions on the basis of diaries, memoirs and contemporary comments on the trial in legal as well as popular journals written by the most influential jurists of the time, and contextualizes them within the wider currents of intellectual and political developments.

Conclusion

By focusing directly on the transnational impact of Asian experiences on (mainly Western) legal personnel, networks and debates, and the contribution this made to emerging expectations about international justice, the present book offers an alternative conceptual framework for understanding the genesis of contemporary international law. International criminal justice, at least in this Asian theatre, is shown to be the result not of a hegemonic intervention by the 'West', but rather as the product of multiple interventions and 'legal flows', often by actors and networks whose histories have been marginalized in existing studies.

A summary of the content of this book reveals that the view that Tokyo was a failure especially because of its 'second best' legal personnel, is a critique that needs to be revised. We see a lot of very devoted and expert men, and some women, who tried to make the utmost of their assignment to the novelty of an international court. It is also true that the Charter for the tribunal itself was contested amongst the judges and formed the basis of concern and criticism on the bench. Sellars points to the limitations of the court and claims that the Tokyo judges were doubly bound: 'by the strictures of the Charter and by the obligation to produce a judgment that would buttress the Nuremberg determination on its most contentious charge. This obligation diminished the judges' autonomy and exacerbated the tensions that at the time seemed to threaten the entire enterprise.'[87]

Many of the lawyers and judges involved had already been in high positions within their home countries, although most of them had no experience with international law, and none of them had ever been to Japan.[88] The political

---

87   Sellars, 'William Patrick and "Crimes Against Peace" at the Tokyo Tribunal', 169.

88   Boister and Cryer, *Tokyo IMT*, p. 78; Horwitz, 'The Tokyo trial', p. 494.

context, formed by old wartime alliances, new frictions and Cold War realities, was highly complex, and resulted in the delay and difficulties which harmed the delivery of justice in court and obscures the Tokyo legacy even now. At the same time, transcultural encounters at the crossroads of Europe, the USA, the USSR, Australia, and East, South-East and South Asia left its mark and developed a certain dynamic during the proceedings. It is therefore high time to reassess the personal commitment of the Tokyo trial's main protagonists and national teams.

Bibliography

Kentarō Awaya, 粟屋憲太郎. *Tōkyō Saiban ron* 東京裁判論 [Views on the Tokyo Trial] (Tokyo: Ōtsuki Shoten, 1989).

Kentarō Awaya, 粟屋憲太郎. *Tōkyō Saiban e no michi* 東京裁判への道 [Road to the Tokyo Trial], 2 vols. (Tokyo: Kōdansha, 2006).

Milinda Banerjee, 'Does International Criminal Justice Require a Sovereign? Historicising Radhabinod Pal's Tokyo Judgment in Light of his "Indian" Legal Philosophy' in Morten Bergsmo, Cheah Wui Ling, and Yi Ping (eds.), *Historical Origins of International Criminal Law*, vol. 2. (Brussels: Torkel Opsahl, 2014), 67-118.

M. Cherif Bassiouni, '"Crimes against Humanity". The Need for a Specialized Convention', *Columbia Journal of Transnational Law,* 31 (1993-1994), 457-94.

M. Cherif Bassiouni, 'From Versailles to Rwanda in Seventy-Five Years: The Need to establish a Permanent International Court', *Harvard Human Rights Journal*, 19 (1997), 11-62.

Herbert Bix, *Hirohito and the Making of Modern Japan* (Hamburg: HarperCollins Publishers, 2000).

Neil Boister and Robert Cryer, *The Tokyo International Military Tribunal: A Reappraisal* (Oxford University Press, 2008).

Neil Boister and Robert Cryer (eds.), *Documents on the Tokyo International Military Tribunal: Charter, Indictment and Judgments* (Oxford University Press, 2008).

Arnold C. Brackman, *The Other Nuremberg: The Untold story of the Tokyo War Crimes Trial* (New York: William Morrow and Company, Inc., 1987).

Timothy Brook, 'Radhabinod Pal on the Rape of Nanking: The Tokyo Judgment and the Guilt of History' in Bob Tadashi Wakabayashi (ed.), *The Nanking Atrocity 1937-38: Complicating the Picture* (New York: Berghahn 2007), pp. 149-78.

Yoshio Chaen (ed.), 茶園義男編. *BC-kyū senpan Gōgun Rabauru saiban shiryō* BC 級戦犯豪軍ラバウル裁判資料 [Documents on Australian military trials of class B and C war criminals at Rabaul] (Tokyo: Fuji Shuppan, 1990).

Yoshio Chaen (ed.), 茶園義男編. *BC-kyū senpan Gōgun Manusu tō saiban shiryō* BC 級戦犯豪軍マヌス等裁判資料 [Documents on Australian military trials of class B and C war criminals at Manus Island] (Tokyo: Fuji Shuppan, 1991).

Yoshio Chaen (ed.), 茶園義男編. *BC-kyū senpan Eigun saiban shiryō* BC 級戦犯英軍裁判資料 [Documents on British military trials of class B and C war criminals (vol. 2)] (Tokyo: Fuji Shuppan, 1989).

Yoshio Chaen and Shigematsu Kazuyoshi, 茶園義男, 重松一義. *Hokan senpan saiban no jissō* 補完戦犯裁判の実相 [Supplement: The true facts about the war crimes trials] (Tokyo: Fuji Shuppan, 1987).

David Crowe, *War Crimes, Genocide and Justice* (New York: Palgrave MacMillan, 2014).

Robert Cryer, 'Röling in Tokyo. A Dignified Dissenter', *Journal of International Criminal Justice*, 8 (2010), 1109-26.

Robert Cryer, 'Röling (The Netherlands)' in Yuki Tanaka, Tim McCormack and Gerry Simpson (eds.), *Beyond Victor's Justice? The Tokyo War Crimes Trial Revisited* (Leiden: Martinus Nijhoff, 2011), pp. 109-26.

John Dower, *Embracing Defeat: Japan in the Wake of World War II* (New York: W.W. Norton, 1999).

Jean Esmein, 'Le Juge Henri Bernard au Procès de Tokyo', *Vingtième Siècle. Revue d'histoire*, 59 (1998), 3-14.

Richard Frank, *Downfall: The End of the Imperial Japanese Empire* (New York: Random House, 1999).

Madoka Futamura, *War Crimes Tribunals and Transitional Justice: The Tokyo Trial and the Nuremberg Legacy* (London/New York: Routledge, 2008).

Marc Gallicchio, *The Unpredictability of the Past: Memories of the Asia-Pacific War in US-East Asian relations* (Durham: Duke University Press, 2007).

Gerrit W. Gong (ed.), *Memory and History in East and South East Asia: Issues of Identity in International relations* (Washington: Center for Strategic and International Studies, 2002).

Meirion Harries and Susie Harries, *Sheathing the Sword: The Demilitarisation of Japan* (New York: Macmillan, 1987).

Tsuyoshi Hasegawa and Kazuhiko Tōgō, *East-Asia's Haunted Present: Historical Memories and the Resurgence of Nationalism* (Westport: Praeger Security International, 2008).

Hirofumi Hayashi, 'British War Crimes Trials of Japanese', *Nature-People-Society: Science and the Humanities*, no. 31, July 2001, online journal at <http://www.geocities.jp/hh hirofumi/engo8.htm> (last accessed 4 August 2016).

Yoshinobu Higurashi, 日暮吉延. *Tōkyō Saiban no kokusai kankei: kokusai seiji ni okeru kenryoku to kihan* 東京裁判の国際関係: 国際政治における権力と規範 [International relations at the Tokyo Trial: Power and norms in foreign policy] (Tokyo: Bokutakusha, 2002).

Yoshinobu Higurashi 日暮吉延, *Tōkyō saiban* [The Tokyo Trial] (Tokyo: Kōdansha, 2008).

Mickael Ho Foui Sang, 'Justice Bernard (France)' in Yuki Tanaka, Tim McCormack and Gerry Simpson (eds.), *Beyond Victor's Justice? The Tokyo War Crimes Trial Revisited* (Leiden: Martinus Nijhoff, 2011), pp. 93-102.

Solis Horwitz, 'The Tokyo Trial', *International Conciliation*, 28 (1950), 475-588.

Chihiro Hosoya, Nisuke Andō, Yasuaki Ōnuma and Richard Minear (eds.), *The Tokyo War Crimes Trial: An International Symposium* (Tokyo: Kodansha, 1986).

Gordon Ireland, 'Uncommon Law in Martial Tokyo', *The Yearbook of World Affairs*, 4 (1950), 54-104.

Takashi Iwakawa, 岩川 隆. *Kotō no tsuchi to narutomo: BC-kyū senpan saiban* 孤島の土となるとも：BC級戦犯裁判 [Even if I perished on a lonely island – The trials of class B and C war criminals] (Tokyo: Kōdansha 1995).

Ichirō Kiyose 清瀬一郎, *Hiroku Tōkyō Saiban* 秘録東京裁判 [A secret history of the Tokyo Trial] (Tokyo: Yomiuri Shinbunsha, 1967).

Keiichirō Kobori, *The Tokyo Trials: The Unheard Defense* (Rockport, Maine: New England History Press, 2003).

Noboru Kojima 児島襄. *Tōkyō Saiban* 東京裁判 [The Tokyo Trial], 2 vols. (Tokyo: Chūō Kōronsha, 1971).

Elizabeth S. Kopelman, 'Ideology and International Law: The Dissent of the Indian Justice at the Tokyo War Crimes Trial', *New York University Journal of International Law and Politics*, 23 (1991), 373-444.

Barak Kushner, 'Pawns of Empire: Postwar Taiwan, Japan and the Dilemma of War Crimes', *Japanese Studies* (Special issue on Japan and Taiwan), vol. 30, no. 1 (May 2010), 111-33.

Barak Kushner, *Men to Devils, Devils to Men: Japanese War Crimes and Chinese Justice* (Harvard University Press, 2015).

Tim McCormack, Georgina Fitzpatrick, and Narrelle Morris, eds., *Australia's War Crimes Trials, 1945-1951* (Leiden: Brill, 2016).

Peter Maguire, *Law and War: An American Story* (New York: University of Columbia Press, 2000).

Richard Minear, *Victors' Justice: The Tokyo War Crimes Trial* (Princeton University Press, 1971).

Sheila Miyoshi Jager and Rana Mitter, *Ruptured Histories: War, Memory and Post-Cold War in Asia* (Harvard University Press, 2007).

Hitoshi Nagai, 'Wasurerareta Tōkyō saiban Firipin hanji: Delfin Jaranilla hanji no shōgai' [The forgotten Filipino judge at the Tokyo trial: A biography of Justice Delfin Jaranilla] in Kentarō Awaya (ed.), *Kingendai Nihon no sensō to heiwa* [War and peace in modern Japanese history] (Tokyo: Gendai Shiryo Shuppan, 2010), pp. 303-66.

Takeshi Nakajima, 'Justice Pal (India)' in Yuki Tanaka, Tim McCormack and Gerry Simpson (eds.), *Beyond Victor's Justice? The Tokyo War Crimes Trial Revisited* (Leiden: Martinus Nijhoff, 2011), pp. 127-44.

Takeshi Nakajima 中島岳志, Pâru hanji Tōkyō saiban hihan to zettai heiwa-shugi パール判事 – 東京裁判批判と絶対平和主義 [Justice Pal: Criticisms of the Tokyo Trial and absolute pacifism] (Tokyo: Hakusuisha, 2007).

Nariaki Nakazato, *Neonationalist Mythology in Postwar Japan: Pal's Dissenting Judgment at the Tokyo War Crimes Tribunal* (Lanham: Lexington Books, 2016).

Ashis Nandy, 'The Other Within: The Strange Case of Radhabinod Pal's Judgment on Culpability', *New Literary History*, 23, 1 (1992), 45-67.

Yasuaki Ōnuma, 大沼保昭. *Tōkyō Saiban kara sengo sekinin no shisō e* 東京裁判から戦後責任への思想へ [From the Tokyo Trial to the doctrine of post-war responsibility] (Tokyo: Yūshindō, 1985).

Philipp Osten, *Der Tokioter Kriegsverbrecherprozeß und die japanische Rechtswissenschaft* (Berliner Wissenschaftsverlag, 2003).

Philip R. Piccigallo, *The Japanese on Trial: Allied War Crimes Operations in the East, 1945-1951* (Austin: University of Texas Press, 1979).

R. John Pritchard, 'The Historical Experience of British War Crimes Courts in the Far East, 1946-1948', *International Relations*, 6 (1978), 311-26.

R. John Pritchard (ed.), *The Tokyo Major War Crimes Trial: The Records for the International Military Tribunal for the Far East with an Authoritative Commentary and Comprehensive Guide*, 124 vols. (Lewinston: Edwin Mellen Press, 1998-2005).

R. John Pritchard, 'The Gift of Clemency Following British War Crimes Trials in the Far East, 1946-1948,' *Criminal Law Forum*, 7:1 (1996), 15-50.

R. John Pritchard and Sonia M. Zaide, *The Tokyo War Crimes Trial: Comprehensive Index and Guide to the Proceedings of the International Military Tribunal for the Far East* (New York: Garland, 1987).

R. John Pritchard, Sonia M. Zaide and D.C. Watt, *The Tokyo War Crimes Trial*, vol. 1 (New York and London: Garland, 1981).

Shamsur Rahman, 'Judgment of Justice Radhabinod Pal at the Tokyo War Crimes Trial, 1946-48', *Journal of the Asiatic Society of Bangladesh*, 55, 1 (2010).

Ann-Sophie Schoepfel, 'La voix des juges français dans les procès de Nuremberg et de Tokyo, Défense d'une idée de justice universelle', *Guerres Mondiales et Conflits Contemporains*, 249 (2013), 101-14.

John Sedgwick, 'A People's Court: Emotion, Participant Experiences, and the Shaping of Postwar Justice at the International Military Tribunal for the Far East, 1946-48', *Diplomacy & Statecraft*, 22. no. 3, (2011), 480-99.

Kirsten Sellars, *'Crimes against Peace' and International Law* (Cambridge University Press, 2013).

Kirsten Sellars, ,William Patrick and "Crimes Against Peace" at the Tokyo Tribunal, 1946-1948', *The Edinburgh Law Review*, 15(2) (2011), 166-96.

Asahi Shinbun, Tōkyō Saiban Kishadan. 朝日新聞東京裁判記者団. *Tōkyō Saiban* 東京裁判 [The Tokyo Trial] (Tokyo: Asahi Shinbunsha, 1995).

Sugamo Hōmuiinkai (Sugamo Law Commission), *The Truth of War Criminals' Trials* (Tokyo: Maki Shobō, 1986).

Yutaka Sugawara 菅原裕, *Tōkyō Saiban no shōtai* 東京裁判の正体 (The truth about the Tokyo Trial) (Tokyo: Kokusho Kankōkai, 2002).

Yuki Takatori, 'The Forgotten Judge at the Tokyo War Crimes Trial', *Massachusetts Historical Review*, 10 (2008), 115-41.

Kenzō Takayanagi 高柳賢三, *Kyokutō saiban to kokusaihō: Kyokutō Kokusai Gunji Saibansho ni okeru benron* 極東裁判と国際法: 極東国際軍事裁判所における弁論 [The Far East Trial and international law: The arguments presented at the International Military Tribunal for the Far East] (Tokyo: Yūhikaku, 1948).

Kayoko Takeda, Interpreting the Tokyo War Crimes Tribunal (Tokyo: Misuzu Shobō, 2010).

Kayoko Takeda, 武田珂代子. *Tōkyō Saiban ni okeru tsūyaku* 東京裁判における通訳 [Interpreting at the Tokyo Trial] (Tokyo: Misuzu Shobō, 2008).

Masajirō Takigawa 滝川政次郎, *Tōkyō Saiban o sabaku* 東京裁判をさばく [A judgment of the Tokyo Trial], 2 vols. (Tokyo: Tōwasha, 1962).

Yuki Tanaka, *Hidden Horrors. Japanese War Crimes in World War II* (Westview: Boulder 1996).

Yuki Tanaka, Tim McCormack and Gerry Simpson (eds.), *Beyond Victor's Justice? The Tokyo War Crimes Trial Revisited* (Leiden: Martinus Nijhoff, 2011).

Yuma Totani, *The Tokyo War Crimes Trial: The Pursuit of Justice in the Wake of World War II* (Cambridge, Mass.: Harvard University Asia Centre, 2008).

Beatrice Trefalt, Sean Brawley and Chris Dixon (eds.), *Competing Voices from The Pacific War* (Berkeley University Press, 2009).

Kei Ushimura, *Beyond the 'Judgment of Civilization'* (LTCB International Library Section no. 14 and published by the International House of Japan in 2003); Original title: 'Bunmei no sabaki' o koete – Tainichi senpan saiban dokkai no kokoromi 「文明の裁き」をこえて – 対日戦犯裁判読解の試み (Chūō kōron shinsha, 2001).

Kei Ushimura, 'Pal's "Dissentient" Judgment Reconsidered: Some Notes on Postwar Japan's Responses to the Opinion', *Japan Review*, 19 (2007), 215-24.

Latha Varadarajan, 'The Trials of Imperialism: Radhabinot Pal's dissent at the Tokyo tribunal', *European Journal of International relations* (Dec. 2014), 1-24.

Lori Watt, *When Empire Comes Home: Repatriation and Reintegration in Postwar Japan* (Harvard University Press, 2009).

Kenneth M. Wells, *Index to the Records of the International Military Tribunal for the Far East* (Christchurch: University of Canterbury Press, 1983).

Annette Wieviorka (ed.), *Les procès de Nuremberg et de Tokyo* (Brussels: A. Versailles, 1999, 2010).

Sandra Wilson, Robert Cribb, Beatrice Trefalt and Dean Aszkielowicz, *Japanese War Criminals: The Politics of Justice after the Second World War* (New York: Columbia University Press, 2017)Urs Mathias Zachmann, *Völkerrechtsdenken und Außenpolitik in Japan, 1919-1960* (Baden-Baden: Nomos, 2013).

CHAPTER 1

Building Blocs: Communities of Dissent, Manufactured Majorities and International Judgment in Tokyo

James Burnham Sedgwick

In July 1946, New Zealand's representative in Washington, Sir Carl Berendsen, met with British and United States authorities to discuss the controversial replacement of American IMTFE Justice John P. Higgins. Berendsen reported that the 'gist' of the meeting was to fill the vacancy as 'a matter of practice and not of inflexible rule'. Despite technical legal doubts, all agreed, 'In this particular case the political circumstances alone would seem to warrant the appointment of a United States representative'.[1] In other words, legal principles suggested Higgins could not be replaced, but pragmatism and politics dictated that the trial needed a replacement American judge. This principle-practice fulcrum came to define international judgment in Tokyo. Ultimately, 'inflexible rule' proved incompatible with trial aims. Breaking legal ground meant improvisation. The resulting ad hoc process forced participants – especially judges – into tight corners. For judges, the Tokyo judgment came down to two factors: buy-in and belonging. High stakes left few choices. Once assigned roles, judges felt compelled to either behave according to expectations (for the majority this meant championing the court's legitimacy and findings) or embrace critique (for dissenters, this meant challenging the court's legitimacy and findings). Judges who accepted the trial found ways to collaborate, compromise, and manufacture a core majority. Misgivings about the tribunal created a different kind of belonging; a community of dissent. Shared outrage among objectors amplified personal doubts. Building blocs behind the scenes came down to social networks defined by personal sensibilities.[2]

---

1 Archives New Zealand (ANZ), Wellington, EA2 1946-30B 106-3-22 Part 3, Carl Berendsen, New Zealand Minister, Washington to Minister of External Affairs, Wellington, 16 July 1946.

2 The idea of 'sensibilities' provides a useful conceptual tool for understanding such complex and contested judicial experiences. 'By bringing together the elements of sense perception, cognition, emotion, aesthetic form, moral judgment, and cultural differences', explains cultural and intellectual historian Daniel Wickberg, sensibilities 'let us dig beneath social actions and apparent content'. Daniel Wickberg, 'What Is the History of Sensibilities? On Cultural Histories, Old and New', *The American Historical Review*, 112, no. 3 (2007), 669.

© KONINKLIJKE BRILL NV, LEIDEN, 2018 | DOI 10.1163/9789004361058_003

A Manufactured Majority

In November 1946, President of the Tribunal William Flood Webb circulated a draft 'judgment' on the defence's challenge to the IMTFE's 'jurisdiction, powers, and authorities'.[3] Webb asked for 'helpful criticism ... [e]ach of us should make his choice of the views open to him and give his reasons for that choice'. He urged colleagues to find true compromise; a task 'more difficult than mere criticism'.[4] In reality, IMTFE judges, including Webb, struggled to accept opposing viewpoints. Throughout the trial, the bench rarely moved discourse beyond 'mere criticism', in how individuals communicated legal opinions, how they received critique, and how the court managed perspectives and approaches to the law. Webb intended his draft to form the foundation of a unified majority judgment. Ironically, the Australian judge's piece exposed a deep rift within the bench. Judges who eventually formed the tribunal majority fiercely upheld the court's validity. They learned to adjust personal, national, and ideological 'rules' to suit international 'practice' and circumstances. They worked hard to find common ground and found strength and direction in numbers.

With certain exceptions, the tribunal followed common law protocols. Anglo-American judges therefore had to bend less principle to fit the IMTFE mold. Unsurprisingly, they formed the majority's bedrock. The common law bloc which stuck closely together – at least in chambers – consisted of Justices Myron C. Cramer (US), Delfin Jaranilla (Philippines), E. Stuart McDougall (Canada), E.H. Northcroft (New Zealand), and Lord Patrick (Britain). The two majority members from other legal systems – Justices Mei Ru'ao (China) and I.M. Zaryanov (USSR) – worked more assiduously to reform personal and national legal precepts into majority arguments. Commitment to the IMTFE mission and conviction of Japanese guilt, locked both common law judges and their Chinese and Russian confreres into the majority.

Judges who 'bought in' to the majority – and to the IMTFE project more generally – fiercely resisted dissent. The stakes in Tokyo felt incredibly high. Judges invested deeply in the experience and every point of divergence became a hotly contested issue. Debate came down to whether a judge thought the IMTFE 'right' or 'wrong', considered inventing law 'good' or 'bad', and believed

---

3   *Bibliothèque de documentation internationale contemporaine* (BDIC), Nanterre, France, Fonds du Juge Henri Bernard: Le Procès de Tokyo, 1946-1949, F°Δ rés 874-10-1-48, W.F. Webb to Henri Bernard, 'The Jurisdiction, Powers and Authorities of the International Military Tribunal for the Far East', 29 November 1946. Hereafter 'Bernard Papers'.

4   Bernard Papers, F Δ rès 874-10-1-48, W.F. Webb to All Members of the Tribunal, 11 December 1946.

Japan to be 'guilty' or 'not guilty'. Judges who believed in the IMTFE attacked sceptics. For instance, the British judge responded severely to even the suggestion by certain colleagues that they had the right to dissent. 'If any Judge could not subscribe to the plain declaration in the Charter under which he was asked to act', Patrick wrote, 'He should not have accepted an appointment under the Charter'. If unwilling to follow the Charter 'at any time', the judge in question 'should tender his resignation to the Allied Powers'. Dissent amounted to 'a "fraud" upon the Charter and upon the Allied Powers'.[5] Canadian judge E.S. McDougall echoed Patrick's sentiments. 'The Charter is the expression of International Law', he opined. 'The Tribunal is bound by the Charter under which it has power to try the offence of waging aggressive war and the other crimes therein set forth'. McDougall explicitly condemned 'Two of the members' who took 'the extraordinary view that notwithstanding their appointment, they are entitled to hold that aggressive war is not a crime and in their opinion it is not a crime'.[6] Open dissent haunted majority members who were concerned with expedient, unified accountability. McDougall complained to Ottawa, 'The other members of the Tribunal have not expressed their views except with destructible criticism of the work of others'.[7] New Zealand's Justice Northcroft echoed the sentiment, 'Everybody is working independently', he wrote. 'I hate to think of the futility of persuading them to shed their pet theories and conclusions'.[8] Building consensus took hard work and willingness to buy in; something a number of judges simply could not manage.

Manufacturing majority while 'being international' in Tokyo challenged even the staunchest IMTFE supporters. Indeed, internal stressors pushed several judges to the brink of quitting. Conditions so frustrated Justice Northcroft that he almost resigned on several occasions. 'Discomfort and embarrassment I have accepted, and, of course, would continue to accept if I thought I could advance the cause of international justice', he reported in March 1947. 'Were I in this position in a Court in New Zealand and subjected without redress to humiliating treatment of this order I would certainly resign from the Court. I am afraid I see no other alternative here'. The New Zealander's anger emerged from petty infighting and personal self-importance and not substantive trial issues. He especially resented non-conforming judges. 'The dignity of this Court is prejudiced by such disturbances between Judges which cannot be kept secret', Northcroft concluded. From Northcroft's perspective, unanimity

---

5   Bernard Papers, F Δ rès 874-10-1-48, Lord Patrick to W.F. Webb, 11 October 1946.

6   ANZ, EA2 1947-26C 106-3-22 Part 5, McDougall to Louis St. Laurent, 19 March 1947.

7   Ibid.

8   ANZ, EA2 1947-26C 106-3-22 Part 5, E.H. Northcroft to H. O'Leary, 18 March 1947.

formed the only way to establish worthwhile post-war justice. 'If [the Tribunal] is to make a useful contribution to international law', he averred, the bench 'must be entirely or substantially of one mind. The chance to secure that, I fear, has gone'.[9] Achieving 'unanimity' proved difficult in Tokyo for a group of judges divided by contrasting sensibilities. Northcroft's closest associates, Justices McDougall and Patrick, also tried to leave their posts for personal reasons. In order to bolster his justification for withdrawal, Northcroft sent Wellington a copy of McDougall's resignation letter, noting 'Lord Patrick has also written to the same effect to his Lord President (the Scottish equivalent of our Chief Justice)'.[10] None of these judges actually resigned. They stayed because they bought in and felt belonging.

The majority relied on interpersonal binders to 'manufacture' consensus and build a sense of belonging together. All IMTFE judges arrived in Tokyo conscious of the tribunal's jurisprudential significance but with entrenched personal opinions on exactly how and why it was important. Unifying such a legally, politically, socially and culturally diverse bench would have required supreme patience and managerial aptitude. President Webb possessed neither. Especially sensitive to challenges to presidential authority, criticism of his November 1946 jurisdiction draft rankled. Webb wrote scathing rebuttals to colleagues, especially to Justice Mei. In response, the Chinese judge demonstrated an equanimity that proved crucial to majority-making. 'I am trying to be outspoken and express my idea as frankly as possible', he explained, 'For, I firmly believe, it is only through absolute frankness and exhaustiveness in discussion among the members that the result of the Tribunal can be best achieved'.[11] Natural compromisers like Mei proved instrumental to Tokyo's judgment by defusing judicial conflict. American Justice Cramer also had a calming influence behind the scenes. 'It would be most unfortunate if this difference of opinion should become public now, not only here in the trial of the case but also for the world public', Cramer reminded colleagues. 'If it once becomes public that our Court is so divided, these various comments will become more numerous ... I am strongly of the view that no opinion should be delivered in open court until the end of the trial'.[12] Cramer's cool presence came to the fore as head of the drafting committee which successfully brought

9   Ibid.
10   ANZ, EA2 1947-26C 106-3-22 Part 5, E.H. Northcroft to Humphrey O'Leary. 21 March 1947.
11   Bernard Papers, F Δ rès 874-10-1-48, Mei to Webb, 8 December 1946.
12   Australian War Memorial Archives, Canberra, Australia, William Webb Papers, AWM 92, Series 1, Wallet 9, Myron C. Cramer to W.F. Webb, 29 January 1947. Hereafter 'Webb Papers'.

together Canadian, Chinese, British, New Zealand, Philippines and Russian judges in support of the majority judgment.

Observers during the tribunal and scholars ever since paint Russian justice Zaryanov as a silent partner in the tribunal's public spectacle.[13] Skewed by Cold War assumptions, accounts portray the Soviet judge's participation as a peculiar combination of playfulness, detachment and menace. IMTFE scholars assume that Zaryanov had little impact on the tribunal's judicial landscape, particularly because the judge had no working knowledge of English or Japanese. In the words of Zhang Wanhong, 'It is hard to imagine how he conducted his work'.[14] A deposit of bench memoranda uncovered in the fonds of French justice Bernard reveals that Zaryanov actually became deeply involved and active in judicial debates. Moreover, he proved instrumental in cementing the majority in Tokyo, both for adapting personal legal sensibilities to fit the majority arguments, and for building consensus behind the scenes. He embodied what it took to be international and invent global justice in the immediate post-war era. Zaryanov emerged as a jurist of unrecognized subtlety inclined to pragmatism; committed to tribunal aims and willing to improvise whatever legal ideas it took to make the IMTFE work. Zaryanov defended the moral roots and social necessity of Tokyo justice. 'It is hardly possible to speak of any mitigating circumstances at the trial where the perpetrators of crimes are those who ruled the state and for a number of years decided the destiny of nations', argued Zaryanov.[15] The 'basic idea' of punishing acts 'so monstrously criminal that they are at variance with all basic natural and moral traits inherent to humanity throughout its history' felt justified. 'Historically changing social relations' created the right conditions for moving international justice forward.[16]

Zaryanov internationalized IMTFE law. The Russian judge worried that dependence on Anglo-American tenets undercut the tribunal's role as the legal expression of global outrage. He contributed jurisprudence for '[a]ggression', 'bandit systems of warfare' (conspiracy), and 'crimes against humanity'. Condemning these acts formed 'an obligatory legal element of various national systems of law', not just common law traditions. 'It is quite obvious', wrote

---

13   Arnold Brackman's description of 'a jovial man, as big and burly – and as dangerous – as a Kodiak bear' is characteristic – and caricatural. A.C. Brackman, *The Other Nuremberg: The Untold Story of the Tokyo War Crimes Trials* (New York: Morrow, 1987), p. 65.

14   W. Zhang, 'From Nuremberg to Tokyo: Some Reflections on the Tokyo Trial (On the Sixtieth Anniversary of the Nuremberg Trials)', *Cardozo Law Review*, 27, no. 42006, 1680.

15   Webb Papers, AWM 92 – Series 1, Wallet 11, I.M. Zaryanov to W.F. Webb, 4 February 1948.

16   Ibid.

Zaryanov, 'that the Non-acceptance by any state of these legal principles in its domestic law would have implied that that was a system of lawlessness a threat to the independence and existence of other nations'.[17] Friend and colleague Justice Northcroft described the Russian judge as 'a vigorous-minded person',[18] deeply committed to the IMTFE. The Charter, argued Zaryanov, 'is the expression of the right of the victorious nations acknowledged by all the civilized peoples to create judicial institutions on the occupied territory to try war criminals and to establish rules of law that are indispensable for the administration of justice'. It represents 'the only source of judicial authority of the members of the Tribunal' and was 'binding upon each of the judges to the same extent to which the codes of substantive law and procedure in a national court are binding upon them'. Zaryanov would not tolerate challenges to court authority.[19]

Zaryanov found an unlikely comrade in justice and sensibility in his Nationalist Chinese colleague. Both tried to find the happy medium between judicial extremes to negotiate complex legal issues in close quarters on the world stage. The Chinese judge became a determined adherent to the IMTFE project. 'Let me repeat my long-cherished stand', Mei avowed. 'We are bound by the provisions of our Charter', even when faced with doubts. 'The Charter in defining our jurisdiction is but an expression of international law, not a violation of [it]'.[20] Elsewhere, Mei expanded his views. 'I am firmly convinced that the Charter is intrinsically sound and its provisions in regard to war-crimes are simply declaratory of principles of law already in existence, instead of creating any new ones', argued Mei. 'I have never been able to agree with the opposite view. Furthermore I believe that this Tribunal, being created by the Charter, is bound to observe the Charter *in toto*, i.e. every article of it'. Sensitive to public relations, Mei emphasized the court's internationalism. 'Protracted citations from well-known decisions of American and British Courts should, in my opinion, be avoided as much as possible, lest it would mar the international character of the Tribunal', Mei wrote. 'Non-English-speaking readers ... might tend to be prejudiced and thereby get a totally wrong impression'.[21]

Judges like Zaryanov and Mei reconciled personal understandings of 'the law' with majority arguments. Mei, for example, worried about the 'peculiari-

---

17   Bernard Papers, F Δ rès 874-10-1-48, I.M. Zaryanov to W.F. Webb, 3 January 1947.
18   NZ Archives, EA2 1946-30B 106-3-22 Part 3, E.H. Northcroft to A.D. McIntosh, 2 July 1946.
19   Bernard Papers, F Δ rès 874-10-49-88, I.M. Zaryanov to W.F. Webb, 31 August 1948.
20   Webb Papers, AWM 92 – Series 4, Wallet 4, Mei Ju-Ao to W.F. Webb 'On Draft Judgment No. 4', 11 March 1948.
21   Bernard Papers, F Δ rès 874-10-1-48, Mei Ju-Ao to W.F. Webb, 8 December 1946. Emphasis in original.

ties of the Anglo-American doctrine of conspiracy', specifically 'how in certain cases, an act to be committed may be itself legitimate, but conspiring to commit it may be deemed criminal'. Mei continued, 'Conspiracy is much wider in scope and application under the Anglo-American law than under other legal systems. Under the Chinese system, mere conspiring, planning or preparing (without act of attempting) to commit ordinary crimes is not punishable'. Ever pragmatic, Mei suggested a compromise. 'I am wondering whether it is necessary or feasible ... to evoke the technical Anglo-American doctrine in regard to "naked conspiracy"', asked the Chinese judge. 'As *a practical* matter, none of the accused is charged solely with "naked conspiracy"'.[22] To square the circle, Mei fell back on moral justifications. 'Aggressive war is a crime of the most heinous kind', Mei explained. 'It is many times more heinous than murder or robbery, treason or revolt'. If conspiracy could be employed to hold individuals accountable for this 'heinous' act, then so be it.[23] Like Mei, Zaryanov found ways to accept the conspiracy charge, despite its novelty in international law. He understood conspiracy was 'one of the pivotal issues of the trial and [of] particular great importance for deciding correctly the question of guilt of individual defendants'.[24] Zaryanov explained:

> [Conspiracy] implies a whole system of far-reaching measures deeply involving all the aspects of the country's life. In Japan, owing to a special part played by the military in the country's public activities, the aggressive schemes of the conspirators found a definite expression in national policy.... It is necessary to emphasize definitely that in this case the *execution of the conspiracy went on ever since it was formed* and that it progressed continuously in various forms.... Throughout the historical period under the Tribunal's consideration.[25]

International justice requires buy-in from all parties. Mei and Zaryanov managed to balance principle for the sake of practicality in Tokyo. Their often overlooked efforts behind the scenes helped build a Tokyo majority.

Imbued with a pragmatic sensibility, the Philippines judge Delfin Jaranilla became another unsung judicial binder in Tokyo. Jaranilla believed in strict accountability. His concurring opinion, which decried IMTFE sentences as 'too

---

22   Webb Papers, AWM 92 – Series 4, Wallet 4, Mei Ju-Ao to W.F. Webb 'On Draft Judgment No. 4', 11 March 1948. Emphasis in original.

23   Ibid.

24   Bernard Papers, F Δ rès 874-10-49-88, I.M. Zaryanov to W.F. Webb, 31 August 1948.

25   Ibid. Emphasis in original.

lenient, not exemplary and deterrent, and not commensurate with the gravity of the offense or offenses committed', revealed a no-nonsense legal ideology; whatever it took to defend IMTFE law. Jaranilla ridiculed Indian justice Pal's dissent. By accepting appointment as a judge, Jaranilla argued, Pal had 'unconditionally accepted not only the validity of the Charter and of all its provisions', but also had agreed to the Allied quest 'for the just and prompt trial and *punishment* of the major war criminals in the Far East'.[26] Dissent poisoned the war's legacy. 'This war is the most hideous, hateful and destructive wherein such untold atrocities have been perpetrated and committed. Shall we overlook and let calmly the international criminal acts go unnoticed and unpunished?', he asked. *'Justice* is the fundamental aim of the courts; in the absence of statutory inhibition, [jurists] may take [extraordinary] steps'.[27] Special circumstances called for exceptional measures. For Jaranilla, ends justified means. Justice meant legal compromise and buy-in.

Community of Dissent

Dissent strengthened majority. Majority behaviour, in turn, hardened dissent. A disparate group of objectors emerged behind the scenes in Tokyo. Like their majority counterparts, Tokyo's community of dissent rested on personal sensibilities and interpersonal relationships. Dissenters would not, or could not, buy into the IMTFE project. Once among like-minded associates, a sense of collective outrage amplified personal frustration. Ground-level considerations outweighed grand-scale politics. Indeed, in most cases, open dissent by judges embarrassed their home governments. Powerful personal forces – principles, obduracy, friendship, acrimony – underlay judicial dissents in Tokyo. Dissent did not happen overnight. It was not predetermined. It emerged and evolved behind the scenes.

Dutch judge B.V.A. Röling arrived in Tokyo with doubts about the proceedings' legality. Yet, he also came convinced the tribunal was necessary. 'The dreadfulness of World War II', he wrote, 'made us realize the necessity of preventing wars in the future.... These horrors of World War II may compel the

---

26   Macmillan Brown Library, University of Canterbury, Christchurch, New Zealand, E.H. Northcroft Papers – MB 1549, Box 324, Delfin Jaranilla, 'Concurring Opinion of the Member from the Philippines', 1 November 1948. Hereafter 'Northcroft Papers' and 'Jaranilla Opinion'. Emphasis in original.

27   Jaranilla Opinion. Emphasis in original.

nations to take the legal steps to achieve the maintenance of peace'.[28] Röling initially tried to work within the bench. In January 1947, Röling told Webb that although 'prepared to write my own judgment', he believed a cohesive final judgment would 'carry more weight' for the future of international justice.[29] 'This trial is of a special importance for the whole world', he further explained, 'We have, if possible, to prove by our activity that representatives of eleven nations can come together and really can cooperate.... We have to do the utmost to come to one "judgment of the majority"'.[30] The 'utmost' proved insufficient. Röling's misgivings deepened over time. 'I have adjusted my opinion and have accepted the charter and its key points are an extension of International Law and have accepted crimes against peace as an idea', he admitted to a friend in July 1948. The compromise being: 'My own special interpretation which separates this crime as a "political crime" distinct from "conventional war crimes"'.[31] He tried at times to buy into the majority, but belonged to the community of dissent in spirit and association. Röling believed that sitting as a Tokyo judge 'does not, and cannot, imply that the Tribunal would be bound to follow the Charter in case it should contain provisions in violation of international law'.[32] He worried that his majority colleagues would push too far too fast. For example, referring to the prosecution's attempt to establish 'murder' as an actionable offence in warfare, Röling protested: 'To assume that every intentional killing in an illegal war, committed with the knowledge of the illegality of that war, is murder would be a negation of the recognition of war in international relations. It would constitute a change in international law which this Tribunal does not have the authority to bring about'.[33] Majority members convinced themselves and each other that the IMTFE could invent new laws. This brashness simply did not feel right to dissenters, despite efforts by some to come onboard. As they shared doubts, they built dissent.

A schism developed regarding the IMTFE's fundamental legitimacy. Judges either felt 'for it' or 'against it'. Indian justice Radhabinod Pal, for one, arrived in

---

28   Northcroft Papers, Box 333, B.V.A. Röling, 'Opinion of Mr. Justice Röling, Member for the Netherlands', 12 November 1948: 179-249. Hereafter 'Röling Dissent'.

29   Webb Papers, Series 1 Wallet 10, Justice B.V.A. Röling to Sir William Webb, 23 January 1947.

30   Nationaal Archief Den Hague, Archief van B.V.A. Röling – 2.21.273, Box 11, Memorandum to Sir William Webb from Justice B.V.A. Röling, 17 February 1947. Hereafter 'Röling Papers'.

31   Röling Papers, Box 27, B.V.A. Röling to Dr. H.N. Boon, Chief of Diplomatic Affairs Division, Ministry of Foreign Affairs, 6 July 1948. I am indebted to Frederik Vermote for help with translation.

32   Northcroft Papers, Box 330, *Bernard and Röling on Judgment*, B.V.A. Röling, 'Judgment Part B, Chapter III: 'Japanese Aggression against the USSR'', 28 July 1948.

33   Northcroft Papers, Box 330, *Bernard and Röling on Judgment*, Röling 'Some Points of Law'.

Tokyo expecting to object. He never seriously considered backing the IMTFE and by trial's end, he unleashed an almost 1,300-page dissenting judgment dismissing nearly every aspect of the trial and calling for the acquittal of all accused. Pal's myopic attack on the tribunal used whatever would strengthen his case.[34] Rooted in deep cynicism about the court's double standards, especially its colonial hypocrisies, Pal's values, background, and reaction to the IMTFE experience itself allowed no other legal response. 'It is perhaps right that we should feel a certain satisfaction and recognize a certain fitness in the suffering of one who has done an international wrong', he wrote. 'It may even be morally obligatory upon us to feel indignant at a wrong done'. However, 'it would be going too far to say that a demand for the gratification of this feeling of revenge alone would justify criminal law'.[35] The Indian judge never tried to collaborate or find common ground with majority members. His presence alone set the tone for other dissenters.

French judge Henri Bernard reflects the built nature of dissent in Tokyo. Bernard seemed even-handed and open-minded in many ways. He accepted arguments from both prosecution and defence teams. He welcomed the court's ambitious claims for moral legitimacy. Yet, Bernard never managed to bend 'rule' to 'practice' at the IMTFE. He struggled to accept unfamiliar evidentiary protocols and objected when British or American concepts were presumed 'universal', 'usual' or 'normal'. 'When invoking their national legislation', Bernard asked judges, '[please] do so not in the name of its nationality but with the assistance of the reasons which have caused its adoption'. Conspiracy without substance seemed 'particularly regrettable' to Bernard because 'we are then apparently invited to compare the alleged facts with the definition of the conspiracy which is presented to us as similar in every country, when on the contrary, it is totally different in many of them'.[36] Bernard consistently tried to bring the court around to a more French civil law mindset, without ever appre-

---

34   For more on Pal's mutable legal ideology, see N. Boister and R. Cryer, *The Tokyo International Military Tribunal: A Reappraisal* (Oxford University Press, 2008), pp. 285-91; T. Brook, 'The Tokyo Judgment and the Rape of Nanking', *The Journal of Asian Studies* 60, no. 3 (2001), 673-700, E.S. Kopelman (Borgwardt), 'Ideology and International Law: The Dissent of the Indian Justice at the Tokyo War Crimes Trial', *New York University Journal of International Law and Politics*, 23, no. 2 (1991), 373-444, A. Nandy, 'The Other Within: The Strange Case of Radhabinod Pal's Judgment on Culpability', *New Literary History*, 23, no. 1 (1992), 45-67, T.S. Rama Rao, 'The Dissenting Judgment of Mr Justice Pal at the Tokyo Trial', *The Indian Yearbook of International Affairs*, 2 (1953), 277.

35   Northcroft Papers, Box: 332a-c, Radhabinod Pal, 'Dissenting Judgment', 30 July 1948.

36   Webb Papers, AWM 92 – Series 4, Wallet 4, Henri Bernard to W.F. Webb, 'Remarks Relative to the Naked Conspiracy', 13 October 1948.

ciating or accepting the court's international character and jurisprudence. When these attempts failed, the French judge eventually committed to dissent.[37] Bernard's objections came from legal disagreements, but social alienation also played a role. His doubts grew stronger, the more the French judge associated with other objectors. Belonging – and not – transformed Bernard's dogmatic legal sensibility into formal judicial dissent.

Majority judges often consciously cut the Bernard, Pal, Röling trio from the loop. In December 1946, for example, Justice McDougall wrote on behalf of the majority to President Webb regarding the tribunal's jurisdiction. 'I am not circulating this draft to other members', McDougall explained, 'preferring to submit it for your consideration first, thus eliminating the spirit of competing judgments'.[38] Both Bernard and Röling tried to work with their colleagues, but they chafed under the unwillingness of other judges to accept differences of opinion. As early as August 1946, both complained to this effect to the president. 'I had the same feeling as Justice Bernard expressed in his memorandum of the 23rd of August', Röling wrote. He continued, 'In my opinion, each judge who has at the end of the trial the duty to make up his mind, has the natural right to ask questions'.[39] The grouping of objectors became so fixed in the minds of their colleagues, that other judges began treating them as a collective. Northcroft, for instance, placed the opinions of Pal, Röling and Bernard together in a separate section of his personal collection of trial material, which included a separate volume, entitled 'Bernard and Röling on Judgment'.[40]

'Otherness' formed a two-way street. Dissenting judges came to revel in their maverick status. Röling's tendency to challenge colleagues irked majority members, especially over politically volatile issues. For instance, Röling incensed his Soviet colleague by disputing prosecution's charges of Japanese aggression against the USSR. 'Justice Röling either did not bother to analize (sic) the ample evidence pertaining to this issue or deliberately ignored it', sniped Zaryanov. 'At any rate Justice Röling reasons in such a way, as if there were no such evidence'. Röling's 'absolutely arbitrary' and 'vicious' argument 'grossly distorts the actual state of affairs' and 'goes even further than the Defense'. More damningly, Zaryanov alleged, 'What Justice Röling proposes to regard as evidence as a matter of common knowledge is actually not evidence but wide-spread slanderous fascists propaganda the repetition of which at this

---

37   Northcroft Papers, 334, Henri Bernard, 'Dissenting Judgment of the Member from France of the International Military Tribunal for the Far East', 12 November 1948.

38   Webb Papers, Series 1, Wallet 9, E.S. McDougall to W.F. Webb, 23 December 1946.

39   Webb Papers, Series 1, Wallet 10, B.V. Röling to W.F. Webb, 26 August 1946.

40   Northcroft Papers, Box 330, Bernard and Röling on Judgment.

time would be trite and cynical'.[41] Justice Bernard similarly angered colleagues
by submitting revisions to early drafts of the majority judgment. He became
particularly unpopular when he questioned preliminary findings regarding the
war in China. The first judge to take offence was McDougall, who was part of
the drafting committee. In one searing passage, the Canadian judge implied
that his colleague was obtuse and dismissed Bernard's arguments as a waste of
time. 'I shall discontinue further comment', McDougall wrote, 'as the investigation of your criticism has taken a great deal of time and your complete
misreading.... is somewhat disheartening'.[42] Responding to the personal tenor
of McDougall's message, Bernard wrote to 'insist' that his views be answered.
'I made them in a spirit of collaboration with the majority and sacrificed considerable time and care which I could have spared if my only desire was to form
my own judgment'.[43] Chinese justice Mei called Bernard's arguments 'purely
speculative' and 'absolutely mistaken'. Even though Mei dismissed Bernard's
work as 'not of sufficient importance to warrant detailed discussion', he took
enough time to scold the French judge: 'One must not see only the tree and
overlook the forest. This attitude is especially important for us who are deciding a case of such vast magnitude'.[44] Eventually, specific objections stopped
mattering. The act of dissent itself angered majority members and the 'other-
ing' of dissenters cemented their opposition.

Objections began to determine personal networks and social sets. The
strong friendship that blossomed between Justices Pal and Röling exemplifies
this development. The two connected immediately and remained lifelong
friends.[45] Both enjoyed poetry and philosophy. Both represented relatively
'minor' powers outside the Occupation establishment and separate from the
Anglo-American cultural majority of the tribunal. They also sat beside each

---

41   Röling Papers, Box 23, Memorandum to the Honorable President and Members of the
      Tribunal from Major-General of Justice Zaryanov, 21 August 1948.

42   Bernard Papers, F° Δ rés 874-10-1-42, Memorandum to The Hon. Mr. Justice Bernard from
      Mr. Justice McDougall RE: Your Memorandum on Part B Chapter II – Draft Judgment,
      7 July 1948.

43   Bernard Papers, F° Δ rés 874-10-1-46, Memorandum to Hon. Mr. Justice McDougall from
      The Member from France RE: Reply to Memorandum of 7 July 1948, 22 July 1948.

44   Bernard Papers, F° Δ rés 874-10-52, Memorandum to The Hon. Mr. Justice Bernard from
      Justice J.A. Mei RE: Comments on 'Remarks Concerning the Draft of Judgment of the
      Majority', 17 August 1948.

45   In 1959, for example, Pal addressed a letter to 'Dear Bert' and signed it off 'With love for
      your children and with the kindest regards to your dear wife and to yourself, Yours affec-
      tionately'. Röling Papers, Box 28, Radhabinod Pal to B.V.A. Röling, 14 August 1959.

other in court.[46] Röling felt evident fondness for Pal. 'I showed your letter to my Indian colleague, sitting next to me here on the bench', Röling wrote to an acquaintance. 'He, as a judge, thought it fair, to answer you. So, you will receive a letter from Justice Pal, who is a poet in his heart'.[47] Pal likewise admired Röling. 'I do not give up hopes that we may yet meet again very soon', he wrote at the trial's end, 'but even if that pleasure be denied me, I would never forget the days I could associate with you'.[48] Mutual criticism of the IMTFE cemented the pair's bond, but a shared sense of dislocation and estrangement in Japan and on the bench fortified the connection. Beyond legal issues and personal sensibilities, emotional dynamics drew people together. Feelings of personal, social and ideological otherness tied dissenters together in Tokyo. The community of dissent in Tokyo became a true community.

Conclusion

Justice (as an ideal) purports to be 'blind'. Yet, courts (as functioning institutions) unfold through negotiated processes and lived experiences. International tribunals navigate especially complex legal, political and social flows to produce definitive judgments on history's most serious crimes. At the Tokyo IMT, judges from eleven countries evaluated two decades of history, a fifty-five count indictment against twenty-eight defendants, thousands of exhibits translated from dozens of languages, hundreds of witness testimonies, and two and half years of trial proceedings. They were expected to produce a single judgment. Instead, the Tokyo bench issued a majority judgment accompanied by five separate opinions.[49] Subjective forces fractured Tokyo's outcomes.

---

46 Seating arrangements should not be dismissed when understanding social dynamics. For example, Justices MacDougall, Patrick, and Cramer – three pillars of the majority – sat beside each other on the IMTFE bench. Likewise, sitting together in court may have helped Justices Mei and Zaryanov overcome the deep political division between their home governments, not to mention their personal politics.

47 Röling Papers, Box 27, B.V.A. Röling to Patricia Daly, 27 August 1946.

48 Röling Papers, Radhabinod Pal to B.V.A. Röling, 11 October 1948, Box 27.

49 Justices Bernard, Pal, and Röling submitted dissenting judgments. Justice Jaranilla submitted a separate concurring opinion. President Webb submitted a 'separate opinion'. Strictly speaking, Webb did not 'dissent'. Nevertheless, he cannot be considered a majority member, having published both a 'separate opinion' and an unpublished three-volume over 600-page alternative 'judgment'. See: Northcroft Papers, Box: 334, W.F. Webb, 'Separate Opinion of the President', 1 November 1948; and Webb Papers, AWM 92 – Series 2, Wallet 1-3, W.F. Webb, Judgment, Volume I-III, 17 September 1948.

Social networks defined by personal sensibilities split its members. Judges either bought into the IMTFE project, or defined themselves by difference. Internal critics formed a distinct community of dissent. Acts of defiance fed off each other; interaction together cemented opposition to the court. The manufactured 'majority', in turn, relied on a shared sense of purpose rather than genuine legal consensus. Judgment in Tokyo meant building blocs amongst dissonant personalities – creating a law unto itself.

The human element of Tokyo's judicial experience may represent the peculiar product of a singular set of circumstances: running a ground-breaking international court in post-war Japan. As a unique moment in history, the IMTFE may hold no lessons for other similar institutions. Japan may have been just far enough on the global periphery to allow trial participants to overlook or downplay directives from home. The scramble to staff and organize the court may have resulted in too many personnel compromises; too little competence, insufficient gravitas. The loneliness of working abroad in a chaotic post-war milieu may have shaped behaviours in unexpected ways as well. The 'strangeness' of life in Japan may have forced people to act outside themselves, resulting in a fragmented judiciary with disjointed findings. The Tokyo judgments may represent accidents of history crafted in an unreplicable space of fluid alliances, friendship-based decision-making, and individual autonomy in international relations. I do not think so. The IMTFE experience may have been special, but history suggests otherwise. Indeed, the problems faced at the IMTFE have proven so common in global affairs, that the best – perhaps only – way to view the Tokyo IMT is as an archetype of all international organizations. The dissenting communities, the majorities manufactured, the blocs built in Tokyo were unique in their time and place, but not their experience; they represent a universal experience of being international.

It is tempting to view and analyse bold political and structural international projects from correspondingly grand political perspectives and visions. In reality, however, such bodies are at least as subject to local contingencies and the human element as they are outgrowths of global forces. My research shows that Tokyo was defined in situ rather than in far-off capitals. Allegiances inside justice were defined by a range of onsite dynamics – convenience, legal objectives, personal sensibilities, social interaction, mutual distrust, even physical proximity – that matched global forces only when also suited to the immediate on the ground needs of participants. The IMTFE's legal world formed an improvised and volatile space where emotions and experiences came to define legal difference in Tokyo as much as fixed notions of jurisprudence and procedure. Inside the raised stakes environment of international justice, judges interpreted the law using spirit as well as training, feeling bound with reason. Judges negotiated a mix of sensibilities rooted in interpersonal relations, all filtered through an internal and institutional logic. This blend of personal judgment and juridical cognition in Tokyo confounds any notion of an objective and sterile legal process. Individual legal responses varied considerably, but the project at hand forced certain broad delineations. Intellectual openness, the willingness to 'create' law, conviction in the IMTFE project, and preconceived views of Japanese guilt drove majority members. Meanwhile, dissenters created an alternate legal experience in Tokyo, leaving a destructive narrative of dysfunction. The exaggerated promise, principles and pragmatics of international justice created an impossible situation for judges expected, and expecting, to produce a conclusive judgment on Japan's crimes and to provide an exemplar for future courts. The resulting personal and legal contradictions helped establish the IMTFE's reputation for cynical victors' justice, an epithet which continues to undermine the tribunal's place in history, law and memory.

Bibliography

Carl Berendsen, *Mr. Ambassador: Memoirs of Sir Carl Berendsen*, edited by Hugh Templeton (Wellington: Victoria University Press, 2009).

Carl Berendsen and Alister McIntosh, *Undiplomatic Dialogue: Letters between Carl Berendsen and Alister McIntosh, 1943-52*, edited by I.C. McGibbon (Auckland University Press, 1993).

Neil Boister and Robert Cryer, *The Tokyo International Military Tribunal: A Reappraisal* (Oxford University Press, 2008).

Arnold C. Brackman, *The Other Nuremberg: The Untold Story of the Tokyo War Crimes Trials* (New York: Morrow, 1987).

Timothy Brook, 'The Tokyo Judgment and the Rape of Nanking', *The Journal of Asian Studies*, 60, no. 3 (2001), 673-700.

Elisabeth S. Kopelman (Borgwardt), 'Ideology and International Law: The Dissent of the Indian Justice at the Tokyo War Crimes Trial', *New York University Journal of International Law and Politics*, 23, no. 2 (1991), 373-444.

Ashis Nandy, 'The Other Within: The Strange Case of Radhabinod Pal's Judgment on Culpability', *New Literary History*, 23, no. 1 (1992), 45-67.

T.S. Rama Rao, 'The Dissenting Judgment of Mr Justice Pal at the Tokyo Trial', *The Indian Yearbook of International Affairs*, 2 (1953), 277.

Daniel Wickberg, 'What is the History of Sensibilities? On Cultural Histories, Old and New', *The American Historical Review*, 112, no. 3 (2007), 661-84.

Wanhong Zhang, 'From Nuremberg to Tokyo: Some Reflections on the Tokyo Trial (On the Sixtieth Anniversary of the Nuremberg Trials)', *Cardozo Law Review*, 27, no. 42006, 1673-82.

CHAPTER 2

Sir William Webb and Beyond: Australia and the International Military Tribunal for the Far East

Narrelle Morris

More than seventy years after the Second World War, there are now some solid legal historical studies of Japanese war crimes and the consequent Allied international and national war crimes investigations and prosecutions, and more are emerging every year. Traditionally, however, there has been little focus on the approaches to Japanese war crimes of the 'smaller' Allied Powers, including Australia. Indeed, an earlier anniversary book on the International Military Tribunal for the Far East (IMTFE) acknowledged the 'glaring gap' in the literature in relation to Australian judge and president, Sir William Flood Webb KBE (1887-1972).[1] What little has been written on Webb generally adopts Richard Minear's views[2] of the trial as a starting point and hence presents a negative view of him.[3] Indeed, Webb is usually damned with the same faint praise as offered by the eminent R. John Pritchard, who summarized Webb at the IMTFE thus: 'Sir William Webb, by all accounts, was coarse, ill-tempered, and highly opinionated. He was hard-working and endeavoured to be conscientious, however'.[4] Yet, as James Sedgwick has pointed out, '[t]he overbearing caricature of Webb is so entrenched in the historiography that it is rarely questioned, let alone explained'.[5] Moreover, the focus on Webb, even as small as it is, has left other aspects of the Australian approach to the IMTFE

---

1 'Editors' Preface' in Y. Tanaka, T. McCormack and G. Simpson, (eds.), *Beyond Victor's Justice? The Tokyo War Crimes Trial Revisited* (Leiden: Martinus Nijhoff, 2011), p. xxix.

2 R. Minear, *Victors' Justice: The Tokyo War Crimes Trial* (Princeton, N.J.: Princeton University Press, 1971).

3 See T. Hewton, '"Webb's Justice": The Role of William Flood Webb in the Tokyo Trial, 1946-1948', unpublished Honours thesis, University of Adelaide (1976); and D. Smith, 'Commentary on "Sir William Webb – Hobbesian Jurist"' in M. White and A. Rahemtula (eds.), *Queensland Judges on the High Court* (Brisbane: Supreme Court of Queensland Library, 2003), pp. 151-70.

4 R. John Pritchard, 'An Overview of the Historical Importance of the Tokyo War Trial', in C. Hosoya, N. Andō, Y. Ōnuma and R. Minear (eds.), *The Tokyo War Crimes Trial: An International Symposium* (New York: Kodansha International Ltd, 1986), p. 92.

5 J. Sedgwick, 'A People's Court: Emotion, Participant Experiences, and the Shaping of Postwar Justice at the International Military Tribunal for the Far East, 1946-48, *Diplomacy & Statecraft*, vol. 22. no. 3, (2011), 491.

understudied, including the role of the Australian associate prosecutor, Justice (later Sir) Alan James Mansfield (1902-80).[6]

Webb was one of the more controversial judicial appointees to the IMTFE, as it was suggested at the time, and frequently since, that he should have refused the appointment or disqualified himself from sitting on the basis that his investigation of Japanese war crimes during the war meant that he had been too closely involved with the issues to be determined at trial and could not be impartial. As the sole judicial 'voice' of the trial – possessing the only microphone on the bench – he was also a controversial president, for many reasons too complex to go into in this brief chapter. This chapter examines, firstly, the selection of Webb as the Australian judge and the issues of apprehended bias that arose. Secondly, it gives a short overview of Webb's approaches to and views of the trial, including his relations with judicial colleagues and counsel. Thirdly, it gives an overview of the prosecution approach of Mansfield. Finally, this chapter deals briefly with Webb's separate judgment.

As Yuma Totani has contended, the Australian participants in the IMTFE 'profoundly shaped the course of the trial and left their deep imprint on its outcome'.[7] Interestingly, correspondence reveals that Webb knew that, due to his wartime work, he probably ought not to sit in judgment on any trial of Japanese war criminals, whether national or international trials. That Webb accepted his nomination suggests that he believed that, as an experienced judicial officer, he was qualified to sit and could appropriately distance himself so as to remain impartial. Yet, if he had acted more conservatively and refused the appointment or recused himself, the IMTFE might have been quite a different tribunal – a hypothetical that underscores how a biographical approach to the IMTFE offers an innovative way of examining it. Whether the trial would have been less criticized overall, however, is unlikely.

Sir William Webb's Appointment

After studying law, Webb was called to the Bar in 1913 and thereafter rose rapidly through the Queensland public service to the office of crown solicitor. His judicial career began with an appointment to the Queensland Court of

---

6 See only F. Cullity, 'Australia's Involvement in the International Military Tribunal for the Far East: The Case of Sir William Webb and Sir Alan Mansfield', *Australian Bar Review*, vol. 41 (2016), 236-45.

7 Y. Totani, *The Tokyo War Crimes Trial: The Pursuit of Justice in the Wake of World War II* (Cambridge, Mass.: Harvard University Asia Centre, 2008), p. 42.

Industrial Arbitration in 1925. He became senior puisne judge of the Supreme Court of Queensland in 1940 and succeeded to the office of chief justice a few weeks later. He was knighted in 1942.[8] The pertinent part of Webb's wartime career commenced in 1943, when he was appointed as Australia's war crimes commissioner to investigate whether the Japanese armed forces were committing atrocities or breaching the rules of warfare. He was appointed a further two times as a war crimes commissioner in 1944-45 and produced three substantial war crimes reports.[9]

Given his role as war crimes commissioner, Webb was accustomed to being consulted regularly by the Australian government on war crimes matters. It probably appeared par for the course in late 1945, therefore, when he was 'urgently'[10] consulted by the Department of External Affairs about a response to the United States' request for Australia to designate military officers or civilians qualified for appointment to the forthcoming international war crimes tribunal for Japanese war criminals.[11] When asked for advice about nominees, Webb suggested 'Judges of High and State Supreme Courts, Kings Counsels and Professors of Law',[12] although, as Chief Justice of the Supreme Court of Queensland, he would have been included on that roster. Webb's name seems to have been put forward in early November 1945 by Professor Kenneth Bailey to the Department of External Affairs, who then consulted Sir George Knowles, then Secretary of the Attorney-General's Department and Solicitor-General.[13] Knowles had initially suggested two judges of the High Court of Australia but then revised his list to include a state judge, two barristers, a professor of law and Webb.[14]

---

8   See H.A. Weld, 'Webb, Sir William Flood (1887-1972)', *Australian Dictionary of Biography*, National Centre of Biography, Australian National University, <http://adb.anu.edu.au/biography/webb-sir-william-flood-11991/text21499>.

9   On Webb's extra-judicial appointments generally, see P. Provis, '"I hope to be of some real assistance to your government": The Extra-Judicial Activities of Sir William Flood Webb, 1942-1948', unpublished PhD thesis, Flinders University (2015).

10   National Archives of Australia (NAA): MP742/1, 336/1/408, cablegram from Department of External Affairs (hereafter Dept Ext Aff) to Evatt, 25 October 1945.

11   NAA, A1066, H45/590/3, cablegram from the Australian Legation, Washington to Dept Ext Aff, 19 October 1945.

12   NAA, MP749/8, 66/431/2, cablegram from Dept Ext Aff to Australian Legation, Washington, 13 November 1945.

13   Evatt Collection, Flinders University Library, 'War. War Crimes' file, letter from Knowles to Evatt, 13 November 1945.

14   NAA, A1066, H45/590/3, record of telephone conversation between Hill and Knowles, 16 November 1945; and memorandum from Knowles to the Secretary, Dept Ext Aff, 21 November 1945.

When the list of proposed civilian nominees was sent in late November 1945 to the Minister for External Affairs and Attorney-General, Dr H.V. Evatt, then overseas, he responded that he was of 'the opinion that experience in criminal jurisdiction was very essential' to the nominees. He suggested, in order, Lord Wright of Durley (Australian representative to and chairman of the United Nations War Crimes Commission (UNWCC) based in London), then Webb, Knowles and several prominent state judges.[15] Webb knew about his possible nomination, as Evatt's response was forwarded to him.[16] Lord Wright was consulted on the idea in late 1945 but he felt that his existing obligations to the UNWCC would not allow him to be absent from the United Kingdom long enough to serve on such a tribunal.[17] Instead, Lord Wright suggested that he 'should not be nominated with the idea that he will be able to sit' but that if both he and Webb were nominated, Webb could 'take an active part at the trial'.[18] That idea appeared to draw no support in Australia. Instead, Evatt's second pick of Webb accepted his prospective nomination on 13 December 1945, 'subject to my being qualified to act'.[19] In doing so, Webb appeared well aware that his nomination might attract criticism due to his war crimes work, pointing out that '[o]f course, I have so far made no finding against any major war criminal'.[20]

With the United States pressing very hard for nominees to be communicated in early January 1946, Evatt approved the nomination of Webb as the Australian judge and Mansfield as associate prosecutor.[21] Mansfield had been admitted to the Queensland Bar in 1924 and was appointed to the Supreme Court of Queensland in 1940. In September 1945, he had also been appointed to join Webb as a war crimes commissioner.[22] An assistant prosecutor to aid Mansfield in Tokyo was selected from the Australian Army: Maj. Thomas Francis Mornane,

---

15 NAA, MP742/1, 336/1/408, cablegram from Australian Legation, Washington to Dept Ext Aff, 29 November 1945.

16 NAA, A1066, H45/590/3, teleprinter message from the Secretary, Dept Ext Aff to Webb, 5 December 1945.

17 NAA, A1066, H45/590/3, reported in cablegram from the External Affairs Officer, London, to Evatt, 14 December 1945.

18 NAA, A6238, 3, reported in letter from Mansfield to Webb, 20 December 1945.

19 NAA, A1066, H45/590/3, letter from Webb to the Secretary, Dept Ext Aff, 13 December 1945.

20 Ibid.

21 NAA, MP742/1, 336/1/408, cablegram from the Secretary, Dept Ext Aff to the Secretary, Department of the Army, 16 January 1946.

22 See J. Greenwood, 'Mansfield, Sir Alan James (1902-1980)', *Australian Dictionary of Biography*, National Centre of Biography, Australian National University <http://adb.anu.edu.au/biography/mansfield-sir-alan-james-11053/text19669>.

then a member of the Australian Army Legal Corps and, ordinarily, an assistant crown solicitor for Victoria.[23]

Webb and Mansfield's nominations were conveyed to the US Department of State on 14 January 1946.[24] The following month, Gen. Douglas MacArthur, the Supreme Commander of Allied Powers, appointed Webb as president of the tribunal.[25] The reasoning behind MacArthur's decision is unclear. MacArthur may have intended to simply select the American judge as the president but changed his mind when he was disappointed with President Truman's nomination.[26] If so, then perhaps Webb was the judge with whom MacArthur was most familiar: Webb and MacArthur had met officially during the war, when MacArthur had been based in Brisbane. While some have described them as 'friends',[27] their direct correspondence is not quite suggestive of that close an acquaintance. Even in private correspondence to Lady Webb, Webb referred to MacArthur formally as 'General MacArthur' or even as 'the Supreme Commander'.[28] Certainly, no degree of their acquaintance induced MacArthur to bend or break the Occupation's regulation about the entry of wives to Japan that, to Webb's annoyance, prohibited Lady Webb's admission for quite some time. Indeed, MacArthur had rejected five written applications in respect of Lady Webb by January 1947.[29]

When Webb's appointment was announced in early 1946, the perception of judicial bias prompted immediate criticism. Even a Supreme Court colleague, the well-known outspoken Justice Frank Brennan, warned that as Webb had investigated and prepared reports on Japanese atrocities, his appointment to the IMTFE 'might place him in a false and invidious position'. While Brennan was 'perfectly satisfied that Sir William, a courteous gentleman, would be just and impartial', he thought that if Webb served, 'foreign nations will be in a

---

23   NAA, MP742/1, 336/1/408, see Mornane's particulars of service and qualifications in memo-
      randum from the Secretary of the Department of the Army to the Secretary, Dept Ext Aff,
      circa 1 February 1946.

24   NAA, MP742/1, 336/1/408, reported in cablegram from the Dept Ext Aff to the Australian
      Legation, Washington, 29 January 1946.

25   Appointment of Members of the International Military Tribunal for the Far East, GHQ,
      SCAP, 15 February 1946, held in R. John Pritchard, S.M. Zaide and D.C. Watt, *The Tokyo War
      Crimes Trial*, vol. 1 (New York and London: Garland, 1981).

26   A.C. Brackman, *The Other Nuremberg: The Untold Story of the Tokyo War Crimes Trials*
      (London: Collins, 1989), p. 70.

27   See, for example, T. Maga, *Judgment at Tokyo: The Japanese War Crimes Trials* (Lexington:
      The University Press of Kentucky, 2001), p. 29.

28   See NAA, M1418, 5, letter from Webb to Lady Webb, 12 December [no year].

29   NAA, M1418, 3, letter from Webb to Latham, 3 January 1947.

position to point the finger of scorn at our conception of British justice'. In his view, Evatt 'may prove to have done a great disservice to Australia' in recommending Webb when:

> [w]e have, in Australia, other excellent and brilliant jurists, any one of whom could fill the judicial role with dignity and distinction. I therefore feel it is my duty to give a timely warning to save our country from contemptuous ridicule.[30]

In response, Evatt pointed out that Webb had made 'no investigation' into major Japanese war criminals and was, therefore, 'completely free to give his judgment on all the matters' that would come before the tribunal.[31]

Evatt's public reassurance about Webb's lack of involvement with Japanese major war criminals was quite disingenuous. In fact, Webb's third war crimes commission granted on 3 September 1945, together with Justice Mansfield and Judge Richard Kirby, specifically authorized them to investigate a set list of war crimes, including at number one on the list:

> Planning, preparation, initiation or waging of a war of aggression or a war in violation of international treaties, agreements or assurances, or participation in a common plan or conspiracy for the accomplishment of any of the foregoing.[32]

This was an instruction to investigate crimes against peace, which logically had to involve major (not minor) war criminals. It is true that, regardless of the typologies of the war crimes under investigation, Webb's commissions did not operate judicially. As Webb repeatedly pointed out, the regulations under which his commissions operated empowered him to inform his mind in any manner he saw fit and he was not bound by the rules of evidence.[33] In his view, this prevented his war crimes work from 'being a judicial proceeding'.[34] Judges had only been chosen as commissioners because they were 'experienced in

---

30 'Judge's Doubts on Webb Appointment', *Sydney Morning Herald* (NSW), 22 March 1946, p. 3.

31 Commonwealth of Australia, House of Representatives, Hansard, 22 March 1946, p. 533 (Evatt).

32 NAA, A11049 ROLL 1, Board of Inquiry, 'Report on War Crimes Committed by Enemy Subjects Against Australians and Others', 31 January 1946, p. 2.

33 *National Security (Inquiries) Regulations*, S.R. 1941, No. 35 (Cth), r 5.

34 NAA, A10943, 1, Sir William Webb, 'A Report on Japanese Atrocities and Breaches of the Rules of Warfare', March 1944, p. 2.

sifting the truth' and were 'not likely to be imposed upon'.[35] As he elaborated at length in one war crimes report:

> The Board [of Inquiry into war crimes] does not try the Japanese; it merely finds as an administrative body whether a war crime has been committed and, if it has, produces the evidence.... Actually then, the Board does not make any finding against any war criminal who will be dealt with ...[36]

Yet Webb was involved in Australia's preparatory work on major Japanese war criminals from mid-1945. In June 1945, for instance, External Affairs asked for Webb's opinion as to whether Japan's leaders could be prosecuted as major war criminals.[37] Webb responded that he had discussed with Lord Wright whether Japanese Cabinet members should be named in his war crimes report, given that the building of the Thai-Burma Railway, for instance, was 'such a large undertaking' that the Cabinet 'must have had full knowledge that it was being built and by what kind of labour, and to have connived at the breach' of international law involved.[38] Webb advised that he thought 'all Japanese offenders, including the Sovereign' could be prosecuted, even though Emperor Hirohito was 'not an actual perpetrator on the spot, but an abettor residing in Tokio [sic]'.[39] Similarly, in September 1945, Webb advised that the evidence he had taken during his commissions:

> strongly suggest[s] that the Japanese armed forces were, to say the least, badly disciplined and that, but for the fact that there were some humane Japanese officers, he would conclude that the atrocities were the policy of the Japanese Government. However, that Government *must in any event be held responsible*, unless they can show they were not aware of them [the atrocities] or that, if they were, then that they did all in their power to prevent them.[40]

---

35   NAA, A6238, 3, letter from Webb to Mansfield, 29 October 1945.

36   NAA, A11049, ROLL 1, Board of Inquiry, 'Report on War Crimes Committed by Enemy Subjects Against Australians and Others', 31 January 1946, pp. 10-11.

37   For the chain of correspondence containing Webb's opinion, see NAA: A6238, 8.

38   NAA, A4611, 747/4, letter from Webb to the Acting Secretary, Dept Ext Aff, 25 June 1945.

39   NAA, A6238, 8, letter from Webb to the Acting Secretary, Dept Ext Aff, 26 June 1945.

40   Italics added for emphasis: NAA, A5954, 671/1, teleprinter message from Webb to the Secretary, Dept Ext Aff, repeated to the Prime Minister and others, 26 September 1945.

If he was asked 'whether the Emperor and his Cabinet Ministers should be placed on the list of war criminals', he said that he would respond 'in the affirmative'.[41]

In September 1945, Webb was approached to help compile a list of names for Australia's first list of major war criminals and was asked specifically to consider including '*Hirohito* as Head of the Army, and as a knowing participant in systematic and barbaric practices in actual warfare'.[42] Webb was provided with a draft – actually compiled by government officials – in late October 1945, which named Hirohito at number seven on the list.[43] At this time, Webb also initialled as 'read' a two-page document entitled 'Tojo's Role as War Criminal', which discussed the culpability of Tōjō Hideki, later a key defendant at the IMTFE.[44] After reviewing the list, Webb requested that its explanatory preface be amended to explicitly acknowledge that the list had been 'passed' by him. Showing a dramatic shift in Webb's thinking, however, he now proposed that the emperor be omitted from the list, as it might be 'desirable to deal with his case at the highest political level'.[45] Yet, without waiting for a response, he approved the list on 24 October 1945.[46] His proposal to omit the emperor was quickly dismissed: he was informed later that same day that 'Emperor on list is in keeping with declared Australian Government policy [sic]'.[47]

Notwithstanding the public characterization of Webb's war crimes investigations as not precluding his nomination, it seems clear that Webb realized in late 1945 that he had probably crossed the line of impartiality in relation to the trials of both minor and major Japanese war criminals. In October 1945, well before his nomination, he indicated to his judicial colleague and co-commissioner, Mansfield, that he would not sit on an Australian military court to try minor Japanese war criminals. Mansfield appears to have raised the topic of their war crimes work and the limitations that it might

---

41   Ibid.

42   Underlining in the original: NAA, A6238, 8, letter from W. Dunk, Dept Ext Aff to Webb, 22 September 1945.

43   The list is in alphabetical order by name, not by prominence.

44   NAA, A6238, 8, 'Tojo's Role as War Criminal', n.d. but initialled by Webb on 24 October 1945.

45   NAA, A6238, 8, letter from Webb to the Acting Secretary, Dept Ext Aff, 24 October 1945.

46   NAA, A1067, UN46/WC/1, memorandum from the Secretary, Dept Ext Aff for the Minister, 'Major Japanese War Criminals – Position of the Emperor', 18 January 1946. Note: there are two copies of this particular memorandum in this file, one with some pencil amendments and marginalia.

47   NAA, A6238, 8, teleprinter message from Acting Secretary, Dept Ext Aff to Webb, 24 October 1945.

impose on their involvement with Australia's future minor war crimes trials.[48] Webb responded to Mansfield that:

> At all events, after visiting England and pressing charges against the Japanese [before the UNWCC] and getting the instructions to military courts altered to facilitate their conviction, I could not accept a membership of a military court to try them.[49]

In early January 1946, after being told he was a prospective nominee, Webb told Mansfield that he had responded: 'I regarded myself as being disqualified and that they had better make another selection'. He told Mansfield that he expected 'Knowles to go as he is next in line and is not disqualified'.[50] Yet Webb partially modified his position about his disqualification only two days later, telling Mansfield:

> I did not regard myself as eligible to try all the Japanese major war criminals. However … it seems that the idea is to try those who are responsible for starting the war as well as those responsible for the way it was conducted. I could deal with the first class but perhaps not with the second … I, of course, have always told Canberra that I thought I was disqualified because of my war crimes activities but they persisted in sending my name to Dr. Evatt. Needless to say, I did not include myself in any recommendations for the international tribunal.[51]

He acknowledged that Lord Wright hoped to visit Tokyo and continued:

> But I certainly do not feel inclined to go with him, great as would be the honour. In the first place, I do not want to become a Major-General or a Lieutenant-General, which the acceptance of the offer appears to involve. Moreover, my wife's health is far from good and I would not improve it by leaving the country although she is anxious for me to go. Further, there are others who can capably fill the position.[52]

---

48   NAA, A6238, 3, letter from Mansfield to Webb, 19 October 1945.
49   NAA, A6238, 3, letter from Webb to Mansfield, 29 October 1945.
50   NAA, A6238, 3, letter from Webb to Mansfield, 6 January 1946.
51   NAA, A6238, 3, letter from Webb to Mansfield, 8 January 1946.
52   Ibid.

As is now clear, someone's persistence, perhaps that of Lady Webb, eventually paid off, as Webb accepted the nomination as Australia's judge.[53] The conclusion that can be drawn from his acceptance is that Webb thought that he would be able to, as an experienced judicial officer, manage any bias; that is, he would be able to appropriately distance himself from the (limited) views on major war criminals he had already formed and expressed so that they would not impact unfairly on the issues to be determined at trial. At the time of his acceptance in early January 1946, however, there was neither a list of defendants to be indicted nor an indictment. The scope of the trial over which Webb thought he could sit impartially was, as yet, entirely unknown, as it was for all the judges.

Once Webb had accepted the nomination, he carefully sought to manage the perception of bias by minimizing any further connection to the major war criminals. For instance, he declined to approve Australia's second list of major Japanese war criminals in January 1946, as 'he did not feel he should do so' now that he had been nominated.[54] He also was careful to point out in his final war crimes report, signed on 31 January 1946, that:

> The Board has not yet obtained any evidence indicating that any Japanese other than those referred to in this report and annexures was guilty of aggression, or a war in violation of International treaties, agreements or assurances or of participating in a common plan or conspiracy for the accomplishment of any of the foregoing.[55]

The appropriateness of Webb's appointment continued to be an issue when the trial opened in May 1946, whereupon the defence sought Webb's disqualification on the grounds of bias. Dr Kiyose Ichirō, the deputy chief defence counsel, suggested that 'it is not proper, from the standpoint of justice and fairness' that Webb should conduct the trial, based on the 'fact that Sir William Webb has investigated the case of Japanese atrocities in New Guinea and has submitted the results of said investigation to the Australian Government'. Webb's atrocities report, he argued, was 'not without connection

---

53   Lady Webb apparently was quite influential, as Webb confided to several correspondents some variation of the account that when he had initially refused appointment to the High Court in 1946, '[t]he Government would not accept the refusal and my wife voted with the Government': see NAA, M1418, 3, letter to 'Reg', 19 September [no year].

54   NAA, A1067, UN46/WC/1, see written note on letter from Dept Ext Aff to Webb, 15 January 1946.

55   NAA, A11049, ROLL 1, Board of Inquiry, 'Report on War Crimes Committed by Enemy Subjects Against Australians and Others', 31 January 1946, p. 146.

with this trial' and 'matters of that kind will influence the decisions taken here'. Alternatively, Kiyose proposed that 'if any references to such incidents in New Guinea' were withdrawn from the indictment, he would withdraw his objection to Webb.[56]

Interestingly, this challenge to Webb was significantly weaker than it could have been: the defence appeared to be considerably underinformed about the actual extent of Webb's war crimes work. Kiyose's references to New Guinea suggest that the defence's objections were based only on Webb's first commission in 1943. However, Webb's second and third commissions in 1944-45 had no geographical limitations at all and ranged broadly.[57] That the defence appeared to have limited knowledge about Webb's war crimes work was not surprising, for only Webb's first commission had received significant publicity by the time the trial opened. While extracts of the first Webb report arising out of that commission were widely published in the press in September 1945, it was extremely unlikely that the defence had read the full version of the report, as it was still classified 'top secret' until April 1947.[58] Crucially, the defence was probably unaware of the second and third war crimes reports, and the confidential advice on major war criminals that Webb had given the Australian government in 1945.

Of course, the strength of the defence's argument was probably irrelevant to the challenge's outcome. The other tribunal members rejected it – without Webb's participation – on the basis that Article 2 of the Charter of the IMTFE prescribed that the tribunal shall consist of members appointed by the Supreme Commander of Allied Powers. As such, the tribunal did not have the power to 'unseat any one appointed by the Supreme Commander'.[59] When Webb returned to the bench after the decision, he advised that he had taken advice on the matter of his appointment prior to taking up his position and had concluded, 'without difficulty', that he was eligible for the position, which was 'supported by the best legal opinion available ... in Australia'.[60] The phrase

---

56   Pritchard et al., *The Tokyo War Crimes Trial*, Transcript, pp. 93-94, 96 (hereafter 'Transcript').

57   See a copy of the instructions in NAA, A10950, 1, 'A Report on War Crimes by Individual Members of the Armed Forces of the Enemy against Australians by Sir William Webb', October 1944, first schedule; and in NAA, A11049, ROLL 1 and ROLL 2, Sir William Webb, 'Report on War Crimes Committed by Enemy Subjects Against Australians and Others', January 1946, pp. 1-3.

58   NAA, A1067, UN46/WC/11, reported in memorandum for the Secretary, Dept Ext Aff, 14 March 1947.

59   Transcript, p. 98.

60   Ibid.

'without difficulty' was patently an exaggeration given the doubts that Webb had earlier privately voiced to Mansfield. Moreover, while the tribunal's decision on the challenge to Webb as a matter of law may have been technically correct, it was a weak outcome, which Webb recognized. In chambers on another matter, Webb stated that he 'would have preferred the facts to have been gone into' and that the challenge had been 'decided on vastly different grounds'.[61] Now knowing the scope of the trial with some precision, and that the indictment did include charges of conventional war crimes, Webb affirmed that he believed that he was not disqualified from the bench. He pointed out:

> I could have said [when challenged]: 'Well, I am objected to; I will get out and go back to Australia,' but I decided, before I came here, I was qualified. I investigated, independently too, and I did not feel in any case that I should have to withdraw.[62]

Webb's Views of the Trial

As the trial commenced, Webb declared that '[t]here has been no more important criminal trial in all history'.[63] Although Arnold Brackman has pointed out the folly of this characterization and suggested that Webb soon regretted it,[64] Webb's hyperbole continued in private. For instance, Webb described the tribunal as the 'greatest criminal court ever constituted'[65] and his own role as president as 'the heaviest responsibility ever cast on a judge',[66] with 'no equal in history, ancient or modern'.[67]

From the outset, Webb seemed to think that relations between the eleven judges were good, writing in early 1946 that he had 'excellent relations with all his colleagues', who were 'all quite good fellows' and that it 'would indeed be hard to improve upon them',[68] although it was unfortunate that 'not one of us

---

61 Motion Suggesting the Disqualification and Personal Bias of the Philippine Justice of the Tribunal, in Pritchard et al, *The Tokyo War Crimes Trial*, vol. 22, p. 22.

62 Ibid, p. 24.

63 NAA, M1418, 10, 'Sir William Webb's Opening Statement at Arraignment', GHQ, USAF, Pacific, Public Relations Office, Special Release, 3 May 1946.

64 Brackman, *The Other Nuremberg*, pp. 103, 230.

65 NAA, M1418, 6, letter from Webb to Evatt, 12 February 1947.

66 NAA, M1418, 6, letter from Webb to MacArthur, 28 June [no year].

67 NAA, M1418, 2, letter from Webb to Evatt, 3 July 1946.

68 NAA, A1067, UN46/WC/15, cablegram from Webb via Australian Political Representative,

can be called an expert in international law'.[69] Webb made similar reports of good judicial relations as time passed. However, the fact that he was officially complimentary did not mean he was oblivious to the increasing disharmony: he observed to Lady Webb, for instance, that '[t]he acidity of one of my colleagues is corrosive'.[70] He was well aware of the difficult task he faced in holding together very diverse judges, telling Lady Webb:

> I have an immense amount of worry ... I have to keep a team of eleven together and to avoid saying one thing that they disapprove. The other day I said something which caused a titter and one judge immediately wrote me a note of protest. Any attempt to relieve the dullness of the proceedings is met that way.... Then, there are all sorts of 'caves', to use the expression of one judge who seems to be a master at making them. If I consult judges on the bench who are English-speaking, I am accused by the foreigners of making an Anglo-American or a British 'bloc'. Yet, I don't think any of them dislike me, but they make my position very difficult. Frequently I am in a tempestuous emotional condition, which is a bad thing for the president of any court.[71]

Several of his colleagues indeed did not hold back in their official reports on Webb and his performance as president. In addition to Justice Röling's well-known views, Lord Patrick called Webb a 'quick-tempered turbulent bully', who had 'antagonised every member of his Tribunal', thereby frustrating the tribunal's purpose.[72] Similarly, Justice Northcroft wrote that Webb had an 'unfortunate manner of expression, generally querulous, invariably argumentative and frequently injudicious'. Moreover, Webb was 'often either, and sometimes both, hostile and unreceptive of our [the judges'] suggestions or incapable of understanding their purport or purpose'.[73]

While Webb also routinely characterized judicial relations with counsel as good, he expressed a certain amount of annoyance towards the defence counsel. Most of his ire appeared to be reserved for the American defence counsel,

---

Tokyo to the Secretary, Dept Ext Aff, 25 May 1946; NAA: M1418, 3, letters from Webb to Latham, 17 April and 8 May 1946.

69   NAA, M1418, 3, letter from Webb to Latham, 17 April 1946.

70   NAA, M1418, 5, letter from Webb to Lady Webb, 30 December [no year].

71   NAA, M1418, 5, letter from Webb to Lady Webb, 1 July [no year but likely 1947].

72   National Archives (UK) (TNA), LCO 2/2992, copy of letter from Lord Patrick forwarded to the Lord Chancellor, circa early 1947, pp. 2, 6.

73   TNA, LCO 2/2992, copy of letter from Justice Northcroft to Chief Justice forwarded to the Lord Chancellor, 18 March 1947, p. 2.

with whom he had several memorable exchanges recorded for posterity in the transcript. In his private view, the Japanese counsel 'never gave much trouble', as they were the '"pick" of the Tokyo Bar', but he wished he could 'say the Americans were the "pick" of the Washington Bar'. He conceded, however, that 'most' of them had 'always behaved well'.[74] He wrote '[i]f I were less firm than I am they [defence counsel] would take possession'.[75] Lord Wright consoled him:

> I should not be too disturbed if some people say you are a little abrupt and peremptory in dealing with objections. You must keep Counsel in order. Someone said it was like driving a four-in-hand: if they took charge, it was impossible to say where it would end, but if you keep them under control things will go well ... I am quite sure that they could never have any reasonable grievance.[76]

Webb's most significant complaint about the trial as it progressed was its duration, as he had originally thought he would be back in Australia in October 1946.[77] Webb generally attributed the length of the trial to a number of factors, including the scope of the indictment, the amount of the evidence presented and the difficulties of translation.[78] One point that he raised often was his belief that the prosecution should have been limited to events after the Japanese attack on Pearl Harbor in December 1941.[79] He lamented a year into the trial that if he had 'known how long it was going to take' he would 'not have accepted [the] appointment'.[80] By May 1947, he described the trial as the 'slowest case in history'.[81]

Many of the criticisms of Webb and his performance at the IMTFE are at extreme odds with views of Webb as a judge in Australia, where he was described, for example, as a 'model of polite, courteous behaviour'.[82] Arguably, the discordance can be partially attributed to fatigue and frustration: even

---

74   NAA, M1418, 3, letter from Webb to Latham, 2 August [no year].

75   NAA, M1418, 3, letter from Webb to Latham, 1 July [no year].

76   NAA, M1418, 4, letter from Lord Wright to Webb, 29 July 1946, p. 2.

77   NAA, M1418, 3, letter from Webb to Latham, 8 May 1946.

78   See, for example, an unsigned document clearly written by Webb: NAA, M1418, 10, 'Length of the Trial', 23 June 1947.

79   NAA, M1418, 4, letter from Webb to McDonald, 21 July 1947.

80   NAA, M1418, 2, letter from Webb to Evatt, 25 April 1947; NAA: M1418, 3, letter from Webb to Latham, 25 April 1947.

81   NAA, M1418, 3 letter from Webb to Fitzgerald, 20 May 1947.

82   Weld, 'Webb, Sir William Flood'.

before the trial, Webb had been working extremely hard for several years, virtually without a break, and had travelled extensively overseas. He then watched – in the position of power but unable to exert much control – as the trial ponderously continued, year after year. As he had personally invested so much time and energy in the trial, as well as sacrificing his personal and professional life in Australia, delays that meant more time in Japan understandably seemed to aggravate him. Moreover, given his view of the trial's importance, he was clearly exasperated by poor press coverage that served to marginalize or stigmatize the trial at home in Australia and elsewhere. For example, he lamented the limited press attention given to the evidence of atrocities being revealed at the trial: 'Some dreadful evidence is being given, but I think the world is tired of hearing even of the worst happenings of the war. Yet it is a terrible crime to forget the dead.'[83] At the same time, Webb loathed some of the press coverage, particularly when reports cast aspersions on him and his handling of the trial or they contained errors or exaggerations about the trial proceedings. He was particularly annoyed by the reporting of Australian journalist Richard Hughes, who depicted him in one article as a Hollywood typecast judge, whose 'blistering observation[s]' from the bench 'crack about the wretched heads of defence attorneys like a tireless stockwhip'.[84]

Mansfield's Approach to the Prosecution

Although Mansfield also had some experience in investigating Japanese war crimes in late 1945, and appeared before the UNWCC, the decision to nominate him as the Australian Associate Prosecutor was uncontroversial. Mansfield's ongoing friendship with and access to Webb in Tokyo would today be regarded as problematic, given that they were now prosecutor and judge. However, all sorts of unusual socializations were the norm amongst the expatriate community in Tokyo during the Occupation, including amongst the judges, counsel and staff of the IMTFE.

With Australia intent on prosecuting the emperor, the task of pressing for his indictment fell upon Mansfield, right up to April 1946, as the trial was about to commence.[85] Mansfield was instructed that:

---

83   NAA, M1418, 4, letter from Webb to Waters, 16 January 1947.

84   'Sir W. Webb in Star Role at War Trial', *Courier-Mail* (Brisbane), 26 August 1946, p. 3.

85   See advice to this point in NAA, A1067, UN46/WC/1, memorandum for the Minister, 'Major Japanese War Criminals', 8 April 1946.

if you are satisfied that there is a case [against the emperor], it is left entirely to you to act upon your considered view. At same time you should avoid any public protest if decision is against indictment or if MacArthur vetoes proposal. You are familiar with the facts and it has always been our view that if the facts warranted indictment, Hirohito is no more entitled to special immunity than the common soldiers who inflicted such cruel barbarities against Allied soldiers and civilians.[86]

Mansfield was reportedly the only prosecutor to urge for a vote on the emperor's inclusion on the list of defendants settled at a prosecutorial meeting[87] but, as is well known, the emperor was not included on the indictment.

Mansfield took the lead in the phase of the trial dealing with offences committed against Allied prisoners of war, which both Australia and the Netherlands reportedly saw as 'one of the most important phases' of the trial.[88] In Mansfield's view, his approach was not to present a 'historical record of atrocities committed by the Japanese in every area' but a 'picture of general conditions under which prisoners-of-war and civilians were confined' which would 'show that the conditions were similar everywhere' and gave the 'irresistible inference' that 'the mistreatment was not the result of the orders of the individual camp and area commanders, but was part of the general policy of the Japanese Government'.[89] Mansfield sought to prove the responsibility of the accused by producing various orders in violation of the laws of war issued by them, their inaction when proof of mistreatment had been conveyed through neutral parties during the war, admissions made by them during interrogation and admissions of breaches of the laws of war made after the surrender by the Japanese government.[90] Mansfield estimated that this 'important phase' could not be 'properly' presented in 'less time than ten weeks'.[91]

In Mansfield's view, the International Prosecution Section 'suffered from many difficulties notably in administration'.[92] He certainly appeared to share the opinion of others at the time, and since, that Joseph Keenan had been a

---

86   NAA, A1067, UN46/WC/1, cablegram from Dept Ext Aff to Australian Political Representa-
      tive, Tokyo, for Mansfield, 9 April 1946.

87   NAA, A1067, UN46/WC/1, cablegram from Mansfield to the Minister of External Affairs, 9
      April 1946.

88   According to Mansfield: see NAA, A1067, UN46/WC/15, memorandum from Mansfield to
      Keenan, 5 November 1946, p. 1.

89   Ibid.

90   Ibid.

91   Ibid.

92   NAA, A1067, UN46/WC/15, letter from Mansfield to Evatt, 18 October 1946, p. 2.

poor choice as chief counsel. Mansfield informed Evatt that Keenan took 'little active part either in the administration of the section or the conduct of the case'[93] and, by November 1946, that Keenan's 'lack of leadership' was 'becoming very serious'.[94] Indeed, Mansfield suggested that Keenan's very presence detracted from the progress of the trial: when Keenan was absent from Japan, the trial progressed 'more smoothly' than if he were there.[95] Interestingly, Mansfield did not suggest to Evatt, even obliquely, that Keenan had a drinking problem.[96] Keenan was, of course, not the only impediment. Mansfield complained that the prosecutors were hampered by 'all sorts of bottle-necks and other difficulties', with the 'greatest obstacle' being the translation and copying of documents. Every document, he pointed out, had to be copied about 125 times in English and about the same in Japanese.[97] He advised that his own staff – Assistant Prosecutor Mornane and his associate Mr A.R. MacDonald – were giving him 'great assistance' and the typists were 'doing excellent work'.[98] Perhaps not unsurprisingly given their close personal history, Webb reported to Evatt that Mansfield was:

> doing a splendid job for the Prosecution.... He is more experienced than most of those associated with him. He is well informed and speaks well. He is also very urbane and tactful. I am very proud of him.[99]

Given that Mansfield attributed a significant part of the prosecution's problems to Keenan, he was demonstrably annoyed when Keenan informed him that the time estimated for the presentation of the prisoner of war phase was 'prohibitively long' and that instructions would be issued as to the 'length of time permitted'.[100] Mansfield responded to Keenan that if five weeks had been taken up by presenting evidence of atrocities in one area alone, he did not think it 'disproportionate' to take up ten weeks to present 'evidence in relation to over 20 other areas in addition to the evidence necessary to impose upon the

---

93   Ibid.

94   NAA, A1067, UN46/WC/15, letter from Mansfield to Evatt, 14 November 1946, p. 1.

95   NAA, A1067, UN46/WC/15, letter from Mansfield to Evatt, 27 December 1946, p. 1.

96   On Keenan's drinking, see N. Boister and R. Cryer (eds.), 'Introduction', in *Documents on the Tokyo International Military Tribunal: Charter, Indictment and Judgments* (Oxford University Press, 2008), p. lvii.

97   NAA, A1067, UN46/WC/15, letter from Mansfield to Evatt, 18 October 1946, p. 2.

98   NAA, A1067, UN46/WC/15, letter from Mansfield to Evatt, 2 December 1946, p. 2.

99   NAA, M1418, 2, letter from Webb to Evatt, 3 July 1946.

100   NAA, A1067, UN46/WC/15, memorandum from Keenan, 6 November 1946.

accused the responsibility for the offence'.[101] Mansfield advised Keenan that he 'would definitely resist an arbitrary limit being placed on the time for presenting this part of the prosecution case'.[102]

The prisoner of war phase finally commenced in December 1946 and took some six weeks. Afterwards, Mansfield reported to Evatt that the Australian witnesses during this phase had given 'excellent evidence' and that the 'whole [prosecution] story as it unfolds is becoming very formidable and when finished will be a very complete picture'.[103] Mansfield had already asked Evatt for his release from Japan after this phase, as his place could be 'satisfactorily taken by a junior' and as the Queensland government had requested his return to the bench of the Supreme Court.[104] He had 'every confidence' in Mornane, he wrote, who had 'worked hard and well and has presented his part of the evidence in a very efficient manner'.[105] When asked for his views on Mansfield's release, Webb advised that he would 'profoundly regret' Mansfield's departure before the end of the trial but understood that there was 'no proper scope' for him after the prosecution case had concluded.[106] Mansfield returned to Australia in early 1947. Mornane was duly appointed as Australian Associate Prosecutor and went on to deliver part of the prosecution's closing address.

Webb's Separate but Concurring Judgment

While Webb had confidently suggested at the early stages that he did 'not anticipate any great difference of opinion' between the judges,[107] there was little unanimity by the end. While Webb drafted several versions of his judgment running to hundreds of pages over time, the first of which was very poorly received by the other judges, his final separate opinion was only ten pages. Pointedly amongst the topics on which Webb eventually differed from the majority was the emperor. Privately, Webb seems to have been fairly consistent in his view – which had been established in late 1945 – that while a case could be made against the emperor, the question of prosecuting him was one for the highest authorities; those authorities had made their decision and he

101   NAA, A1067, UN46/WC/15, memorandum from Mansfield to Keenan, 7 November 1946.

102   Ibid.

103   NAA, A1067, UN46/WC/15, letter from Mansfield to Evatt, 27 December 1946, p. 1.

104   NAA, A1067, UN46/WC/15, letter from Mansfield to Evatt, 2 December 1946, p. 2.

105   NAA, A1067, UN46/WC/15, letter from Mansfield to Evatt, 27 December 1946, p. 1.

106   NAA, A1067, UN46/WC/15/1, cablegram from Webb to Attorney-General, 30 November 1946.

107   NAA, M1418, 2, letter from Webb to Evatt, 3 July 1946.

would not go against it. He wrote to MacArthur in August 1947, for instance, that he had advised the Australian government that there was a prima facie case against the emperor but that 'the matter might be one for decision at the highest political level'. He continued:

> I have no desire to see the Emperor of Japan put on trial. If he were I would refuse to try him if asked to do so. It is quite immaterial to me that the decision at the highest political level was in the Emperor's favor ...[108]

Yet, in a section of Webb's judgment headed 'Immunity of the Emperor', he stated that he thought that the emperor's authority in Japan had been 'proven beyond question' by his ending of the war. He reiterated, however, that:

> the Prosecution also made it clear that the Emperor would not be indicted ... I do not suggest that the Emperor should have been prosecuted. That is beyond my province. His immunity was, no doubt, decided upon in the best interests of all the Allied Powers. Justice requires me to take into consideration the Emperor's immunity when determining the punishment of the accused found guilty: that is all.[109]

Given that the emperor had escaped prosecution and punishment, he pressed for the death penalty not to be given to the convicted, in which he was, of course, unsuccessful.

Conclusion

While Webb's performance as Australian judge and as president of the IMTFE, as well as the contribution of Mansfield, remain to be explored at length, there is no doubt that it may have been wiser, particularly in relation to the long-term historical and legal perceptions of the IMTFE, for Australia to have appointed a judge with a lesser or no connection at all to investigating Japanese war crimes. Yet would displacing Webb from the biographical narrative make a significant difference to how the trial has been critically perceived? If Webb had refused the nomination or recused himself early on, another Australian judge would have been selected. But this may well have created new problems.

---

108   NAA, M1418, 6, letter from Webb to MacArthur, 6 August 1947, p. 2.
109   Sir William Webb, 'Separate Opinion of the President', in Boister and Cryer (eds.), Documents on the Tokyo International Military Tribunal, pp. 638-39.

Perhaps Sir George Knowles, the 'next in line' according to Webb, would have packed his bags for Tokyo instead of South Africa as Australian High Commissioner? However, Knowles died there in November 1947, long before the IMTFE concluded – an event that would have left the tribunal bereft of a judge at a point when a replacement could not have been appointed. The presiding hand of any other judge, given the prominence of the position, would have certainly resulted in some differences. Perhaps Lord Patrick, who MacArthur (unsuccessfully) favoured to act as president in Webb's absence from Japan, would have taken the position? Yet, Lord Patrick has been described as 'aloof' and 'exceptionally reserved' (and likewise loathed the press).[110] In the end, the trial is unlikely to have been less contentious, minus the presence of Sir William Webb.

Bibliography

Neil Boister and Robert Cryer (eds.), 'Introduction', in *Documents on the Tokyo International Military Tribunal: Charter, Indictment and Judgments* (Oxford University Press, 2008) pp. xxxiii-lxxxiv.

Arnold C. Brackman, *The Other Nuremberg: The Untold Story of the Tokyo War Crimes Trial* (New York: William Morrow and Company, Inc., 1987).

Finian Cullity, 'Australia's Involvement in the International Military Tribunal for the Far East: The Case of Sir William Webb and Sir Alan Mansfield', *Australian Bar Review*, 41 (2016), 236-45.

John Greenwood, 'Mansfield, Sir Alan James (1902-1980)', *Australian Dictionary of Biography*, National Centre of Biography, Australian National University <http://adb.anu.edu.au/biography/mansfield-sir-alan-james-11053/text19669>.

Terry Hewton, '"Webb's Justice": The Role of William Flood Webb in the Tokyo Trial, 1946-1948', unpublished Honours thesis, University of Adelaide (1976).

Chihiro Hosoya, Nisuke Andō, Yasuaki Ōnuma and Richard Minear (eds.), *The Tokyo War Crimes Trial: An International Symposium* (New York: Kodansha International Ltd, 1986).

Timothy Maga, *Judgment at Tokyo: The Japanese War Crimes Trials* (Lexington: The University Press of Kentucky, 2001).

Richard Minear, *Victors' Justice: The Tokyo War Crimes Trial* (Princeton, N.J.: Princeton University Press, 1971).

R. John Pritchard, Sonia M. Zaide and Donald C. Watt, *The Tokyo War Crimes Trial*, vol. 1. (New York and London: Garland, 1981).

---

110   Brackman, *The Other Nuremberg*, p. 73.

Peter Provis, '"I hope to be of some real assistance to your government": The Extra-Judicial Activities of Sir William Flood Webb, 1942-1948', unpublished PhD thesis, Flinders University (2015).

James Sedgwick, 'A People's Court: Emotion, Participant Experiences, and the Shaping of Postwar Justice at the International Military Tribunal for the Far East, 1946-48, *Diplomacy & Statecraft*, vol. 22. no. 3 (2011), 480-99.

Dayle Smith, 'Commentary on "Sir William Webb – Hobbesian Jurist"' in Michael White and Aladin Rahemtula (eds.), *Queensland Judges on the High Court* (Brisbane: Supreme Court of Queensland Library, 2003), pp. 151-70.

Yuki Tanaka, Tim McCormack and Gerry Simpson (eds.), *Beyond Victor's Justice? The Tokyo War Crimes Trial Revisited* (Leiden: Martinus Nijhoff, 2011).

Yuma Totani, *The Tokyo War Crimes Trial: The Pursuit of Justice in the Wake of World War II* (Cambridge, Mass.: Harvard University Asia Centre, 2008).

H.A. Weld, 'Webb, Sir William Flood (1887-1972)', *Australian Dictionary of Biography*, National Centre of Biography, Australian National University, <http://adb.anu.edu.au/biography/webb-sir-william-flood-11991/text21499>.

CHAPTER 3

MacArthur, Keenan and the American Quest for Justice at the IMTFE

David M. Crowe

In the summer of 1946, John H. Higgins, the recently appointed US judge to the International Military Tribunal for the Far East (IMTFE; Tokyo trial), hastily resigned to return to his position as Chief Justice of the Superior Court of Massachusetts. Joseph B. Keenan, the tribunal's chief prosecutor, who had opposed Higgins's appointment, was incensed, as was Tom C. Clark, the Attorney General of the United States, who had insisted on it. Though Higgins stated in his letters to Gen. Douglas MacArthur, the Supreme Commander for the Allied Powers (SCAP), Clark and Keenan that his decision was based solely on the fact that he had been misled about the potential length of the trial and problems replacing him on the Massachusetts court. He told his daughter in a private letter in July that he was also deeply troubled by Keenan's 'organizing ability and tact for the difficult task of molding the confidence of associate prosecutors'. Keenan, he went on, also 'failed in his contact and associations with his fellow Americans'. He also told her that though Keenan's staff had gathered a remarkable body of evidence, these problems led to a prosecutorial 'failure in the presentation of this case' before the tribunal. This, coupled with what Higgins said were 'several instances of [Keenan's] conduct that I don't care to mention', left him with serious doubts about the future of the trial.[1]

Such criticisms were not isolated. Arthur Comyns-Carr, the British associate prosecutor and president of the prosecution's executive committee, and his Australian peer, Alan J. Mansfield, met with MacArthur soon after they learned of Higgins's resignation to express opposition to the appointment of a new US judge 'at this stage of the trial'. They also raised concerns about Keenan's ability to oversee the prosecution's case. MacArthur told them that the decision to replace Higgins would be made solely by the US government, while Washington

---

1 Quoted in Y. Takatori, 'The Forgotten Judge at the Tokyo War Crimes Trial', *Massachusetts Historical Review*, 10 (2008), 115-41, footnote 39 as from her private collection, letter by John P. Higgins to Eleanor Higgins, July 2, 1946, p. 1; John P. Higgins to General Douglas MacArthur, June 21, 1945, p. 1; John P. Higgins to The Honorable Tom C. Clark, June 28, 1946.

left it up to him 'to adjudge the competency of the membership' of the court. The same was true, he implied, when it came to Keenan.[2]

These criticisms underscored some of the problems of one of the most contentious international trials in modern history. The US hoped that the Tokyo trial would enjoy similar success to the Nuremberg trial, and help not only to show the Japanese the merits of democratic institutions in action, but also reveal the horrors of illegal aggressive war. This is not to say, of course, that the trial did not succeed in doing this. But it did underscore the fact that the US, by relying far too heavily on MacArthur and Keenan to conduct a fair trial in the midst of the American occupation of Japan, created problems that haunted it from 1946-48.

Until recently, very little has been written about MacArthur's role in the planning of the trial. In his *Reminiscences* he says that

> From the moment of my appointment as supreme commander, I had formulated the policies I intended to follow, implementing them through the Emperor and the machinery of the imperial government. I was thoroughly familiar with Japanese administration, its weaknesses and its strengths, and felt the reforms I contemplated were those which would bring Japan abreast of modern progressive thought and action. First destroy the military power. Punish war criminals. Build the structure of representative government.[3]

Courtney Whitney, SCAP's major domo and chief apologist, seconded this impression, noting in his hagiographic *MacArthur: His Rendezvous with History* that on their flight to Japan on 30 August 1945 he recalled

> vividly the sight of that striding figure as he puffed on his corncob pipe, stopping intermittently to dictate to me the random thoughts that crowded his mind and were destined to become the basis of the occupation. I can see now in retrospect that those terse notes I took formed the policy under which we would work and live for the next six years.[4]

The reality, unfortunately, was quite different, and many of the policies that MacArthur implemented, particularly in the early years of the occupation,

---

2 Douglas MacArthur Archives, RG5, Box 27, Folder 3, OMS Files, C.W. Higgins, Acting Chief of Counsel IPS to Chief of Staff, 15 July 1946, 'Higgins', 1 p.

3 D. MacArthur, *Reminiscences* (New York: McGraw-Hill, 1964), pp. 282-83.

4 C. Whitney, *MacArthur: His Rendezvous with History* (New York: Alfred A. Knopf, 1956), p. 213.

were dictated by Washington. This was particularly the case when it came to the planning of the IMTFE and the question of the indictment of Emperor Hirohito as a war criminal.

Certainly one of the most storied and controversial figures in American military history, William Manchester described MacArthur as

> a great thundering paradox of a man, noble and ignoble, inspiring and outrageous, arrogant and shy, the best of men and the worst of men, the most protean, most ridiculous, and most sublime. No more baffling, exasperating soldier every wore a uniform. Flamboyant, imperious, and apocalyptic, he carried the plumage of a flamingo, could not acknowledge errors, and tried to cover up his mistakes with sly, childish tricks.[5]

D. Clayton James, who wrote the definitive biography of MacArthur, was far less critical, though he did note that he had no qualms withholding 'bouquets or brickbats on some specific episodes and issues'.[6]

Yet none of this should diminish his remarkable achievements in Japan during his six years as SCAP. What he achieved during that period is nothing less than remarkable. Soon after his dismissal in 1951, the liberal Japanese newspaper, *Asahi*, published an editorial, 'Lament for General MacArthur'.

> We lived with General MacArthur from the end of the war until today… When the Japanese people faced the unprecedented situation of defeat, and fell into the kyodatsu condition of exhaustion and despair, it was General MacArthur who taught us the merits of democracy and pacifism and guided us with kindness along this bright path. As if pleased with his own children growing up, he took pleasure in the Japanese people, yesterday's enemy, walking step by step toward democracy, and kept encouraging us.[7]

American planning for the occupation of Japan and the trial of its war criminals began in the fall of 1942, just months after the US strategic victories in the battles of the Coral Sea and Midway. Convinced now that Japan's offensive

---

5   W. Manchester, *American Caesar: Douglas MacArthur, 1880-1964* (Boston: Little Brown, 1978), p. 3.

6   D.C. James, *The Years of MacArthur*, vol. 3, *Triumph & Disaster, 1945-1964* (Boston: Houghton Mifflin, 1985), p. vii.

7   J.W. Dower, *Embracing Defeat: Japan in the Wake of World War II* (New York: W.W. Norton, 1999), pp. 548-49.

threat had been blunted,[8] specialists in the Department of State began to ask questions about the possible occupation of Japan. In early 1943, State Department officials created an Interdivisional Area Committee on the Far East to prepare studies of the various options the US might consider for such an occupation. The War Department was also studying an occupation, and in early 1944, State Department specialists were asked to share their research with the military, particularly the US Navy. This ultimately led the Secretaries of State, War and the Navy to create the State-War-Navy Coordinating Committee (SWNNC) to discuss the political and military implications of an occupation. SWNCC created a Sub-Committee on the Far East that was responsible for coordinating the sharing of research on this question. Political reports were to be reviewed by State Department specialists, while those on military questions were studied by their peers in the War Department. These reports were then sent on to SWNCC which, if approved, became 'official United States policy'.[9] Among the most important SWNCC reports were 'The Instrument of Surrender (IS)', which was signed in Tokyo Bay on 2 September 1945, and SWNCC/150/4 (22 September 1945), 'Politico-Military Problems in the Far East: United States Initial Post-defeat Policy relating to Japan'.[10]

SWNCC also played a role in the discussions about the terms of surrender, which were included in the Potsdam Agreement of 26 July 1945, which became the general roadmap for the surrender and occupation of Japan. After an SWNCC meeting in late April 1945, James Forrestal, the Secretary of the Navy, said that what the committee did not want to do was to '[hand] Morgenthau those islands',[11] a reference to the Treasury Secretary's earlier plan to transform Nazi Germany into '"a primarily a pastoral community" too weak to threaten

8   Ian W. Toll, *Pacific Crucible: War at Sea in the Pacific, 1941-1942* (New York: W.W. Norton, 2012), pp. 43-45, 59, 374, 478-79.

9   Hugh Bolton, 'Preparation for the Occupation of Japan', *The Journal of Asian Studies*, 25, no. 2 (February 1966), 203-12, 204.

10   State-War-Navy Coordinating Committee, 'Political-Military problems in the Far East: United States Initial Post-Defeat Policy Relating to Japan', SWNCC 150, pp. 1-3. <http://www.ndl.go.jp/constitution/e/shiryo/009/009tx.html#001>; The State-War-Navy Coordinating Committee, SWNCC 150/4, 6 September 1945, 'Memorandum for the Secretary of State', pp. 1-4. <http://www.ndl.go.jp/constitution/e/shiryo/01/022/022tx.html>; National Diet Library, 'U.S. Initial Post-Surrender Policy for Japan', pp. 1-4. <http://ndl.go.jp/constitution/e/shiryo/01/022.shoshi.html>; Bolton, 'Preparation for the Occupation of Japan', 205-6.

11   Michael Neiberg, *Potsdam: The End of World War II and the Remaking of Europe* (New York: Basic Books, 2015), p. 238.

Europe and the world'.[12] According to Forrestal, no one on the SWNCC 'desired the permanent subjugation of Japan, the enslavement of its people, or any attempt to dictate what kind of government the country should have'. This, he went on, raised serious questions about what the US meant by its demand for 'unconditional surrender', something he urged the president to clarify at Potsdam.[13]

The Potsdam Proclamation of 26 July 1945 warned Japan's leaders that their nation would face 'prompt and utter destruction' if they refused to accept 'unconditional surrender'. But these terms were balanced with more moderate terms that had been part of earlier SWNCC discussions. While the Allies were determined to remove those leaders who had led Japan to war, and mete out 'stern justice... to all war criminals', the proclamation also pledged to

> remove all obstacles to the revival and strengthening of democratic tendencies of the Japanese people. Freedom of speech, of religion, and thought, as well as respect for fundamental human rights shall be established.[14]

The Proclamation also did not mention Emperor Hirohito and the 'emperor institution', something that had been a prominent topic in SWNCC discussions for quite some time.

This was not the case with the 'Japanese Instrument of Surrender' of 2 September 1945. The emperor was mentioned three times, while his authority and that of the 'Japanese Government to rule the state shall be subject to the Supreme Commander for the Allied Powers who will take such steps as he deems proper to effectuate these terms of surrender'. This, coupled with portions of the first paragraph, which pledged the emperor, the government and Japanese Imperial Headquarters 'to accept the provisions' of the Potsdam Proclamation, set the stage for the vast powers that SCAP would wield in rebuilding Japan and bringing its war criminals to justice.[15]

The question of the fate of the emperor and the 'emperor institution' was one of the first topics discussed by specialists in the State Department as they

---

12   David M. Crowe, *War Crimes, Genocide, and Justice: A Global History* (New York and London: Palgrave Macmillan, 2013), p. 154.

13   Neiberg, *Potsdam*, p. 238.

14   N. Boister and R. Cryer (eds.) *Documents on the Tokyo International Military Tribunal: Charter, Indictment and Judgments* (Oxford University Press, 2008), pp. 1-2.

15   Ibid., pp. 3-4.

explored ideas about the occupation of Japan. Hugh Bolton, one of these experts, wrote on 26 April 1944 that a week earlier

> the Postwar Program Committee considered my document on the Institution of the Emperor in which it was recommended that the imperial family be placed under protective custody but the Emperor be given access to his advisers. Furthermore, he should delegate to his subordinates the carrying out of their administrative duties so the occupation forces would be able to use a maximum number of Japanese officials. If this plan is impracticable, then the occupying authorities could suspend all of the functions of the Emperor.[16]

Bolton added that these ideas prevailed in US governing circles when it came to the question of Hirohito over the next two years.[17]

SWNCC/150/4 certainly left the door open for MacArthur to follow the committee's suggestions about adopting a more moderate stance on Hirohito. His lenient treatment of the emperor, who was not even required to appear onboard the *Missouri* on 2 September to sign the IS, created a firestorm in the US. One common thread for those who advocated the abolition of the imperial system or proposed maintaining it was that 'the Emperor was clearly an important figurehead in the Japanese consciousness'.[18] MacArthur, who recalled in his memoirs the almost universal call for the dissolution of the imperial system when he arrived in Japan in late August 1945, added that he had already decided when he was appointed SCAP that he would implement his reforms of Japan 'through the Emperor and the machinery of the imperial government'.[19] Moreover, he was convinced that if the emperor was tried and hanged as a war criminal, guerilla war would probably break out, which would require 'at least one million reinforcements should such action be taken'.[20]

In reality, MacArthur was not initially convinced of the wisdom of keeping the emperor on the throne and using him as part of his rebuilding strategy. He had not been consulted on the terms of SWNCC/150/4, and while he generally agreed with most of them, his opinions were more driven by SWNCC's 22 September directive, 'Identification, Apprehension and Trial of Persons

---

16   Bolton, 'Preparation for the Occupation of Japan', 205.

17   Ibid., p. 205.

18   N. Berlin, 'Constitutional Conflict with the Japanese Imperial Role: Accession, Yasukuni Shrine, and Obligatory Reformation', *Journal of Constitutional Law*, 1, no. 2 (Fall 1998), 391.

19   MacArthur, *Reminiscences*, pp. 279-80.

20   Ibid., p. 288.

Suspected of War Crimes', which stated quite specifically that he was to 'take no action against the Emperor as a War Criminal pending receipt of a special directive concerning his treatment'.[21] This memorandum also laid out fairly detailed guidelines being discussed in Washington about the charges being considered for alleged Japanese war criminals, as well as guidelines for the identification, investigation, apprehension and detention of those considered war criminals. It also gave SCAP the power to create special 'International Military Courts' and 'to prescribe or approve the rules of procedure for such tribunals'.[22]

MacArthur had his first meeting with the emperor on 22 September, and later wrote that he accepted full responsibility 'for every political and military decision made and action taken by my people in the conduct of the war'.[23] He then explained that he was a constitutional monarch and, as such, had to do what his ministers advised him, 'even if I don't like it.'[24] But John W. Dower, using the highly secret minutes of the meeting prepared by Okumura Katsuzo, the emperor's household interpreter, says that 'at best' this was 'a creatively ornamented version of what actually was said', meaning the emperor never accepted responsibility for the war.[25] Regardless, both men established a strong rapport that resulted in annual meetings. MacArthur would later call the emperor 'the First Gentleman of Japan in his own right',[26] while Hirohito came deeply to respect the general for not blaming him for the war and for his peaceful occupation policies.[27]

But even after the first meeting, MacArthur still seemed a little uncertain about the fate of the emperor and the 'emperor institution'. In the early days of the occupation, E.H. Norman, a Canadian specialist on Japan who had worked in the Canadian embassy in Tokyo from 1940 until he was repatriated in 1942, was assigned to MacArthur's staff to head up temporarily the Research and Analysis Section of the Office of the Chief Counter-Intelligence Officer of the Occupation.[28] A year earlier, Norman had anonymously co-authored an article

---

21   MacArthur Archives, SWNCC, RG9, Box 159, Folder 'War Crimes, Sept 45–June 46', 'Identification, Apprehension and Trial of Persons Suspected of War Crimes', 22 September 1945, pp. 1-2.

22   Ibid., pp. 1-2.

23   Berlin, 'Constitutional Conflict', 395.

24   Ibid., p. 395; MacArthur, *Reminiscences*, p. 287.

25   Dower, *Embracing Defeat*, pp. 295-96.

26   MacArthur, *Reminiscences*, p. 288.

27   James, *Years of MacArthur*, 3, p. 322.

28   J. Price, 'E.H. Norman, Canada and Japan's Postwar Constitution', *Pacific Affairs*, 74, no. 3 (Fall 2001), 383-405, at 391-92.

in *Pacific Affairs* in which he said that if the emperor and his institution, which he considered 'the linch-pin of the whole system of Japanese imperialism', was preserved after the war, it would mean that Japan would remain a 'dangerous problem for the rest of the world'. But after his assignment to MacArthur's staff, he wrote to his wife that the Allies should take a neutral stance when it came to the demands of some Japanese leftists who called for the emperor to be deposed because he did not think the Japanese people were ready for such a move.[29]

Brig. Gen. Bonner F. Fellers, MacArthur's military secretary and member of his inner circle, argued that to try Hirohito would be an act of religious sacrilege given his importance to the Japanese people as 'the living symbol of the race in whom lies the virtues of their ancestors'. The war, he went on, did not 'stem from the Emperor himself', who was also responsible for the 'bloodless' occupation of the Japanese home islands. To try him for war crimes would not only be a 'breach of faith', but would also ensure the collapse of the Japanese 'governmental structure' and lead to 'a general uprising' that would result in 'chaos and bloodshed'. It would also force the US to send in a much larger military force which would prolong the occupation and alienate the Japanese.[30]

In the end, this was the rationale that MacArthur used when later confronted with questions about the fate of Hirohito. Armed with orders from SWNCC and the Joint Chiefs of Staff (JCS) 'not to remove the Emperor without prior consultation with and advice of the JCS',[31] MacArthur warned members of the newly created Far Eastern Commission (FEC) on 30 January 1946 of the dangers of any action against Hirohito, whom he considered 'the most perfect example of a stooge or Charlie McCarthy', a reference to one of the wooden puppets used by famed American ventriloquist and comedian Edgar Bergen. The emperor, he told the FEC, was prepared to stand trial, and, if convicted, go to his death 'as a man'. But, MacArthur added, such a decision would have to be made by all nine countries involved in the occupation. And once made, they all would have to share equally in the costs for what would become an 'indefinite military occupation' involving a million Allied troops. Personally, he thought that in the not too distant future, the Japanese people would strip the 'emperor

---

29   M.S. Bates and K.S. Latourette, 'The Future of Japan', *Pacific Affairs*, 17, no. 2 (June 1944), 190-203, at 202-3.

30   MacArthur Archives, RG5, Box 2, Folder 2, Bonner F. Fellers, 'Memorandum to the Commander-in-Chief', 2 October 1945, 'O.C. 45', 1 p.

31   National Diet Library. Joint Chiefs of Staff, 'Basic Directive for Post-Surrender Military Government in Japan Proper', 3 November 1945, p. 2. <www.ndl.go.jp/constitution/e/shiryo/01/036/036tx.html>.

institution' of all of its 'spiritual and temporal power', which would make it more like the system in England. On the other hand, if the Allies chose to try and later execute Hirohito, it would ensure that the imperial institution in Japan would emerge from the 'scaffold stronger and more potent to the Japanese people than ever before in Japanese history'. He compared the result 'to the crucifixion of Christ'.[32]

And if there was any doubt about the position the US should take on the fate of Hirohito, it was pretty much set in stone after President Truman sent Keenan a note that ordered him to 'lay off Hirohito, and that meant laying off the whole Imperial Household as well'. Robert Donihi, a member of Keenan's staff, said that he told him personally 'not [to] attempt to interrogate any of them'. Keenan also told his staff that if anyone did not agree with this decision, then they 'should "by all means go home immediately"'.[33]

This decision, of course, had nothing to do with the prosecution of the other Japanese leaders responsible for the Pacific War. In mid-September, Washington sent SCAP a detailed list of possible Japanese war crimes suspects, followed by the 22 September guidelines for identifying, apprehending and trying them. A few days later, the War Department asked MacArthur if he needed help choosing 'counsel under your authority' who would assume a role similar to that of Justice Robert Jackson in Nuremberg. Washington also wanted to know if it would be helpful to appoint a liaison officer from Nuremberg to help plan the Japanese trials.[34]

MacArthur never responded to this query, and instead appointed Col. Alva C. Carpenter to oversee SCAP's Legal Section to handle all war crimes matters. MacArthur then asked Washington for permission to begin proceedings against Prime Minister Hideki Tōjō, who had served as Japan's minister of war from 1940 to 1944 and prime minister from 1941 to 1944. He was told that this and other matters related to the question of major war crimes trials would be discussed in meetings in Tokyo with John J. McCloy, the assistant secretary of war, and Abraham M. Goff, the deputy director of the Judge Advocate General's war crimes office.[35]

---

32   National Diet Library. 'Memorandum of Interview with General of the Army Douglas MacArthur', 30 January 1946, pp. 3-4. <http://www.ndl.go.jp/constitution/e/shiryo/03/066/066_001r.html>.

33   Crowe, *War Crimes*, pp. 203-4.

34   MacArthur Archives, RG9, Box 159, Folder 'War Crimes, Sept. 45–June 46', Assistant Secretary of War to MacArthur, 27 September 1945, 1 p.

35   MacArthur Archives, RG9, Box 159, Folder 'War Crimes, Sept. 45–June 46', 'MacArthur to WARCOS', 7 October 1945, 1 p.; RG 9, Box 159, Folder, 'War Crimes, Sept. 45–June 46', Washington to CINCAFPAC [MacArthur], 11 October 1945, 1 p.

By the time that they met in late October, Carpenter was already moving ahead with plans to try General Tomoyuki Yamashita, a Japanese war hero who had commanded the 14th Army Group in the Philippines during the last year of the war, and Gen. Masaharu Homma, commander of the same unit during the battle for Corregidor in 1942. When the Japanese invaded the Philippines on 8 December 1941, MacArthur was in Manila as the recently appointed commander of US Army Forces in the Far East. The Japanese quickly forced him to retreat to the Bataan peninsula and Corregidor Island to protect the entrance to Manila harbour. MacArthur, who was ordered by President Roosevelt to flee to Australia in early 1942 to coordinate Allied resistance there, was deeply affected by the fall of Corregidor and the Bataan Death March after his departure. He later wrote that the 'bitter memories and heartaches [of these losses and tragedies] will never leave me'.[36]

Yamashita, whose trial took place in Manila from 29 October to 7 December 1945, was formally charged with unlawful disregard and failure 'to discharge his duty as commander to control the operations of the members of his command, permitting them to commit brutal atrocities and other high crimes against people of the US and of its allies and dependents; particularly the Philippines'. He 'thereby violated the laws of war'.[37]

However, according to Gary Solis, there 'was no precedent in U.S. military law for this charge [now, command responsibility or respondent superior], since Yamashita was not charged with giving orders to commit such crimes or even knew of them.' His alleged criminality centred simply around the fact that he was in command when the crimes took place.[38]

The Yamashita trial was extremely controversial. According to Robert Shaplen, a *Newsweek* reporter who attended the trial, most of his colleagues who covered it were convinced that the military 'commission went into the courtroom the first day with the decision already in its collective pocket'.[39] The same was true of Homma's trial in early 1946. Both men, who were found guilty and sentenced to death, appealed their cases to the US Supreme Court, which ruled against them. However, two justices, Wiley Rutledge and Frank Murphy, wrote dissenting opinions that pointed out that the structure and

---

36   MacArthur, *Reminiscences*, p. 146.

37   United Nations War Crimes Commission (UNWCC), *Law Reports of Trials of War Criminals*, vol. 4 (London: The United Nations War Crimes Commission, 1948), pp. 3-4.

38   G.D. Solis, *The Law of Armed Conflict: International Humanitarian Law in War* (Cambridge University Press, 2010), p. 383.

39   P. Maguire, *Law and War; International Law & American History*, Revised Edition (New York: Columbia University Press, 2010), p. 107.

haste of the trials robbed both men of the most elemental rights of due process guaranteed by the Fifth Amendment of the US constitution.[40] MacArthur, who had final say on the commissions' decisions, said both trials were extremely fair and just, and confirmed them.[41]

But questions about the fairness of the Yamashita and Homma trials continued to haunt MacArthur, particularly after Justice Hugo Black told Col. Frederick B. Weiner, who was handling two similar cases (Uyeki and Cantos), that he and other justices now had doubts about the "legal underpinning[s]' of both trials. In fact, Black went on, if the cases now came before the Supreme Court, he and at least three or four of the other Supreme Court judges would 'vote against the rationale of the earlier decisions'. This led secretary of War Robert P. Patterson to order MacArthur to turn the Uyeki and Cantos cases over to the new Philippine government to avoid further controversy about his handling of sensitive war crimes trials.[42]

Such concerns about the handling of the trials of major Japanese war criminals was one of the reasons that Goff and McCloy met with MacArthur in Tokyo in the fall of 1945. Keenan had just been named chief prosecutor and Goff wanted MacArthur to approve his appointment and lay the organizational groundwork for the trial.[43] MacArthur had no problem with Keenan's appointment, and saw him 'as a counterpart for Jackson in the trial of 1A criminals [accused of crimes against peace]'. But Keenan had to understand, he told Goff, that he 'distinctly [had to] be under the Commanding General to work effectively'.[44]

But MacArthur sought further clarification about Keenan's authority from Secretary of War Robert P. Patterson. His principal concern was that Keenan might compromise or undercut the work and position of Col. Carpenter, whom MacArthur argued had done a 'brilliant', efficient job gathering evidence for and organizing Class B and C trials [for those accused of crimes other than crimes against peace] as well as the Yamashita and Homma trials. Patterson reassured the general that Keenan would be fully under his command and that he was only responsible for the trial of 1A war criminals before an international

---

40   UNWCC, Case no. 21, 'Trial of General Tomoyuki Yamashita', *Law Reports*, 4, pp. 37-63 passim; Hampton Sides, 'The Trial of General Homma', *American Heritage Magazine*, 58, no. 1 (February/March 2007), 2, 17-19. <http://www.americanheritage.com/print/61812> [accessed 8/4/2011].

41   Hampton Sides, "The Trial of General Homma", American Heritage Magazine, Vol 58, No 1 (February/March 2007), 19.

42   James, *Years of MacArthur*, 3, p. 101.

43   Joseph B. Keenan Papers, Harvard Law School Library, Box 2, Abe M. Goff, 'Memorandum', 29 October 1945, pp. 1-6.

44   Ibid., p. 2.

or US tribunal. Patterson admitted that he had misunderstood the function of Carpenter's Legal Section and that Keenan's appointment in no way would affect him or the work of his office. He added that

> it is essential that these [1A] cases be given preponderant consideration and that counsel in them should enjoy priority as to the determination of the defendants' designation of witnesses, evidence and other facilities for their prosecution in the event of conflicting claims from other agencies.[45]

McCloy followed this up with a personal letter to MacArthur reassuring him that he had final power on all matters dealing with the occupation of Japan and the forthcoming trials 'subject to the directives you may receive from the Joint Chiefs of Staff'. Moreover, he had President Truman's assurances that Keenan's job was only to 'conduct the main trial', which would in no way interfere with Carpenter's work. And when it came to trying Tōjō, he said that the US government wanted to adhere to a policy similar to the one in Nuremberg, which was to emphasize 'international responsibility for the type of conspiracy which resulted in the attacks on Poland by Germany and on Pearl Harbor and the Malay by Japan'.[46]

Keenan, who was putting together his prosecution team in the US, hoped to arrange the same kind of support 'found essential by Justice Jackson in Europe'.[47] He was well aware of MacArthur's concerns and had no intention of doing anything to run afoul of him. MacArthur wrote to the JCS on 9 December that his first meeting with Keenan was both 'comprehensive and thoroughly satisfactory'. They both agreed that the war crimes trials in Japan should 'proceed without delay', and that invitations had to be sent out to interested Allied nations to participate in the 1A trials.[48]

---

45   MacArthur Archives, RG 9, Box 159, Folder 'War Crimes, Sept. 45–June 46', CINCAFPAC ADV to WARCOS, 25 October 1945, 1 p.; RG 9, Box 159, Folder 'War Crimes, Sept. 45–June 1946', CINCAFPAC ADV (MACARTHUR PERSONAL) to Washington (SECRETARY OF WAR), 2 November 1945, 1 p.; RG 9, Box 159, Folder 'War Crimes, Sept. 46–June 46', WASHINGTON (SECRETARY OF WAR) to CINCAFPAC ADV (PERSONAL FOR MACARTHUR), 14 November 1945, 1 p.; RG 9, Box 159, Folder 'War Crimes, Sept. 45–June 46', CINCAFPAC ADV to WARSEC, 17 November 1945, pp. 1-2.; RG 9, Box 159, Folder 'War Crimes, Sept. 45–June 46', WASHINGTON (SECRETARY OF WAR PATTERSON), 18 November 1945, 1 p.

46   MacArthur Archives, RG 5, Box 2, Folder 2, 'John J. McCloy to General Douglas MacArthur', 19 November 1945, pp. 1-3.

47   MacArthur Archives, RG 9, Blue Binders, 'War Crimes, Nov. 45', WASHINGTON (SECRETARY OF WAR) to CINCAFPAC (PERSONAL FOR MACARTHUR), 14 November 1945, 1 p.

48   MacArthur Archives, RG 9, Box 159, Folder, 'War Crimes, Sept. 45–June 46', CINCAFPAC ADV to WARCOS (JOINT CHIEFS OF STAFF), 9 December 1945, pp. 1-2.

Keenan, a World War I veteran, got his law degree at Harvard, and entered private practice in Cleveland, Ohio a year later. An 'ardent' supporter of President Franklin Roosevelt, he was appointed special assistant to Roosevelt's first attorney general, Homer S. Cummings, soon after Roosevelt took office in 1933. Keenan's job was to develop a programme to deal more aggressively with 'an outbreak of crime throughout the United States, which resulted in numerous bank robberies, kidnaping[s] and other methods of predatory crimes of violence'. He worked closely with J. Edgar Hoover and advised Congress on a series of laws designed to strengthen Federal efforts to deal with the rise in major crimes. He later became head of the Justice Department's Criminal Division, and was actively involved in some of the most famous criminal trials in the 1930s. He returned to private practice in 1939 with offices in Washington and Cleveland.[49]

Soon after he arrived in Tokyo in December 1945, he began to encounter problems that haunted him throughout much of the trial. In a letter to Senator Kenneth McKella, he admitted that the 'work over here is difficult and contains an organization problem of some size'. He also had serious doubts about not indicting Hirohito, and considered the emperor institution 'still highly dangerous and one that will have to be done away with before there will be any solid foundation for reasonable expectation of peace'.[50]

Such doubts periodically surfaced during the trial. During his cross-examination of Kochii Kido, the Keeper of the Privy Seal and Hirohito's personal adviser, Keenan pressed him on the emperor's role in the attack on Pearl Harbor. His questioning became so intense that the president of the court, William Webb, intervened, reminding Keenan that 'we are not trying the Emperor'.[51] Keenan regained his footing during his questioning of Tōjō, after the former prime minister admitted that no one in Japan had the power to oppose the emperor. Webb wondered out loud if this meant that Hirohito could have stopped Japan's drift to war. Keenan quickly intervened and was able to get Tōjō to retract his statement.[52]

Concerns about Keenan's ability to organize an effective prosecution led British Prosecutor Arthur Comyns-Carr to send him a memorandum in late February 1946 from the Commonwealth prosecutors about the conduct of their phase of the trial.[53] They were concerned that Keenan and his team had

49   Keenan Papers, Box 2, n.d., 'Joseph B. Keenan Biography', pp. 1-8.

50   Keenan Papers, Joseph B. Keenan to Kenneth McKellar, Box 2, 26 December 1945, pp. 1-2.

51   R.J. Pritchard (ed.) *The Tokyo Major War Crimes Trial: The Records of the International Military Tribunal for the Far East* (Lewiston, N.Y.: Edward Mellen Press, 1998), 13, p. 31331.

52   Ibid., 77, pp. 36779-36781.

53   Ibid., pp. 34-46.

become bogged down in time-consuming interrogations of individual suspects, and wanted him to focus on securing 'the ruling that planning and
waging aggressive war constituted a crime in international law'.[54]

The memorandum suggested that he select a group of fifteen to twenty
defendants who were 'representative of the responsibility of the various criminal acts or incidents'. Comyns-Carr added that while the Japanese public
generally supported the prosecution of such criminals, this could quickly
change if there was a prolonged trial. Equally important, he argued, was the
fact that a trial in Japan would not enjoy the interest or prestige of the
Nuremberg trial, and once the German trial was over 'world interest, as distinct
from the purely Japanese interest, in the whole subject of International Trials'
would 'fall to a vanishing point'.[55] He thought that whether one was or was
not a major war criminal was a question 'of degree'. Once a set number of
defendants were chosen, the prosecutors could then begin investigating their
individual criminality prior to the selection a final list for trial. Comyns-Carr
argued that it was important to have defendants who were involved in Japan's
various acts of aggression. Those selected for trial, he noted, should be Japan's
'principal leaders' who bore the 'primary responsibility for the acts committed',
and for whom the prosecution's case was 'so strong as to render negligible the
chances of acquittal'. Those most eligible would be members of the highest
organs of state and war, including the emperor's Imperial Conference and
Privy Council.[56]

Keenan agreed with most of these ideas, but also thought that the British
wanted to 'run' the trial.[57] Regardless, he asked Comyns-Carr, along with
Carlisle W. Higgins, the American deputy chief prosecutor, to handle the prosecution's day-to-day presentations of its case against the defendants. For
Keenan, the reason was simple – both prosecutors had 'wide experience and
ability as trial lawyers'.[58]

Yet none of this masked the serious problems that the prosecution faced
during the trial. And though Keenan was quite sensitive to the mounting criticism of his role as chief prosecutor, particularly his long absences and alleged
drinking problems, he was protected by MacArthur, who took any criticism of

---

54   Y. Totani, *Tokyo War Crimes Tribunal: The Pursuit of Justice in the Wake of World War* II
        (Cambridge: Harvard University Press, 2008), p. 66.

55   Ibid., pp. 66-67.

56   Boister and Cryer, *Tokyo International Military Tribunal*, pp. 53-54; Totani, *Tokyo Major
        War Crimes Trial*, pp. 67-69.

57   Keenan Papers, Box 2, Joseph B. Keenan to Joseph Bossong, 13 August 1946, p. 2.

58   Keenan Papers, Box 2, 'Keenan Memorandum', 4 February 1947, p. 1.; Box 2, Joseph B.
        Keenan to Mrs. Joseph B. Keenan, 16 December 1947, pp. 1-2.

Keenan personally. Keenan met with MacArthur about once a week for an hour or two, and, over time, they developed a close relationship. In late 1947, Keenan wrote to Tom Clark about mounting criticism of the trial, and told him that he thought it was important to conduct the rest of it 'most scrupulously... to avoid justifiable criticism'. This also led Keenan and MacArthur to conclude that it would be unwise to conduct any further international trials in Asia or Europe.[59]

This did little to still Keenan's critics, particularly Owen Cunningham, one of the trial's defence attorneys. During the last months of the trial, he gave a devastating speech before the American Bar Association about it. He said that he considered it a sham, and was critical of every phase of it. The Charter, he argued, was an exercise in ex post facto law, while the judges ensured that the defendants were never 'afforded a fair trial'. He challenged his audience 'to inspect the sloppy record upon which the Tokyo tribunal bases its power'.

> The two sets of rules of procedure were novel and flexible – one liberal set was applied to the prosecution's evidence and a very strict set imposed upon the defense. They were constantly changed in favor of the prosecution as the case progressed. No one knew from one day to the next what was the 'law of the case'.

The overarching goal of the prosecution, he added, was 'conviction, not justice'. He added that the 'greatest evil of the Tokyo trials rests in the creation and the composition of the court itself'. This, and the lack of a serious appeal process 'reduced the trial to a political football with eleven nations outdoing each other to air their international grievances, and transformed what was intended to be a judicial inquiry into a political battleground'.[60]

Earlier that year, Ronald H. Quilliam, New Zealand's associate prosecutor, wrote prime minister Peter Fraser a detailed report on the trial. While he said that all nations involved in it shared some blame for its problems, the United States, in particular, 'failed' properly and fairly to discharge 'its responsibility in connection with the appointment of a Chief of Counsel'. If Washington had made a better choice, he went on, 'many of the difficulties which seriously affected the conduct of the Trial would never have arisen or would have been overcome without the successful conduct of the proceedings being prejudiced'. He added that by the time he arrived in Tokyo with his staff in early February

---

59   Keenan Papers, Box 2, Joseph B. Keenan to Tom C. Clark, 3 December 1947, pp. 1-2.
60   National Archives of the United States. Owen Cunningham, RG 153, Series 118-7, Box 124, Book 3, 'The Major Evils of the Tokyo Trial', 7 September 1948, pp. 1-3.

1946, it became very apparent that the chief of counsel and his staff had done 'very little planning and that there was lacking any competent leadership or direction'. Keenan, he told Fraser, was simply incompetent.[61]

Keenan and MacArthur were unaware of Quilliam's comments but were stung by the critiques of the trial in the dissenting opinions of several of the judges, particularly the separate judgment of Indian judge Radhabinod Pal, who was extremely critical of most of the findings of the tribunal. He was particularly incensed when it came to the issue of crimes against peace and argued that the defendants should all be found not guilty.[62]

For the most part, MacArthur remained silent about such criticism, though in a somewhat reflective meeting with Keenan in December 1947, he said that as people learned more about the trial, they would see its educational value and its 'exemplary' role in 'deterring or perhaps preventing military aggression in future years'.[63] A year later, he wrote to Keenan and thanked him for the outstanding, distinguished role he had played as chief prosecutor.[64]

The first major criticism of MacArthur came in 1949, when A. Frank Reel, a member of Yamashita's American defence team, published *The Case of General Yamashita*. Courtney Whitney, prompted by his boss, responded in *The Case of General Yamashita: A Memorandum*, calling Reel's book 'an attack on our American system of jurisprudence'.[65] Keenan followed this up with a study of the Tokyo trial in 1950, co-authored with Prof. Brendan F. Brown, who had served as his judicial consultant during the trial. They concluded that the IMTFE deserved a 'distinctive place... in the history of Jurisprudence and international law'.[66]

---

61   Justice Northcroft, Tokyo War Crimes Trial Papers, 112497, Prosecution Documents, University of Canterbury. MB 1549, R.H. Quilliam to Prime Minister Peter Fraser, 29 January 1948, *Report on the Proceedings of the International Military Tribunal for the Far East*, pp. 1, 3,4.

62   'Judgement of the Honorable Mr. Justice Pal, Member of India', in Boister and Cryer, *Documents on the Tokyo International Military Tribunal*, pp. 809-1421 passim.

63   Keenan Archives, Box 2, Keenan to Mrs. Keenan, 16 December 1947, pp. 1-2.

64   MacArthur Archives, RG 5, Box 32, Folder 1, 'OMS KE-KEL', Douglas MacArthur to Joseph B. Keenan, 26 November 1948, 1 p.

65   A.F. Reel, *The Case of General Yamashita* (New York: Octagon Books, 1971). Reprint of 1949 edition; James, *Years of MacArthur*, 3, p. 97; C. Whitney, *The Case of General Yamashita: A Memorandum* (Tokyo: General Headquarters, Supreme Commander for the Allied Powers, Government Section, 1949), p. 1.

66   J.B. Keenan and B.F. Brown, *Crimes against International Law* (Washington, D.C. Public Affairs Press, 1950), p. 1.

The criticism of MacArthur and Keenan affected the former's decision to publish the trial transcripts, something that had already been done for the Nuremberg IMT trial.[67] When Keenan learned of these plans, he wrote to MacArthur that he should include his opening statement, the indictment, the judgment, and the opinions of the judges. He was concerned that if this was not done, then

> the dissenting opinion of Judge Pal would be given undue emphasis and could be extremely misleading and could well cause a conclusion to be reached by a reviewer that the majority decisions were not warranted and subject the entire prosecution to misconception.[68]

MacArthur responded that the JAG (the US Army's Judge Advocate General's Corps which handled issues dealing with military justice) had recommended a much more expansive publication of the trial records. And though he agreed that these should have the 'widest circulation' because of the trial's 'historic importance', he also felt that care should be taken with the selection of what material from the trial would be included so that 'undue emphasis' should not be placed on 'certain facets' of the trial. He added that Justice Jackson had played an important role in the selection of the trial material for the Nuremberg publication, which included the full trial transcripts, and suggested that Keenan now consider the same for the Tokyo trial publication.[69]

In the meantime, the State Department pushed hard to expand the publication to include prosecution and defence summations 'to obviate any criticisms [that] defense views [were] not publicized or that [the] defense [was] not given adequate opportunity [to] present its side of the case'. The State Department also thought it was important to publish a more complete set of transcripts 'to avoid inference of too great [a] difference [in] importance between [the] German and Japanese trials'. If the cost of printing bound volumes, which was to be borne by SCAP, was too expensive, then it suggested doing an offset publication.[70]

---

67 MacArthur Archives, RG 5, Box 32, Folder 1, 'OMS, KE-KEL', Douglas MacArthur to Joseph B. Keenan, 6 May 1950, 1 p.

68 MacArthur Archives, RG 5, Box 32, Folder 1, 'OMS, KE-KEL', Joseph B. Keenan to Douglas MacArthur, 21 April 1950, 1 p.

69 MacArthur Archives, RG 5, Box 32, Folder 1, 'OMS-KE-KEL', Douglas MacArthur to Joseph B. Keenan, 4 May 1950, pp. 1-2.

70 MacArthur Archives, RG 9, Box 160-F, 'War Crimes, Nov 48–May 50', DA (SAOUS OUS FE) WASH DC to SCAP TOKYO JAPAN, 13 May 1950, p. 1.

In the end, MacArthur decided not to publish the trial records for 'financial and practical reasons'. According to Alva Carpenter, the 'basic principles involved [in the Tokyo trial] have all been embodied in the historical presentation of the German trial and it is believed there is little independent interest in the Japanese version'.[71] This decision further damaged the reputation of the trial since it deprived legal scholars and others of the documentation necessary to thoughtfully study and analyse the trial transcripts. In the end, at least until R. John Pritchard completed his monumental publication of the transcripts, there were literally only a handful of such documents in the world, which robbed historians and experts in international criminal law of the opportunity to study what still remains one of the benchmark trials in modern legal history.

Bibliography

M. Searle Bates and Kenneth Scott Latourette, 'The Future of Japan', *Pacific Affairs*, 17, no. 2 (June 1944), 190-203.

Noah Berlin, 'Constitutional Conflict with the Japanese Imperial Role: Accession, Yasukuni Shrine, and Obligatory Reformation', *Journal of Constitutional Law*, 1, no. 2 (Fall 1998), 383-414.

Neil Boister and Robert Cryer (eds.) *Documents on the Tokyo International Military Tribunal: Charter, Indictment and Judgments* (Oxford University Press, 2008).

Hugh Bolton, 'Preparation for the Occupation of Japan', *The Journal of Asian Studies*, 25, no. 2 (February 1966), 203-12.

David M. Crowe, *War Crimes, Genocide, and Justice: A Global History* (New York and London: Palgrave Macmillan, 2013).

John W. Dower, *Embracing Defeat: Japan in the Wake of World War II* (New York: W.W. Norton, 1999).

D. Clayton James, *The Years of MacArthur*, vol. 3, *Triumph & Disaster*, 1945-1964 (Boston: Houghton Mifflin, 1985).

Joseph Berry Keenan and Brendan Francis Brown, *Crimes against International Law* (Washington, D.C. Public Affairs Press, 1950).

Douglas MacArthur, *Reminiscences* (New York: McGraw-Hill, 1964).

Peter Maguire, *Law and War; International Law & American History*, Revised Edition (New York: Columbia University Press, 2010).

---

71   MacArthur Archives, RG 9, Box 160-F, 'War Crimes, Nov. 48–May 50', Alva C. Carpenter to DA WASH DC, 22 May 1950, 1 p.

William Manchester, *American Caesar: Douglas MacArthur, 1880-1964* (Boston: Little Brown, 1978).

Michael Neiberg, *Potsdam: The End of World War II and the Remaking of Europe* (New York: Basic Books, 2015).

John Price, 'E.H. Norman, Canada and Japan's Postwar Constitution', *Pacific Affairs*, 74, no. 3 (Fall 2001), 383-405.

R. John Pritchard (ed.) *The Tokyo Major War Crimes Trial: The Records of the International Military Tribunal for the Far East* (Lewiston, N.Y.: Edward Mellen Press, 1998).

Hampton Sides, 'The Trial of General Homma', *American Heritage Magazine*, 58, no. 1 (February/March 2007) <http://www.americanheritage.com/print/61812> [accessed 8/4/2011].

Gary D. Solis, *The Law of Armed Conflict: International Humanitarian Law in War* (Cambridge: Cambridge University Press, 2010).

Yuki Takatori, 'The Forgotten Judge at the Tokyo War Crimes Trial', *Massachusetts Historical Review*, 10 (2008), 115-41.

Ian W. Toll, *Pacific Crucible: War at Sea in the Pacific, 1941-1942* (New York: W.W. Norton, 2012).

Yuma Totani, *Tokyo War Crimes Tribunal: The Pursuit of Justice in the Wake of World War II* (Cambridge: Harvard University Press, 2008).

Courtney Whitney, *The Case of General Yamashita: A Memorandum* (Tokyo: General Headquarters, Supreme Commander for the Allied Powers, Government Section, 1949).

Courtney Whitney, *MacArthur: His Rendezvous with History* (New York: Alfred A. Knopf, 1956).

CHAPTER 4

On a 'Sacred Mission': Representing the Republic of China at the International Military Tribunal for the Far East

Anja Bihler

As one of the victorious Allies in the Second World War, the Republic of China was among the eleven nations represented at the International Military Tribunal for the Far East (IMTFE). Building on a number of excellent legal and historical studies that have emerged over the last two decades, the following chapter explores China's participation in the tribunal – a topic rarely touched upon in available literature.[1] In line with the overall methodological approach of this volume, the following chapter focuses on the Chinese legal staff posted to Tokyo. Part I introduces the main legal actors, their personal as well as their professional backgrounds, and discusses the actors' self-perceived role and function at the IMTFE. Providing the larger framework, Part II outlines the Chinese government's strategical interest in and support for the IMTFE and explores to what degree the legal staffs' personal opinions were aligned with national policy. Part III continues to portray the Chinese judge over the course of the proceedings, discussing his legal standpoints and interaction with fellow judges.

Prisoners of their Own Experiences?[2]

On 22 October 1945, the Chinese ambassador to the United States Wei Daoming 魏道明 sent a telegram to the Ministry of Foreign Affairs (MOF) in Chongqing

---

1   This chapter predominantly relies on Chinese language material. For a general introduction in English, see N. Boister and R. Cryer, *The Tokyo International Military Tribunal: A Reappraisal* (Oxford University Press, 2008), Y. Totani, *The Tokyo War Crimes Trial: The Pursuit of Justice in the Wake of World War II* (Cambridge, MA: Harvard University Press, 2008), B. Kushner, 'Chinese War Crimes Trials of Japanese, 1945-1956 – A Historical Summary', in M. Bergsmo, W.L. Cheah and P. Yi (eds.), *Historical Origins of International Criminal Law*, vol. 2 (Brussels: Torkel Opsahl, 2014), pp. 243-65.

2   The subtitle is adapted from a passage in S.M. Schwebel, *Justice in International Law: Further Selected Writings* (Cambridge University Press, 2011), p. 21. 'Every judge is a prisoner of his or

conveying the US State Department's wish that the Republic of China designate five representatives qualified for membership on the international military courts planned at the time.[3] The MOF solicited suggestions from, inter alia, the Chinese Ministry of Judicial Administration and the Ministry of Military Orders. The MOF also suggested three candidates they considered distinguished members of the Chinese legal sphere and who they thought would do justice to the 'prestige of the court and the dignity of the Republic of China'.[4] On 29 November, the Minister of Foreign Affairs, Wang Shijie 王世杰, presented a final list of five candidates to Chiang Kai-shek, the chairman of the National Government, for further deliberation.[5] One of the candidates on the list, Xiang Zhejun 向哲濬,[6] was approached and asked to indicate a preference for either a position on the bench or in the prosecution section of the IMTFE, of which he chose the latter.[7] Following his decision, the Chinese suggested Xiang Zhejun and Mei Ru'ao 梅汝璈 [8] for appointment as associate prosecutor and judge respectively.[9]

---

her own experience.... The judge sees the facts and applies the law to those facts with his own limited vision, a vision inevitably affected by his genetic endowment and environmental influences, his nationality, education, experience, not to speak of more evanescent factors such as his relations with his colleagues. Perfect objectivity is unattainable.'

3 Xiang Longwan 向隆万 and Sun Yi 孙艺, 'Dongjing shenpan zhong de zhongguo daibiaotuan 东京审判中的中国代表团' [The Chinese delegation at the Tokyo Trial], *Minguo dang'an*, 1 (2014), 62 - 71, at 62.

4 Guoshiguan 国史馆 (Academia Historica, Taiwan) [henceforth AH], 020-010117-0029-0070, Ministry of Foreign Affairs, Memorial, undated. A compiled list of recommendations contained the following eight names: Wu Jingxiong (John C.H. Wu) 吴经熊, Yan Shutang 燕树棠, Mei Ru'ao 梅汝璈, Xiang Zhejun 向哲濬, Ni Zhengyu 倪征燠, Liu Fangju 刘方矩, Shi Yusong 石毓崧, Lü Jie 吕节.

5 Xiang and Sun, 'Dongjing shenpan zhong de zhongguo daibiaotuan', 62. Those recommended were: Mei Ru'ao 梅汝璈, Xiang Zhejun 向哲濬, Ni Zhengyu 倪征燠, Liu Fangju 刘方矩 and Lü Jie 吕节.

6 This chapter uses the modern standard romanization, the name may otherwise also appear as Hsiang Che-chun.

7 Zhou Fang 周芳, 'Liangshi ailü yi mingsi – Xiang Zhejun furen Zhou Fang huiyi jilu 良师爱侣忆明思 – 向哲濬夫人周芳回忆录' [A good teacher and companion – Mrs. Xiang Zhejun Zhou Fang's memories] in Xiang Longwan 向隆万 (ed.), *Dongjing shenpan: zhongguo jianchaguan Xiang Zhejun* 东京审判—中国检察官向哲濬 [Tokyo Trial: The Chinese prosecutor Xiang Zhejun] (Shanghai jiaotong daxue chubanshe, 2010), pp. 215-308, at p. 254.

8 This chapter uses the modern standard romanization, the name may otherwise also appear as Mei Ju-ao.

9 L. Xiang and M.L. Houle, 'In Search of Justice for China: The Contributions of Judge Hsiang Che-chun to the Prosecution of Japanese War Criminals at the Tokyo Trial', in M. Bergsmo, W.L. Cheah and P. Yi (eds.), *Historical Origins of International Criminal Law*, vol. 2 (Brussels: Torkel Opsahl, 2014), pp. 143-75 at p. 149.

Born in 1904, Mei was prepared for overseas studies at the predecessor institution of Tsinghua University in Beijing before receiving his undergraduate degree from Stanford University in 1926 and his doctorate in law from the University of Chicago in 1928.[10] Mei was politically active in student organizations in both China[11] and the US,[12] sympathizing with leftist ideas. In the 1930s, he taught law at various institutions in China, including the Kuomintang-led Central Political Institute, before returning to Shanghai in 1945, where he continued to work as a law professor at Fudan University. During his early career, he assumed various political positions, including advisor for the Interior Ministry, member of the Legislative Yuan, and special member of the Supreme National Defence Council.[13] Mei Ru'ao had an excellent command of the English language and a solid legal education in common law, but no experience as a legal practitioner or judge. Convinced that he lacked the necessary judicial experience and freshly married, he decided to decline the offer to be posted to Tokyo and attempted to resign as a member of the Legislative Yuan.[14] The President of the Legislative Yuan eventually convinced him that a place on the bench in Tokyo was a blessing in disguise, a 'golden opportunity to leave his mark on history'.[15]

Xiang Zhejun obtained his B.A. in American and English literature from Yale University in 1920 and his LL.B. from George Washington University Law School

---

10   For a short overview over his life and career, as well as his major publications, see Mei Xiao'ao 梅小璈 and Fan Zhongxin 范忠信 (eds.), *Mei Ru'ao faxue wenji* 梅汝璈法学文集 [Mei Ru'ao's collected writings on law] (Beijing: Zhongguo zhengfa daxue chubanshe, 2007), pp. 410-16.

11   He was a core member of the leftist student organization called Weizhen Xuehui 唯真学会 (Truth-Only Society). See Qinghua daxue xiaoshi yanjiushi 清华大学校史研究室, *Qinghua Manhua* 清华漫话 [Talking about Tsinghua], vol. 1 (Beijing: Tsinghua University Press, 2009), pp. 233-34.

12   During his time at Stanford he acted as the editor in chief of the 'Chinese Students' Monthly', a publication of the Chinese Students Alliance in the US. See H.M. Lai, *Chinese American Transnational Politics* (Urbana: University of Illinois Press, 2010), p. 75. Speaking of Mei's time as editor, the author suggests that articles sympathetic to the Marxist left began to predominate.

13   He was released from his positions at the Legislative Yuan for the duration of the trial.

14   Mei Ruao 梅汝璈, *Dongjing da shenpan – yuandong guoji junshi fating zhongguo faguan Mei Ruao riji* 东京大审判－远东国际军事法庭中国法官梅汝璈日记 [The Tokyo Trial – Diary of the Chinese judge Mei Ru'ao at the IMTFE] (Nanchang: Jiangxi jiaoyu chubanshe, 2005), p. 130.

15   Li Lingling 李伶伶, *Ta jiang zhanfan songshang jiaojia-guoji fayuan faguan Ni Zhengyu* 他将战犯送上绞架-国际法院法官倪征噢 [Sending war criminals to the gallows – Judge Ni Zhengyu of the Court of International Justice] (Beijing: Zhongguo qingnian chubanshe, 2006), p. 6.

in 1925.[16] Upon his return to China, he worked, inter alia, as a secretary at the Ministry of Judicial Administration.[17] In 1933, he became Chief Prosecutor at the Shanghai Special District court and when Shanghai fell to the Japanese, he was appointed secretary to the Supreme National Defence Council.[18] He became a Kuomintang (KMT) party member around 1942.[19] After the war, he was named chief prosecutor of the Shanghai Supreme Court before being offered the position at the IMTFE.

The Chinese associate prosecutor, Xiang Zhejun, arrived in Tokyo on 7 February 1946, accompanied only by his secretary.[20] Mei Ru'ao and his designated secretary, Fang Fushu 方福枢, were ready to take up their positions shortly afterwards in March 1946.[21] Xiang soon found himself overwhelmed with work and in September and October of 1946 he requested that additional Chinese assistants be sent to Tokyo.[22] In reaction to his demands, the Chinese government selected additional translators and secretaries and eventually appointed four legal advisors to further assist the Chinese prosecution section. Ni Zhengyu 倪征燠, who possessed an advanced law degree from Stanford University, was selected as head advisor.[23] Prior to his appointment, he had worked at the Ministry of Judicial Administration in Nanjing and served as a judge in Shanghai.[24] His fellow advisors, E Sen 鄂森, a practising lawyer from Shanghai, and Gui Yu 桂裕, a judge at the Shanghai High Court, were also able to contribute much needed practical trial experience.[25] The fourth advisor, Professor Wu Xueyi 吴学义 from Nanjing Central University, had been educated at the Imperial University in Kyoto and was familiar with the workings

---

16   Xiang and Houle, 'In Search of Justice for China', 146.

17   Ni Zhengyu 倪征燠, *Danbo congrong li haiya* 淡泊从容莅海牙 [Arriving in The Hague with a peaceful mind] (Beijing: Falü chubanshe, 1999), p. 104.

18   Xiang and Houle, 'In Search of Justice for China', 147-48.

19   Zhou Fang 周芳, 'Liangshi ailü yi mingsi', 244.

20   Xiang and Sun, 'Dongjing shenpan zhong de zhongguo daibiaotuan', 62. Xiang was initially only accompanied by his secretary, Qiu Shaoheng 裘劭恒.

21   Ibid., p 62.

22   Telegrams, 12 September 1946 and 3 October 1946, Xiang Zhejun to Ministry of Foreign Affairs, reproduced in: Xiang Longwan 向隆万 (ed.), *Xiang Zhejun dongjing shenpan han dian ji fating chenshu* 向哲浚东京审判函电及法庭陈述 [Xiang Zhejun's letters, telegrams and court statements at the Tokyo Trial] (Shanghai jiaotong daxue chubanshe, 2015), p. 23 and p. 25-26.

23   Xiang and Sun, 'Dongjing shenpan zhong de zhongguo daibiaotuan', 63.

24   Li, *Ta jiang zhanfan songshang jiaojia*, p. 114.

25   Ibid., p. 28.

of the Japanese legal system. Over the course of the proceedings, several members of the advisory team also appeared in court on behalf of China.[26] Because of the duration of the trial, there was a relatively high fluctuation of support staff, with several members of the team returning to China before the trial was over.[27] The special nature of the IMTFE and the stringent language requirements naturally restricted the number of suitable candidates in the Republic of China and led to a certain homogeneity in educational backgrounds, legal training and understanding of the law.[28] Wudong University, at the time famous for teaching comparative and common law in China, was a common denominator amongst many of those appointed. Xiang and Ni had at some point in their career taught at the institution, while another six appointees were graduates of Wudong University. Mei, Xiang and Ni were also members of an elite group of Chinese legal scholars educated at top institutions in the US. Even though the Republic of China was a civil law country, they were partially, or even exclusively, trained in the Anglo-American common law tradition. Xiang and Ni had worked together in Shanghai[29] before they were both forced to leave for Chonqing by the invading Japanese forces.[30] Mei's diary entries also reveal that he had a close personal relationship with Xiang.

Judges in international courts and tribunals are commonly expected to rise above their national identities, but as the legal scholar Milan Markovic has argued, they 'are unlikely to act as true representatives of the international

---

26   The Chinese associate prosecutor, Xiang Zhejun, appeared in court on twenty occasions, the main advisor to the Chinese delegation, Ni Zhengyu, on sixteen, the advisor Gui Yu on four. See Xiang Longwan 向隆万 and Sun Yi 孙艺, 'Zhongguo jianchaguan Xiang Zhejun 中国检察官向哲浚' [The Chinese prosecutor Xiang Zhejun] in Dongjing shenpan yanjiu zhongxin 东京审判研究中心 (ed.), *Dongjing shenpan zai taolun* 东京审判再讨论 [Re-evaluating the Tokyo Trial] (Shanghai: shanghai jiaotong daxue chubanshe, 2015), pp. 188-223, at p. 205.

27   Over the course of the trial, China was represented by the following persons: The Chinese Judge: Mei Ru'ao 梅汝璈, Secretaries to the Judge: Fang Fushu 方福枢, Luo Jiyi 罗集谊, Yang Shoulin 杨寿林; Chinese Associate Prosecutor: Xiang Zhejun 向哲浚, Secretaries to the Prosecutor: Qiu Shaoheng 裘劭恒 (Chiu Henry), Liu Zijian 刘子健 (Liu T.C. James), Zhu Qingru 朱庆儒, Gao Wenbin 高文彬; Advisors: Ni Zhengyu 倪征噢 (Nyi Judson) (Main Advisor), E Sen 鄂森, Gui Yu 桂裕, Wu Xueyi 吴学义; Translators: Zhou Xiqing 周锡卿, Zhang Peiji 张培基, Gao Wenbin 高文彬, Zheng Luda 郑鲁达, Liu Jisheng 刘继盛. See Xiang and Sun, 'Dongjing shenpan zhong de zhongguo daibiaotuan,' p. 63.

28   For biographical information on the members of the Chinese prosecution section, see Xiang, *Xiang Zhejun donjing shenpan han dian ji fating chenshu*, pp. 297-302.

29   Ni, *Danbo congrong li haiya*, p.104.

30   Zhou Fang, 'Liangshi ailü yi mingsi', 242. They fled together from Shanghai when the Japanese entered the international settlement in December 1941.

community in cases involving crimes allegedly committed by or against their fellow nationals'.[31] Even though the IMTFE was clearly an international tribunal, Mei considered his fellow judges first and foremost to be representatives of their respective countries. In his later writings on the IMTFE, he stated that of the eleven judges, there was not a single member of the bench he was willing to consider a truly 'international judge'.[32] Mei considered himself both a representative of the Republic of China and a representative of the Chinese People. Xiang Zhejun also strongly identified himself as a Chinese representative in Tokyo, an attitude that became clear on the occasion when US judge Cramer replaced the former judge Higgins on the bench. Speaking in court, Xiang stated: 'as the Chinese prosecutor I do not speak for the prosecution as a whole. I merely speak for China. China welcomes the full representation of eleven nations represented in this Tribunal. China especially does not like to see the non-representation of the United States of America on the bench.'[33] The British liaison mission in Tokyo reported back to the Foreign office: 'the Chinese prosecutor ... caused considerable embarrassment to the prosecutors by publicly welcoming Cramer in court, in despite of agreement among the prosecutors themselves to say nothing at all.'[34] The Dutch justice Röling later remarked that he thought the Japanese defence lawyers had mainly sought to protect the honour of their country and the Japanese emperor. The individuals on trial, Röling argued, were of secondary importance, 'their main interest was to save Japan'.[35] The American defence lawyers, on the other hand, Röling found, were mainly preoccupied with the defendants' individual fate.[36] Ni Zhengyu later wrote that he had found it hard to understand why the allied defence counsels were willing to place the Japanese defendants' interest above their own national interest.[37]

---

31 M. Markovic, 'International Criminal Trials and the Disqualification of Judges on the Basis of Nationality', *Washington University Global Studies Law Review*, 13 (2014), 1-48, at 48.

32 Mei Ru'ao 梅汝璈, *Yuandong guoji junshifating* 远东国际军事法庭 [International Military Tribunal for the Far East] (Beijing: Falü chubanshe, 2005), p. 61.

33 Transcript of proceedings, 22 July 1946, p. 2350. Available at: <http://www.legal-tools.org/doc/3bbeda/>.

34 TNA London, WO 311/ 537, Telegram from Gascoigne (head of the British liaison mission) to Foreign Office, 24 July 1946.

35 B.V.A Röling, *Tokyo Trial and Beyond: Reflections of a Peacemonger*, ed. A. Cassese (Cambridge: Polity Press, 1993), p. 37.

36 Röling, *Tokyo Trial and Beyond*, p. 37.

37 Ni, *Danbo congrong li haiya*, p. 105-6.

The Chinese media portrayed Mei Ru'ao and Xiang Zhejun as joint representatives of the Republic of China, without duly acknowledging the different and
at times conflicting roles they played as judge and member of the prosecution
section at an international tribunal. Aware of public perception and international expectations, they tried to maintain a professional distance. While Xiang
and Mei had initially both stayed at the Imperial Hotel in Tokyo, Xiang eventually moved because Mei feared it would be deemed inappropriate for a judge
and an associate prosecutor to live in such close physical proximity.[38] In his
diary, however, Mei reveals that he also thought of the Chinese representatives
as a team jointly representing their country. Expressing doubt about the prosecution section's ability to make a strong case against the defendants, he noted:
'*Our* [emphasis added] evidentiary material is not at all much', 'will the prosecution section in the future be able to fully confirm the indictments?'[39]

To 'Repay Evil with Kindness' – A Nation's Weakness or Virtue?

When the St James Declaration called for the punishment of German war
criminals 'through the channel of organized justice' on 13 January 1942,[40] China
publicly declared her intention to eventually 'apply the same principles to the
Japanese occupying authorities in China'.[41] In the Potsdam Declaration on 26
July 1945, the US, the UK and China warned that 'stern justice shall be meted
out to all war criminals'. By the time Japan finally surrendered, however, Chiang
Kai-shek started to promote a more generous and forgiving attitude towards
Japan, that became known as the strategy 'to repay evil with kindness'. In his
famous 'victory' speech that was broadcast on 15 August 1945, Chiang Kai-shek
appealed to his countrymen 'not to remember evil deeds of the past'.[42] To a

---

38   Mei, *Dongjing da shenpan*, p. 62.

39   Ibid., p. 138.

40   Full text of the declaration reprinted in 'The Inter-Allied Conference, January 13 1942', in
      the *Bulletin of International News*, 19 (1942), 50-53.

41   Telegram, The Ambassador to the Polish Government in Exile (Biddle) to the Secretary of
      State, 14 January 1942, in United States Department of State, *Foreign Relations of the
      United States Diplomatic Papers, 1942 General; the British Commonwealth; the Far East*
      (Washington: US Government Printing Office, 1960), p. 45.

42   Huang Zijin 黄自进, *Jiang Jieshi yu riben – yi bu jindai zhongri guanxi shi de suoying* 蒋介
      石与日本一部近代中日关系史的缩影 [Chiang Kai-shek and Japan – the epitome of
      the history of modern Sino-Japanese relations] (Taibei: Zhongyang yanjiuyuan jindaishi
      yanjiusuo, 2013), p. 337.

certain extent, this lenient approach also extended to suspected war criminals. The Chinese government policy suggested that ordinary war criminals should be handled with leniency, while major war criminals and those connected to well-known atrocities, such as the Nanjing Massacre, were to be treated harshly.[43] Mei's opinion concerning his government's general policy towards Japan was ambivalent and he noted in his diary:

> The Japan Times carried a report entitled 'The Chinese people are not seeking revenge', describing how magnanimously China treated Japan after her surrender and how China decided to 'treat her enemy as a friend'. To show leniency is surely a virtue, but to be indulgent and fearful is cowardice. When I read this article I did not know whether to laugh or cry.[44]

Chiang Kai-shek selected twelve names for a list of Japanese 'major war criminals' on 16 October 1945.[45] The list was sent to the US Department of State for submission to the Allied Forces in Japan.[46] While the US occupying forces were responsible for the arrest of suspects, it was the executive committee of the International Prosecution Section (IPS), of which Xiang Zhejun was also a member, which decided on the defendants.[47] Out of the twelve names

---

43   See Zhanzheng zuifan chuli weiyuanhui dui rizhanfan chuli zhengci huiyi jilu 战争罪犯
     处理委员会对日战犯处理政策会议记录 [Minutes of the Commission on War Crimi-
     nals Meeting Concerning the Strategy for Handling Japanese War Criminals], reprinted in
     Guo Biqiang 郭必强 and Jiang Liangqin 姜良芹 (eds.), *Nanjing datusha shiliaoji* 南京大
     屠杀史料集 [Collection of historical documents on the Nanjing Massacre], vol. 14 (Nan-
     jing; Jiangsu renmin chubanshe, 2006), pp. 25-30, at 28.

44   Mei, Dongjing da shenpan, p. 80.

45   Chiang Kai-shek selected the following twelve persons from a list of twenty: 土肥原賢二
     (Doihara Kenji), 本莊繁 (Honjo Shigeru), 谷壽夫 (Tani Hisao), 橋本欣五郎 (Hashi-
     moto Kingoro), 板垣征四郎 (Itagaki Seishiro), 磯谷廉介 (Isogai Rensuke), 東條英機
     (Tojo Hideki), 和知鷹二 (Wachi Takaji), 影佐禎昭 (Kagesa Sadaaki), 酒井隆 (Sakai
     Takashi), 喜多誠一 (Kita Seiichi), 畑俊六 (Hata Shunroku). The remaining eight were:
     梅津美治郎 (Umezu Yoshijiro), 多田駿 (Tada Hayao), 秦彦三郎 (Hata Hikosaburo),
     小磯國昭 (Koiso Kuniaki), 大谷光瑞 (Otani Kozui), 阿部信行 (Abe Nobuyuki), 南次
     郎 (Minami Jiro), 甘粕止彦 (Amakasu Masahiko). Reprinted in Qin Xiaoyi 秦孝仪,
     Zhonghua minguo zhongyao shiliao chubian-duiri kangzhan shiqi 中华民国重要史料初
     编-对日抗战时期 [First collection of important historical documents of the Republic of
     China] Post-War China, vol. 4 (Taipei: zhongguo guomindang zhongyang weiyuanhui
     dangshi weiyuanhui, 1981), p. 395.

46   NARA RG 84, Box 21, Note, Ministry of Foreign Affairs to the American Embassy Nanking,
     9 February 1946.

47   The members of the IPS decided on the defendants by a majority vote on 8 April 1946. See
     G. Townsend, 'Structure and Management' in L. Reydams, J. Wouters and C. Ryngaert

suggested by the Chinese, five were eventually selected as defendants: Tojo Hideki, Itagaki Seishirō, Hashimoto Kingorō, Doihara Kenji and Hata Shunroku. During the war years and leading up to the trial, there was an expectation amongst China's bureaucrats as well as the general public that the Japanese emperor Hirohito would be tried as a war criminal.[48] And while the emperor's name had appeared on earlier lists of war crimes suspects in Chinese official circles, he was neither among those selected by Chiang Kai-shek nor among those eventually indicted by the IMTFE.[49]

According to Article 8 (a) of the IMTFE Charter, 'The Chief of Counsel ... is responsible for the investigation and prosecution of charges against war criminals'. With the IMTFE's seat in Tokyo and all crimes under investigation committed overseas, the IPS under Keenan was dependent on state cooperation for the collection of war crimes evidence. While some of the associate prosecutors brought evidence with them to Japan, the Chinese prosecutor Xiang arrived in Tokyo without any sizeable amount of evidentiary material. This peculiar situation was a clear source of distress to Xiang, who was convinced that after fifteen years of conflict with Japan, the Republic of China should have been the country able to present the largest amount of relevant evidence.[50] Xiang's role in the prosecution section was marginalized, causing Mei Ru'ao to concede that the Chinese prosecution team was merely playing a subordinate role. 'The overwhelming majority of investigative work', Mei concluded, 'was undertaken by the head of the prosecution office and his American staff; the Chinese team was merely assisting from the sidelines.'[51] The scarcity of material necessitated several trips by the international prosecution staff to China where they collected additional evidence. In March 1946, the American prosecutor Joseph Keenan and members of his staff embarked on an initial

---

(eds.), *International Prosecutors* (Oxford University Press, 2012), pp. 171-318, p. 219.

48   Riben tianhuang ying lie wei zhanfan zhi yi 日本天皇应列为战犯之一 [The Japanese Emperor should be listed as a war criminal] *Shenbao*, 20 March 1946, reprinted in: Dui ri zhanfan shenpan wenxian congkan bianweihui 对日战犯审判文献丛刊编委会, *Erzhan hou shenpan riben zhanfan baokan ziliao xuanbian* 二战后审判日本战犯报刊资料选编 [A collection of press materials on the post-war trials against Japanese war criminals], vol. 1 (Beijing: Guojia tushuguan chubanshe, 2014), p. 90.

49   Zuo Shuangwen 左双文, 'Guomin zhengfu yu chengchu riben zhanfan jige wenti de zai kaocha' 国民政府与惩处日本战犯几个问题的再考察 [A reinvestigation of certain questions concerning the National Government and the punishment of Japanese war criminals], *Shehui kexue yanjiu*, 6 (2012), 144-156, at 149.

50   Mei, *Dongjing da shenpan*, p. 74.

51   Mei Xiao'ao 梅小璈 and Mei Xiaokan 梅小侃 (eds.) *Mei Ru'ao dongjing shenpan wengao* 梅汝璈东京审判文稿 [The Tokyo Trial manuscripts of Mei Ru'ao] (Shanghai: Shanghai jiaotong daxue chubanshe, 2013), p. 205.

voyage.[52] One month later, several American prosecutors arrived in China for a longer tour of a number of major Chinese cities to collect further evidence. The lack of preparation on the Chinese side did not go unnoticed. *The New York Times* reported in April 1946 that 'the work of building up China's case against major Japanese war criminals soon to be tried in Tokyo is proving to be a slow and complicated task.'[53] Chiang Kai-shek gave orders to assist the visitors from Tokyo in their work and expressed support and appreciation for the work of the IMTFE.[54] There were, however, clear limits to China's willingness to cooperate where it meant compromising national interests. When Tokyo requested Okamura Yasuji, the Supreme Commander of the Japanese forces in China, to appear in court as a witness, the Chinese government deliberately prevented extradition to Japan.[55] They declared Okamura was still needed in his position as Chief of the Central Liaison Office for the Japanese Military[56] in China and that he was unfit to travel due to health issues.[57]

Over time, the members of the Chinese prosecution section used increasingly frank words to express their dissatisfaction with the progress of the trial. 'By its midway point in the summer of 1947, James T.C. Liu ... observed that the trial had become a "second-rate show" that no longer commanded public interest'.[58] In January 1948, a newswire from Tokyo again raised the issue of how little evidence the Chinese prosecution section had contributed to the trial. Quoting an unnamed judge, the newswire predicted that 'the lack of sufficient concrete evidence might place China in an unfavourable position when the final judgment is drafted.' It went on to say: 'The Chinese prosecution sec-

---

52 'Keenan in Chungking-Seeking Evidence on The "China Incident" ', 南华早报 (South China Morning Post & The Hongkong Telegraph), 26 March 1946, reprinted in *Erzhan hou shenpan riben zhanfan baokan ziliao xuanbian*, vol. 1, p. 40.

53 D. Tillman, 'War Crimes Case Delayed in China', 1 April 1946, *The New York Times*, p. 11.

54 'Keenan in Chungking – Seeking Evidence on The China "Incident"', 南华早报 (South China Morning Post & The Hongkong Telegraph), 26 March 1946, reprinted in: *Erzhan hou shenpan riben zhanfan baokan ziliao xuanbian*, vol. I, p. 40.

55 Gangcun Ningci 冈村宁次, *Gangcun ningci huiyilu* 冈村宁次回忆录 [The memory of Okamura Yasuji] (Shanghai: zhonghua shuju, 1981), p. 146.

56 B. Kushner, *Men to Devils, Devils to Men: Japanese War Crimes and Chinese Justice* (Cambridge: Harvard University Press, 2015), p. 96.

57 AH, 020-010117-0023-0015, SCAP (diplomatic section) to the Chinese Mission in Japan, undated. Okamura eventually remained in China until 1948 where he was indicted for war crimes by a military court in Shanghai. Eventually, after an ominous acquittal, he returned to Japan.

58 T. Brook, 'The Tokyo Judgment and the Rape of Nanking', *The Journal of Asian Studies*, 60 (2001), 673-700 at 675.

tion, in an interview with Central News, attributed the lack of atrocity evidence to the "un-cooperative and indifferent" attitude of the competent authorities in China toward the trial in Tokyo'.[59] Several English newspapers in China picked up on the story and Xiang was at pains to explain that neither of the Chinese representatives had actually spoken to the journalist in question.[60] With regard to the question of indicting the emperor, Mei was at odds with his government's decision, but initially willing to accept the realities in Tokyo. In a private conversation with Xiang he stated: 'This is a political question. If we purely speak about the legal concepts, I am honestly unable to perceive how the emperor could have no responsibility for Japan's aggressive warfare.'[61] Once the trial was over, Mei was willing to state this opinion in public, openly contradicting his government's position on the matter. Three days after the reading of the judgment in 1948, Mei stated in an interview with the major Chinese newspaper *Shenbao* 申报 that 'the emperor Hirohito should face trial by the court just as the other important war crimes suspects'. The article further stated that Mei 'supports the president of the court Webb's opinion that the emperor's guilt was no less than those of the other twenty-five major war criminals and that he therefore should be punished by the court ... the court has a large amount of evidence proving the emperor's different war crimes.'[62]

A Tale of Eleven 'Charming Brothers'[63]

While Roosevelt had entertained hopes for the Republic of China to eventually live up to the status of one of the 'Big Four' in the post-war era, China's situation turned out to be unpredictable at best. In the words of the China historian Rana Mitter: 'In August 1945 China was simultaneously in the strongest global position it had ever occupied and weaker than it had been for nearly a century.'[64] Mei personally thought of China as one of the important powers, but was at

---

59   AH, 020-010117-0026-0111, collected news wire 'China's evidence of atrocities', 9 January 1948.

60   Telegram, Xiang Zhejun to Ministry of Foreign Affairs, 22 January 1948 and 23 January 1948, reprinted in Xiang Longwan, *Xiang Zhejun dongjing shenpan han dian ji fating chenshu*, pp. 51 and 52.

61   Mei, *Dongjing da shenpan*, p. 74.

62   Mei Ru'ao fabiao yijian 梅汝璈发表意见 [Mei Ru'ao gives his opinion] *Shenbao*, 15 November 1948.

63   Term used by Mei Ru'ao to refer to his fellow members of the bench.

64   Rana Mitter, *Forgotten Ally: China's World War II, 1937-1945* (Boston: Houghton Mifflin Harcourt, 2013), p. 362.

the same time extremely concerned about the country's ability to uphold its newfound political status in the future.[65] Seeing himself primarily as a representative of China, Mei perceived the level of respect shown to himself in Tokyo as a direct reflection of the national prestige of the Republic of China. Article 2 of the IMTFE Charter specified: 'The Tribunal shall consist of not less than six nor more than nine Members, appointed by the Supreme Commander for the Allied Powers from the names submitted by the Signatories to the Instrument of Surrender'.[66] For Judge Mei, this reference to the Japanese Instrument of Surrender apparently gave rise to the expectation that the judges would be seated following the order of signatures: United States of America, Republic of China, United Kingdom and so on.[67] When the time came to decide on the seating arrangement, however, President Webb wished to depart from this order. Judge McDougall described the conflict that ensued in a telegram to the Canadian authorities in the following manner: 'From the diplomatic angle the seating of the judges and their seniority has been a bit of a problem. Our president ... has solved the problem by departing from the Instrument of Surrender to suit his own convenience and placing the judges in the order of his opinion of the importance of the Countries which they represent. In the result China is moved down one place, changing places with United Kingdom and Canada moved down below France and the Netherlands'.[68] Eventually, the judges were seated according to the order of signatures. The Chinese media happily reported that Judge Mei was seated right next to the president of the court. This arrangement, one Chinese article explained, was a sign of the 'participating nations' understanding of the important role the Republic of China played in trying Japanese war criminals'.[69] In an interview with *Shenbao* in July 1947, Mei Ru'ao pointed out that he was very content with the treatment he was receiving in Tokyo.[70]

---

65   Mei, Dongjing da shenpan, p. 61.

66   N. Boister and R. Cryer (eds.), *Documents on the Tokyo International Military Tribunal: Charter, Indictment and Judgments* (Oxford University Press, 2008), pp. 7-11. Article 2 was amended by General Order No. 20 on 26 April 1946 to allow for two additional judges from India and the Philippines.

67   Order of signature of the country representatives: C.W. Nimitz (United States), Hsu Yung-Chang (Republic of China), Bruce Fraser (United Kingdom), K. Derevyanko (Union of Soviet Socialist Republics), [rest omitted].

68   Library and Archives Canada [LAC], RG 25, vol. 3641, File 4060-C-40, telegram McDougall to Robertson (Canadian Under Secretary of State for External Affairs), 23 April 1946. Special thanks to Yuki Takatori for graciously sharing the material.

69   Riben zhanfan de shenpan 日本战犯的审判 [Trial of Japanese War Criminals] *Shenbao*, 9 May 1946.

70   Yuandong guoji junshi fating wo faguan 远东国际军事法庭我法官 [Our judge at the International Military Tribunal for the Far East] *Shenbao*, 16 July 1947.

Judge Mei also showed great concern about the judicial outcome of the IMTFE. In a memorandum to the president of the court, Mei enthusiastically articulated what he believed to be the importance of the trial: 'the Tokyo trial, like the Nuremberg trial should also be considered as the greatest thing that comes out from the world war to borrow a phrase of President Truman.'[71] In the Chinese media he pointed out that the significance of the trial went far beyond determining the fate of the defendants. He pointed towards the role of the trial for the development of international law and the importance of firmly establishing aggressive warfare as a crime.[72] Mei proved a stern supporter of the IMTFE when the court was faced with challenges to its jurisdiction. Even though he was absent when the judges passed the decision to dismiss all motions lodged by the defence in chambers, he did not fail to register with Webb, that he was 'all-out for a complete dismissal of those motions.'[73] Mei stated he was 'firmly convinced that the charter is intrinsically sound and its provisions in regard to war-crimes are simply declaratory of principles of law already in existence, instead of creating any new ones'.[74] In an interview with the Chinese newspaper *Shenbao*, Mei said the IMTFE was not only of 'great historical significance' but had a 'sacred mission' to fulfil.[75]

For Mei it was thus of utmost importance to ensure that the judges in Tokyo spoke with one voice, leaving no doubts about the factual or legal issues at stake. While some scholars have suggested that judicial dissent may also serve to strengthen the legitimacy of international adjudicating bodies,[76] it is hard to argue away the fact that a divided bench does to a certain extent diminish the authority of a court in the eyes of the public. The New Zealand judge Northcroft was also deeply worried about the effects of judicial dissent on public perception and the legacy of the court: 'I fear the result of this long trial will be futile and valueless or worse.... If a Court of this standing is seriously divided, and I feel sure it will be, then the modern advances in international law towards the outlawry of war may suffer a serious setback'.[77] The judges initially agreed to draft a joint judgment, but with the Indian judge Pal's firm intention to write a

---

71   AH, 020-010117-0027-0112 Confidential Memorandum, Mei Ru'ao to Webb, undated.

72   Shenpan ri zhanfan qingxing 审判日战犯情形 [The current situation with trying Japanese war criminals] *Shenbao*, 6 January 1947.

73   AH, 020-010117-0027-0106 Confidential Memorandum, Mei Ru'ao to Webb, undated.

74   Ibid.

75   Mei Ru'ao jin chen fei dongjing fanren 梅汝璈今晨飞东京返任 [This morning Mei Ru'ao is flying to Toyko to return to his post] *Shenbao*, 26 January 1948.

76   H. Mistry, 'The Paradox of Dissent: Judicial Dissent and the Projects of International Criminal Justice', *Journal of International Criminal Justice*, 13 (2015), 449-74.

77   Northcroft to O'Leary, 18 March 1947, quoted in K. Sellars, *'Crimes against Peace' and International Law* (Cambridge University Press, 2013), p. 238.

dissenting opinion, the united front on the bench quickly began to crumble.[78] Initially looking towards Webb as the president of the court, a group of five common law judges from the US, the UK, Canada, New Zealand and the Philippines eventually started to work on a joint draft judgment.[79] Webb's own drafts failed to fruitfully engage the other judges, eliciting outspoken critique instead. Like most of his colleagues, Mei was little impressed by Webb's draft judgment calling it 'too lengthy and involved', and 'essentially patch-work, consisting chiefly of protracted citations from well-known authors, popular works and famous cases'.[80] Mei notified the Chinese MOF that his own views were at variance with those of the president of the court[81] and he eventually joined the group of common law judges in drafting the majority judgment.[82]

Since the International Military Tribunal in Nuremberg passed judgment before the IMTFE, there was the sensitive question of the extent to which Tokyo should follow and endorse the judgment in Nuremberg. Worried about the gravitas and the legacy of the court, Mei argued that 'the two trials should be regarded as independent of each other and their results should be reached separately ... we must not follow Nuremberg slavishly, at least not in appearance. In my opinion, we should avoid copying Nuremberg's exact wording whenever we can and employ our own language as much as possible'.[83] In the Chinese media, Mei described Tokyo, when compared to Nuremberg, as yet another step forward and a further contribution to the development of modern international law.[84]

Besides his concerns about the legacy of the court, Mei also showed a high level of emotional involvement with the trial. Even though Mei had not directly lived under Japanese occupation, he felt strongly about the Nanjing Massacre and privately resented the Japanese troops for having destroyed his family home.[85] On seeing the defendants assembled in court on the first day of trial, he felt a sense of hatred. In his diary he noted:

> the group of (defendants) seated opposite to me create boundless resentment, boundless feelings in my heart. These people are all veterans of the

78   Sellars, *Crimes against Peace*, p. 244.

79   Ibid.

80   AH, 020-010117-0027-0106 Confidential Memorandum, Mei Ru'ao to Webb, undated.

81   AH, 020-010117-0027-0007, Telegram, Mei Ru'ao to the Ministry of Foreign Affairs, 15 June 1948.

82   Boister and Cryer, *Documents on the Tokyo International Military Tribunal*, p. lxviii.

83   AH, 020-010117-0027-0112 Confidential Memorandum, Mei Ru'ao to Webb, undated.

84   Ri zhanfan caipan jingguo 日战犯裁判经过 [The jugment against Japanese war criminals] *Shenbao*, 30 November 1948.

85   Mei, *Dongjing da shenpan*, p. 30.

invasion of China who poisoned the country for several decades, millions and tens of millions of compatriots died under their hands, so my resentment is also the resentment of my fellow countrymen. The opportunity to sit on the bench and punish these arch-criminals and arch-enemies has been paid for with the blood and flesh of many million Chinese. I have to be vigilant! I have to be solemn![86]

A widely held assumption in legal scholarship is that 'the essence of the adjudicator's role ... is to avoid writing personal predilections, biases and prejudices into the law that they are entrusted to administer and safeguard or surrendering to considerations of personal or political expediency.'[87] In reality, however, these are extremely high expectations that not every judge can realistically be expected to fulfil. Especially if trials involve 'horrific crimes allegedly committed by or against members of a judge's national polity', some scholars have argued, it is extremely difficult 'for professional detachment to triumph over the natural tendency to view a conflict and the crimes committed therein through the prism of national identity'.[88]

There was a pervasive feeling amongst the Chinese representatives that unless the defendants were found guilty and punished sternly, their task in Tokyo was unfulfilled.[89] Mei Ru'ao's firm stance on the matter was well known to his fellow judges. Judge Röling, for instance, noted that the Chinese judge was 'in favour of very severe judgements'.[90] Leading up to the deliberation of punishments, Mei was exceedingly worried about his colleagues' attitude toward the death penalty. In an interview with the major Chinese newspaper *Zhongyang Ribao* 中央日报 Mei stated:

> Because of this question, I have spent I do not know how much time and efforts on my colleagues. For a whole week, I was so worried that I could not even find sleep at night. If not even these major Japanese militarists who invaded China and are guilty of the most heinous crimes are condemned to death, how can I return to my country and face our elders?[91]

---

86   Ibid., p. 133.

87   G.I. Hernández, 'Impartiality and Bias at the International Court of Justice', *Cambridge Journal of International and Comparative Law*, 1 (2012), 183-207, at 184.

88   M. Markovic, 'International Criminal Trials and the Disqualification of Judges on the Basis of Nationality', *Washington University Global Studies Law Review*, 13 (2014) 1-48 at 25.

89   Ni, *Danbo congrong li haiya*, p. 115.

90   Röling, *Tokyo Trial and Beyond*, p. 29.

91   *Zhongyang Ribao*, 30 November 1948, reprinted in *Erzhan hou shenpan riben zhanfan baokan ziliao xuanbian*, vol. 3, pp. 549-50, at 550.

When Webb later considered accepting mitigating evidence, Mei, together with Northcroft, Zaryanov and Cramer opposed the notion.[92]

Conclusion

By the time the trial ended, the Chinese mainland was deeply embroiled in the last stages of the civil war. With the communist victory looming, the representatives of the Chinese Nationalist government at the IMTFE were faced with the difficult decision to either return to the mainland, retreat with the Nationalist forces or to emigrate. Mei Ru'ao was offered the position of Minister of Judicial Administration,[93] but instead travelled to Beijing where he became a legal advisor to the new communist government.[94] Xiang Zhejun and Ni Zhengyu both declined much coveted prosecutorial positions: Xiang because he had nearly reached retirement age and Ni because he decided to return to a teaching career.[95] Ni remained in mainland China, where he went on to work as a legal advisor to the Ministry of Foreign Affairs, before finally becoming the first PRC judge at the International Court of Justice in The Hague. In 1948, official and public interest in the IMTFE had reached a low point and when Ni and Xiang returned to Nanjing they orally reported on the results of the proceedings to the Minister of Legal Administration Xie Guansheng 谢冠生. At the Ministry of Foreign Affairs, however, they could no longer find anyone responsible for the matter.[96]

Bibliography

English

Neil Boister and Robert Cryer (eds.), *Documents on the Tokyo International Military Tribunal: Charter, Indictment and Judgments* (Oxford University Press, 2008).

---

92   N. Boister and R. Creyer, *The Tokyo International Military Tribunal: A Reappraisal* (Oxford University Press, 2008), p. 92.

93   Xin ge quanti mingdan jueding 新阁全体名单决定 [Complete name list for the new cabinet has been decided] *Shenbao*, 22 December 1948.

94   He Qinhua 何勤华, 'Mei Ru'ao yu yuandong guoji junshifating 汝璈与远东国际军事法庭' [Ru'ao and the International Military Tribunal for the Far East], *Faxue* (2005), 3-19, at 4. He was targeted during the Anti-rightist campaign and the Cultural Revolution and was not able to continue his academic career in law.

95   Li, *Ta jiang zhanfan songshang jiaojia-guoji fayuan faguan Ni Zhengyu*, p. 124.

96   Ni, *Danbo congrong li haiya*, p. 127.

Neil Boister and Robert Cryer, *The Tokyo International Military Tribunal: A Reappraisal* (Oxford University Press, 2008).

Timothy Brook, 'The Tokyo Judgment and the Rape of Nanking', *The Journal of Asian Studies*, 60 (2001), 673-700.

Gleider I. Hernández, 'Impartiality and Bias at the International Court of Justice', *Cambridge Journal of International and Comparative Law*, 1 (2012), 183-207.

Barak Kushner, 'Chinese War Crimes Trials of Japanese, 1945-1956 – A Historical Summary', in Morten Bergsmo, Cheah Wui Ling and Yi Ping (eds.), *Historical Origins of International Criminal Law*, vol. 2 (Brussels: Torkel Opsahl, 2014), pp. 243-66.

Barak Kushner, *Men to Devils, Devils to Men: Japanese War Crimes and Chinese Justice* (Cambridge, MA: Harvard University Press, 2015).

Him Mark Lai, *Chinese American Transnational Politics* (Urbana: University of Illinois Press, 2010).

Milan Markovic, 'International Criminal Trials and the Disqualification of Judges on the Basis of Nationality', *Washington University Global Studies Law Review*, 13 (2014) 1-48.

Hemi Mistry, 'The Paradox of Dissent: Judicial Dissent and the Projects of International Criminal Justice', *Journal of International Criminal Justice*, 13 (2015), 449-74.

Rana Mitter, *Forgotten Ally: China's World War II, 1937-1945* (Boston: Houghton Mifflin Harcourt, 2013).

Luc Reydams, Jan Wouters, and Cedric Ryngaert (eds.) *International Prosecutors* (Oxford University Press, 2012).

B.V.A. Röling and Antonio Cassese, *Tokyo Trial and Beyond: Reflections of a Peacemonger* (Cambridge: Polity Press, 1993).

Kirsten Sellars, *Crimes against Peace* (Cambridge University Press, 2013).

Stephen M. Schwebel, *Justice in International Law: Further Selected Writings* (Cambridge University Press, 2011).

United States Department of State, *Foreign Relations of the United States Diplomatic Papers, 1942 General: the British Commonwealth – the Far East* (Washington: US Government Printing Office, 1960).

Yuma Totani, *The Tokyo War Crimes Trial: The Pursuit of Justice in the Wake of World War II* (Cambridge, MA: Harvard University Press, 2008).

Xiang Longwan and Marquise Lee Houle, 'In Search of Justice for China: The Contributions of Judge Hsiang Che-chun to the Prosecution of Japanese War Criminals at the Tokyo Trial' in Morten Bergsmo, Cheah Wui Ling and Yi Ping (eds.), *Historical Origins of International Criminal Law*, vol. 2 (Brussels: Torkel Opsahl, 2014), pp. 143-76.

Chinese

Dui ri zhanfan shenpan wenxian congkan bianweihui 对日战犯审判文献丛刊编委会, *Erzhan hou shenpan riben zhanfan baokan ziliao xuanbian* 二战后审判日本战犯报

刊资料选编 [A collection of press materials on the post-war trials against Japanese war criminals] (Beijing: Guojia tushuguan chubanshe, 2014).

Gangcun Ningci 冈村宁次, *Gangcun ningci huiyilu* 冈村宁次回忆录 [The memory of Okamura Yasuji] (Shanghai: Zhonghua shuju, 1981).

Guo Biqiang 郭必强 and Jiang Liangqin 姜良芹 (eds.), *Nanjing datusha shiliaoji* 南京大屠杀史料集 [Collection of historical documents on the Nanjing Massacre], vol. 19 (Nanjing: Jiangsu renmin chubanshe, 2006).

He Qinhua 何勤华, 'Mei Ru'ao yu yuandong guoji junshifating 梅汝璈与远东国际军事法庭 ' [Mei Ru'ao and the International Military Tribunal for the Far East], *Faxue* (2005), 3-19.

Huang Zijin 黄自进, *Jiang Jieshi yu riben – yi bu jindai zhongri guanxi shi de suoying* 蒋介石与日本一部近代中日关系史的缩影 [Chiang Kai-shek and Japan – the epitome of the history of modern Sino-Japanese relations] (Taibei: Zhongyang yanjiuyuan jindaishi yanjiusuo, 2013).

Li Lingling 李伶伶, *Ta jiang zhanfan songshang jiaojia-guoji fayuan faguan Ni Zhengyu* 他将战犯送上绞架-国际法院法官倪征噢 [Sending war criminals to the gallows – Judge Ni Zhengyu of the Court of International Justice] (Beijing: Zhongguo qingnian chubanshe, 2006).

Mei Ru'ao 梅汝璈, *Dongjing da shenpan – yuandong guoji junshi fating zhongguo faguan Mei Ru'ao riji* 东京大审判远东国际军事法庭中国法官梅汝璈日记 [The Tokyo Trial – Diary of the Chinese judge Mei Ru'ao at the IMTFE] (Nanchang: Jiangxi jiaoyu chubanshe, 2005).

Mei Ru'ao 梅汝璈, *Yuandong guoji junshifating* 远东国际军事法庭 [International Military Tribunal for the Far East] (Beijing: Falü chubanshe, 2005).

Mei Xiao'ao 梅小璈 and Fan Zhongxin 范忠信 (eds.), *Mei Ru'ao faxue wenji* 梅汝璈法学文集 [Mei Ru'ao's collected writings on law] (Beijing: Zhongguo zhengfa daxue chubanshe, 2007).

Mei Xiao'ao 梅小璈 and Mei Xiaokan 梅小侃 (eds.) *Mei Ru'ao dongjing shenpan wengao* 梅汝璈东京审判文稿 [The Tokyo Trial manuscripts of Mei Ru'ao] (Shanghai: Shanghai jiaotong daxue chubanshe, 2013).

Ni Zhengyu 倪征噢, Danbo congrong li haiya 淡泊从容莅海牙 [Arriving in The Hague with a peaceful mind] (Beijing: Falü chubanshe, 1999).

Qinghua daxue xiaoshi yanjiushi 清华大学校史研究室, *Qinghua Manhua* 清华漫话 [Talking about Tsinghua] (Beijing: Tsinghua University Press, 2009).

Qin Xiaoyi 秦孝仪, *Zhonghua minguo zhongyao shiliao chubian-duiri kangzhan shiqi* 中华民国重要史料初编-对日抗战时期 [First collection of important historical documents of the Republic of China], vol. 4 (Taipei: zhongguo guomindang zhongyang weiyuanhui dangshi weiyuanhui, 1981).

Xiang Longwan 向隆万 (ed.), *Dongjing shenpan: zhongguo jianchaguan Xiang Zhejun* 东京审判—中国检察官向哲浚 [Tokyo Trial: The Chinese prosecutor Xiang Zhejun] (Shanghai jiaotong daxue chubanshe, 2010).

Xiang Longwan 向隆万 (ed.), *Xiang Zhejun dongjing shenpan han dian ji fating chenshu* 向哲浚东京审判函电及法庭陈述 [Xiang Zhejun's letters, telegrams and court statements at the Tokyo Trial] (Shanghai jiaotong daxue chubanshe, 2015).

Xiang Longwan 向隆万 and Sun Yi 孙艺, 'Dongjing shenpan zhong de zhongguo daibiaotuan 东京审判中的中国代表团 ' [The Chinese delegation at the Tokyo Trial]', *Minguo dang'an* 1 (2014), 62-71.

Xiang Longwan 向隆万 and Sun Yi 孙艺, 'Zhongguo jianchaguan Xiang Zhejun 中国检察官向哲浚 ' [The Chinese prosecutor Xiang Zhejun], in Dongjing shenpan yanjiu zhongxin 东京审判研究中心 (ed.), *Dongjing shenpan zai taolun* 东京审判再讨论 [Re-evaluating the Tokyo Trial] (Shanghai: shanghai jiaotong daxue chubanshe, 2015), pp. 188-223.

Zhou Fang 周芳, 'Liangshi ailü yi mingsi – Xiang Zhejun furen Zhou Fang huiyi jilu 良师爱侣忆明思—向哲浚夫人周芳回忆录 ' [A good teacher and companion – Mrs. Xiang Zhejun Zhou Fang's memories] in Xiang Longwan 向隆万 (ed.), *Dongjing shenpan: zhongguo jianchaguan Xiang Zhejun* 东京审判—中国检察官向哲浚 [Tokyo Trial: The Chinese prosecutor Xiang Zhejun] (Shanghai: jiaotong daxue chubanshe, 2010), pp. 215-308.

Zuo Shuangwen 左双文, 'Guomin zhengfu yu chengchu riben zhanfan jige wenti de zai kaocha 国民政府与惩处日本战犯几个问题的再考察 ' [A reinvestigation of certain questions concerning the National Government and the punishment of Japanese war criminals], *Shehui kexue yanjiu*, 6 (2012), 144-56.

CHAPTER 5

Managing Justice: Judge William Patrick, Prosecutor Arthur Comyns-Carr and British Approaches to the IMTFE

Kerstin von Lingen

British Foreign Secretary Ernest Bevin, when asked early in 1946 to nominate candidates for the Tokyo tribunal, framed it as follows:

> This trial is of considerable significance to us, because of the important role which we play in the Far East, and also because of the tremendous effect which the Pacific War had on large numbers of British subjects and on important British territories.[1]

Participation in the trial was seen as an enhancement of Britain's prestige in Asia.[2] Whitehall was also surely on a mission to strengthen the Nuremberg principles, set down in the London Charter of August 1945. Although Britain had agreed relatively late to the establishment of an International Military Tribunal in Nuremberg and in Tokyo,[3] it was now determined to hold up this legacy. Tokyo was thus envisioned as a 'second Nuremberg'.

This chapter discusses the role of the British team in Tokyo, whose task was drafting the indictment and planning the prosecution's strategies for the trial, as well as framing the majority judgment. The British role in the trial mirrors London's effort to 'manage' the trial's outcome, while at the same time trying to balance the difficult equilibrium between the national teams coming from not only different cultural and political backgrounds, but also fundamentally different legal traditions.

The British team in Tokyo was dominated by two very different personalities as judge and prosecutor. As the US journalist and observer of the Tokyo trial, Arnold Brackman, noted, Judge Patrick was a 'remote, aloof figure who seemed

---

1 The National Archives at London (TNA), LCO 2/2986 Bevin to Patrick, 7 February 1946.

2 K. Sellars, 'William Patrick and "Crimes Against Peace" at the Tokyo Tribunal, 1946-1948', *The Edinburgh Law Review*, 15 (2011, 2), 166-96, here 170.

3 A. Kochavi, *Prelude to Nuremberg: Allied War Crimes Policy and the Question of Punishment* (Chapel Hill: University of North Carolina Press, 1998).

to have come directly from central casting. In his black robes, he looked like and acted as a judge – tall, somber, gray-haired, crisp, and authoritative'.[4] Patrick was crucial in drafting the majority judgment, with the concepts of crimes against peace and conspiracy as the central elements. Prosecutor Arthur Comyns-Carr was another 'major power behind the scenes in Tokyo', as Pritchard points out.[5] He had respectable diplomatic skills, drafted the indictment, led the prosecution section, and was responsible for key defendants and their cross-examination; in this regard, it is fair to say that he acted as the manager of the Tokyo tribunal.

Patrick found his adversary in the court's president William Webb from Australia; Comyns-Carr had his counterpart in US chief counsel Joseph Keenan. Thus, another element of Britain's role at Tokyo is that its team – different from Nuremberg – clashed with its long-time allies.

Although British strategy has been analysed in depth in the scholarship,[6] the individual roles of the British lawyers at Tokyo has been understudied. A first glimpse is available, however, from Kirsten Sellars,[7] and also from Lord Bonomy's recollections on Judge Patrick.[8] Sellars points to the role of the Foreign Office and its liaison officer to Japan, Alvary Gascoigne, as well as Patrick's moderating effect in managing the split in the judge's bench in the summer of 1947. However, the role of the British associate prosecutor, Arthur Comyns-Carr, has not yet been highlighted. Thus, this paper gives credit to the role of both men in the context of their government's expectations and the overall British strategy for Japan and the delivery of justice, by focusing on key events such as the selection process, the drafting of the indictment, the crisis on the judge's bench in 1947, and the struggle for a majority judgment.

---

4   A.C. Brackman, *The Other Nuremberg: The Untold Story of the Tokyo War Crimes Trial* (New York: William Morrow, 1987), p. 67.

5   J.R. Pritchard, 'The Historical Experience of British War Crimes Courts in the Far East, 1946-1948', *International Relations*, 6 (1978), 311-26, here 315.

6   For example, in Y. Totani, *The Tokyo War Crimes Trial: The Pursuit of Justice in the Wake of World War II* (Harvard University Press, 2008); N. Boister and R. Cryer, *The Tokyo International Military Tribunal: A Reappraisal* (Oxford University Press, 2008); K. Sellars, *'Crimes against Peace' and International Law* (Cambridge University Press, 2013).

7   Sellars, 'Patrick and "Crimes against Peace"'.

8   I. Bonomy, 'Justice Patrick (United Kingdom)' in Y. Tanaka, T. McCormack and G. Simpson (eds.), *Beyond Victor's Justice? The Tokyo War Crimes Trial Revisited* (Leiden: Nijhoff, 2011), pp. 103-8.

Appointment of the British Staff and British Mission

Given the importance London placed on a successful outcome to the Tokyo trial, it was crucial to find suitable candidates. The experience of the Nuremberg tribunal had already given a taste of the consequences of longer absences within the home district courts,[9] thus Lord Chancellor William Jowitt suggested the selection of someone from the Scottish Court of Session, which was the Supreme Civil Court.[10] After short consultations, Jowitt came up with three candidates and named Judge McIntyre (Lord Sorn), Lord Keith and Lord Patrick, all of them able to 'play... the part which Lawrence is playing at Nuremberg'.[11] Normand agreed Patrick was the most suitable amongst the candidates as he was firstly not married, and secondly had in court no dependants, which would facilitate a month-long absence. He also thought that Patrick would make the 'better member of a team'.[12] Patrick was approached with concrete salary proposals, and agreed merely days later.[13] Shawcross reacted very enthusiastically to the idea that a Scotsman was to be nominated, as this would silence critique 'against the case being left exclusively in English hands'.[14] He emphasized that Patrick's appointment would serve as 'a source of pride in Scotland'.[15]

Up to that point, Patrick's career had been fairly mundane. Born as William Donald Patrick on 29 June 1889 in Dalry, Ayrshire, he attended Glasgow University, where he acquired his LLB.[16] He suffered from tuberculosis in 1930 and had to retire to a sanatorium for at least a year.[17] In 1939, he was elevated to the Scottish bench – a 'remarkable achievement', as Bonomi summarizes.[18] Lord Cameron characterized Patrick as follows:

---

9   Sellars, 'Patrick and "Crimes against Peace"', 170.

10   TNA, LCO 2/2986, Letter Normand to Jowitt, 16 January 1946.

11   TNA, LCO 2/2986, Letter Jowitt to Shawcross, 14 January 1946.

12   TNA, LCO 2/2986, Letter Normand to Jowitt, 16 January 1946.

13   TNA, LCO 2/2986, Letter Patrick to Jowitt, 22 January 1946.

14   TNA, LCO 2/2986, Letter Judge Advocate to Jowitt, 22 January 1946.

15   TNA, LCO 2/2986, Letter Jowitt to Lord Cooper, the Right Honourable Lord President of the Court of Session, 24 January 1946.

16   All following biographical details by Sellars, 'Patrick and "Crimes against Peace"', 170-71 and Bonomy, 'Justice Patrick', 103. See for details 'Biography of Captain William Donald Patrick', in *The University of Glasgow Story*, at <http://www.universitystory.gla.ac.uk/ww1-biography/?id=4523> (last accessed 3 December 2015).

17   Sellars, 'Patrick and "Crimes against Peace"', 171.

18   Bonomy, 'Justice Patrick', 104.

To a wide knowledge of law and of legal principle he added a calm and balanced mind... Though patient and courteous he did not... permit the time of the court to be wasted in discussing irrelevancies, and he was quick to spot the fallacies of an unsound argument.[19]

These qualities were important with regard to the troubled nature of the later Tokyo tribunal.

Arthur Strettel Comyns-Carr was born in 1882 in London and 'combined a versatile legal career with regular forays into politics', as the biography puts his numbered efforts to run for the Liberal Party in elections in the thirties.[20] Comyns-Carr, who was a barrister at Grays Inn, was offered the position of chief British prosecutor at Tokyo. He met for a first briefing with his team and Shawcross in London on 14 January 1946, when details of the charges and British strategy to be adopted were discussed.[21] In this meeting, it was agreed to model the Tokyo Charter on the Nuremberg one and follow the three-charges model outlined earlier, thus 'crime of aggression' could (again) be made the centrepiece of legal strategies.[22]

Arrival at Tokyo made clear to the team that not pleasure but duty was to be expected. Comyns- Carr wrote back in intense frustration to Shawcross:

This is a frightful job you have let me in for. I have already been here as long as you said the whole trip would take, and there is no sign of the proceedings even beginning. On arrival I found the Americans with a huge staff engaged in an enormous research with a stack of documents which have never even been listed or translated.[23]

However, he was surely aware of the British mission of disseminating the legacy of Nuremberg. His biography notes: 'He was said to have been deeply affected by the experience but believed that such trials, by upholding international law in an international tribunal, were of "the utmost importance, not so much in relation to the past as to the future" as he revealed in an interview.'[24]

---

19   Cited after Sellars, 'Patrick and "Crimes against Peace"', 171.

20   See his biography at <http://www.oxforddnb.com/view/article/61800> (last accessed 4 December 2015).

21   Sellars, *Crimes against Peace*, p. 183.

22   Ibid.

23   Cited after M. Harries and S. Harries, *Sheathing the Sword: The Demilitarisation of Japan* (New York: Macmillan, 1987), p. 118.

24   Comyns-Carr's biography at <http://www.oxforddnb.com/view/article/61800>, citing *The Times*, 4 Aug 1948, 3b.

The British aim was a confirmation of the Nuremberg legacy. Judge Patrick, after intense briefing in London had left for Japan convinced that the Tokyo tribunal needed to sustain the idea that Nuremberg's justice was right.[25] He was especially eager to adopt the view of Shawcross's opening statement from Nuremberg, foreclosing the argument that it was a retrospective enactment, and the message thus would have been, as Sellars summarises, 'first, aggression was a crime; and second, individuals could be held responsible for it.'[26]

Patrick wrote to Normand in January 1947:

> The essence of the Charter of this Tribunal, as of that which sat at Nure[m]berg, is (first) its declaration that the planning or waging of a war of aggression is a crime, and (second) its declaration that there shall be individual responsibility for what used to be considered acts of state, for which there was no individual responsibility.[27]

The focus on aggression was one of the core points of British strategy, mirrored clearly in Comyns-Carr's draft for the indictment, and the idea was of course bound to have the Tokyo tribunal emphasize the Nuremberg Court's finding by giving the same prominence to 'crimes against peace'.[28] The Foreign Office had made it clear that failure to prove aggression would be devastating. Senior Legal Advisor Eric Beckett warned that this:

> would inter alia mean that the Tokyo tribunal was saying that the judgment of the Nuremberg tribunal was based at any rate in part upon bad law, and that the Allies had been guilty of infringing the principle 'nulla poena sine lege', which is supposed to be one of the fundamental principles of justice.[29]

The Tokyo judges were therefore doubly bound, as Sellars notes: 'by the strictures of the Charter and by the obligation to produce a judgment that would buttress the Nuremberg determination on its most contentious charge. This obligation diminished the judges' autonomy and exacerbated the tensions that at the time seemed to threaten the entire enterprise.'[30]

---

25   Sellars, 'Patrick and "Crimes against Peace"', 171.

26   Ibid., 172.

27   TNA, LC02/2992, Letter Patrick to Normand, without date, presumably January 1947.

28   Sellars, 'Patrick and "Crimes against Peace"', 169.

29   TNA, FO 371/66552, Memorandum Beckett, 5 May 1947.

30   Sellars, 'Patrick and "Crimes against Peace"', 169.

Drafting the Indictment: Comyns-Carr

Although their national teams were much smaller than the US team, the British
and Australian prosecutors immediately took the lead in forming an Executive
Commission for drafting the indictment, with Comyns-Carr and Mansfield
leading the team.[31]

Drafting of the indictment was without doubt a major legal achievement
and is the long-lasting legacy of Comyns-Carr, who used the Tokyo trial to rise
from mid-range barrister to real star. In a meeting in early March 1946, Comyns-
Carr and his assistant Christmas Humphreys laid out the basic criteria for
determining this representative defendant group.[32] In order to avoid merely
following orders, and after witnessing how Keenan had neutralized the able
US counsels John A. Darsey and John W. Fihelly by appointing Eugene Williams
as Chief Administrator, Comyns-Carr had formed a bloc with the other Commonwealth lawyers, thus dominating the legal argument of the prosecution.[33]
Additionally, he suggested the establishment of a Drafting Committee (also
chaired by himself), an Incidents and Treaties Committee (chaired by the Australian Associate Prosecutor, Alan Mansfield) and an Evidence and Defendants
Committee (also chaired by Mansfield).[34]

Rivalries are clearly visible here: Keenan was especially watchful of Comyns-
Carr and 'eager to restore his dignity, and if necessary, to do so by pushing aside
the Commonwealth prosecutors or anyone else who might steal the limelight
from him', as Totani underlines.[35] The Commonwealth judges, in turn, tried to
remove Keenan from office as 'incompetent' on at least three occasions.[36]

When drafting the indictment, Comyns-Carr drew his conclusions from a
meticulous analysis of the first 1500 of the prosecution's IPS documents. In a
meeting in late February 1946, Comyns-Carr received backing from the other
Commonwealth prosecution teams from Australia, Canada, New Zealand and
India[37], and proposed a strategy for the whole trial. In a memorandum given
to the Executive Committee on 1 April 1946, he exemplified the selection criteria further.[38]

---

31   Boister and Cryer, *Tokyo IMT*, p. 52; Totani, *Tokyo Trial*, p. 18.
32   Totani, *Tokyo Trial*, p. 68.
33   Harries and Harries, *Sheathing the Sword*, p. 118.
34   Sellars, *Crimes against Peace*, p. 187.
35   Totani, *Tokyo Trial*, p. 36.
36   Sellars, *Crimes against Peace*, p. 188.
37   Boister and Cryer, *Tokyo IMT*, p. 52-53; Sellars, *Crimes against Peace*, p. 187.
38   University of Virginia Acrhive (UVA), Law Library, Morgan, MSS 93-94, IMTFE (IPS), Mem-
      orandum Comyns-Carr to Executive Committee re Selection of Defendants, 1 April 1946.

Comyns-Carr emphasized that the trial needed to show the world that Japan was guilty of the crime of aggression, and should start quickly, to have an educating effect on the Japanese population.[39] He observed: '[A]t the present moment we understand that the Japanese themselves support the prosecution', but 'if the trial is delayed or prolonged, they may swing around in their sympathy and end by regarding the men as martyrs whom at present they wish to see condemned.'[40]

Altogether, there were 55 charges, which were divided into three related groups. The first group, Counts 1 to 36, explained the charge of crimes against peace, by citing crimes that the defendants had committed over a seventeen-year period, from 1 January 1928 until the moment of the official surrender on 2 September 1945. Unsurprisingly, Count 1 was the most numerous.[41] With Counts 2, 3 and 4, the charge of conspiracy, divided for domination between Manchuria, China, and the rest of the Pacific Sphere; while Count 5 stands on its own at a tangent to Count 1, alleging a conspiracy for world domination by having aligned with the Nazis.[42]

In Comyns-Carrs's understanding, the Japanese situation, however, differed substantially from the German case, not only by the fact that while in Nazi Germany there was only one ruling party at the time, but also in that there was no comparable pyramidal state structure.[43] This had important consequences for the conspiracy charge: the defendants in Tokyo, unlike those in Nuremberg, did not immediately appear to be linked to any specific group or organization, thus proving a 'grand conspiracy' was difficult.

Given the criticism in Nuremberg of the charge of crimes against peace (not to mention crimes against humanity), Comyns-Carr enforced the conventional war crimes charge. Looking back on the Tokyo trial, he underlined:

> In the first place it was considered simpler and better that those who initiate aggressive wars should be recognized as ordinary murderers as

---

39   The meetings of 2 March and 9 March 1946, presided over by Arthur Comyns-Carr, which took place in the theatre room at the Meji Building in Tokyo, are somehow lost in the UK and US archives but are reprinted in a Japanese Document Compilation for the Tokyo trial, which Yuki Takatori kindly made available. The book is Awaya Kentarō, Hitoshi Nagai and Masayuki Toyoda (eds.), *Tōkyō Saiban e no michi: Kokusai Kensatsukyoku, seisaku kettei kankei bunsho* (Tokyo: Gendai Shiryō Syuppan, 1999), vol. 3, pp. 160-71, and vol. 4, pp. 129-48.

40   Cited after Totani, *Tokyo Trial*, p. 67.

41   Sellars, *Crimes against Peace*, p. 188.

42   Harries and Harries, *Sheathing the Sword*, p. 119.

43   Sellars, *Crimes against Peace*, p. 193; Harries and Harries, *Sheathing the Sword*, p. 122.

well as being in a special criminal category. Secondly, if this view of their conduct is accepted it removes any possible doubt as to the charge being ex post facto or based upon a legislative act of the victorious powers.[44]

Comyns-Carr thought the American staff very inefficient with their task of establishing charges against all subjects and investigating war crimes, but proposed instead forming a steering committee (headed by himself) which would define the group of defendants[45] – individuals who would serve as representatives for the various crimes under consideration.[46]

Debate about including the emperor within the defendants group was especially heated[47]: Britain was opposed to indicting him for monarchical considerations, and was backed by the Americans who saw the political benefits of holding him in place, while Australia and especially China were very interested in removing him and putting him on trial.[48] In the British view, indicting the emperor would have been 'a capital political blunder'; and not even the Russians, who had trumpeted Hirohito's war guilt in the media, had pressed for the inclusion of his name in the list of accused when they had finally arrived in Japan.[49]

The indictment was fleshed out in a meeting between some of the prosecutors in March 1946. The New Zealand assistant prosecutor Quilliam, recorded them as 'very difficult'. Quilliam's impression was 'that the Chinese, Dutch, and French prosecutors did not understand some of the disputed points of law at all and the Philippines prosecutor threatened to resign unless his addition, couched "in picturesque extravagant and loose language", was added to the original draft indictment'.[50] The result was a compromise, and the indictment finally delivered to the court on 29 April 1946.

Keenan bitterly resented the loss of authority and the formation of a 'British justice bloc', his thoughts about which he voiced privately a year later:

Although they have differences among themselves from time to time ... they all gather together under one roof and the vote is five to one, and

---

44   A. Comyns-Carr, 'The Tokyo war crimes trial', *Far Eastern Survey*, 18 (1949), 109-14, here 110.

45   Sellars, *Crimes against Peace*, p. 187.

46   Totani, *Tokyo Trial*, p. 67.

47   For an overview, see H. Bix, *Hirohito and the Making of Modern Japan* (Hamburg: HarperCollins Publishers, 2000).

48   Sellars, *Crimes against Peace*, p. 191.

49   Harries and Harries, *Sheathing the Sword*, p. 129.

50   A. Trotter, 'New Zealanders and the International Military Tribunal for the Far East', *New Zealand Journal of History*, 23 (1989, 2), 142-56, here 149.

they know it and take full advantage of it. It is simply impossible to get the idea out of their minds that this is not a British trial to be held according to British rules and practices.[51]

However, back in London there was satisfaction. Maurice Reed cabled to Shawcross that Comyns-Carr had succeeded at an exceptionally difficult task[52], and went beyond what was to be expected. Harries summarizes: 'For a lawyer schooled in the domestic criminal courts of London, whose natural habitat was the Old Bailey, it represented a quantum leap into the unknown.'[53]

Issues of the Trial

Regarding the work environment, translation difficulties seem to have been the greatest obstacle for prosecution and defence alike. A complaint by the Canadian judge McDougall from March 1947 reveals a constant shortage of translators, the slow process of documents and a lack of overall organization.[54] The New Zealand judge Northcroft also criticized the bad quality of the US counsel, and summarized that '[t]he degree of disorganisation … is disturbing'.[55] Comyns-Carr, as head of the IPS, thus ordered that documents needed to be shorter, given that the translation of one page of double-spaced text took a single linguist two days.[56]

Comyns-Carr is reported to have gotten along quite well with the Soviet team (a photo of him and Zaryanov at a reception has survived, and he reported back to Shawcross that 'the Russians were extremely friendly'[57]), and he seems to have been on good terms with the Dutch judge Röling with whom he shared a passion for mountain climbing.[58] Patrick, in antithesis, detested socializing, and Brackman reports that at Allied diplomatic receptions,

51 Cited after Sellars, *Crimes against Peace*, p. 187, quoting a letter from Keenan to his wife of 4 November 1947, Keenan papers HLS, Doc. 752, Box 2.
52 Cited after Sellars, *Crimes against Peace*, p. 203.
53 Harries and Harries, *Sheathing the Sword*, p. 118.
54 TNA, LCO 2/2992, Memorandum to all members of the tribunal from McDougall, 27.03.1947.
55 TNA, LCO 2/2992, Letter Northcroft to Chief Justice, 28 March 1947.
56 Harries and Harries, *Sheathing the Sword*, p. 117.
57 TNA, LCO 2/2992, Letter Comyns-Carr to Attorney General, 2 January 1948.
58 Brackman, *The Other Nuremberg*, p. 66.

Lord Patrick was exceptionally reserved. As one of the attorneys at the trial later observed, 'He never permitted anyone to get close to him.' He also detested the press and on one occasion described news photographers as 'dogs'.[59]

However, the longer the trial lasted, the more tense the atmosphere became. Comyns-Carr after eighteen months complained about the food and cited his permanently bad relations with Keenan as a reason to resign: 'I think my public part in it is over.'[60] Also, complaints about Keenan's drunkenness were voiced.[61]

Crisis on the Bench

The diverging opinions on the bench became more and more apparent, and Patrick observed them with growing concern. In January 1947, he told Normand in confidence that the court was hopelessly divided, and the goal of a second Nuremberg was fading. He claimed:

> The President will sustain the Indictment upon a special ground of contract, useless as a precedent for the future, the Frenchman will sustain it as being in accord with his 'bon coeur'. Russia ... because of Japan's dastardly attack on democracy. The Philippines will sustain it on I know not what grounds. And Holland and India will deliver a detailed attack on the grounds of the Nur[em]berg judgment.[62]

Patrick was particularly unsettled by the position of the Indian judge, who had made his dissent clear from the first moment.[63] He didn't hold back that he thought Pal was a poor choice.[64] In the very same report to Normand, Patrick continues on Pal: 'He has made his position quite clear since first he was appointed,' he wrote, 'so why the Government of India ever nominated him... is difficult to see'.[65] And he concluded: 'Britain should never go into an endea-

---

59   Ibid., p. 67.
60   TNA, LCO 2/2992, Letter Comyns-Carr to Attorney General, 6 October 1947.
61   TNA, LCO 2/2992, Letter Maurice Reed to Attorney General, 11 November 1947.
62   TNA, LCO 2/2992, Letter Patrick to Normand, without date, presumably January 1947.
63   Sellars, 'Patrick and "Crimes against Peace"', 175.
64   Harries and Harries, *Sheathing the Sword*, p. 167.
65   TNA, LCO 2/2992, Memorandum Patrick to Normand, without date, title: Imperial Hotel Toyko Charter, 7 pages, presumably January 1947.

vour such as Tokyo again without more screening of the calibre of its other participants'.[66]

Patrick even thought that the whole court had only been set up to prove that war was illegal, and feared that this message was being damaged by a unanimous judgment. He saw it as 'rank dishonesty'.[67] Judge Patrick's argumentation line, or the line of the British bloc, is clearly visible, when his letter goes on, emphasizing:

> The judges must be taken to have accepted the validity of the Charter when they accepted their appointments... and it is absurd therefore that some of them should contemplate a finding that the preparation or waging of aggressive war is not a crime according to international law.[68]

He continued, 'the matter is a political one, and I can express no final view on it'.

Back in London, officials were alarmed. The covering letter from Jowitt to Normand deplores: 'It's indeed lamentable that these proceedings should undo much of the good of Nuremberg ... the hopes with which we started this trial seem to have failed'.[69] The Lord President expressed his worry that 'if Tokyo fails it may discredit Nuremberg'.[70]

Two months later, in March 1947, tensions between the judges and the president had grown to the point that three judges from the Commonwealth nations – Patrick, Northcroft and McDougall – threatened their resignation.[71] The deeper motivations behind that crisis had grown out of frustration about Webb's failed leadership, as the three saw it, but the conversations also reveal an attitude towards the trial and its mission as 'a British Justice approach'.

The problem of resignation had already come up in the summer of 1946, when US judge Higgins had resigned only a few weeks after the opening of the trial, to take over a post at the court in his US home district; he had been replaced by Judge Myron Cramer.[72] This crisis must have been the catalyst for the spring crisis of 1947 of the three Commonwealth judges.

---

66   Ibid., p. 7.

67   Ibid.

68   Ibid.

69   TNA, LCO 2/2992, Letter Jowitt to Normand, 6 February 1947.

70   TNA, LCO 2/2992, Letter Lord President to Jowitt, 17 April 1947.

71   Sellars, 'Patrick and "Crimes against Peace"', 176.

72   Y. Takatori, 'The Forgotten Judge at the Tokyo War Crimes Trial', *Massachusetts Historical Review*, 10 (2008), 115-41.

As Sellars has shown, the main points of criticism against Webb were his failed action when early unanimity might have been consolidated; his wavering over the Charter, which had prevented him from leading from the front; and his 'irascibility, stubbornness and unwillingness to collaborate' which 'had soured relations with some of the other members'.[73]

New Zealand judge Northcroft complained: 'The court is in effect in two parts, the president and the rest'.[74] Writing to his government (but sending copies also to London), Northcroft claimed he could not go on with the trial as it was. Judge McDougall also asked Ottawa for permission to resign.[75] Northcroft was especially unhappy about the growing dissent among the judges.[76] In his view, the whole legacy of the Tokyo trial was at stake:

> I fear the result of this long trial will be futile and valueless or worse. This court will not speak with a clear voice upon any topic whether of law or fact. If a Court of this standing is seriously divided ... then the modern advances in international law towards the outlawry of war may suffer a serious setback.... Varying opinions from this Court including sharp dissent from Nuremberg must be disastrous.[77]

The British Foreign Office had received a letter from Patrick, which confirmed all claims made by Northcroft. Patrick had suggested three possible exit scenarios: 'that the United Kingdom stick with the trial to the end even though the outcome would be regrettable; that it withdraw from the trial and jettison the chance to mobilise support for the Nuremberg line; or that it ask Australia to withdraw Webb, "who sets us all by the ears"'.[78] In April, Patrick reiterated these three scenarios, pointing to the 'serious friction between Mr. Webb and his fellow judges'.[79]

In London, indignation was profound. Foreign Office Assistant Undersecretary Esler Dening found the threat of a triple resignation 'little short of disastrous', and feared it would harm Allied prestige in Asia, which was already damaged by the military debacles in Pearl Harbor and Singapore.[80] Dening

---

73   Sellars, 'Patrick and "Crimes against Peace"', 176.

74   TNA, LCO 2/2992, Letter Northcroft to Chief Justice, 18 March 1947.

75   Sellars, 'Patrick and "Crimes against Peace"', 174.

76   Ibid.

77   TNA, LCO 2/ 2992, Letter Northcroft to Chief Justice, 18 March 1947.

78   Sellars, 'Patrick and "Crimes against Peace"', 175; see also letter in TNA, LCO 2/2992 Patrick to Cooper, 29 March 1947.

79   TNA, LCO 2/2992, Telegram top secret by Gascoigne on Patrick, 25 April 1947.

80   Sellars, 'Patrick and "Crimes against Peace"', 177.

emphasized that this situation was particularly sensitive in regard to the recently reclaimed Western Colonies in Asia, where strong independence movements challenged the returning old colonial powers, and summarized:

> Here we have a predominantly Western tribunal sitting in the Far East to try Japanese war criminals. If the tribunal fails to fulfil its task, Western justice will become the laughing-stock not only of Japan but of the Far East in general.[81]

The Foreign Office agreed that failure would deliver 'a shattering blow to European prestige' and 'proclaim to the world that Japanese militarism had been justified since we had tried to convict it and failed'.[82]

The claims of the Commonwealth judges, however, had two consequences. London felt it necessary to bring all judges back to the initial commitment, and to let MacArthur know, that a successful end to the trial was under threat, should the dissent prevail. The Dutch representative was summoned to make sure Röling was 'under control' and would not issue a dissenting judgment.[83]

In general, London hoped that the 'tragic farce' at Tokyo[84] would be solved by Patrick somehow holding the judge's bench together and 'persuading his colleagues'.[85] Foreign Secretary Ernest Bevin underlined that Patrick needed to stay where he was, as well as the other Commonwealth judges, otherwise 'all his time will be wasted': 'If we withdraw our judge, for whatever reason, New Zealand and Canada will almost certainly withdraw theirs, and the trial will become a farce'.[86] Bevin underlined that in his view, Patrick was the only figure holding the bench together and preventing the other judges from deserting the Nuremberg legacy. 'Lord Patrick is undertaking a campaign to convert these judges to the right attitude.'[87] As a result, after consulting with London, New Zealand as well as Canada rejected resignation requests of their judges, as this would harm the whole legacy of the trials.[88]

---

81 TNA, FO 371/66552, Letter Dening to Sargent, 30 April 1947.
82 TNA, FO 371/66553, Letter Garner to Addis, 22 May 1947.
83 Sellars, 'Patrick and "Crimes against Peace"', 179, and TNA, FO 371/66553, letter Dening to Sargent, 21 May 1947.
84 TNA, LCO 2/2992, Letter Jowitt to Attorney General, 8 May 1947.
85 TNA, LCO 2/2992, Letter Jowitt to A. Napier, 18 June 1947 ('persuade'), and letter Jowitt to Lord Cooper, 24 June 1947: 'No-one but Patrick could convert his colleagues.'
86 TNA, LCO 2/2992, Letter Bevin to Joseph Westwood MP, 24 July 1947.
87 Ibid.
88 FO 371/66553, Letter Garner, 11 June 1947.

Contrast with Keenan

In the meantime, the tribunal entered its busiest period for the prosecution, with various cross-examinations commencing. Comyns-Carr was responsible for two important defendants, Kido and Togo, for which he prepared for several months.[89] He employed a brisk style of questioning defendants, which prompted Aristides Lazarus, the American counsel for Field Marshal Hata, to call Comyns-Carr's strategy 'vicious'.[90] His deep contrast with Keenan's strategy of running the prosecution became apparent in the cross-examination of Kido, which Keenan took away from him.[91] As Brackman reports: 'Comyns-Carr planned to conduct the cross-examination, and it had the makings of a great match up between two sophisticated, cunning, and wily adversaries. But Joseph Keenan could not resist the spotlight and shunted Comyns-Carr aside.'[92] During the cross-examination, Keenan was ill-prepared, and Kido didn't reveal anything helpful.[93]

Thus, when the cross-examination of Kido was over, Comyns-Carr cabled back to London on 21 October 1947: 'Everything has worked out even more disastrously than I anticipated'.[94] He went on, openly criticizing Keenan: 'When you agreed that the Nuremberg system should be replaced by having one chief of counsel, I suppose you had no idea of the kind of man under whose heel I was to be placed. If I had known I would never have come.'[95] He concluded: 'Keenan has been playing merry hell with the case.' His personal remarks to Shawcross are even more revealing on the subject of Keenan's incompetency, as he saw it:

> [T]he trouble is (a) this man is a rather important and difficult case, requiring a great knowledge of detail which he can't possibly acquire in the time and would be incompetent to handle if he did, and (b) his obvious reasons are (1) he wants to prevent the British Commonwealth from figuring too prominently in the case, and (2) he wants to develop a row he has started with Webb ... over the question of the Emperor's responsibil-

---

89   Harries and Harries, *Sheathing the Sword*, p. 118.

90   Brackman, *The Other Nuremberg*, p. 305.

91   David Crowe, *War Crimes, Genocide and Justice* (New York: Palgrave MacMillan, 2014), p. 213.

92   Brackman, *The Other Nuremberg*, pp. 332-33.

93   Totani, *Tokyo Trial*, p. 38.

94   Cited after Harries and Harries, *Sheathing the Sword*, p. 154.

95   TNA, LCO 2/2992, Letter Comyns-Carr to Attorney General, 21 October 1947.

ity.... The case is thus in danger of being finally reduced to a laughing stock, if it wasn't already.[96]

Despite all complaints, there was nothing to be done against Keenan's interference, thus the long-awaited cross-examination of Tōjō Hideki on 26 December 1947 was a lost opportunity for the prosecution. Many visitors came to see the verbal battle and the accused behaved like a war hero, smiling at friends and photographers, and signing autographs for American souvenir hunters.[97] Comyns-Carr reports that Keenan decided at the very last moment that he himself would lead the cross-examination, ordered Fihelly to leave the courtroom and continued himself.[98] Keenan claimed that he had simply wanted to 'ask some questions', although he himself had given the one-counsel rule.[99] Comyns-Carr reported to London 'equally disastrous results' and complained that in general Keenan was ill-prepared and had not 'set foot in the courtroom in months'.[100] Even MacArthur, otherwise a loyal supporter of Keenan, remarked that the triumphant Tōjō cross-examination had wrought devastating effects as it confirmed for the Japanese public the view that the accused bore no war guilt at all.[101]

Patrick as Court President?

While the prosecution struggled with battles of hierarchy, it wasn't much better on the judges' bench. In late October 1947, the Australian government temporarily recalled William Webb for 'High Court duties', angering the other judges, as Webb would 'miss important parts of the case, and should be prevailed upon to resign', as Patrick criticized.[102] Patrick had revealed to Gascoigne his views that Webb's 'running away' was 'against all English laws'.[103]

---

96   Ibid., and Harries and Harries, *Sheathing the Sword*, pp. 153-54.

97   Harries and Harries, *Sheathing the Sword*, p. 160.

98   Crowe, *War Crimes, Genocide and Justice*, p. 218.

99   Harries and Harries, *Sheathing the Sword*, p. 162, quote the following statement of Webb to Keenan: 'Only one counsel for each party may cross-examine a witness.... A majority of the Court is against you, Mr Chief of Counsel. You will not have the assistance of Mr Fihelly. A majority of the Court has intimated to me that it is opposed to your application being granted, and I have announced the results.'

100   TNA, LCO 2/2992, Letter Comyns-Carr to Attorney General, 2 January 1948.

101   Harries and Harries, *Sheathing the Sword*, p. 163.

102   TNA, FO 371/63820, Letter Gascoigne to FO, 10 November 1947.

103   TNA, LCO 2/ 2992, Telegram Gascoigne to FO, 10 November 1947.

His absence, however, also nourished hopes of a proper replacement for Webb. Liaison Officer Gascoigne cabled to the FO back home that it: 'would be in the interests of a happy ending of the trial that Webb should no longer remain in charge'.[104]

From the point of view of seniority, the New Zealand judge Northcroft would have been the next in line to take the seat, but MacArthur rejected this as he thought New Zealand 'too insignificant to merit the position'[105] and proposed Patrick for the position instead.[106] When Patrick was notified of this decision on 7 November 1947, a press release was issued without his knowledge. Nevertheless, Patrick rejected the position, claiming poor health.[107] As a consequence, an angry MacArthur appointed the US judge Myron Cramer instead, not holding back on his views that he saw Patrick's refusal as a sign that Patrick 'couldn't handle the responsibility'.[108]

Although Gascoigne was understanding of Patrick's poor health, he regretted the missed opportunity, as well as the fact that they had not convened beforehand either. The presidency, Gascoigne claimed, 'would have given a much needed fillip to the United Kingdom prestige'.[109]

However, the affair revealed much deeper rifts. Patrick showed a degree of deep frustration when he told Gascoigne that 'he could hardly be expected to proceed with work of framing judgments on Nuremb[e]rg lines, only to have them quashed by Webb on his return.'[110]

General MacArthur let London know that he was 'dumbfounded' by Patrick's refusal and that he should have 'risked sudden death in court rather than turn down the appointment'.[111] MacArthur used the occasion for some blunt words on Britain's fading authority, adding that he felt Patrick's selection would have been especially welcome in Britain given 'the trials and setbacks which the United Kingdom was now undergoing all over the world'. With these comments, MacArthur had, however, crossed a thin red line. Foreign Office Legal Secretary John Killick observed that MacArthur's 'patronizing remarks... about the United Kingdom, and his rather callous attitude towards Lord Patrick ... have done nothing to improve a delicate situation'.[112]

---

104   TNA, LCO 2/ 2992, Telegram Gascoigne to FO, 9 October 1947.
105   Reported by Gascoigne in FO 371/63820, Letter Gascoigne to FO, 11November 1947.
106   Sellars, 'Patrick and "Crimes against Peace"', 181.
107   Sellars, 'Patrick and "Crimes against Peace"', 182.
108   TNA, LCO 2/2992, Telegram from Gascoigne to FO, 11 November 1947.
109   TNA, FO 371/63820 Letter Gascoigne to FO, 10 November 1947.
110   Ibid.
111   TNA, FO 371/63820, Letter Gascoigne to FO, 11 November 1947.
112   TNA, FO 371/63820, Letter Killick, 13 November 1947.

Considering the split on the bench, and at the same time the problems in the prosecutors' department after the cross-examination debacles of Keenan, Whitehall remarked sarcastically: 'It is difficult to decide which is more fantastic – the relationship between the judges or the behaviour of the chief of counsel'.[113]

Verdicts and Sentences

When Webb returned to Tokyo on 18 December 1947, he resumed his duties, 'but he never recaptured his former authority over his colleagues', as Sellars underlines.[114] The mistrust was deep, and the three Commonwealth judges Patrick, McDougall and Northcroft started drafting their own judgment, as they assumed that Webb would likely fail to produce an adequate judgment.[115] This move was prompted by earlier experience, as Northcroft explained: 'Naturally we would all like to see one judgment, but I am afraid none of us have [sic] sufficient confidence in the President to leave it to him, and from past experience we know he will not accept any advice or suggestions.'[116]

As Sellars points out, drafting a judgment was 'a high-risk strategy because these judges could not have predicted Webb's response, and their faction was initially in the minority'.[117] Only when Myron Cramer, Delfin Jaranilla, Mei Ru'ao of China and Judge Zaryanov of the Soviet Union joined them, was the faction transformed into a majority, and finally Webb agreed on 24 March 1948 to the draft being handled by that group.[118] Although these judges shared a common objective, they did not always share a common approach, which meant that some legal issues continued to excite debate, especially the discussion of conspiracy to commit crimes against peace, which dragged on for

---

113   TNA, LCO 2/2992, Law's Office Department to Lord Chancellor, 18 November 1947.

114   Sellars, 'Patrick and "Crimes against Peace"', 183.

115   This was backed up by the fact that Webb had already circulated a draft verdict in December 1946, which in the eyes of his colleagues lacked basic legal standards. Patrick ridiculed the document as a quote compilation on natural law (see Sellars, 'Patrick and "Crimes against Peace"', 174, and the letter at TNA, LCO 2/2992, Patrick to Normand, without date, presumably January 1947), and Harvey Northcroft was even more blunt when he remarked that this document 'read like a student's not very good essay on international law' (see Trotter, 'New Zealanders', 142-56)

116   Cited after Sellars, Patrick and "Crimes against Peace", 183, quoting from NANZ, AAOM 7130 ACC W4676 Box 1: Northcroft to O'Leary, 18 March 1948.

117   Sellars, 'Patrick and "Crimes against Peace"', 183.

118   Ibid., 184.

almost a year.[119] The judges were divided over the central question of responsibility for the Asia-Pacific war.[120]

Another special issue was the question of conspiracy itself, as Sellars has shown; Patrick argued that 'conspiracy was made up of two elements: naked or unexecuted conspiracy (a conspiracy to commit a crime that was not actually carried out) and executed conspiracy (a conspiracy to commit a crime that was carried out)'.[121] He reassured his fellow judges that by agreeing to executed conspiracies they would be applying rules of responsibility common to all their legal systems.[122] Bonomy states that Patrick left his mark by determining both the 'fact, and the extent, of criminal responsibility of members of the military and political leadership',[123] pointing out that the concept has a place even today in the 'fragmented debate about the nature of joint criminal enterprise liability in international criminal law'.[124]

In the final weeks, when drafting the judgment, the majority stopped consulting the remaining judges altogether. Dutch judge Röling found out in an article he read in the US newspaper *Stars and Stripes* that the majority had already sent it to the translators. He complained that the judgment had been decided 'without some members even knowing its final contents', and that in his opinion, 'this procedure is in violation of the Charter'.[125] French judge Bernard also objected on the same grounds, however, both protests were in vain.

In addition to the judgment of the majority faction, there were five separate opinions: two concurring (Webb and Jaranilla), two partially dissenting (Bernard and Röling) and one dissenting (Pal). The majority judgment did not offer any new interpretations of international law, but 'carefully duplicated the Nuremberg Judgment's pronouncements',[126] as Sellars concludes.

Judge Patrick's illness, a recurrence of his tuberculosis,[127] was aggravated by the fact that he could not wait for the handing down of the sentences. The conversation about calling him home shows the completely changed British

---

119   Ibid.
120   Ibid., 188.
121   Cited after Sellars, 'Patrick and "Crimes against Peace"', 184, quoting AWM, Webb papers, 3DRL 2481 Series 1/2/14 Patrick 'Planning' and 'conspiracy in relation to criminal trials, and specially in relation to this trial', 30 January 1948.
122   Sellars, 'Patrick and "Crimes against Peace"', 184.
123   Bonomy, 'Justice Patrick', 107.
124   Ibid.
125   Sellars, 'Patrick and "Crimes against Peace"', 187.
126   Ibid., 188.
127   Harries and Harries, *Sheathing the Sword*, p. 172.

attitude towards the Tokyo tribunal by the end of 1948. The Judge Advocate approached Jowitt and urged him to call Patrick home, stating he 'sacrificed his health by his long exile.... All of us who took part in sending Patrick on this ill-fated enterprise will, I am sure, be anxious to assist in this matter.'[128] Passage on the *Lancashire* hospital ship was organized for October 1948, and the Lord Chancellor summarized to Lord Cooper 'we owe Patrick all possible consideration in view of the onerous work he has undertaken for us'.[129]

In December 1948, the sentences were handed down, and all twenty-five Japanese leaders were found guilty.[130] Seven of the accused were condemned to death, sixteen more were given life sentences. No defendant was acquitted. The split on the bench was also reflected in the judge's votes on death sentences.[131] In view of the Cold War realities, the Allies were looking to Japan as a future ally.

Conclusion

Although Tokyo's majority judgment duplicated the legal principles set out in the Nuremberg judgment, the trial left, in Sellars' view, 'a highly ambivalent legacy on the question of aggression, shaped by the dissenting judgments as well as by the exigencies of the Cold War'.[132]

In concluding the Tokyo tribunal, Liaison Officer Gascoigne showed his disappointment and described the tribunal as a 'political failure'. Shawcross remarked that the tribunal was in his eyes a 'complete disaster', and Keenan 'hopelessly incompetent'.[133] Jowitt replied in confirming the debacle of the 'gloomy affair at Tokyo' that 'the sooner the thing is ended the better'.[134] The debate was concluded with qualms over the horrendous costs of the trial. Fortifying the Nuremberg legacy was a failure in Tokyo.

However, the criticism of dominance of a 'British bloc' within the judges' bench, pointing at the three Commonwealth judges might be overestimated. While it is true that its nature was one of cultural formations and understanding, it was more likely a deep obligation to the mission accepted which is

---

128   TNA, LCO 2/2986, Letter Judge Advocate to Jowitt, 22 September 1948, see also TNA, LCO
         2/2986, Letter Jowitt to Shinwell, 23 September 1948.
129   TNA, LCO 2/2986, Letter Jowitt to Cooper, 7 October 1948.
130   Sellars, 'Patrick and "Crimes against Peace"', 192.
131   Sellars, 'Patrick and "Crimes against Peace"', 192.
132   Sellars, *Crimes against Peace*, p. xi.
133   TNA, LCO 2/2992, Letter Shawcross to Lord Chancellor Jowitt, 23 January 1948.
134   TNA, LCO 2/2992, Letter Jowitt to Shawcross, 29 January 1948.

described in the term 'British bloc', rather than a real strategy. In the views of the three Commonwealth judges, taking a seat on the Tokyo bench had implied that one subscribed to the Charter and its charges, and challenging the Charter was neither morally nor legally justified.[135] It was thus unthinkable for these three judges to give dissenting votes, and the only exit strategy seemed to be to resign. As this was rejected, they decided to take the lead in drafting the judgment, following the model given at Nuremberg and fulfilling their task of advancing international law.

The British mission to fortify the Nuremberg judgment, however, was jeopardized by the split on the Tokyo bench. This, from British points of view, confirmed the decline of British authority not only in the Commonwealth family, but also with its American ally and in its old colonial realm in the Pacific. As Sellars states, Tokyo was more to be seen as a 'façade'; unlike at Nuremberg, where Allied unity at least in the Western bloc was intact, 'the Japanese war crimes trials showed visible divisions, rather than just giving the impression of an alliance'.[136] Although the British representatives had done their utmost to get the mission accomplished, it proved highly disappointing, and the 'gloomy affair' was thus silenced for decades.

Bibliography

Herbert Bix, *Hirohito and the Making of Modern Japan* (Hamburg: HarperCollins Publishers, 2000).

Neil Boister and Robert Cryer, *The Tokyo International Military Tribunal: A Reappraisal* (Oxford University Press, 2008).

Iain Bonomy, 'Justice Patrick (United Kingdom)' in Yuki Tanaka, Tim McCormack and Gerry Simpson (eds.), *Beyond Victor's Justice? The Tokyo War Crimes Trial Revisited* (Leiden: Nijhoff, 2011), pp. 103-8.

Arnold C. Brackman, *The Other Nuremberg: The Untold Story of the Tokyo War Crimes Trial* (New York: William Morrow and Company, Inc., 1987).

Arthur Comyns-Carr, 'The Tokyo War Crimes Trial', *Far Eastern Survey*, 18 (1949), 109-14.

David Crowe, *War Crimes, Genocide and Justice* (New York: Palgrave MacMillan, 2014).

Meirion Harries and Susie Harries, *Sheathing the Sword: The Demilitarisation of Japan* (New York: Macmillan, 1987).

---

135   Sellars, 'Patrick and "Crimes against Peace"', 174.
136   Ibid., 193.

Awaya Kentarō, Hitoshi Nagai and Masayuki Toyoda (eds.), *Tōkyō Saiban e no michi: Kokusai Kensatsukyoku, seisaku kettei kankei bunsho* (Tokyo: Gendai Shiryō Syuppan, 1999), vol. 3., pp. 160-71, and vol. 4, pp. 129-48.

Arieh Kochavi, *Prelude to Nuremberg: Allied War Crimes Policy and the Question of Punishment* (Chapel Hill: University of North Carolina Press, 1998).

John R. Pritchard, 'The Historical Experience of British War Crimes Courts in the Far East, 1946-1948', *International Relations*, 6 (1978), 311-26.

James Burnham Sedgwick, 'A People's Court: Emotion, Participant Experiences, and the Shaping of Postwar Justice at the International Military Tribunal for the Far East, 1946-1948', *Diplomacy & Statecraft*, 22 (2011, 3), 480-99.

Kirsten Sellars, *'Crimes against Peace' and International Law* (Cambridge University Press, 2013).

Kirsten Sellars, 'William Patrick and "Crimes Against Peace" at the Tokyo Tribunal, 1946-1948', *The Edinburgh Law Review*, 15 (2011, 2), 166-96.

Yuki Takatori, 'The Forgotten Judge at the Tokyo War Crimes Trial', *Massachusetts Historical Review*, 10 (2008), 115-41.

Yuma Totani, *The Tokyo War Crimes Trial: The Pursuit of Justice in the Wake of World War II* (Harvard University Press, 2008).

Ann Trotter, 'New Zealanders and the International Military Tribunal for the Far East', *New Zealand Journal of History*, 23 (1989, 2), 142-56.

CHAPTER 6

The Soviets at Tokyo: International Justice at the Dawn of the Cold War

Valentyna Polunina

In his memoirs, Anatoly Nikolaev, a Soviet clerk at the International Military Tribunal for the Far East, recalled that 'the vast majority of Americans whom I encountered... made a good impression on me: professional, outgoing and friendly, in their mentality and character they were just like Russians'.[1] Despite the common belief that the Soviet government perceived the trial in Tokyo as 'detrimental to world peace' and tried 'to undermine that which it could not control',[2] its representatives cooperated with their Western colleagues to a much greater extent than the Soviets previously assumed. Of course, they had ulterior motives.

Despite the fiasco of the Soviet performance in Nuremberg due to the lack of well-trained and experienced staff combined with Moscow's attempts to control the Soviet delegation,[3] the Soviet leadership expressed a somewhat surprising willingness to participate in the common prosecution of Japanese war criminals even though it clearly understood the leading role of the United States in the tribunal.[4] Despite their unfamiliarity with the IMTFE, the Soviets assured the Americans, who had invited them, that their 'interest was more than formal', and they wanted to know much more about the role of the USSR in the proposed trial.[5] This unexpected willingness can be explained by the

---

1   A.N. Nikolaev, *Tokio: sud narodov. Po vospominaniiam uchastnika protsessa* (Moscow: Iuridicheskaia literatura, 1990), p. 16.

2   P.R. Picigallo, *The Japanese on Trial: Allied War Crimes Operations in the East, 1945-1951* (Austin: University of Texas Press, 1979), p. 146.

3   Francine Hirsch, 'The Soviets at Nuremberg: International Law, Propaganda, and the Making of the Postwar Order', *American Historical Review*, 2 (2008), p. 701-30.

4   Despite the fact that the Soviet Union was not as heavily involved in the Pacific theatre of World War II as the other Allies, it was still very much interested in shaping postwar justice in Asia. Further reading: T. Hasegawa, *Racing the Enemy: Stalin, Truman, and the Surrender of Japan* (Harvard: Belknap Press, 2005); B.N. Slavinskii, *The Japanese-Soviet Neutrality Pact: A Diplomatic History, 1941-1945* (London and New York: Routledge, 2004); P. Duara, 'The New Imperialism and the Post-Colonial Developmental State: Manchukuo in Comparative Perspective', in *Japan Focus* <http://www.japanfocus.org/-Prasenjit-Duara/1715>.

5   Picigallo, *The Japanese on Trial*, p. 145.

Soviet belief that the ideological and geopolitical benefits of participation in an international war crimes tribunal exceeded the possible risks.

In Europe, the post-war trials of Nazi war criminals and their collaborators had been aimed primarily at obtaining justice for the (mainly Soviet) victims and delivering retribution for the crimes.[6] The Japanese war crimes trials, on the other hand, were critical for Soviet authorities as a political platform at the start of the Cold War because of the relatively minor participation of the Soviet troops in the war against Japan. The Soviet Union had not entered the Pacific War until 9 August 1945, when it invaded Manchuria. During and after the so-called Soviet-Japanese War of 1945, the Red Army imprisoned about 600,000 Japanese military personnel from the Kwantung Army.[7] In Tokyo, the most important propaganda aims of the Soviets were to persuade the international community that the Soviet Union was the only power interested in delivering justice to the victims of Japanese occupation, preventing the spread of 'American imperialism' and re-militarization of Japan, as well as protecting its allies from attacks and new colonization.[8]

In general, the Soviets had an ambivalent attitude towards the Tokyo trial. On the one hand, there was an overall approval of its outcome. It was broadly recognized in the Soviet Union that the conviction of the Japanese war criminals played an important historical role. Together with the International Military Tribunal in Nuremberg (IMT), the Tokyo trial created an important precedent in international law for bringing to justice war criminals, regardless of their rank or official position.

In an article written several months after the tribunal had finished its work, Aleksandr Vasilyev, the Soviet prosecutor at the IMTFE, summarized the major positive results of the trial. He argued that the verdict had been 'received by the progressive world community with great appreciation as an act of real historical and political significance that serves to protect peace and democracy.'[9] The author stressed that 'the indisputable upside of the verdict is the uncondi-

---

6   See Tanja Penter, 'Collaboration on Trial: New Source Material on Soviet Postwar Trials against Collaborators', *Slavic Review*, 64, 4 (Winter 2005), pp. 782-90; Penter, '"Das Urteil des Volkes." Der Kriegsverbrecherprozess von Krasnodar 1943', *Osteuropa*, 60 (2010), 117-32.

7   A. D. Coox, *Nomonhan; Japan Against Russia, 1939* (Stanford University Press, 1985), p. 1176.

8   M.Y. Raginsky, S.Y. Rosenblit and L.N. Smirnov, *Bakteriologicheskaia voina – prestupnoe orudie imperialisticheskoi agressii. Khabarovskii protsess iaponskikh voennykh prestupnikov* (Moscow: Izdatel'stvo Akademii nauk SSSR, 1950), p. 11. All Russian sources are translated by the author.

9   A.N. Vasilyev, 'O skorom sude i nakazanii vinovnikov agressii (K itogam Tokiyskogo protsessa)', *Sovetskoye gosudarstvo i pravo*, 3 (1949), p. 40.

tional recognition of Japan's aggression against the Soviet Union',[10] keeping silent about the fact that the Soviet prosecution team had only partially fulfilled the goals set in Moscow. Nevertheless, Vasilyev praised the Soviet contribution to the trial's outcome: the fact that 'the tribunal ultimately found the right solution to the main issues of the charges shows how great was ... the power of truth on the side of humanity, led by the Soviet Union in the struggle against aggression for peace and democracy'.[11]

On the other hand, the setting of the trial, its conduct and some results of the IMTFE were heavily criticized by the Soviets. Whereas the main points of criticism from the Dutch, French and Indian judges referred to 'victor's justice' or the newly created charges of crimes against peace and conspiracy or tendentious interpretation of history, the Soviet criticism was focused on blaming the Western Allies, especially the USA, for using the tribunal to pursue their own political agenda.

The Soviet Delegation at the IMTFE

According to archival documents, the Soviets had started preparing for the trial already in January 1946 on Stalin's instructions. On 25 January 1946, the Deputy People's Commissar for Foreign Affairs Vladimir Dekanozov sent a letter to the Chief of the Main Directorate of Counter-Intelligence 'SMERSH'[12] Vladimir Abakumov mentioning the upcoming participation of the Soviet delegation at the IMTFE and a list of fifty-seven potential defendants. Furthermore, Dekanozov asked his colleague to start selecting and summarizing available 'documents and other factual material evidence that could be used by our prosecutor at the trial as prosecution materials. I ask you to urgently send all these materials to the People's Commissariat of the USSR.'[13] On the same day Dekanozov sent identical letters to the heads of military intelligence, state security and the ministry of the interior.[14]

---

10   Ibid.

11   Ibid., p. 49.

12   'SMERSH' (Death to Spies) – a military counter-intelligence agency that was officially created on 19 April 1943 and was subordinate directly to Stalin. The organization existed until 4 May 1946 when its duties were transferred back to the NKGB.

13   AVP RF, F. 0146, Op. 30, F. 282, D. 28, p. 1. Cited from A.E. Kirichenko, Za kulisami tribunala, <http://histrf.ru/uploads/media/default/0001/26/a2ccdec73923b964017f4b0ce1c6e4232 751e7a3.pdf, p. 218>. Achival materials translated by the author.

14   Ibid.

Surprisingly enough, the Soviet Union was relatively cooperative during the negotiations leading up to the establishment of the trial and afterwards throughout the proceedings. When the United States government distributed a policy document concerning the punishment of war criminals in the Far East in mid-October 1945, the only thing the Soviets objected to was the granting of equal rights to judges and prosecutors. After intense US-Soviet negotiations, the government of the USSR decided to send a delegation to Tokyo. Even if this decision was made at the last moment, it does not necessarily mean that the Soviet government had a completely different view of the Tokyo tribunal or was against the leading role of MacArthur at that time. The USSR was still eager to cooperate as long as 'the United States could promise equal rights of representation'.[15]

The Soviet delegation was willing to go to any lengths to secure a guilty verdict, including cooperating with their ideological enemies and making compromises. According to the Soviet position, war criminals to be tried in Nuremberg and Tokyo were all guilty and the tribunals were created merely to 'establish the magnitude of each prisoner's culpability ... and not wrestle with the issue of innocence or guilt since a summary determination by the Allied triumvirate had already decided that the latter was the case'.[16] The Soviets were well aware that their Western allies were capable of organizing their own war crimes tribunal without Moscow's help but 'such excommunication was to be avoided at any cost, which explained why the Soviet members of the cast repeatedly opted for accommodation whenever the United States and its friends refused to budge'.[17] Participation in an event of such importance along with other members of the winner's camp had a symbolic meaning in itself: the Soviet Union emerged as a new superpower that had a say in the determination of the post-war order not only in Europe but also in Asia. Moreover, proving the guilt of the accused would support Soviet propaganda claims of being the only power genuinely interested in delivering justice to victims of Japanese occupation, frustrating 'American imperialism', and preventing the re-militarization of Japan.[18]

---

15   Not only the Soviets insisted on provision of equal rights to their representatives in Tokyo. This aspect was also important to the French government which started negotiations with the Americans as well. Yuma Totani, *The Tokyo War Crimes Trial: The Pursuit of Justice in the Wake of World War II* (Harvard University Press, 2008), p. 27.

16   George Ginsburgs, *Moscow's Road to Nuremberg: The Soviet Background to the Trial* (The Hague, Boston, London: Martinus Nijhoff Publishers, 1996), p. 117.

17   Ibid., pp. 107-8.

18   Raginsky, Rosenblit and Smirnov, *Bakteriologicheskaia voina – prestupnoe orudie imperialisticheskoi agressii*, p. 11.

The Soviet delegation in Tokyo consisted of about seventy people: military and civilian judges, prosecutors, investigators, experts, interpreters, administrative and technical staff. Major-General of Justice Ivan Zaryanov, member of the Military Collegium of the Supreme Court of the USSR, was appointed as the Soviet judge to the International Military Tribunal for the Far East. Previously, he had been the head of the Military Law Academy of the Red Army.

The Soviet delegation at the IMTFE was headed by Professor Sergey Golunsky, a member of the Board of the Ministry of Foreign Affairs of the USSR, Chief of the Department of Legal Affairs of the Ministry, and a member of the Academy of Sciences of the USSR. He was a well-educated lawyer and diplomat, author of several books on criminal procedure and legal theory who had extensive work experience not only in the Ministry of Foreign Affairs but also in the Prosecutor's Office and different judicial bodies. Golunsky participated in the Yalta and Potsdam conferences, where he worked as Stalin's consultant and interpreter: Golunsky was fluent in English, French and German. At the IMTFE, he was appointed as the Soviet Associate Prosecutor.

In his memoirs, Anatoly Nikolaev describes Golunsky as follows:

> Having good command of foreign languages and a lot of experience at international conferences, he quickly came into contact with foreign colleagues upon his arrival in Tokyo and enjoyed their great respect. Particularly obvious was the sympathy for him from the Chief Prosecutor Keenan.[19]

A possible explanation for such behaviour might be Keenan's desire to 'pus[h] ... aside the Commonwealth prosecutors or anyone else who might steal the limelight from him'.[20] In this situation, looking for allies in the Soviet camp did not seem like such a bad idea. Moreover, at least at the very beginning of the tribunal's work, the relations of the Soviet prosecutor were friendly, not only with Keenan, but also with other fellow prosecutors. Golunsky's wish to maintain these fruitful relations, which is evident from his correspondence with Moscow, was without doubt an important factor in the cooperative approach of the Soviet delegation to the work of the IMTFE.[21] However, Sergey Golunsky did not stay in Tokyo until the end of the trial: after the Soviet part of the prosecution was over in October 1946, he was recalled to Moscow and replaced by the former prosecutor of the city of Moscow, Aleksandr Vasilyev.

---

19   Nikolaev, *Tokio: sud narodov*, pp. 52-53.
20   Totani, *The Tokyo War Crimes Trial*, p. 36.
21   GARF, Delo 155, Opis 2, Fond 7867, p. 836.

Previous experience of participation in war crimes trials was a crucial factor for the Soviet leaders in making an important decision on the composition of the delegation. It is possible that they had learned a lesson from the first negative experience at the Nuremberg trials where the lack of professionalism of the Soviet delegation members was one of the reasons why the IMT 'turned into an embarrassment for the USSR'.[22] Therefore, some of the members of the Soviet delegation already had valuable experience of participation in international war crimes trials. Lev Smirnov, Deputy Prosecutor in Tokyo, previously worked as an assistant to the Chief Prosecutor from the USSR at the Nuremberg trial Roman Rudenko. Solomon Rosenblit was also a member of an investigation team under the Chief Prosecutor from the USSR at the IMT in Nuremberg. Since 1941, he had held senior positions at the Main Military Prosecutor's Office of the USSR and had also been a member of an investigation team under the Chief Prosecutor from the USSR at the Nuremberg IMT.

Nevertheless, archival documents show that the Soviet leadership still tried to control every aspect of their delegation's work at international tribunals. This had been the case at the Nuremberg trial proceedings and was one of the reasons for the fiasco of Soviet propaganda there.[23] The USSR delegation at the IMTFE was subordinate to a governmental commission consisting of people from Stalin's closest circle: the commission's chairman, Andrey Vyshinsky, at that time the Deputy Foreign Minister of the USSR; the Prosecutor General of the Soviet Union, Konstantin Gorshenin; and the Minister of Justice, Nikolay Rychkov.[24] After studying archival materials such as the correspondence between the delegation in Tokyo and the governmental commission in Moscow, it seems that the control from the centre was less strict in comparison to the experience of the Soviet lawyers in Nuremberg. This slight policy change was most probably due to the lesser political importance of the IMTFE for the USSR, the negative experience at the IMT, and the logistical distance between Moscow and Tokyo.

Considering the attempts to control the activities of the Soviet delegation from Moscow, it is difficult to know to what extent the personal experiences and beliefs of Soviet lawyers influenced their work. As previously stated, the high professional level and the previous experience of participation in war crimes tribunals was certainly an important factor for Moscow in taking a decision about the composition of the delegation. At the same time, it seems reasonable to believe that individual members were seen rather as transmitters

---

22   Hirsch, *The Soviets at Nuremberg*, p. 703.

23   Hirsch, *The Soviets at Nuremberg*, p. 701-30.

24   GARF, Delo 155, Opis 2, Fond 7867, pp. 727, 827.

of the Soviet policy and not as independent actors. One should also not forget to mention, for example, the 'personal' opposition of Judge Zaryanov to the death penalty. In Tokyo, Ivan Zaryanov openly opposed all death sentences in general, as capital punishment was abolished in the Soviet Union at the time.[25] It is difficult to say what exactly his personal opinion was, but the sincerity of his convictions is doubtful, taking into account Zaryanov's participation in purge trials during his work in the Military Collegium of the Supreme Court of the USSR in the 1930s, where he handed down death sentences on a mass scale. During the period of Khrushchev's Thaw and the dismantling of Stalin's personality cult, the work of Ivan Zaryanov was 'acknowledged' by stripping him of his rank of Major General of Justice and expelling him from the Communist Party for 'gross violations of socialist legality while working in the Military Collegium of the Supreme Court'.[26]

As Russian historian Vasiliy Molodyakov argues, Zaryanov (and all other members of the Soviet delegation) had to follow strict instructions from Stalin. They were not to vote for death sentences, not to express any special opinion or public disagreement with the final decision of the tribunal, and to include as much evidence as possible in the verdict about Japan's aggressive intentions towards the USSR.[27] The last point was necessary because the Soviet Union had to justify the entry into the war at the very last stage and its violation of the Neutrality Pact.

One problem for the whole Soviet delegation was the fact that Judge Zaryanov did not speak any foreign languages and relied on interpreters. During the trial hearings it was often necessary to quickly submit a personal opinion to Chairman Webb. In this case, Zaryanov had to call for a soldier who would bring his note to the Soviet interpreters sitting in a special box. It would be translated, brought back to Zaryanov and finally after this cumbersome detour the Soviet judge was able to pass his note to Webb. This was very time-consuming and he admitted bitterly: '[I]t does not matter how well and convincingly I speak, it still does not reach them. In fact, I am talking to the interpreter but I have no idea how he translates my speech. Maybe I want to focus on one word, and he emphasizes a completely different one. That is my misfortune.'[28]

---

25   N. Boister and R. Cryer, *The Tokyo International Military Tribunal: A Reappraisal* (Oxford University Press, 2008), p. 258. K. Sellars, 'William Patrick and "Crimes against Peace" at the Tokyo Tribunal, 1946-1948', *The Edinburgh Law Review*, 15 (2011), p. 192.

26   'Odin den' Voyennoy kollegii Verkhovnogo suda SSSR', Sakharov Center <http://www. sakharov-center.ru/blogs/main/all/odin-den-voennoy-kollegii-verhovnogo-suda-sssr/>.

27   V. Molodyakov, *Rossiia I Iaponiia: mech' na vesakh* (Moscow: 2005), excerpts from the book can be found in the author's blog: <http://molodiakov.livejournal.com/17796.html>.

28   Nikolaev, *Tokio: sud narodov*, p. 46.

It should be noted that at the beginning the Russian interpreting was very weak, inconsistent and sometimes simply incomprehensible. Translation and editing of the court's transcripts in Russian caused great difficulties as well and resulted in some curious errors: for example, the word 'ambassador' (posol) was translated as 'donkey' (osel), etc.[29] Nonetheless, after a few months of work at the tribunal, Soviet translators made a lot of progress in interpretation and translation.

The peculiarity of the Soviet legal practice of the time which gave state prosecutors a leading role in a trial caused difficulties for the Soviet leaders. Appointing Sergey Golunsky as the head of the delegation, they hoped that his previous experience and mastery of foreign languages would help him in this responsible position to establish contacts with other delegations and promote the interests of the USSR at the tribunal. Nevertheless, the Soviets did not count on the fact that *judges* were expected to be at the head of the delegations and therefore were quite surprised on arrival in Tokyo.[30]

Anatoly Nikolaev recalls:

> When we were coming down from the frigate, the prosecutor from the Soviet Union, who was also the head of the delegation S.A. Golunsky, was ahead of our delegation followed by the Judge I.M. Zaryanov. It should be noted that Golunsky spoke English fluently and, therefore, immediately entered into conversation with foreign representatives of the Tribunal. Zaryanov, conversing with the help of an interpreter, of course, just could not take such an active role in the conversation, however, as soon as the representatives of the International Military Tribunal found out who from the visitors was a judge, and who the prosecutor, Zaryanov immediately became the centre of attention. A comfortable American car and a luxury room in 'The Imperial', the best hotel in Tokyo, were promptly provided at his disposal, while Golunsky did not enjoy any special care and lived in an ordinary American hotel 'Daiichi', using a car from the garage of our embassy.[31]

At this point it is important to mention that the Soviet delegation, for instance the judge and the prosecutor, saw themselves rather as a team with a common goal and not as independent people from different institutions.

---

29   Ibid.
30   Ibid., pp. 48-49.
31   Ibid.

The composition of the delegation was constantly changing during the trial: some members left for various reasons, while others came to take their place. Besides Ivan Zaryanov, Sergei Golunsky and Aleksandr Vasilyev, the delegation of the USSR included numerous assistants of the Soviet prosecutors and investigators who later would become the authors of the first published works on the Tokyo trial in the Soviet Union.

The Soviet prosecution team was in charge of Counts 35 and 36 of the indictment, namely waging 'a war of aggression and a war in violation of international law, treaties, agreements and assurances'[32] against the USSR and the Mongolian People's Republic during the summer of 1938 and 1939. This respectively refers to two Soviet-Japanese border clashes at Lake Khasan and Khalkin-gol (also known as Nomonhan Incident) which resulted in a defeat of the Japanese and the signing of the Soviet-Japanese Neutrality Pact in April 1941.

At the same time, the Soviet leadership hoped to obtain in court a condemnation of Japanese actions committed not only during the 1938 and 1939 incidents but also throughout all the conflicts between the USSR and Japan that happened over the period of time covered by the indictment (1 January 1928-2 September 1945). Prosecutor Golunsky, addressing the court on 8 October 1946, emphasized the long history of 'Japanese aggression against the Soviet Union' going back to the Russo-Japanese war (1904-5) when 'a young Japanese imperialist predator grew teeth and attacked Russia'.[33]

Another important goal of the Soviet prosecutors was to prove that starting an offensive in Manchuria against the Japanese forces did not constitute a violation of the Neutrality Pact between the two powers. In this regard, Sergey Golunsky based his assertion on three claims. First of all, that Japan used the Neutrality Pact in order to disguise its military preparations against the Soviet Union. Secondly, that the USSR declared a war on 'Japanese aggressors' being faithful to its duties as an ally of the USA and the United Kingdom for the sake of 'accelerating the end of the war, from which the humanity had been bleeding for six years'.[34] The last-mentioned reason was the wish to 'spare the Japanese people from dangers and destruction that had been witnessed by Germany after its refusal of the unconditional surrender'.[35]

---

32   Indictment from the International Military Tribunal for the Far East, World War II File, Bontecou Papers, Harry S. Truman Presidential Museum & Library, available online: <http://bit.ly/1GJTtlW>.

33   'Na protsesse glavnykh yaponskikh voyennykh prestupnikov', *Pravda* (11 October 1946), p. 4.

34   Ibid.

35   Ibid.

The goal of the Soviet leadership in Moscow was also to persuade the court and, more importantly, world public opinion that 'the Soviet Union had borne the brunt of the aggressors and played a decisive role in defeating them, in saving mankind from the fascist barbarism;[36] as Prosecutor Vasilyev articulated in his speech on the Japanese aggression against the USSR delivered on 17-18 February 1948.

Archival documents make it clear that Soviet leaders were aware of the challenges their delegation would face in Tokyo due to the changing political situation, especially the sharp deterioration in relations with the United States and the United Kingdom.[37] During the trial the hostile atmosphere became even more pronounced. Aleksandr Vasilyev complained in a memo from July 1947 that the 'famous speech of Truman and the declaration of active struggle against the spread of communism found their reflection in the work of the tribunal very quickly. American defence lawyers made it the cornerstone of their opening speech during the Russian phase of the prosecution, trying to prove that Japan was forced in the past to do something that the United States has to do today.'[38]

Moreover, Soviet lawyers in Tokyo identified other problems that could endanger the mission to secure the guilty verdict. Besides the atmosphere of the Cold War, Soviet prosecutors pointed to the fact that many important documents had been destroyed before Japan's capitulation; 'the remaining documents are in Japanese archives under the control of SCAP and submitting them to the trial depends entirely on its consideration.'[39] Furthermore, being forced to work with ten delegations and not just three as in Nuremberg was seen as an additional obstacle that could significantly complicate following the official line at the tribunal. Members of the Soviet delegation in their letters to Moscow mentioned at times uneasy relations with their colleagues:

> Some judges (Röling, Pal) took from the very beginning a position of justification and defence of the Japanese aggression. A number of others (mainly the French judge Bernard, partly the American judge Kramer and Canadian judge McDougal) at first occupied a wavering intermediate position but in recent years have come closer to the right-wing group due to changes in the international political situation and the political

---

36   *Pravda*, 17 February 1950, p. 4.

37   GARF, Delo 155, Opis 2, Fond R7867, 'Perepiska s inostrannymi delegatsiyami obvineniya v MVT. Tom 2', p. 675.

38   Ibid., p. 678.

39   Ibid.

situation in the respective countries. Only the Chinese judge Mei occu-
pies a relatively stable democratic position. The president of the tribunal,
Webb, though he sometimes emphasizes his friendly attitude to the Soviet
Union, almost always joins the majority and in the best case just tries to
reconcile the most acute divergences between the opposing camps.[40]

Despite the incipient Cold War atmosphere and their inability to control the
course of the tribunal, the Soviet lawyers often put aside ideological differences and preferred cooperation over rivalry.

As we will learn later, not only did the Soviet team fail to reach positive
results on the smaller border conflicts in the period of 1928 to 1945, but it was
dragged by the defence into a very unpleasant argument about breaching the
Neutrality Pact by declaring war on Japan and launching the Manchurian
Offensive. These and some other failures, which will be discussed in greater
detail, caused the wave of criticism of the Tokyo trial in the Soviet Union that
started to emerge during its latest phases of the tribunal and reached its peak
after the trial was over.

Soviet Criticism of the Tokyo Trial

Immediately after the verdict had been handed down in Tokyo, Soviet legal
scholars and practitioners started to produce their assessments of what happened just some months ago at the IMTFE. It should be noted that all these
early commentaries reflected the official attitude to the Tokyo trial in the
Soviet Union and thus can be used as an indicator of Moscow's position. The
majority of articles and books on the trial were published by former members
of the Soviet delegation in Tokyo – prosecutors, clerks, investigators. But two
prosecutors involved in the Tokyo tribunal were particularly productive –
Solomon Rosenblit and Marc Raginsky.[41]

Before the Soviet criticism of the Tokyo trial is addressed, it is important to
highlight the fact that the Soviets never questioned the findings and the outcome of the trial. Ultimately, they themselves were actively contributing to this
outcome and were even willing to cooperate with their ideological enemies

---

40   Ibid., pp. 675-76.

41   Marc Raginsky came to Tokyo directly from Nuremberg where he worked as an assistant
      of the Soviet Chief Prosecutor in order to 'compile the BW information'. P. Williams and
      D. Wallace, *Unit 731: Japan's Secret Biological Warfare in World War II* (New York: Free Press,
      1989), p. 198. Solomon Rosenblit was member of the Soviet prosecutor's team in Tokyo.

just to avoid any acquittals.[42] Finding any of the defendants not guilty would have done more harm to the whole Soviet narrative about the war in Asia than compromises with the Americans in the courtroom and beyond. Recognizing Japan as an aggressor was crucial for the justification of the Soviet entry into the Pacific War.

Just like their colleague Aleksandr Vasilyev, Rosenblit and Raginsky emphasized the importance of the tribunal that 'collected a huge amount of evidence, revealed the secret sources of the criminal foreign policy of Japan, and Japan's role as an ally of Hitler's Germany in a general conspiracy against peace and humanity; exposed the atrocities of the leaders of the ruling clique of imperialist Japan who unleashed the Second World War [...] This, of course, is the positive role of the trial.'[43] Most importantly, the trial 'condemned aggression as an international crime' and found that 'imperialist Japan was closely associated with Nazi Germany, with which it had sought to conquer and enslave entire nations'.[44]

In the circumstances of the incipient Cold War they naturally paid special attention to the failures of the IMTFE, in particular to those connected to the American dominance in Tokyo.[45] First of all, the whole setting of the trial was unjust and undemocratic since the judges were not able to elect their court president as in Nuremberg, but had to agree with the decision of General Douglas MacArthur to appoint Australian William Webb. Moreover, the participating countries had to agree to having only one chief prosecutor – American Joseph Keenan, again, not elected by everyone but nominated by US president Harry Truman. Soviet authors also expressed their dissatisfaction with the fact that the Charter was not jointly elaborated but was imposed on the participants by American legal scholars. For them, the fact that the Charter was based on the 'Anglo-American legal system'[46] allowed defence lawyers to protract the trial.[47] One of the major points of criticism from the Soviet side was the issue

42   The Soviet judge, Ivan Zaryanov, actively concurred with the majority judgment.

43   M.Y. Raginsky and S.Y. Rosenblit, 'Protsess glavnykh yaponskikh voyennykh prestupnikov', *Sovetskoye gosudarstvo i parvo*, 7 (1948), p. 66.

44   M.Y. Raginsky and S.Y. Rosenblit, *Mezhdunarodniy prozess glavnih yaponskih voennih prestupnikov* (Moscow-Leningrad: Izdatelstvo akademii nauk SSSR, 1950), p. 9.

45   For more on the Soviet criticism of the Tokyo trial, see Valentyna Polunina 'The Khabarovsk Trial: The Soviet Riposte to the Tokyo Tribunal' in Sellars (ed.), *Trials for International Crimes in Asia* (Cambridge University Press, 2015), pp. 121-45.

46   Raginsky and Rosenblit, *Mezhdunarodniy protsess*, p. 79.

47   Ibid., p. 78.

of selective justice: from their point of view, an important group of perpetrators managed to escape justice – *zaibatsu*, Japanese leading industrial tycoons.[48]

At this point, another omission should be noted that surprisingly enough did not evoke Soviet criticism during the trial – the atomic bombing of Japanese cities Hiroshima and Nagasaki in August 1945 by American forces. The official reaction in the Soviet Union was remarkably reserved. The biggest Soviet daily newspapers *Pravda* and *Izvestiya* published a summary of Truman's statement that an atomic bomb was dropped on Hiroshima with an aim to destroy Japan's capacity to continue fighting.[49] Even though brief overviews of the Pacific theatre of war were published in the Soviet media on a regular basis after the USSR declared war on Japan on 9 August 1945, they did not mention the bombing of Hiroshima and Nagasaki.

Even though this topic became a popular example of 'aggressive plans' of 'American imperialists'[50] in the Soviet propaganda of the Cold War period, Soviet prosecutors did not raise this issue at the Tokyo IMT. One possible reason for this was that they did not want to play into hands of the defence lawyers. In fact, the defence had compared the sensitive issue of atomic bombings with the attack on Pearl Harbor, suggesting that there was no difference between the two. By doing so, Major Ben Bruce Blakeney, American member of the defence counsel, tried to prove that killing in war could not be considered murder:

> If the killing of Admiral Kidd by the bombing of Pearl Harbor is murder, we know the name of the very man whose hands loosed the atomic bomb on Hiroshima, we know the chief of staff who planned the act, we know the chief of the responsible state. Is murder on their consciences? We may well doubt it. We may well doubt it, and not because the event of armed conflict has declared their cause just and their enemies unjust, but because the act is not murder.[51]

---

48   Ibid., p. 67.
49   *Pravda*, 8 August 1945, p. 4.
50   Raginsky, Rosenblit and Smirnov, *Bakteriologicheskaia voina*, p. 17.
51   International Military Tribunal for the Far East. Transcript of proceedings (14.05.1946), Legal Tools Project, p. 212. Available online: <https://www.legal-tools.org/uploads/tx_ltpdb/TR01-006-a_04.pdf> (last accessed on 9.09.2016). The strategy of the defence can be summarized in the following main arguments. First of all, defence attorneys claimed that a trial composed of victorious nations was biased and thus not able to organize a fair and just trial. Moreover, they denied the criminality of aggressive wars, criminal responsibility of individuals for initiating wars and for killing in war except those that may be considered a violation of the laws and customs of war. Furthermore, they insisted that the

Furthermore, he used the topic of atomic bombing in his argument against possible violation of the Hague Convention of 1907 by his clients:

> If we could concede that officials of Japan were violating Hague Convention IV as they are charged with violating it, in planning certain measures violative of its provisions, we should find ourselves in the same dilemma when we find that the high officials of the United States were planning the use of this [atomic – author's addition] weapon from 1941...[52]

Only after the trial did the Soviets change their official position with regard to the bombing of Hiroshima and Nagasaki due to the beginning of the nuclear arms race between the two superpowers in 1949, the year when the first Soviet atomic bomb was successfully tested. The same people who did not say a word about the Japanese nuclear tragedy at Tokyo, started fiercely criticizing the USA for causing the tragedy. So, former members of the Soviet prosecution team at the IMTFE Solomon Rosenblit, Marc Raginsky and Lev Smirnov, published in 1950 a common volume in which they accused the Americans of deliberate 'brutal mass extermination' of Japanese civilians.[53]

But most strongly Raginsky and Rosenblit criticized those who challenged the Soviet version of the war in Asia and had doubts about the Japanese aggression against the Soviet Union. They attacked the Japanese defence attorneys, who, they said, belonged to the same 'ruling circles of imperialist Japan' as the defendants.[54] Anatoly Nikolaev, a member of the Soviet delegation's Secretariat at Tokyo mentioned in his memoirs, published in the heat of *perestroika*, that the Japanese counsel 'fully shared the ideas of the major Japanese war criminals and thus vigorously defended' their clients' outlook and beliefs.[55] Correspondence between the governmental commission and Prosecutor

---

defendants could not be charged with war crimes when no war had been officially declared. Finally, the defence rejected charges related to Mongolia, the Philippines and India as the lawyers had doubts about their sovereignty. International Military Tribunal for the Far East. Transcript of proceedings (13-15.05.1946), Legal Tools Project, pp. 118-317. Available online: <https://www.legal-tools.org/uploads/tx_ltpdb/TR01-005-a_05.pdf>, <https://www.legal-tools.org/uploads/tx_ltpdb/TR01-006-a_04.pdf>, <https://www.legal-tools.org/uploads/tx_ltpdb/TR01-007-a_04.pdf> (last accessed on 18.09.2016).

52   International Military Tribunal for the Far East. Transcript of proceedings (03.04.1947), Legal Tools Project, pp. 17658-17659. Available online: <https://www.legal-tools.org/uploads/tx_ltpdb/TR09-171-a_04.pdf> (last accessed on 9.09.2016).

53   Raginsky, Rosenblit and Smirnov, *Bakteriologicheskaia voina*, p. 18.

54   Ibid.

55   A.N. Nikolaev, *Tokio: sud narodov*, p. 61.

Vasilyev shows that the prosecution team went even further, internally calling most of the defence witnesses for the section of Japan's aggression against the USSR 'accomplices of the defendants'.[56]

Worst of all, the defendants received help not only from their defence counsel, but also from 'many high officials from the USA and England who ... did not shun dirty slanders against the USSR and other nations'.[57] It is true that the former American general, George C. Marshall, provided an affidavit that was used by a defence lawyer in court which substantially damaged the Soviet position. In the affidavit, Marshall argued that the Soviet Union violated the Neutrality Pact and Japan preferred not to provoke conflict with the Soviet Union.[58]

The Soviet delegation was well aware of these tactics of the defence, built on 'the counter-accusations of democratic countries in aggression against Japan'.[59] The governmental commission in Moscow therefore recommended not engaging in any debates with the defence on this issue in order not to be forced to explain why the Soviet Union was not an aggressor.[60] In order to support the claim that it was the USSR who was a victim of aggression and not Japan, it was important to find among captured Japanese servicemen those who would corroborate this argument.

In early 1946, the Soviet government instructed the Ministry of the Interior to start searching for prospective witnesses in POW camps. In April 1946, it put forward a preliminary list of seventy-seven possible witnesses, and submitted various affidavits. Initially, they only produced three witnesses in court: Colonel Sejima Ryūzō, a staff officer in the Kwantung Army; Lieutenant-General Kusaba Tatsumi, Commander of the 4th Army of the Kwantung Army (who committed suicide shortly after his arrival in Tokyo); and Major-General Matsumura Tomokatsu, Deputy Chief of Staff of the Kwantung Army. They did not produce the other seventy-four witnesses – despite the defence's insistence that they appear so that they could be cross-examined over the contents of their affidavits[61] – presumably because it was felt that the Japanese witnesses could not be trusted not to make surprise statements in court if transported back home.[62]

---

56   GARF, D 155, Op 2, R 7867, p. 396.

57   M.Y. Raginsky, *Militaristy na skam'e podsudimih: po materialam Tokiyskogo I Habarovskogo protseddov* (Moscow: Yuridicheskaya literatura, 1985), p. 45.

58   K. Sellars, *'Crimes against Peace' and International Law* (Cambridge University Press, 2013), pp. 229-30.

59   GARF, D 155, Op 2, R 7867, p. 401.

60   Ibid.

61   Sellars, *Crimes against Peace*, pp. 228-29.

62   Kuznetsov, *Problema voennoplennih*, p. 127.

Archival documents show that at least two of the witnesses – Sejima Ryudzo and Matsumura Tomokatsu – were carefully prepared for the trial. They were isolated from other POWs in July 1946 and enjoyed better living conditions than other inmates.[63] There is evidence that interrogators put pressure on future witnesses who were afraid to be handed over to the Americans and subsequently prosecuted. After assurances from the Ministry of Interior that they would not be handed over, they 'calmed down'.[64]

However, their preparation was futile: Matsumura's performance in the courtroom was so counterproductive to the strategy of the prosecutors (in his testimony, he was not certain enough about the decision of the Japanese to attack the USSR) that the Soviets sentenced him to a long spell in a labour camp.[65] Sejima Ryūzō suffered the same fate; in July 1949, he was sentenced to twenty-five years in prison by a military tribunal for espionage and counter-revolutionary activities.[66] It is particularly interesting that the tribunal considered counter-revolutionary his 'development of war plans against the Soviet Union, Britain and America' as a representative of the General Staff of Japan.[67] Sejima Ryudzo and Matsumura Tojekazu returned to Japan only in 1956 after the establishment of diplomatic relations between the USSR and Japan.

In his letter to the governmental commission from 25 June 1947, Prosecutor Vasilyev pointed out that the problem of absent witnesses whose affidavits were presented by the Soviet prosecution was 'the most challenging' one.[68] He noted that:

> if the testimony of these witnesses was not submitted at all, it certainly would be a significant disadvantage to our evidence, especially for the section on planning a war of aggression, but it would not have been required to remove the charges. The refusal from these testimonies at present, in order not to present witnesses for cross-examination will entail not only the aforementioned consequences, but it will be understood by the majority of the tribunal in a way that will make the prospects for our continued participation in the trial very unfavourable.[69]

---

63   Ibid., p. 128.
64   Ibid., p. 126.
65   S.I. Kuznetsov, *Problema voennoplennykh v rossiisko-iaponskikh otnosheniiakh posle Vtoroi mirovoi voiny* (Irkutskii universitet, 1994), pp. 127-28, 130.
66   Kuznetsov, *Problema voennoplennih*, p. 129.
67   Ibid.
68   GARF, D 155, Op 2, R 7867, p. 759.
69   Ibid., pp. 759-60.

He proposed bringing three or four Japanese witnesses to Tokyo and offering them freedom in exchange for 'correct' testimonies (in the case they were prisoners of war and had not been accused of committing crimes themselves).[70] His suggestion was then taken into account.

In 1947, after the beginning of the defence phase, the Soviet prosecution team started looking for new witnesses from among the Japanese POWs to withstand the strategy of the defence lawyers. In autumn 1947, three people were brought to Tokyo: Lieutenant-General Murakami Keisaku, former commander of the Third Army in Manchuria; Takeba Ryūzō, a clerk in the Government of Manchukuo; and Matsura Kusuo, head of a department in the Staff of the Kwantung Army. After giving their testimony, all of them were sent back to the USSR and put back in POW camps despite the attempts of the SCAP to release them during their stay in Tokyo. But the Soviets feared that in this case the Japanese witnesses would refuse to testify, so they promised to repatriate them in the near future.[71] Nevertheless, Murakami, Takeba, and Matsura shared the fate of the first group of Japanese witnesses: General Murakami died in the prison, Takeba was handed over to the government of Mongolia, and Matsura returned to Japan only in 1950 with one of the last groups of returnees. Soviet prosecutors had an ace up their sleeve with their other witness: Pu Yi, the last emperor of China and the final ruler of the Qing dynasty who was captured by the Soviet Red Army on 16 August 1945 while attempting to flee to Japan. Just like the aforementioned Japanese witnesses, Pu Yi was afraid of being extradited from the Soviet Union, in his case to China into the hands of Chiang Kai-shek and potentially receiving a more severe punishment than in the USSR.[72] The appearance of such a prominent figure in Tokyo in early August 1946 attracted international media attention. 'Flanked constantly by a Russian soldier and a Russian civilian'[73], Pu Yi spent a month in Tokyo. Soviet prosecution hoped that his testimony would help them prove that by invading Manchuria, Japan had been preparing a military attack on the USSR.[74] Yet, his testimony proved to be not particularly useful.[75] Nonetheless, in 1950, Pu Yi was handed over to the PRC where he spent ten years in the Fushun

---

70   GARF, D 155, Op 2, R 7867, p. 760.

71   Kuznetsov, *Problema voennoplennih*, p. 130.

72   S.V. Karasyev, 'Imperator Pu I v sovetskom plenu', *Voprosy istorii*, 6 (2007), p. 124.

73   *Chicago Tribune*, 10 August 1946, p. 9.

74   Karasyev, 'Imperator Pu I v sovetskom plenu', p. 124.

75   Adam Cathcart, 'Resurrecting Defeat: International Propaganda and the Shenyang Trials of 1956' in Kerstin von Lingen (ed.), *War Crimes Trials in the Wake of Decolonization and Cold War in Asia, 1945-1956: Justice in Time of Turmoil* (Basingstoke: Palgrave Macmillan, 2016), pp. 261-278, at p. 267.

prison. For the Soviets, Pu Yi's imprisonment and his extradition to China had a political value and strengthened their position in Asia.[76] They could claim that to them, all people, emperors included, were equal before the law. Moreover, for the Chinese Communist Party 'merely possessing him' had its political benefits too.[77]

Besides the Japanese witnesses, several Soviet and Mongolian military servicemen supported the prosecution at Tokyo. Among them were Hero of the Soviet Union Tereshkin and Hero of the Mongolian People's Republic Uogdon who testified about the border clashes between the USSR and Japan near the Khalkhin-gol River (or Nomonhan) and Lake Khasan.

Above all previously mentioned grounds, the Soviets criticized the IMTFE for the following two reasons: 'its equivocal determination of "crimes against peace" against the Soviet Union, and more importantly its failure to address Japan's biological weapons programme'[78], also considered 'an instrument of imperialist aggression' against the Soviet Union.[79] They also criticized, among other things, the reluctance of American prosecutor David Sutton to elaborate on the crimes committed in the so-called Tama detachment or Unit 1644 stationed in Nanjing. Indeed, on 29 August 1946 a remarkable dialogue took place between Judge Webb and Prosecutor Sutton that could have initiated the prosecution of the Japanese BW programme:

THE PRESIDENT: Mr. Sutton.
MR. SUTTON: (Reading)
'Particulars Regarding Other Atrocities.
The enemy's TAMA Detachment carried off their civilian captives to the medical laboratory, where the reactions to poisonous serums were tested. This detachment was one of the most secret organizations. The number of persons slaughtered by this detachment cannot be ascertained.'

---

76 S.V. Karasyev, *Problemy plena v sovetsko-yaponskoy voyne i ikh posledstviya (1945-1956 gody)* (Izdatel'stvo Irkutskogo gosudarstvennogo tekhnologicheskogo universiteta, 2006), p. 131.

77 Adam Cathcart, 'Resurrecting Defeat', p. 267.

78 Polunina, *The Khabarovsk Trial*, p. 121.

79 'Bacteriological warfare – a criminal tool of imperialist aggression' or 'Bakteriologicheskaya voyna – prestupnoye orudiye imperialisticheskoy agressii' is the title and the main message of the book written by the above-mentioned Soviet prosecutors involved in the Tokyo tribunal, Lev Smirnov, Solomon Rosenblit, and Marc Raginsky. It was published in 1950, immediately after the end of the Khabarovsk trial. The book illustrates well that the Soviets were interested in prosecuting members of the Japanese BW programme as long as they could frame their bacteriological experiments as aggression against the USSR.

THE PRESIDENT: Are you going to give us any further evidence of these alleged laboratory tests for reactions to poisonous serums? That is something entirely new, we haven't heard before. Are you going to leave it at that?

MR. SUTTON: We do not at this time anticipate introducing additional evidence on that subject.[80]

It is not exactly known why Sutton decided not to dwell on this subject; most likely he was not completely sure that the allegations were true.[81]

Interestingly enough, the public accusations of wilfully omitting the topic of biological weapons emerged only after the trial had ended. So, only in 1950 Raginsky and Rosenblit claimed in their book that in autumn 1946 the Soviet prosecution sent Keenan testimonies of Major General Kiyoshi Kawashima and Major Tomio Karasawa which contained information about human experiments conducted in Unit 731.[82] The authors criticized the decision of Keenan not to present the documents to the trial and to reject any further investigation even though 'he could not be unaware' of the mentioned facts.[83] But the Soviet critics of the Tokyo trial omitted the fact that the USSR delegation didn't raise this issue during the trial when it was still possible to bring the perpetrators to justice.

Correcting Tokyo's 'Failures'

In order to correct these 'failures' and to address the crimes not properly considered at Tokyo, the so-called Khabarovsk trial was held in December 1949 in the Russian Far East.[84] It was the only trial that was entirely dedicated to the

---

80   International Military Tribunal for the Far East. Transcript of proceedings (29.08.1946), Legal Tools Project, pp. 4546-7. Available online: <https://www.legal-tools.org/uploads/tx_ltpdb/TR03-059-a_04.pdf> (last accessed on 19.09.2016).

81   Tsuneishi Kei-ichi, 'Reasons for the Failure to Prosecute Unit 731 and its Significance', in Yuki Tanaka, Tim McCormack and Gerry Simpson (eds.), *Beyond Victor's Justice? The Tokyo War Crimes Trial Revisited* (Leiden: Brill, 2011), p. 198.

82   Raginsky, Rosenblit and Smirnov, *Bakteriologicheskaya voyna – prestupnoye orudiye imperialisticheskoy agressii*, p. 102.

83   Ibid.

84   More on the Khabarovsk trial: V. Polunina, 'Soviet War Crimes Policy in the Far East: The Bacteriological Warfare Trial at Khabarovsk, 1949' in M. Bergsmo, W.L. Cheah and P. Yi (eds.), *Historical Origins of International Criminal Law*, vol. 2 (Brussels: Torkel Opsahl, 2014), pp. 539-562; Polunina 'The Khabarovsk Trial', pp. 121-45.

Japanese wartime biological weapons programme, the implementation of which was primarily carried out by Unit 731 of the Kwantung Army. Twelve defendants who served in medical units of the Kwantung Army stood trial for preparations for bacteriological war and medical experiments on human beings 'punishable under Article I of the Decree of the Presidium of the Supreme Soviet of the USSR of 19 April 1943' (Ukaz 43), and were sentenced to labour camp internments ranging from two to twenty-five years. The Japanese defendants were thus charged with aggressively 'manufacturing and employing bacteriological weapons' against the Soviet Union and China.[85] While earlier Soviet-sponsored military courts dealing with crimes committed in Europe were seen as an extension of the Nuremberg tribunal,[86] the Khabarovsk trial dealing with crimes committed in Asia was conceived as a corrective to the Tokyo tribunal.

The Soviet's inability to impact the agenda of the IMTFE and American control over it didn't prevent the state from planning subsequent international tribunals, just as was the case with the US-led Nuremberg Military Trials. After reaching the verdict at Khabarovsk, the Soviet leadership insisted on establishing an international tribunal that would correct the failures of the IMTFE.

On 1 February 1950, the Soviet Ambassador in Washington, Aleksandr Panyushkin, handed a diplomatic note to the US Secretary of State, Dean Acheson, in which Moscow proposed establishing another international tribunal, this time for the Japanese emperor and those who bore major responsibility for the biological warfare programme, among them Ishii Shirō. In a formal statement, the State Department claimed that 'the Russian demand was merely a propaganda cloak to hide Soviet failure to explain the fate of more than 370,000 Japanese war prisoners.'[87]

A peculiar response to the note to the Soviet Union from the United States was the publication on 7 March 1950 of circular letter number 5, which stated that all Japanese war criminals, serving their sentences would be released.[88] It provoked a note from the USSR to the US on 11 May 1950, in which such intentions were condemned as an attempt to change or even reverse the deci-

---

85   *Materials*, p. 7.

86   According to Andreas Hilger, there were 38 Soviet trials of Germans in 1945, 245 in 1946, 841 in 1947, 2432 in 1948, 15145 in 1949 and 1416 in 1950. (Andreas Hilger, '"Die Gerechtigkeit nehme ihren Lauf?": Die Bestrafung deutscher Kriegs- und Gewaltverbrecher in der Sowjetunion und der SBZ/DDR' in N. Frei (ed.) *Transnationale Vergangenheitspolitik. Der Umgang mit deutschen Kriegsverbrechern in Europa nach dem Zweiten Weltkrieg* (Göttingen: Wallstein Verlag, 2006), pp. 180-246, at p. 182.

87   'Hirohito demand by Soviet called propaganda', *Daily Boston Globe*, 4 February 1950, p. 2.

88   Raginsky, *Militaristy*, pp. 46-47.

sion of the International Military Tribunal in Tokyo, a gross violation of basic norms and principles of international law.[89] As in the previous case, the note was ignored by the Americans, symbolically ending Soviet attempts to create another international tribunal on Japanese war-related crimes.

Conclusion

The International Military Tribunal in Tokyo, as well as the International Military Tribunal in Nuremberg, were seen in the Soviet Union as important historical precedents that condemned aggressive war as the gravest international crime and established a legal framework for prosecuting war criminals. According to the official Soviet position:

> [T]he Tokyo trial revealed the political, economic, ideological and military machinery behind Japan's preparations for a war of aggression; the nature and objectives of the Japanese militarism and its plans for the enslavement of other nations, criminal cynical wars that resulted in innumerable human casualties and huge material losses among Japanese people and people of other countries.[90]

From the first days of the Soviet state, its leaders were fully aware of the didactic, geopolitical, and propaganda benefits of open political trials. Generally, war crimes tribunals were treated by the USSR as a tool for achieving their goals on the international stage. Japanese war crimes trials were 'made to fit into the overall national and foreign policy objectives of each Allied country'[91] and the Soviet Union was no exception. From the 1930s, the Soviet government began to elaborate a practical approach to international trials and from that time saw them as a good opportunity to present the benefits of a communist state as well as the Soviet version of the past to the world.[92]

However, some outcomes of the tribunal caused heavy criticism: the Soviets were of the opinion that the dissenting votes in Tokyo indicated the absence of unity among the judges and, therefore, the need for compromises while passing the verdict. As a result, some contradictions between the outcomes of the

---

89   'Nota Sovetskogo Pravitel'stva pravitel'stvu SSHA', *Pravda* (13 May 1950).

90   Nikolaev, *Tokio: sud narodov*, pp. 392-93.

91   Picigallo, *The Japanese on Trial*, p. xiii.

92   See A. Prusin, 'The Holocaust and "Public Education" in Soviet War Crimes Trials' in Norman Goda (ed.), *Writing Retribution. Holocaust Justice and its Meaning* (forthcoming).

tribunal and the facts established by said tribunal could be observed. The Soviets were outraged that while the judgment recognized a military alliance between Germany and Japan and their aggressive politics of waging a war to establish their domination over other countries and nations, the tribunal did not find that the existence of a general conspiracy between Japan and Germany against peace was an established fact. Instead, the court emphasized the role of the military in the Japanese-German alliance while downplaying that of the government, emperor, and heavy industry.

Chief Prosecutor Keenan described in April 1946 a peculiar characteristic of how the Soviets viewed the forthcoming Tokyo trial. For them, he wrote, it was 'a landmark in international relations and international justice', 'far more important than the Nuremberg proceedings' due to its multinational nature.[93] Just some ten years later his assistant at the IMTFE Brendan F. Brown came to a completely different conclusion, claiming that the Tokyo trial was used by the Soviets 'merely as a means for furthering political objectives', especially 'to advance the hegemony of the Communist party' in Asia.[94]

While the IMT in Nuremberg attracted a lot of attention in the USSR, the Tokyo trial faded from memory over time. Only three books on the IMTFE and several articles were published in the Soviet Union by Russian authors, mostly from former members of the Soviet delegation in Tokyo, describing the trial as a triumph of justice and exaggerating the role of the USSR in it.

Despite their considerable experience in arranging political trials, in the long run the Soviets did not succeed in taking advantage of the post-war international military tribunals as a political and ideological platform. They failed to clearly distinguish between domestic trials, where they could control every step, and jointly organized international tribunals where it was difficult to monopolize the course of events. This was particularly true for the Soviet participation at the International Military Tribunal for the Far East.

For the Soviet Union, the Tokyo trial was another attempt to correct mistakes made in Nuremberg and gain as much as possible from a trial that they could not control in the situation of the coming Cold War. Despite all efforts, the IMTFE proved to be even less successful for the Soviets than the Nuremberg tribunal, which was used to portray the Soviet Union as the sole liberator of Europe and a genuine fighter against fascism. The Tokyo trial, on the contrary, turned out to be a failure of the Soviet propaganda machine. Its role turned out to be supplementary to later Soviet domestic prosecutions of captured Japanese citizens and the associated propaganda campaigns directed at the

---

93   Picigallo, *The Japanese on Trial*, p. 149.

94   Ibid.

new Asian allies of the USSR – for instance, the People's Republic of China and
North Korea.

Bibliography

Neil Boister and Robert Cryer, *The Tokyo International Military Tribunal. A Reappraisal*
(Oxford University Press, 2008).

Adam Cathcart, 'Resurrecting Defeat: International Propaganda and the Shenyang Trials
of 1956', in Kerstin von Lingen (ed.), *War Crimes Trials in the Wake of Decolonization
and Cold War in Asia, 1945-1956: Justice in Time of Turmoil* (Basingstoke: Palgrave
Macmillan, 2016), pp. 261-78.

Alvin D. Coox, *Nomonhan; Japan Against Russia, 1939* (Stanford University Press: 1985).

George Ginsburgs, *Moscow's Road to Nuremberg: The Soviet Background to the Trial* (The
Hague, Boston, London: Martinus Nijhoff Publishers, 1996).

Andreas Hilger, '"Die Gerechtigkeit nehme ihren Lauf?": Die Bestrafung deutscher
Kriegs- und Gewaltverbrecher in der Sowjetunion und der SBZ/DDR', in N. Frei (ed.)
*Transnationale Vergangenheitspolitik. Der Umgang mit deutschen Kriegsverbrechern
in Europa nach dem Zweiten Weltkrieg* (Göttingen: Wallstein Verlag, 2006),
pp. 180-246.

Francine Hirsch, 'The Soviets at Nuremberg: International Law, Propaganda, and the
Making of the Postwar Order', *American Historical Review*, 2 (2008), 701-730.

S.V. Karasyev, 'Imperator Pu I v sovetskom plenu', *Voprosy istorii*, 6 (2007), 120-27.

S.V. Karasyev, *Problemy plena v sovetsko-yaponskoy voyne i ikh posledstviya (1945-1956
gody)* (Izdatel'stvo Irkutskogo gosudarstvennogo tekhnologicheskogo universiteta,
2006).

A.E. Kirichenko, Za kulisami tribunala <http://histrf.ru/uploads/media/default/0001/26/
a2ccdec73923b964017f4b0ce1c6e4232751e7a3.pdf>.

S.I. Kuznetsov, *Problema voennoplennykh v rossiisko-iaponskikh otnosheniiakh posle
Vtoroi mirovoi voiny* (Irkutskii universitet, 1994).

Vasiliy Molodyakov, *Rossiia I Iaponiia: mech' na vesakh* (Moscow: 2005), excerpts from
the book in the author's blog: <http://molodiakov.livejournal.com/17796.html>.

A.N. Nikolaev, *Tokio: sud narodov. Po vospominaniiam uchastnika protsessa* (Moscow:
Iuridicheskaia literatura, 1990).

Tanja Penter, 'Collaboration on Trial: New Source Material on Soviet Postwar Trials
against Collaborators', *Slavic Review*, 64, 4 (Winter 2005), 782-90.

Tanja Penter, '"Das Urteil des Volkes". Der Kriegsverbrecherprozess von Krasnodar 1943',
Osteuropa, 60 (2010), 117-32.

Philip R. Picigallo, *The Japanese on Trial: Alled War Crimes Operations in the East, 1945-
1951* (Austin: University of Texas Press, 1979).

Valentyna Polunina 'The Khabarovsk Trial: The Soviet Riposte to the Tokyo Tribunal' in
    Kirsten Sellars (ed.), *Trials for International Crimes in Asia* (Cambridge University
    Press, 2015), pp. 121-45.

Valentyna Polunina, 'Soviet War Crimes Policy in the Far East: The Bacteriological
    Warfare Trial at Khabarovsk, 1949' in Morten Bergsmo, Cheah Wui Ling, and Yi Ping
    (eds.), *Historical Origins of International Criminal Law*, vol. 2 (Brussels: Torkel Opsahl),
    pp. 539-62.

Alexander Prusin, 'The Holocaust and "Public Education" in Soviet War Crimes Trials'
    in Norman Goda, (ed.), *Writing Retribution: Holocaust Justice and its Meaning*
    (forthcoming).

M.Y. Raginsky, S.Y. Rosenblit and L.N. Smirnov, *Bakteriologicheskaia voina – prestupnoe
    orudie imperialisticheskoi agressii. Khabarovskii protsess iaponskikh voennykh
    prestupnikov* (Moscow: Izdatel'stvo Akademii nauk SSSR, 1950).

M.Y. Raginsky and S.Y. Rosenblit, *Mezhdunarodniy prozess glavnih yaponskih voennih
    prestupnikov* (Moscow-Leningrad: Izdatelstvo akademii nauk SSSR, 1950).

M.Y. Raginsky, *Militaristy na skam'e podsudimih: po materialam Tokiyskogo I Habarovskogo
    protseddov* (Moscow: Yuridicheskaya literatura, 1985).

Kirsten Sellars, 'William Patrick and "Crimes against Peace" at the Tokyo Tribunal, 1946-
    1948', *The Edinburgh Law Review*, 15.2 (2011), 166-96.

Kirsten Sellars, *'Crimes against Peace' and International Law* (Cambridge University
    Press, 2013).

Tsuneishi Kei-ichi, 'Reasons for the Failure to Prosecute Unit 731 and its Significance',
    in Yuki Tanaka, Tim McCormack and Gerry Simpson (eds.), *Beyond Victor's Justice?
    The Tokyo War Crimes Trial Revisited* (Leiden: Brill, 2011).

Yuma Totani, *The Tokyo War Crimes Trial: The Pursuit of Justice in the Wake of World War
    II* (Harvard University Press, 2008).

A.N. Vasilyev, 'O skorom sude i nakazanii vinovnikov agressii (K itogam Tokiyskogo
    protsessa)', *Sovetskoye gosudarstvo i pravo*, 3 (1949), 40-49.

Peter Williams and David Wallace, *Unit 731: Japan's Secret Biological Warfare in World
    War II* (New York: Free Press, 1989).

Indictment from the International Military Tribunal for the Far East, World War II File,
    Bontecou Papers, Harry S. Truman Presidential Museum & Library, available online:
    <http://bit.ly/1GJTtlW>.

*Materials on the trial of former servicemen of the Japanese Army charged with manufac-
    turing and employing bacteriological weapons* (Moscow: Foreign Languages Publishing
    House, 1950).

'Odin den' Voyennoy kollegii Verkhovnogo suda SSSR', Sakharov Center, <http://www.
    sakharov-center.ru/blogs/main/all/odin-den-voennoy-kollegii-verhovnogo-suda-
    sssr/>

CHAPTER 7

'Little Useful Purpose Would be Served by Canada': Ottawa's View of the Tokyo War Crimes Trial

Yuki Takatori

Reluctant Participant

In August 1945, when the Big Four (France, the United Kingdom, the United States and the Soviet Union) signed the Agreement of London, to which was attached 'The Charter of the International Military Tribunal', commonly known as 'The Nuremberg Charter', all the nations with representatives on the United Nations War Crimes Commission (UNWCC) promptly adhered to this historic pact. With the exception of Canada. Vincent Massey, the high commissioner for Canada, started despatching messages to the Department of External Affairs, advising that Ottawa follow suit. The British government, too, repeatedly urged Canadian acceptance. Ottawa's reaction to the accord, however, was lukewarm interest, scepticism, reluctance and caution. At that time, Canada did not even have any 'acts or statutes allowing for the trial of war crimes suspects'.[1] Though his department's legal advisor, E.R. Hopkins, supported the 'Jackson plan', finding it one in keeping with customary international law, Secretary of State for External Affairs Louis St Laurent noted that 'little useful purpose would be served by Canada adhering to this agreement and it is therefore very unlikely that adherence will come forward'.[2] John E. Reed, another legal advisor to St Laurent (and later elected a member of the International Court of Justice), weighing the pros and the cons of abiding by the accord, concluded that, on the one hand, Canada would 'protect our technical position', but that, on the other, it would have to shoulder responsibility for all the matters that had been discussed and decided on without prior consultation with the Crown. Shortly before the Nuremberg trial began, the high commissioner's office proposed that a Canadian judge be appointed as the alternate to

---

1   M. Sweeney, 'The Canadian War Crimes Liaison Detachment – Far East and the Prosecution of Japanese "Minor" War Crimes', unpublished thesis, University of Waterloo (2013), p. 37; P. Brode, 'Bruce Macdonald and the Drafting of Canada's War Crimes Regulations – 1945', *Gazette*, 29 (1995), 276-77.

2   Library and Archives Canada (LAC), RG 25/vol. 3182/ File 4896-40, Memorandum to the High Commissioner, 14 December 1945.

the United Kingdom's member on the bench, but Reed was not at all interested in taking forward such a proposal. One of the consequences of not joining the Big Four, as Massey pointed out, would be Canada's ineligibility to send official observers to the Nuremberg trial. Eventually, a senior military officer did go to Nuremberg to observe the trial, but his visit was approved 'on understanding that he is going in strictly private capacity'.[3] In the end, Canada did not ratify the agreement, and was never more than a reluctant and diffident participant in the Allied undertakings to determine in courts of law the guilt or innocence of the German architects of war and their minions. The only progress made during this period, thanks to the tireless efforts of Lieutenant Colonel Bruce Macdonald, was the introduction of the Canadian War Crimes Regulations to the House of Commons. This law was to become the nation's first 'war crimes apparatus'.[4]

Several reasons can be advanced as to why there was so little enthusiasm for participation in this Allied post-war task. In part, Canada's reluctance emanated from a lingering 'timid Dominion' mentality – a self-perception that Canadians were too 'reticent to engage with the world' – and from a consciousness that an ocean separated it from the European theatre.[5] And, in part, it was a reflection of the world view of William Lyon McKenzie King, the wartime prime minister, who saw as dubious the value of Canada's international commitments, fearing that embroilment in conflicts beyond its national boundaries might reduce its autonomy. An absence of reports of systematic mistreatment of Canadian POWs by the Germans – some repatriated former POWs even praised their treatment in German camps – might also have contributed to the government's minimal interest in European war crimes trials.[6]

---

3   LAC, RG 25/vol. 3182/ File 4896-40, Note for the Under Secretary of External Affairs, 29 August 1945; Letter to the High Commissioner, 11 September 1945; Letters from the High Commissioner, 4 September, 26 November 1945.

4   Brode, 'Bruce Macdonald', 276.

5   P. Brode, *Casual Slaughters and Accidental Judgments: Canadian War Crimes Prosecutions, 1944-1948* (Toronto: University of Toronto Press, 1997), pp. 35-53; J. Stanton, 'Reluctant vengeance: Canada at the Tokyo War Crimes Tribunal', *The Journal of American and Canadian Studies*, 17 (1999), 61-62.; H. Forsey, *Eugene Forsey, Canada's Maverick Sage* (Toronto: Dundurn Press, 2012), p. 226.

6   Brode, *Casual Slaughters*, p. 32; *Globe and Mail*, 11 January 1944: 'Mates free 15 Canadians in Ortona and Nazi captors become captives'.

Canada and the Far Eastern War Crimes Trial

In contrast, Canada deemed the punishment of Japanese war crimes of greater importance. Having had two battalions captured in the fall of Hong Kong, it had 'suffered more at the hands of the Japanese than any other nation against whom [its] forces had been sent'; the atrocities committed by the Japanese forces and the appalling conditions in their prisoner-of-war camps had had 'no parallel in either Germany or Italy'.[7] Moreover, Canada, which had not been invited to participate in the diplomatic conference that resulted in the London Agreement, was party to the negotiations over the setting up of Far Eastern war criminal courts. Nonetheless, the cabinet moved at a dawdling pace; and when eight of the other Allies decided in 1944 to launch an 'extensive publicity campaign on atrocities in the hopes of shaming the Japanese government into improving camp conditions', it at first balked, asking for more time to consider the matter. Canada was the only nation that did not join the effort immediately.[8]

Canadian involvement in the trials of Japanese war criminals officially began on 18 October 1945, when the United States despatched a memorandum, requesting that Britain, China, and the Soviet Union each nominate five judges, and Australia, Canada, France, the Netherlands, and New Zealand three. Together, they would form a panel from which General Douglas MacArthur, Supreme Commander for the Allied Powers (SCAP), would choose justices to preside over a tribunal. (Correspondence between the United Kingdom, Canada, and the United States seems to suggest that the Allied Powers originally contemplated holding multiple international tribunals simultaneously in different localities. In the end, the '[idea] of nominating panels of judges [was] tacitly abandoned'.) By and large, however, the recipients did not respond to the call for jurists for more than two months, partially because they were not being furnished with full details on the compensation, messing, billeting, and transportation of judges. Feeling somewhat put out, Joseph B. Keenan, President Harry S. Truman's appointee as chief prosecutor at the trial, confided to Group Captain C.M.A. Strathy and Lieutenant Colonel R.D. Jennings, two Canadian military lawyers visiting Washington in November 1945, that the United States was ready to proceed, with or without the participation of other nations, and urged that Canada hasten to select a judge for the upcoming trial.

---

7 W.P. McClemont, 'War Crimes Trials: Criminals Brought to Justice', *Canadian Army Journal*, 1 (3) (1947), 16-20, 17-18.

8 J.F.W. Vance, *Objects of Concern: Canadian Prisoners of War through the Twentieth Century* (University of British Columbia Press, 1994), pp 189, 292.

Finally, on 14 December, the United States issued an ultimatum, giving the Allied nations until 5 January 1946 to decide on their representatives.[9]

Selecting the Canadian Representative on the Bench

Ottawa, having received this final notice from the US, immediately set out to select a justice to be sent to the International Military Tribunal for the Far East (IMTFE). However, one qualification for the nominee – that he be a military officer with a rank of major general or higher – proved so difficult to meet that the Department of National Defence could find no suitable candidate. Citing the example of the New Zealand and Chinese governments, both of which had selected a jurist not in the military, it proposed choosing a civilian who had once been an officer and who could be granted an honorary rank upon nomination, and advanced the names of two supreme court of Ontario justices, both of them World War I veterans: John Andrew Hope, '[a former] company commander of a Canadian infantry battalion', and John Keiller MacKay, a major, '[formerly] commanding three artillery brigades'.[10] By 7 January, Deputy Minister of Justice F.P. Varcoe, after discussion with National Defence, notified Prime Minister McKenzie King of his decision to recommend Justice Andrew Hope. The next day, the Privy Council Office advised Hopkins that the chief justice of Ontario had to be 'consulted regarding the appointment of Mr Justice Hope'. The journey to the announcement of the Canadian judge, however, had to deal with a few more delays, not unlike the miscommunications and crossed wires that occurred during the selection process of the American who would sit on the bench, John P. Higgins.[11]

Once an agreement was reached on who to send to Tokyo, the sequence of events quickened. On 8 January, the cabinet approved the nomination of Justice Hope, who, anxious to discuss his assignment in person, had left

---

9   LAC, RG 25/vol. 3641/ File 4060-C-40, Memorandum from the Secretary of State for Dominion Affairs, 4 December 1945; Telegram from the Canadian Ambassador, 28 December 1945; The National Archives of the United Kingdom (TNA), FO 371/57422, From Washington to Foreign Office, 6 January 1946.

10   LAC, RG 25/vol. 3641/File 4060-C-40, From Department of National Defence, 5 January 1946; C. Moore, *The Court of Appeal for Ontario: Defining the Right of Appeal, 1792-2013* (Toronto: University of Toronto Press, 2014), pp. 236, 249.

11   LAC, RG 25/vol. 3641/File 4060-C-40, Memorandum for the Prime Minister, 7 January 1946; Memorandums from Privy Council Office, 8 January 1946; Y. Takatori, 'The Forgotten Judge at the Tokyo War Crimes Trial', *Massachusetts Historical Review*, 10 (2008), 115-41, at 118-22.

Toronto for Ottawa the previous evening. Just as the issue which had been pending since the Note of 18 October appeared to be settled, the prime minister's office experienced a shock: the chief justice of Ontario had vetoed the choice. In the words of Deputy Minister Varcoe, the consent of approval was declined because 'the administration of justice in Ontario will suffer if [Justice Hope] is absent for three months at this time'.[12]

Within a few days, E. Stuart McDougall of the Court of King's Bench of Québec, was called on to fill the void. There is no documentation for the discussions that led to his selection; perhaps, since the deadline for nominations had already passed when Justice Hope was eliminated from consideration, the necessity to act quickly forced the decision-makers to engage in face-to-face or telephone consultations only: a clue that this was the case is a note handwritten by E.R. Hopkins on a 11 January teletype message to Washington instructing the ambassador to inform the American authorities of the choice of McDougall: 'Mr. Justice Hope not being available, the appointment of Mr. Justice McDougall was cleared by telephone. E.R.H.'[13]

There is no sign that Justice Hope was aware of the rapidly executed search for his replacement after Ottawa heard of the negative vote of his superior. A week after his trip to the capital, he sent a letter to the legal branch of the Department of External Affairs, relating a personal meeting he had had with the chief justice, who 'while realizing the difficulties of the Court short of Judges, felt that he had not irrevocably closed the door to my nomination', and asking to 'let the appointment proceed'. Apparently believing that he had not made his eagerness sufficiently clear in his earlier message by mail, Hope sent another one the very next day by Canadian Pacific Telegraph: 'Please withhold any action based on... my letter of yesterday.'[14] By this time, however, the door to his nomination had been 'irrevocably closed'. On 22 February, Justice McDougall left for Tokyo on a Douglas C-54 Skymaster from Hamilton Army Airfield in California in the company of Higgins, whose selection had been made public only four days earlier, and B.V.A. Röling, the Dutch justice.[15]

A native of Montréal and graduate of McGill University, where he earned the bachelor of civil law (BCL), McDougall served during World War I in the

---

12   LAC, RG 25/vol. 3641/File 4060-C-40, Letter from Deputy Minister of Justice, 10 January 1946.

13   LAC, RG 25/vol. 3641/File 4060-C-40, Teletype message to the Canadian Ambassador, 11 January 1946.

14   LAC, RG 25/vol. 3641/File 4060-C-40, Letter from Andrew Hope, 14 January 1946; Telegram from A. Hope, 15 January 1946.

15   *Diary of John P. Higgins*, 22 February 1946 (Private collection).

Canadian Armed Forces from June 1915 to November 1918, achieving the rank of major. A specialist in mining and corporation law, he had no experience in criminal or international law, and had been in private practice until appointed a puisne judge of the Court of King's Bench in 1942. A one-page curriculum vitae prepared for External Affairs contained nothing remarkable; other than 'Political career' (provincial treasurer in 1936) and 'General' (counsel to Royal Commission investigating labour troubles), it was for the most part a list of 'Clubs', 'Recreations', 'Athletic activities in earlier days', and 'Avocation'. When compared with Justice Hope, who had more than ten years of experience on Ontario's highest court, he was wanting in distinction. McDougall himself looks to have been mindful of the gaps in his knowledge, both new and long-standing, since he requested from the government, before departing for Japan, a copy of the judgment of the trial of General Tomoyuki Yamashita in the Philippines and of the Criminal Code.[16]

The appointment of someone with such a 'relatively undistinguished record as a jurist' to a position of international prestige must have puzzled those not involved in his selection. Patrick Brode speculates that McDougall owed his nomination to McKenzie King's Liberal Party. As mentioned above, he had been a provincial treasurer in Québec in the Adélard Godbout govern-ment, which had lent unstinting support to King in 1944 on the immensely controversial issue of conscription and backed him on Québec autonomy. A McDougall tie to King grows in plausibility when one takes into account his strong background in labour relations, especially in mining, an area in which King himself had been deeply involved, not only as Canada's first labour min-ister but also as a consultant to the Rockefellers during the bloody 1913-14 strike against their mining operations in Ludlow, Colorado. It is therefore not unlikely that McDougall had struck up a friendship or formed a political alli-ance with King sometime prior to his nomination. Notwithstanding his snap appointment under exigent circumstances, with (to go by the evidence) little cabinet discussion, McDougall came to be admired by his peers in Tokyo; an American attorney in the International Prosecution Section (IPS) and another in the defence were to call him 'one of the better judges'.[17] As we shall see, he was to play an important role in the formation of the bloc of so-called majority judges, and whereas, as has often been noted in criticisms of the trial, some of the judges took absences in excess, McDougall did not, being one of the two

---

16   LAC, RG 25/vol. 3641/File 4060-C-40, Letters from McDougall to Hopkins, 19 January, 5 Feb-
        ruary 1946.
17   A.C. Brackman, *The Other Nuremberg: The Untold Story of the Tokyo War Crimes Trial* (New
        York: William Morrow and Company, Inc., 1987), p. 66; Brode, *Casual Slaughters*, p. 192.

(the other being Röling, one of his two companions on the flight to Japan) who missed only fourteen court sessions.[18]

Trouble in Tokyo

Shortly before the opening of the trial on 3 May 1946, McDougall sent two letters to Norman Robertson of the Department of External Affairs; neither was a harbinger of things to come. In the first, after mentioning the 'big strides [that] have been made in the matter of accommodation', he described the relations among the judges as 'excellent, everyone showing the best spirit of cooperation'. He did express some concern over the possibility that the trial might not be over in three months as originally promised, but it was a pretext for an additional funding request that occupied three quarters of the letter. The second letter, much shorter, was in the same vein; it mentions important amendments to the Charter of the tribunal as if in afterthought.[19] From the outset, however, the proceedings went anything but smoothly, and on 19 March 1947, less than a year after the trial got underway, McDougall wrote to St Laurent a third letter that, dispensing with even a modicum of pleasantries, began with 'I have hesitated to write to you concerning my troubles as a member of the [tribunal].'

In his letter, the severest criticism was directed against President William Webb, whom he described as someone 'in whom no one has any trust or confidence: his lack of experience and ability, we know; and his sincerity, we suspect', and as someone who 'refuses to discuss or is incapable of discussing any question and has ... antagonized the Members'.[20] But, his disparagement of the president was not confined to derogating the man's competence and character. McDougall could not understand why Webb would advocate the application of natural law theory in determining whether the actions of the defendants were crimes. Naming no names, he also gave vent to his differences with three other justices: one, presumably Justice Röling, he criticized for taking the 'extraordinary view' that aggressive war was not a crime, a position shared by the second, Justice Radhabinod Pal, whom McDougall only referred to as 'the member

---

18   The trial was in session for 417 days. As for the remaining judges, Cramer missed 28 days, Bernard 32 days, Jaranilla 38 days, Patrick 43 days, Mei and Northcroft 49 days, Webb 53 days and Pal 109 days. M. Harries and S. Harries, *Sheathing the Sword: the Demilitarisation of Japan* (New York: Macmillan Publishing, 1987), p. 149.

19   LAC, RG 25/vol. 3641/File 4060-C-40, Letters from McDougall to Robertson, 23, 24 April 1946.

20   LAC, RG 25/vol. 5762/ File 104-J-(s), Letter to Rt. Hon. Louis St Laurent, K.C., 19 March 1947.

from India'. McDougall additionally faulted Pal for not signing a pre-trial agreement to keep secret all deliberations in chambers. The third judge subject to McDougall's disfavour was Henri Bernard of France, who was, like Webb, a natural law advocate; it was Bernard's belief that the proceedings ought to be governed neither by the Charter nor by international law but by 'the feelings in the heart of each man (le bon coeur)'. As for the remaining judges, he complained that they did not '[express] their views except with destructive criticism of the work of the others'. He concluded with a request to be relieved of his duties so that 'Canada would avoid in the future the opprobrium of having her representative participate in a judgment which will do credit to no nation'.[21]

This was not the first time that McDougall had indicated a desire to quit. Nine months earlier, when John P. Higgins (McDougall's other trans-Pacific companion) tendered his resignation, which was accepted by MacArthur, McDougall confided in Higgins that he too was contemplating a return home. Higgins took a cynical view of this confidence, observing in his diary, 'McDougall all talk and no action said he thought of getting out etc, etc. He will do nothing for he looks henpecked and glad to be away but has to say something big.'[22]

St Laurent was so alarmed by McDougall's missive that he sent a handwritten note, barely legible, to the cabinet, asking, 'Who is the President "in whom no one has any trust or confidence"?',[23] but not everyone shared his sense of urgency. The Canadian ambassador in Washington responded with archetypical bureaucratic complacency that '[the] War Department, not the State Department, appears to have the main responsibility for the conduct of the trials in Japan, and we have not got any contacts there of the sort which we could use in a question like this', and that the embassy's opposite number in the State Department 'has been moved elsewhere'. Since the ambassador had not heard such 'adverse reports' from the British or New Zealand representatives on the Far Eastern Commission (FEC), he concluded that 'there is no source of information in Washington on which we could draw concerning the dissension and manifestation of incompetence in the Tribunal itself which are alluded to by Judge McDougall in his letter', and that his inquiries 'have probably gone far enough to show at least there is no widespread concern on the

---

21   Ibid.
22   *Diary of Higgins*, 26 June 1946.
23   LAC, RG 25/vol. 5762/File 104-J-(s), Note written by St Laurent, 29 March 1947.

matter here', even though he did admit that lack of information may be 'due to ignorance of the facts'.[24]

It seems McDougall's letter was delivered first among those by the three Commonwealth justices who requested their governments to recall them. When the cabinet members in Ottawa were scrambling to find out the latest on Tokyo, the British government, still unaware of the discord in chambers, had no idea what was meant by the Canadian government's '[inclination] to withdraw from the trials', and theorized that the continual friction in the tribunal they were agitated about might be in reference to the 'old troubles' about 'the absence of the U.S. Chief Prosecutor, Mr. Keenan' or 'the suspension of a U.S. counsel for the defence', implying that Canada was not always (or was not making efforts to be) brought up to date with respect to the trial.[25]

E.H. Norman

The most comprehensive first-hand account of the situation in Tokyo was provided by another Canadian of consequence at the tribunal, E.H. Norman, a scholar of Japanese history and the head of the Canadian Liaison Mission in Japan. Born in Japan, and having spent his formative years there, Norman had acquired a native command of Japanese. When the apprehension of suspects got underway in November 1945, Norman played a not insignificant role in effecting the incarcerations of two individuals who were key figures: ex-premier Prince Konoe Fumimaro and Lord Keeper of Privy Seal Kido Kōichi, the emperor's closest advisor. In a seven-page single-spaced memorandum to MacArthur, Norman argued with a vigour that bordered at times on immoderation for Konoe's designation as a major war crimes suspect, portraying him as an insincere, chameleonic figure upon whom responsibility for the attack on China, 'the second great step toward World War II', should fall. So forceful and cogent was his brief that it convinced George Atcheson, acting United States political advisor to SCAP, to place Konoe's name on a list of major war crimes suspects, despite his having earlier advised President Truman to the contrary.[26]

---

24   LAC, RG 25/vol. 5762/File 104-J-(s), Personal and confidential letter from Canadian Embassy, 21 April 1947.

25   TNA, FO 371/57426, Minutes, [Date unknown] April 1947; FO 371/69833, From Tokyo to Foreign Office, 17 April 1947.

26   Konoe committed suicide by taking poison the night before he was to report to prison.

It was also Norman's guidance that led to the arrest of Marquis Kido. His memo on Kido, though much less vehement in its tenor and wording, was nonetheless impassioned in its identification of its subject as the man who had strongly urged that General Tōjō Hideki be named as successor to Konoe. Once again, a Norman memorandum, although not directly recommending his arrest, nudged Atcheson into taking action; on 6 December 1945 he listed Hirohito's confidante as a suspect.[27] Awaya Kentarō, a pioneering researcher on the Tokyo trial, praised Norman's thesis for its insight into the 'system of irresponsibility' among Japan's wartime leaders, the passing of accountability to immediate superiors, or to others, until it reached the head of state, the emperor, who could not be legally held answerable for the actions and decisions of his subordinates.[28]

Soon after his arrest, Kido came forward with a 5,920-page diary he had begun keeping in 1930. It turned out to be a windfall of immeasurable value to the Allied prosecutors, giving them the means to untangle the complicated web of machinations behind Japanese aggression in the 1930s and 1940s. It has since proved to be, as well, a treasure trove of primary-source material for historians studying the politics of the Shōwa Era.

As an English-Japanese bilingual speaker, a rarity at that time, Norman was one of the very few people in the courtroom able to listen to and understand the trial in both languages simultaneously. In a letter to External Affairs dated 5 April 1947, he showed much less sympathy to Justice McDougall than to Sir William Webb, whom, just a few weeks before, the former had deprecated with such force. Norman explained that the president 'must constantly endeavour to reconcile the views of the whole Tribunal', a body consisting of judges from eleven different nations, 'many of whom do not follow either the same legal system or procedure in their own national Courts'. Writing of the resignation of Justice Higgins which 'caused bitter criticism in Tokyo, and particularly amongst Americans themselves, although he was at once replaced by Major-General Cramer', he judged that McDougall's exit would 'impair the prestige of the court' and was 'exceedingly difficult to justify'.[29] He went on to summarize the course of the trial for his readers, presenting intelligence by then long pos-

---

27   National Archives and Records Administration, College Park, Maryland (NARA II), RG 59/ Box 3641/ Decimal File 740.00116 PW/11-545, Office of the United States Political Adviser to Truman, 5 November 1945; Decimal File 740.00116 PW/11-1945, Prince Konoye as a War Criminal Suspect, 5 December 1945; War Guilt of Marquis Kido, Lord Keeper of Privy Seal, 19 November 1945.

28   K. Awaya, Tōkyō saibanron (Tokyo: Ōtsuki Shoten, 1989), pp. 63-64.

29   LAC, RG 25/vol. 5762/File 104-J-(s), Letter from the Canadian Liaison Mission, 5 April 1947.

sessed by their counterparts in the United Kingdom and New Zealand; that the indictment covered the period beginning in 1928, that American attorneys had been appointed to assist the Japanese defence lawyers, that the prosecution had rested and the defence had started their case, and so on. That Norman took the trouble to give a kind of 'survey course' on the tribunal further supports the theory that Canada had had, from the beginning, no great interest in what was occurring in Tokyo. The mindset of scant concern may have extended beyond keeping up with tidings from Japan, for due care was not always exercised in the routing of messages; a top-secret telegram transmitted from the Department of National Defence to Norman during this period was deciphered and delivered to him carelessly through Australian army channels. When Norman's complaint was conveyed to National Defence via External Affairs, the judge advocate general defensively replied that the cable was 'quite innocuous' and that 'if at the time I had been aware of what you have subsequently told me, it would have been sent through your Department'.[30]

Autonomy and Neutrality

Between the end of the pre-trial period and the onset of the dispute, no record exists of correspondence between McDougall and the government. What does this silence mean? Whereas Ottawa's silence was a sign of its general indifference toward the prosecution of war criminals, it is plausible that McDougall's was indicative of personal and professional rectitude. Since he was not, evidently, a man particularly averse to writing letters, having penned six between January and April, the cessation of outgoing missives after May 1946 is, at the least, suggestive of an ethical choice; he might well have thought it improper for a judge to exchange information with his government, which technically represented one of the prosecuting nations. The following examples may bolster, if not prove, a theory about how seriously he took obligations of confidentiality. Within a week of Canada notifying the US government of his nomination, McDougall asked that 'authority for the press release ... be given very soon'. It was not that he craved the public spotlight. He had in fact kept his new assignment a secret, but someone in the government was leaking, putting him at risk of embarrassment if he continued to feign ignorance while the rumours spread. In his letter to Hopkins, he expressed his resentment toward those people 'who occupy such positions [but are] unable to keep confidential

---

30   LAC, RG 25/vol. 5762/File 104-J-(s), Message from the Canadian Liaison Mission, 28 May 1947; Message from R.J. Orde, 29 May 1947.

information to themselves'. As already mentioned, he led off his 19 March 1947 letter to External Affairs by declaring how hesitant he had been to write to them because 'as a member of the Tribunal my duties and functions are entirely judicial and any defect in its organization or operations are matters non-political which must be remedied, if remedy is possible, by the members of the Tribunal themselves on their own initiative'. In case it should appear to St Laurent that he was 'unethical in disclosing ... the opinions of my colleagues before the judgment is delivered', he referred to Justice Pal's refusal to subscribe to the disclosure agreement, 'freeing the remainder from their undertaking'. In a letter Norman wrote to Ottawa about the bench's decision to take a six-week summer recess in 1947, he asked to 'have from you our Judge's considered opinion regarding aspects of trial'. It may sound odd that Norman, who was never far from McDougall in Tokyo, had to obtain information the latter might have through the Crown more than 10,000 kilometres away, but despite frequent meetings between the two, Norman believed the judge 'might feel more disposed to discuss the problem of the Court in Ottawa than in Tokyo'. His long-distance request implies that McDougall was not sharing information with him on anything that happened inside the courtroom.[31]

McDougall's at-arm's-length behaviour stood in sharp contrast with that of his fellow judges. For instance, when a San Francisco news broadcast reported 'so much of the truth [about the judgment] that it can hardly be attributed to guess work', he composed a memo to President Webb, entitled 'Secrecy of Decision', suggesting that a 'thorough investigation be conducted in order that we may take whatever steps are necessary to ensure that our verdicts and sentences will not become public knowledge until they are pronounced by the Tribunal'. In response, Sir William, though agreeing, asserted that 'everything in the broadcast does not disclose a "leakage"' and admitted that he himself 'frequently told persons outside the Tribunal, that is to say, my own Government ... and others interested, when the Judgment might be expected to be given'.[32] Similarly, neither Justice Erima Northcroft (New Zealand) nor Justice W.D. Patrick (UK) thought twice about the impropriety of such ex parte communications. In what he called 'the casual notes of a judicial resident in Tokyo', Northcroft regularly reported his disappointment with the trial to

---

31   LAC, RG 25/vol. 3631/File 4060-C-40, Letter to Hopkins, 15 January 1946; RG 25/vol. 5762/ File 104-J-(s), Letter to Rt. Hon. Louis St. Laurent, K.C., 19 March 1947; Letter to External Affairs, 16 June 1947.

32   Australian War Memorial (AWM), Papers of Sir William Webb, 3DRL-2481/Series 4/Wallet 11 of 20, Memorandum to the president, 13 October 1948; Memorandum to the member for Canada, 13 October 1948.

Wellington, describing the performance of Keenan and of American defence attorneys in such derogatory terms as 'incompetent', 'poor', 'unseemly', and 'stupid'. Having received such reports, it is doubtful that the New Zealand government was surprised when it learned Northcroft wanted to resign.[33] While not the prolific writer that Northcroft was, Patrick was contacting the officials at the United Kingdom Liaison Mission in Japan, telling them what he hoped to do to shorten the defence phase of the trial once it began.[34] The Chinese judge, Mei Ru'ao is believed to have prematurely disclosed to the Chinese press who among the defendants had been sentenced to death. Higurashi commented that Mei's understanding of confidentiality was probably very weak.[35] If true, this was an egregious leak of the worst kind by a keeper of the law.

The situation was more or less the same in the court's minority bloc. Röling was in correspondence with the secretary-general of the Justice Ministry in the Netherlands, revealing his 'reservations concerning the crime against peace and the Nuremberg judgment', and seeking advice regarding the repercussions a dissenting opinion from him might cause. Pal did not write about the trial in his personal letters to his family; however, he did let the Indian government know early on that he supported the objections filed by the defence. Bernard, on the other hand, as Ōoka pointed out, kept in such close contact with the French associate prosecutor that his conduct would be considered unbecoming in 'ordinary trials'.[36] However, in a trial with political implications where 'justice' was practically synonymous with 'guilty verdict', few people might have seen cooperation between judges and prosecutors as a violation of legal ethics. Under these circumstances, Canada's lack of enthusiasm ended up, although unintentionally, enabling McDougall to maintain the appearance of the most autonomous and neutral judge of all.

---

33   R. Kay (ed.), *Documents on New Zealand External Relations*, vol. 2, *The Surrender and Occupation of Japan* (Wellington: Historical Publications Branch, Department of Internal Affairs, 1982), pp. 1610-15.

34   TNA, FO 371/57429, Telegram from Tokyo to Foreign Office, 23 November 1946.

35   Y. Higurashi, *Tōkyō Saiban no kokusai kankei* (Tokyo: Mokutakusha, 2002), p. 472.

36   B. v. Poelgeest, 'The Netherlands and the Tokyo Tribunal', *Japan Forum*, 4 (1) (1992), 81-90, at 87-88; N. Nakazato, *Paru Hanji, Indo nashonarizumu to Tōkyō Saiban* (Tokyo: Iwanami Shoten, 2011), pp. 100, 107-8; Y. Ōoka, *Tōkyō Saiban furansujin hanji no muzairon* (Tokyo: Bungei Shunjū, 2012), pp. 119, 194-95.

McDougall as a Majority Justice

Justice McDougall succeeded in maintaining judicial autonomy in a trial political in nature; his skill in assessing the credibility of the witnesses and the arguments of the prosecution and the defence, and in shaping the judgment is also noteworthy. Though, prior to the tribunal, some questioned whether he was qualified to grapple with the complexities of international criminal proceedings, he met the challenge admirably, proving himself one of the most active judges. McDougall got into a heated exchange, in writing, with Bernard over the legitimacy of Japan's colonial rule in Manchuria and the probative value of the Lytton Report. He was also the instigator of a linguistic dispute that brought the proceedings almost to a halt: when a suggestion was made that 'the Tribunal [would] permit each counsel (other than Japanese) whose native language is not English to read in his own language his opening address and all documents in such language tendered by him', McDougall alerted Webb to a possible violation of a provision in the Charter.[37] Unquestionably, his most important contribution was his participation in authoring the court's final judgment. For instance, during the summation, McDougall, together with Patrick, submitted to the other judges a paper, entitled simply 'The Law', propounding their reasons as to why the preliminary motions in June 1946, challenging the very establishment of the tribunal, could not be sustained. An unqualified declaration of conformance to all the relevant opinions of the Nuremberg trial, the majority adopted it for the most part verbatim in Chapter II of the final judgment.[38]

He also took the initiative in disregarding Counts 6 to 17 (which pertained to planning and preparing for aggressive wars) and 18 to 26 (which pertained to initiating such wars) in the indictment, streamlining the thirty-six conspiracy counts to fifteen, and eventually to eight. In a similar manner, he proposed that Counts 45 through 50 (concerning the killing of civilians and disarmed soldiers) be included in Count 54 (concerning conventional war crimes and crimes against humanity). Finally, he took issue with two separate but related counts: Count 27 (having to do with the hostilities against the Republic of China which started on 18 September 1931) and Count 28 (having to do with the hostilities against the Republic of China which started on 7 July 1937). McDougall argued

---

37   Ōoka, *Tōkyō Saiban furansujin hanji no muzairon*, pp. 160-73; AWM, Papers of Sir William Webb, 3DRL-2481/Series 1/Folder 9 of 17, Memorandum from McDougall, 28 September 1946; Brackman, *The Other Nuremberg*, pp. 214-18.

38   AWM, Papers of Sir William Webb, 3DRL-2481/Series 1/Folder 9 of 17, Memorandum from McDougall and Patrick, 18 March 1948.

that these counts, should they be retained, could be awkwardly interpreted to hold that Japan was waging two separate wars simultaneously against the same country. Accepting his reasoning, the majority decided to consider only the 'fuller charge contained in Count 27'.[39] By the end of the process, culling had eliminated forty-five of the original fifty-five counts.

McDougall made a sensible decision and exercised leadership in another situation involving the judgment. Shortly after the translation of the judgment into Japanese commenced, an officer from the Civil Information and Education Section of General Headquarters (CIE) offered to prepare a summary of the judgment (and of its translation) for the press. At least seven justices, from both the majority and the minority, concurred; some had reservations, but none that referred to the fundamental desirability of a summary.[40] McDougall was the sole voice against it. In a lengthy memorandum to the president, he presented four main objections: (1) summarizing the findings of facts – a section which would occupy a large part of the judgment – would be 'too dangerous' because '[to] summarize or reduce such statement of facts could only be done by omitting some facts'; (2) should any errors be made, the tribunal would be held responsible for them; (3) should the judgment be summarized, its translation would have to be prepared 'by the present translation organization. That would have to be done after complete translation of the judgment itself. The time element would, therefore, be of importance'; and finally, (4) it is often the case that 'on the opening day the reports are headlines, on the second day they are found on the inside pages of the papers, and on subsequent days, barely noted, and [this] judgment would seem to be one in which history will probably repeat itself'.[41]

Eventually, '[as] no member of the Tribunal has signified any objection to the [proposal]', Webb gave his consent to the CIE to summarize the final judgment 'for press purposes in the manner proposed by [the CIE]' on the condition that it 'will be distributed only when reading commences, and then only piecemeal with related parts of the Judgment'.[42] However, there is no evidence that press summaries of the judgment were ever produced. It is probable that the

---

39   AWM, Papers of Sir William Webb, 3DRL-2481/Series 1/Folder 9 of 17, Memorandums from McDougall. 19 and 23 August 1948; R.J. Pritchard and S.M. Zaide (eds.), *The Tokyo War Crimes Trial*, 22 vols. (New York: Garland, 1981), vol. 22, p. 49771.

40   The seven justices were Cramer, Röling, Bernard, Zaryanov, Jaranilla, Northcroft and Mei. Pal and Patrick did not respond, at least not in writing.

41   AWM, Papers of Sir William Webb, 3DRL-2481/Series 4/Wallet 17 of 20, Memorandum from McDougall, 10 August 1948.

42   AWM, Papers of Sir William Webb, 3DRL-2481/Series 4/Wallet 17 of 20, Memorandum to General Secretary, 20 September 1948.

CIE recognized at some point how challenging the project would be and quietly abandoned it, for the judgment came to be of a length – some 1,445 pages – far exceeding that of Nuremberg. Not only did it take over six months to draft, but each of its sections was forwarded to the translators as it was completed, and not necessarily in the order in which it would appear in the table of contents. For instance, the section on the law, which was designated 'Part A – Chapter II', was finished last, and the discussion on sentences had not even begun until after the commencement of the reading of the judgment.[43]

The Aftermath

On 22 November, General Douglas MacArthur met with members of the FEC, whom he had summoned to canvass for their recommendations in regard to the verdicts. A division similar to the one seen on the bench – what James Burnham Sedgwick calls 'the manufactured majority' and 'the community of dissent'[44] – was formed at this meeting. While the members of the former group each offered up a terse 'No change', those of the latter either made specific recommendations or expressed a general agreement but with exceptions, such as 'No change, but would not oppose reduction in sentences.' The Indian representative, B.N. Chakravarty, recommended commutation of all death sentences to life imprisonment. The Dutch representative, Baron Evert Joost Lewe van Aduard, notwithstanding the government's strong opposition to Röling's separate dissenting opinion,[45] asked for mitigation of the sentences of five defendants, including the four Röling had found not guilty. The French representative, Zinovy Peshkoff, despite the Quai d'Orsay's disapproval of his request for commutation recommendations,[46] stated, 'Officially no change; personal appeal for clemency.'[47] Perhaps these diplomats thought it would be politic to show a united front with their justices.

The only exception to this majority-minority dichotomy was Canada. E.H. Norman had requested the cabinet's opinion five days prior to the meeting, but E.R. Hopkins did not reply to Norman as he thought a press release of 16 November, issued the day after St Laurent was sworn in as the new prime

---

43   Higurashi, *Tōkyō Saiban*, p. 430.
44   Sedgwick (this volume)
45   Poelgeest, 'The Netherlands and the Tokyo Tribunal', 87-88.
46   Schoepfel (this volume).
47   W. Sebald, *With MacArthur in Japan* (New York: W.W. Norton & Compnay, 1950), pp. 168-69.

minister, to be adequate.[48] He was prepared to discuss mitigation, only to be made to feel inhibited by MacArthur from expressing any view other than 'Not opposed to reduction in sentences.'[49] Nevertheless, unable to give up on mitigation, he later wrote a letter to the supreme commander pleading for the commutation of sentences and arguing that mercy 'will reveal to the Japanese public in a practical manner that the victorious powers are not motivated by a general and indiscriminate sense of revenge'.[50] There is no evidence that MacArthur replied to the letter; in the end, the general upheld all sentences. However, when two of the prisoners on death row appealed to the US Supreme Court for permission to apply for writs of habeas corpus as prisoners of war, the FEC was asked by the US Justice Department to submit an opinion as to whether the IMTFE was an international court. Once again, Canada adhered to its one basic principle on all things related to the punishment of war criminals: to do nothing. Lester Pearson, the new secretary of state for External Affairs, instructed the Canadian ambassador in Washington to 'abstain if this matter is pressed to a vote'.[51] The reason for abstention was that Canada did not consider it 'appropriate that the FEC should in a matter of this kind render an opinion to the United States Department of Justice which was to be used in a domestic court of the United States'.[52] Only Canada and India chose not to cast a vote.

Postscript

While the resumé of E.H. Norman, who had already been known as a prominent Japanologist, might not have been enhanced much by his stint in Tokyo, there is no doubt that the career of Justice E. Stuart McDougall was, as an obituary put it, 'brightened by his appointment as Canadian representative on the Japanese War Crimes Commission between 1946 and 1948'.[53] Each, unfettered by government instructions, left his mark on the Tokyo war crimes trial: McDougall was one of the primary authors of the court's judgment; Norman assisted with vigour the prosecution of some defendants but earnestly pursued

---

48   LAC, RG 25/vol. 3642/File 4060-C-40, Telegram from Norman, 17 November 1948.

49   Sebald, *With MacArthur in Japan*, pp. 168-69.

50   LAC, RG 25/vol. 3642/File 4060-C-40, Letter from Norman to MacArthur, 23 November 1948; Letter from Norman to SEEA, 24 November 1948.

51   LAC, RG 25/vol. 3642/File 4060-C-40, Teletype message from Canadian ambassador, 11 December 1948; RG 25/vol. 5762/File 104-J-(s), Message to Canadian ambassador, 14 December 1948.

52   LAC, RG 25/vol. 5762/File 104-J-(s), Message to Canadian ambassador, 14 December 1948.

53   *Gazette*, 15 February 1957: 'Mr. Justice E.S. McDougall, soldier, scholar dies at 70.'

clemency for others. It is ironic that Ottawa's policy of non-engagement, born of a conviction that 'little useful purpose would be served by Canada' becoming involved in the prosecution of war criminals, freed these two Canadians to accomplish much of consequence.

Bibliography

Kentarō Awaya, *Tōkyō saibanron* (Tokyo: Ōtsuki Shoten, 1989).

Arnold C. Brackman, *The Other Nuremberg: The Untold Story of the Tokyo War Crimes Trial* (New York: William Morrow and Company, Inc., 1987).

Patrick Brode, 'Bruce Macdonald and the Drafting of Canada's War Crimes Regulations – 1945', *Gazette*, 29 (1995), 274-82.

Patrick Brode, *Casual Slaughters and Accidental Judgments: Canadian War Crimes Prosecutions, 1944-1948* (Toronto: University of Toronto Press, 1997).

Helen Forsey, *Eugene Forsey, Canada's Maverick Sage* (Toronto: Dundurn Press, 2012).

Meirion Harries and Susie Harries, *Sheathing the Sword: The Demilitarisation of Japan* (New York: Macmillan Publishing, 1987).

Yoshinobu Higurashi, *Tōkyō Saiban no kokusai kankei* (Tokyo: Mokutakusha, 2002).

Robin Kay (ed.), *Documents on New Zealand External Relations*, vol. 2, *The Surrender and Occupation of Japan* (Wellington: Historical Publications Branch, Department of Internal Affairs, 1982).

W.P. McClemont, 'War Crimes Trials: Criminals Brought to Justice', *Canadian Army Journal*, 1 (3) (1947), 16-20.

Christopher Moore, *The Court of Appeal for Ontario: Defining the Right of Appeal, 1792-2013* (Toronto: University of Toronto Press, 2014).

Nariaki Nakazato, *Paru Hanji: Indo nashonarizumu to Tōkyō Saiban* (Tokyo: Iwanami Shoten, 2011).

Yūichirō Ōoka, *Tōkyō saiban furansujin hanji no muzairon* (Tokyo: Bungei Shunjū, 2012).

Bart van Poelgeest, 'The Netherlands and the Tokyo Tribunal', *Japan Forum*, 4 (1) (1992), 81-90.

R. John Pritchard and Sonia M. Zaide, *The Tokyo War Crimes Trial*, 22 vols. (New York: Garland, 1981).

B.V.A. Röling and Antonio Cassese, *The Tokyo Trial and Beyond* (Cambridge: Polity Press 1993).

William Sebald, *With MacArthur in Japan* (New York: W.W. Norton & Compnay, 1950).

John Stanton, 'Reluctant vengeance: Canada at the Tokyo War Crimes Tribunal', *The Journal of American and Canadian Studies*, 17 (1999), 61-87.

Mark Sweeney, 'The Canadian War Crimes Liaison Detachment – Far East and the Prosecution of Japanese "Minor" War Crimes', unpublished thesis, University of Waterloo (2013).

Yuki Takatori, 'The Forgotten Judge at the Tokyo War Crimes Trial', *Massachusetts Historical Review*, 10 (2008), 115-41.

Jonathan F. Vance, *Objects of Concern: Canadian Prisoners of War through the Twentieth Century* (Vancouver: University of British Columbia Press, 2014).

Illustrations

FIGURE 1   *President William F. Webb (AUST) sitting at his office desk.*

FIGURE 2
Judge William D. Patrick (GB).

FIGURE 3 *Judge Erima H. Northcroft (NZ) at his office desk.*

FIGURE 4 *Judge Radhabinod Pal (IND) sitting at desk.*

FIGURE 5
Judge Bernard V.A. Röling (NL)
standing at desk.

FIGURE 6   *Judge Ivan Zaryanov* (SU) *seated at desk.*

FIGURE 7
Judge E. Stuart McDougall
(*CAN*).

FIGURE 8
Judge Delfin Jaranilla (*PHIL*).

FIGURE 9   *Judge Myron C. Cramer (USA) at desk.*

FIGURE 10   *Judge MEI Ru'ao (CHN).*

FIGURE 11   *Judge Henri Bernard (F) sitting at desk.*

FIGURE 12   *Cramer (US) and Zaryanov (SU) laughing at a party together.*

FIGURE 13   *Group shot of British Commonwealth Judges: McDougall, Patrick, Webb, Northcroft and Pal, 27 August 1946.*

FIGURE 14   *All eleven Judges, formal group photo (Pal, Röling, McDougall, Bernard, Northcroft, Jaranilla, Patrick, Cramer, Webb, Mei, Zaryanov).*

FIGURE 15   *Group photo of Prosecutors (IPS), 22 Oct 1946: Golunsky, Comyns-Carr,*
Keenan, Borgerhoff-Mulder, Mansfield, Quilliam, Chiu (assistant to
prosecutor Xiang), Oneto, Pedro Lopez and Nolan.

FIGURE 16   *Defense lawyers at table: Uzawa Sōmei; two men unknown; Aristide*
Lazarus; James L. Freeman; Ben B. Blakeney.

FIGURE 17   Webb reading the judgment, with Mei and Zaryanov in background, 5 Nov
1948.

FIGURE 18   Party at Philippine embassy, 9 Sept 1947, guests: McDougall, Mei, Ruperto
Kangleon (Philippine Secretary of National Defense), Webb, Mrs Jaranilla,
Röling, Cramer, Jaranilla, some of Kangleon's staff.

FIGURE 19   *US Congressional Party visits* IMTFE, *Reception, 26 August 1946* (*Cramer left and Pal right, unknown*).

FIGURE 20   *US Congressional Party Reception, 26 August 1946* (*Röling right*).

FIGURE 21   *Oneto at lectern addressing in French, 30 Sept 1946.*

FIGURE 22   *Group of judges around a table: Northcroft, Webb, Higgins, McDougall, 4 March 1946.*

FIGURE 23   *All eleven judges seated at bench in court: Pal, Röling, McDougall, Patrick,*
Cramer, Webb, Mei, Zaryanov, Bernard, Northcroft, Jaranilla, Sept 1946.

FIGURE 24   IPS *Group (Prosecutors) at table, with female attorney.*

FIGURE 25
Keenan and MacArthur taking a stroll and talking.

FIGURE 26 *Allied dignitaries at Russian Embassy party celebrating anniversary of October Revolution: Lt Gen EC Whitehead, Mrs Whitehead, Brig Gen SB Akin, Webb, 7 Nov 1946.*

FIGURE 27   *Judges and Gen* HDC *Crerar (Canada): Jaranilla, Webb, Cramer, Röling, Crerar,*
             Bernard, Pal, Mei and Patrick, 6 Aug 1947.

FIGURE 28   *Courtroom with Court in session.*

FIGURE 29 *Japanese Defendants: Doihara, Hata, Hirota, Minami; Tōjō, Oka, Umezu, Araki, Mutō, Hoshino, Hashimoto, Koiso, Nagano, Ōshima, Matsui, Hiranuma, Tōgō, Shigemitsu, Satō, Shimada, Shiratori, Suzuki, Itagaki.*

FIGURE 30 *Photo of partial bench showing judges listening, thinking, reading papers and writing during defense's final summation, 30 March 1948.*

CHAPTER 8

New Zealand's Approach to International Criminal Law from Versailles to Tokyo

Neil Boister *

Why do small states like New Zealand participate in attempts to impose criminal liability on the leaders of major powers for aggression? A cynic might respond that they do so to toady up to their more powerful allies engaged in laundering their own past aggressive behaviour. Yet these strategic outliers that are as defenceless against foreign predation as Belgium was to Germany in 1914, or New Zealand was to potential invasion by Japan in 1941, also act out of self-interest. The deterrent value of international criminal law appeals to them. They try to switch from always having to be 'price takers' – states that have little influence over international affairs – to 'price makers' – states that do influence international affairs.[1] They perceive international law's granting of interest-laden rights to both the weak and powerful alike as an opportunity to try to control the depredations of the more powerful political outliers that threaten them.[2] This chapter explores the extent to which New Zealand self-consciously resorted to international criminal law post the First and Second World Wars to try to both punish and deter leaders of global powers that threatened it. Taking a biographical approach, it focuses on the actions and thoughts of Prime Minister William Massey, who co-chaired the International Commission on Responsibility of the Authors of the War and on the Enforcement of Penalties that sat in 1919 at the preliminary Peace Conference at Versailles, and various New Zealand officials who worked in the International Military Tribunal for the Far East from 1946-48 in Tokyo. In this way it examines how key officials attempted to influence the discourse of realist lawlessness among self-interested states in international society through the agency of international criminal law.

---

* My thanks to Roger Clark and the participants in the Conference 'Law Biography and a Trial: Tokyo's Transnational Histories' held at the University of Heidelberg in December 2015 for their comments.

1 See Y-K. Heng and S.M.A. Aljunied, 'Can Small States be more than Price Takers in Global Governance?' *Global Governance*, 21(2015), 435.

2 I. Hull, *A Scrap of Paper: Breaking and Making International Law during the Great War* (Ithaca: Cornell UP, 2014), p. 320.

Massey in Paris

As early as 1916 it appears that the 'public mind' in New Zealand had some thought of holding individual Germans accountable for war crimes and that Prime Minister Massey favoured the application of the 'the Mosaic law ... to the very letter'.[3] Realizing this goal, however, proved difficult. One of the strategies of small states seeking to be 'price makers' in international relations is to 'bandwagon',[4] and the bandwagon in this case became the attempt to hold the Kaiser accountable for starting the war made at the post-war Peace Conference held at Versailles. Before leaving New Zealand for Europe in 1918, Massey had clarified his feelings about war responsibility: 'The Kaiser was a criminal, and should be made to answer for his crimes.'[5] The Allies had to break the power of Germany 'so that she will not again become dangerous for a century, or centuries, to come'.[6]

As a member of the 'Empire Delegation', Massey became an alternative British representative on the Commission on the Responsibility of the Authors of the War and the Enforcement of Penalties, which studied the question of war guilt and investigated war crimes prior to the Peace Conference.[7] The Commission was riven by two fractures: between those who favoured criminal prosecution for the authors of the war and those who could find no legal precedent for doing so, and between those who felt that the sovereigns of the central powers enjoyed no immunity from prosecution for 'violations of the law and customs of war and principles of humanity' and the dissenting US and Japanese delegates who thought otherwise.[8] Massey was chair of Sub-Commission I on Criminal Acts, mandated to assemble the evidence of the culpable conduct in the inception of the war and in its execution.[9] Sub-Commission II on the Responsibility for the War and Sub-Commission III on the Responsibility for the Violation of the Laws and Customs of War were then to decide on whether and if so how to prosecute. Massey's work as fact-finder

---

3 *New Zealand Parliamentary Debates* (*Hansard*), 7 July 1916, p. 580.

4 Heng and Aljunied, 'Can Small States be more than Price Takers', 136.

5 *Hansard*, 5 December 1918, p. 822.

6 *Hansard*, 28 November 1918, pp. 538-40.

7 Archives New Zealand (ANZ), Lloyd George Papers 404.2, Massey to Lloyd George, 24 Jan 1919.

8 See 'Report of the Commission to the Preliminary Peace Conference', reprinted in *American Journal of International Law* 14 (1920), 95; K. Sellars, *Crimes against Peace and International Law* (Cambridge University Press, 2013) pp. 2-11.

9 R. Kay, 'Caging the Prussian Dragon: New Zealand and the Paris Peace Conference 1919' in J. Crawford and I. McGibbon (eds.), *New Zealand's Great War: New Zealand and the Allies and the First World War* (Auckland: Exisle, 2007), p. 135.

underpinned the Commission's overall finding that the war was 'premeditated by the Central powers', all attempts at peace were deliberately frustrated and Belgium's neutrality deliberately violated.[10] Massey was in favour of trial and punishment; the *Daily Telegraph* reported at the time that 'no one has been more insistent on securing the trial and punishment of those guilty of crimes against the laws and customs of war'.[11] However, the Commission concluded that without a positive legal obligation forbidding wars of aggression 'the acts which brought about the war should not be charged against their authors'.[12]

Massey was among those who sought to ascribe legal responsibility for the war to the Kaiser and who lost the debate to the legal experts in the Commission who were less sanguine about legal responsibility.[13] The US delegates had grumbled about the criticism of their legalistic approach by other delegates;[14] Massey, resentful of US influence at Paris,[15] was among their critics: 'I was quite astonished to find that there were representatives from civilized communities who were strongly of the opinion that heads of States should be exempted from punishment no matter what crimes had been committed.'[16] He felt strongly that the decision to forgo criminal liability and try the Kaiser only for 'a supreme offence against international morality and the sanctity of treaties' was not the 'right thing' to do because of the latter's responsibility 'for the horrors of the war'.[17] Back in New Zealand in 1919 he said:

> I do not think I am a particularly vindictive individual, and if it rests with me alone, and I was quite certain that Germany would not go to war again and was not going to repeat the crimes and offences she committed during the four years and a quarter of war I would say, 'Go, and sin no more.' But I know perfectly well we are not done with Germany. I know perfectly well that if we fail in our duty so far as punishment for the crimes committed is concerned that other nations looking on to-day who only want

---

10   See 'Report of the Commission', pp. 107, 112.

11   H.J. Constable, *From Ploughboy to Premier: A New Life of The Right Hon. William Ferguson Massey, PC* (London: John Marlowe Savage & Co Ltd, 1925), pp. 13-14.

12   See 'Report of the Commission', p. 120.

13   G. Simpson, 'International Criminal Justice and the Past' in G. Boas, W. Schabas and M. Scharf (eds.), *International Criminal Justice: Legitimacy and Coherence* (Cheltenham: Edward Elgar, 2012), p. 123, p. 132.

14   See 'Report of the Commission', p. 149.

15   G.A.R. Riddell, *Lord Riddell's Intimate Diary of the Peace Conference and After: 19-18-1923* (London: Gollancz, 1931), p. 307.

16   *Hansard*, 2 September 1919, p. 41.

17   Ibid., pp. 41-43.

leaders and who would be willing to take the risks that Germany took and be guilty of the deeds Germany was guilty of in the hope they would be successful where Germany failed. We have to do something to those nations of which I am thinking – something that will frighten them; make them understand that if they commit a crime against humanity and law and order, so far as nations are concerned, they will be held responsible and punished accordingly.[18]

Although New Zealand joined the League of Nations, Massey doubted the capacity of a League made of small powers to guarantee peace and did not share the faith of its supporters that its foundation heralded a new era of peace.[19] It would not 'put an end to war'[20]; only a combination of great powers including the US could enforce peace.[21] Ironically, however, in Massey's view it was New Zealand's post-war involvement at Versailles that cemented her status as an equal partner within rather than a dependency of the British Empire,[22] while the League provided the authority for New Zealand to take mandated control of former German territories in the South Pacific, territory Massey considered a valuable prize of the Great War.[23]

New Zealand at Tokyo

The idea of imposing a punitive peace through the application of war crimes was resurrected when New Zealand was asked to participate in the Tokyo war crimes trials at the end of World War II. In the inter-war period, New Zealand had begun to take a more independent approach in international affairs, aligning herself with small powers against Britain in the League, and favouring imposition of sanctions on Germany, Italy and Japan for violating the international prohibitions on the use of force.[24] Future prime minister Walter Nash recalled:

---

18   Ibid., p. 41.
19   G. Chaudron, *New Zealand in the League of Nations: The Beginnings of an Independent Foreign Policy, 1919-1939* (London: McFarland & Co, 2012), p. 44.
20   *Hansard*, 2 September 1919, pp. 39, 40.
21   Ibid., p. 51.
22   Ibid., p. 36.
23   G.H. Scholefield, *William Ferguson Massey MP PC Prime Minister of New Zealand, 1912-1925: A Personal Biography* (Wellington: Harry H. Thombs Ltd, 1925), p. 15.
24   G. Daniels, 'New Zealand and the Occupation of Japan' in I. Nish (ed.), *The British Commonwealth and the Occupation of Japan, 1945-1952: Personal Encounters and Government*

New Zealand called for League action in support of China: New Zealand urged the League to take up the cause of Republican Spain. New Zealand banned the shipment of scrap iron to Japan as far back as 1936. The policy of appeasement as it was pursued during these years in both in Europe and the Far East was vigorously opposed.[25]

During the war, New Zealand joined other small states within the UN War Crimes Committee (UNWCC) in support of the failed attempt by the Czechoslovakian delegate, Bohuslav Ečer, to get the UNWCC to adopt a resolution condemning aggression as a crime.[26] At war's end New Zealand remained anxious about Japanese imperialism.[27] In a letter to the British Minister for Dominion Affairs, Prime Minister Peter Fraser called for 'radical changes in Japanese political, social and economic institutions ... to prevent the rebirth of Japanese aggression and to promote conditions which will ensure that a co-operative Japan may later come into being.'[28] New Zealand attended the signing of the Instrument of Surrender on the USS *Missouri* in Tokyo Bay and participated in the Far Eastern Advisory Committee (FEAC) and then the Far Eastern Commission (FEC).[29]

Eschewing war crimes trials itself because most of its regular soldiers had fought in Europe and Africa and ex-prisoners of Japan were unwilling to return to give evidence,[30] in 1946 New Zealand was invited by General MacArthur, Supreme Commander of the Allied Powers (SCAP), to nominate a judge and prosecutor to the International Tribunal to be held at Tokyo.[31] Initially reluc-

---

        Assessments (Leiden: Brill, 2013), p. 64.

25   W. Nash, *New Zealand: A Working Democracy* (New York: Duel, Sloan and Pearce, 1943), p. 36.

26   W.A. Schabas, 'Origins of Criminalization of Aggression: How Crimes Against Peace Became the "Supreme International Crime"', in M. Politi and G. Nesi (eds.), *The International Criminal Court and the Crime of Aggression* (Aldershot: Ashgate, 2004), p. 17, p. 31, fn. 55.

27   F.S. Dunn, *Peace-making and the Settlement with Japan* (Princeton University Press, 1963), p. 125.

28   R. Kay (ed.), *Documents on New Zealand External Relations*, vol. 2, *The Surrender and Occupation of Japan* (Wellington: Government Printer, 1982), Minister of External Affairs (Fraser) to Secretary of State for Dominion Affairs (Addison), 11 August 1945, p. 289, fn. 1.

29   See 'Statement on the Establishment of the Far Eastern Commission to Formulate Policies for the Carrying out of Surrender Terms', *US Department of State Bulletin* 13 (1945), 545.

30   ANZ, EA 106/3/22, Part 1, 'JB', *Japanese War Crimes: Interim Report and Critique*, to NZ Dept. of External Affairs.

31   ANZ, EA 106/3/22, Part 1, UNWCC, Special Far Eastern and Pacific Committee, *Summary of Recommendations Concerning Japanese War Crimes and Atrocities*, SFEC 1, 13 August 1945,

tant, once the process was underway New Zealand's political leaders became more enthusiastic about joining, asserting an interest in prosecution of Japan's wartime leaders.[32] Announcing Justice Harvey Northcroft's appointment, then Acting Prime Minister Walter Nash justified New Zealand's participation out of its 'special interest in the settlement in Japan and in the maintenance of peace and security in the Pacific' and through a desire 'to establish once again and ensure recognition for all time of the rule of law in the relations of nations and peoples of the world.'[33] According to Foss Shanahan, Deputy Head of External Affairs, the goal was to engender public support for participation because '[o]ur people are singularly apathetic in matters of this kind and, in view of the importance of the Pacific'.[34] Count 10 of the indictment laid at Tokyo charged planning, preparing, initiating or waging an aggressive war against New Zealand; however, both the hope of engaging New Zealand's people and of ensuring recognition of the rule of law at an international level were to prove vain.[35] New Zealand proved somewhat powerless and rather timid in realizing these goals. Pleading lack of information, it declined the invitation to send a list of war criminals to Tokyo,[36] and although its officials on the ground in Tokyo and Washington strongly favoured indictment of Emperor Hirohito, Wellington accepted the US view that he was a mere puppet.[37] The New Zealand prosecutor made an implicit protest against this decision through an objection he made to the initial US draft indictment which joined Japan with the Allies in bringing charges. He felt that doing so would perpetuate the myth that the emperor could not be charged and that Japan was innocent.[38]

Paragraph VI(a).

32   ANZ, File no. EA 106/3/22, Part 1, Secretary of State for Dominion Affairs to Minister for External Affairs, 24 October 1945.

33   Kay (ed.), *Documents II*, no. 650, Statement by the Acting Prime Minister on Nominations to the IMTFE, 18 January 1946, pp.1507-8.

34   Ministry of Foreign Affairs Archive, 59/2/49 Pt.1, Shanahan to Quilliam, 25 October 1946, cited in A. Trotter, 'New Zealanders and the International Military Tribunal for the Far East', *New Zealand Journal of History*, 23 (2) (1989), 143.

35   Trotter, 'New Zealanders and the IMT', 143.

36   Kay, *Documents II*, no. 651, New Zealand Member of the Far Eastern Commission, Tokyo, to Minister of External Affairs, 18 January 1946, and no. 652, Minister of External Affairs to New Zealand Member, FEC, Tokyo, pp. 1508-10.

37   ANZ, EA 106/3/22, Part 2, Memorandum from Department of External Affairs, Wellington, to NZ High Commission, London, 2 February 1946.

38   ANZ, EA 106/3/22, part 2, *Explanatory Memorandum on Indictment* accompanying Quilliam's letter to NZ External Affairs of 29 April 1946.

The Prosecutor: Ronald Quilliam

The Associate Prosecutor for New Zealand, Brig. R.H. Quilliam, crown prosecutor in Taranaki and former Deputy Adjutant-General of the New Zealand Army,
was one of New Zealand's leading criminal law barristers.[39] Quilliam understood that New Zealand's goal was to 'demonstrate the importance New
Zealand attaches to the trials, and ... show that Japanese and Pacific affairs are
of vital interest to us'.[40] As a member of the International Prosecution Section
(IPS) executive committee, he was well positioned to comment on progress
towards these goals. But the political nature of the enterprise did not sit well
with him. He did not like the decision not to indict the emperor[41] or the charges
relating to the Mongolian hostilities of 1938 and 1939 included at the behest of
the Russians (who thought they were vulnerable to charges of aggression),[42]
and reported with unease Tribunal President Webb's view that MacArthur was
trying to sabotage the trials to please a conservative Japanese government
upon which SCAP had come to rely to implement occupation policy.[43]

Most of his feedback was of a more technical kind, however, and it was
entirely negative. While his appointment was lauded in his home town of New
Plymouth as an opportunity to reaffirm the standards of 'British' justice,[44] he
was quick to damn the US effort after he arrived in Tokyo. The indictment was
'in no way ready, and ... little progress had been made with the collection of
evidence and the selection of defendants.'[45] Highly critical of the trial set-up,
with Webb in control of the sole microphone,[46] he thought Webb incompetent,[47]
the IPS 'a United States organization'[48], US defence counsel intent upon obtain-

---

39   Trotter, 'New Zealanders and the IMT', 147.

40   Kay, *Documents II*, no. 692, New Zealand Associate Prosecutor, IMTFE, to Secretary of
      External Affairs, 26 August 1946, pp. 1637-38.

41   ANZ, 106/3/22, Part 6, Quilliam to Foss Shanahan, External Affairs, Wellington, 31 October
      1947.

42   ANZ, EA 106/3/22, Part 7, Brigadier R.H. Quilliam, *Report on the Proceedings of the Interna-
      tional Military Tribunal for the Far East*, p. 17; Kay, *Documents II*, no. 709, New Zealand
      Associate Prosecutor, IMTFE, to Secretary of External Affairs, 3 June 1947, p. 1671-72.

43   Kay, *Documents II*, no. 680, New Zealand Associate Prosecutor, IMTFE, to Secretary of
      External Affairs, 2 July 1946, p. 1606 at p. 1607.

44   'Brigadier Quilliam Honoured', *New Zealand Law Journal*, 22 (3) (1946), 40.

45   Quilliam, *Report*, p.2.

46   Ibid., pp.7-8.

47   Ibid., pp. 9-10.

48   Ibid., p. 5.

ing 'notoriety',[49] Japanese defence counsel evasive,[50] and was disparaging about by the prosecutors from other legal and linguistic traditions[51] and unable to fathom the Japanese public whom he thought 'inscrutable and inexplicable'.[52] His spleen was directed principally at Chief Prosecutor Joseph Keenan[53] whom he considered 'quite unsuitable'.[54] Keenan, in his view, deliberately sidelined British Commonwealth lawyers,[55] kept the other prosecutors in the dark,[56] made little arrangement for his absences,[57] performed weakly in court,[58] and was a drunk.[59] In July 1946, Keenan's principal antagonist,[60] Quilliam failed in an attempt to depose him upon his absence in Washington.[61] Quilliam vented his frustration to Wellington that the US was making 'a very bad job of' the trial for which they 'must be held responsible'. Wellington made it clear that the US continued to support Keenan and Quilliam backed off.[62] He made then withdrew a request to be relieved,[63] before, having done all in his opinion that he usefully could,[64] returning home in December 1947 with the prosecution incomplete. His legacy was a trenchantly put view that there should be no further trials of Class A prisoners, which became the official New Zealand standpoint.[65] Once home he kept his criticism of US conduct of the trial

---

49   ANZ, EA 106/3/22, Part 2, Quilliam to External Affairs, 5 June 1946.

50   Kay, *Documents II*, no. 708, New Zealand Associate Prosecutor, IMTFE, to Secretary of External Affairs, 9 May 1947, p. 1669.

51   Kay, *Documents II*, no. 669, New Zealand Associate Prosecutor, IMTFE, to Secretary of External Affairs, 24 April 1946, pp. 1559-64.

52   Kay, *Documents II*, no. 680, New Zealand Associate Prosecutor, IMTFE, to Secretary of External Affairs, 2 July 1946, p. 1606, at p. 1608.

53   Quilliam, *Report*, p. 11.

54   Ibid., p. 12.

55   Ibid.

56   ANZ, EA 106/3/22, Part 1, Legation Washington to External Affairs, 26 January 1946.

57   Quilliam, *Report*, p. 12.

58   Ibid.

59   ANZ, EA 106/3/22, Part 3, Quilliam to McIntosh of 25 June 1946.

60   Kay, *Documents II*, no. 678, New Zealand Associate Prosecutor, IMTFE, to Secretary of External Affairs, 25 June 1946, pp. 1601-4.

61   ANZ, EA 106/3/22, Part 3, Quilliam to McIntosh, 25 June 1946.

62   ANZ, EA 106/3/22, Part 3, Quilliam to McIntosh, 26 July 1946.

63   Kay, *Documents II*, no. 725, Former New Zealand Associate Prosecutor, IMTFE, to Secretary of External Affairs, 22 March 1948, pp. 1712-13.

64   Trotter, 'New Zealanders and the IMT', 152.

65   Kay, *Documents II*, no. 701, New Zealand Associate Prosecutor, IMTFE, to Secretary of External Affairs, 24 January 1947, p. 1652.

private,[66] but his experience had transformed him into a public critic of US conduct in Japan. In *The Times* of 4 February 1948 he commented: 'The Emperor has renounced his divinity. It has been taken up by General MacArthur.'[67]

Quilliam's response to the trial was not limited to the carping of a displaced professional. Alive to the importance of establishing the criminality of wars of aggression in East Asia and the Pacific through the trial,[68] he was also aware of the historical background to this effort: 'The demand that arose during the 1914-1918 World War for the punishment of the Kaiser and the many efforts made since to outlaw war and bring world security, cannot be disregarded.'[69] But he clearly thought that a shorter, simpler, rougher process would have achieved these goals. Mindful of the difficulties caused by the scope and complexity of the events covered in the indictment,[70] he argued that this flowed from a flaw in the Tokyo Charter. It had broken with the assumptions in the Cairo and Potsdam Declarations by failing to proclaim that Japan's actions during the period amounted to aggression. He felt that the IPS should have been left only to prove the individual responsibility of the accused. When the Charter left it to the IPS to try to prove that Japan's actions were aggressive, it introduced a discomforting uncertainty into the proceedings:[71]

> If the Prosecution are required to discharge the onus of proving affirmatively that Japan was guilty of waging an aggressive war, it would appear to follow that the Tribunal has the power to find that in fact Japan was guiltless, and that on the other hand, the countries of the United Nations in fighting against Japan were guilty of initiating and waging aggressive war. It would probably shock the people of those countries if they realised that such a finding is legally possible. They would understand that the Tribunal might decide that on the evidence submitted to it, a particular individual was not guilty. They would, however, be unable to understand how it could come about that Japan could be exonerated, and their own countries held guilty. It would appear to be scarcely credible that the Governments of the countries of the United Nations have agreed, by

---

66   Quilliam, *Report*, p. 8.
67   L.C. Green, 'Law and Administration in Present-Day Japan', *Current Legal Problems*, 1 (1948), 188-96, fn. 23.
68   Quilliam, *Report*, p. 15.
69   Ibid., p. 17.
70   Ibid., p. 4.
71   Ibid., pp. 17-18.

undertaking the prosecution, to the Tribunal deciding the question of the responsibility of the War.[72]

The abstract possibility of opening the question of responsibility for the war influenced Quilliam's view that serious consideration should be given before the laying of a charge of crimes against peace again.[73] He appeared unconvinced of the goal of developing a crime of aggression that had universal applicability, including to the Allies themselves.

The Judge: Erima Harvey Northcroft

Justice Northcroft was a decorated World War I veteran who had been appointed to the bench in New Zealand in 1935.[74] Selected for the IMTFE in early 1946,[75] he came to Tokyo ignorant of international law, but according to Trotter with a strong sense of his function as a representative of a 'Common law' country intent upon establishing itself as a Pacific nation with an interest (in this case) in Japan.[76] Schooled in the British legal tradition, Northcroft struggled to assimilate to US modes of running a court.[77] He was uncomfortable with the propagandistic theatricality of the trial, which he considered 'derogatory of the dignity of the court'[78] and thought the behaviour of the US defence counsel 'technical and obstructive to the greatest degree'.[79] Condemning the US administration of the trial,[80] he warned that 'the Prime Minister and New Zealand must be prepared for a disappointment' and hoped

---

72   Ibid., pp. 18-19.

73   Ibid.

74   A. Trotter, 'Justice Northcroft' in Y. Tanaka, T. McCormack and G. Simpson (eds.), *Beyond Victor's Justice? The Tokyo War Crimes Trial Revisited* (Leiden and Boston: Nijhoff, 2011), p. 81.

75   ANZ, EA 106/3/22, Part 1, Letter of Appointment to Justice Northcroft, 18 January 1946.

76   Trotter, 'New Zealanders and the IMT', 147-48.

77   ANZ, EA 106/3/22, Part 3, Extract from Periodical Report no.6 of the UK Liaison Minister in Japan, para. 138, June 1946.

78   ANZ, EA 106/3/22, Part 3, Northcroft to AD McIntosh, Secretary for External Affairs, Wellington, 2 July 1946.

79   ANZ, EA 106/3/22, Part 5, Northcroft to Chief Justice Sir Humphrey O'Leary, 18 March 1947.

80   ANZ, EA 106/3/22, Part 5, Northcroft to Chief Justice Sir Humphrey O'Leary, 21 March 1947.

only that the judgment itself would be of value to future students of international law and indicate that the bench had done its work properly.[81]

Although aware of their linguistic shortcomings, Northcroft was on the whole moderate in his view of his fellow judges.[82] The exception was President Webb. His pre-trial acceptance of Webb when they had worked closely together,[83] switched to denunciation during the course of the trial as Northcroft, together with the Canadian McDougall and the Scot Lord Patrick, fell out completely with Webb.[84] Northcroft blamed many of the trial's shortcomings on Webb's poor control of proceedings[85] and absences from Tokyo[86], which he thought would 'condemn the trial utterly'.[87] Webb in turn was bitingly critical of Northcroft's doubts as to whether Australia and New Zealand had been attacked or had been attackers because they had declared war against Japan pre-emptively.[88] Northcroft's strongest criticism was of Webb's failure to immediately give reasons for dismissing the defence motions to the jurisdiction of the court made *ad litem*:[89]

> A strong or even sensible President would have cleared off the questions of law at the time we heard the argument. There is a simple view which most of us regard as unanswerable. We think the Charter declares the law and that we are merely a fact finding body. If the law of the Charter is bad we are not empowered to review it. Our appointment is only to implement the Charter and we are given no authority to pronounce upon its statement of the law. If any of us disagreed with the law of the Charter we should have declined to accept office under it. Others, including some who hold the foregoing conclusions, think this is an opportunity to write learned treatises on international law in defence of the Charter, but each

---

81   Kay, *Documents II*, no. 681, New Zealand Member, IMTFE, to Secretary of External Affairs, 2 July 1946, p. 1610, at pp. 1611-13.

82   ANZ, EA 106/3/22, Part 5, Northcroft to M Myers, Wellington, 18 May 1947.

83   Australian National Library, MS/5192, Rough drafts of letters from Webb to MacArthur, Webb to Department of External Affairs, Canberra, 7 March 1946; ANZ, EA 106/3/22, Part 1, Northcroft to Prime Minister Peter Fraser, 11 March 1946.

84   See N. Boister and R. Cryer, *The Tokyo International Military Tribunal: A Reappraisal* (Oxford University Press, 2008), pp. 82-83.

85   ANZ, EA 106/3/22, Part 5, Northcroft to Chief Justice O'Leary, 18 March 1947.

86   ANZ, EA 106/3/22, Part 6, Northcroft to Foss Shanahan, 24 December 1947.

87   ANZ, 106/3/22, Part 6, Northcroft to Chief Justice O'Leary, Wellington, 10 November 1947.

88   Australian War Memorial (AWM), Papers of William Flood Webb, Series 4, Wallet 19, 3DRL/248, Memorandum to: All Judges, From: The President, 13 September 1948.

89   Trotter, 'Justice Northcroft', 85-86.

upon different grounds. Still others, one of whom was of the original nine, deny the law of the Charter and our right to try these accused at all. One of these dissentients has written a draft 'dissenting judgment' of no less than 250 pages and another dissentient has written not so lengthily but still at very considerable length. This Tribunal, if it is to make a useful contribution to international law, must be entirely or substantially of one mind. The chance to secure that, I fear, has gone.[90]

In a letter to Chief Justice O'Leary of New Zealand, he noted:

> If a Court of this standing is seriously divided, and I feel sure it will be, then the modern advances in international law towards the outlawry of war may suffer a serious setback. The Judgment of the Nuremberg Court seems to be generally approved and considered a valuable contribution to international law. Varying opinions from this Court including sharp dissent from Nuremberg must be disastrous. This I feel sure will happen.[91]

He too sought permission to resign.[92] Prime Minister Fraser consulted the retired Chief Justice Sir Michael Myers who recommended Northcroft remain in Tokyo to try to preserve the trial's legitimacy and relations with the US and Australia; Northcroft reluctantly agreed.

This episode reveals that when Northcroft signalled to Wellington that the broader goals that New Zealand had set out with were not going to be satisfactorily achieved, Wellington shifted the goal to keeping its alliances intact,[93] a segue Massey would have been entirely familiar with. Whether the Allies valued that alliance to the same degree is doubtful. When Webb was recalled to Australia, the less senior and less experienced American Judge Cramer was appointed as acting President over Northcroft's head because of MacArthur's view of New Zealand's 'insignificance ... as a world power'.[94]

Northcroft then limited his goals to trying to ensure the production of a properly written final judgment.[95] Excluding Webb, Northcroft, Lord Patrick

---

90   ANZ, EA 106/3/22, Part 5, Northcroft to Chief Justice O'Leary, 18 March 1947.

91   Ibid.

92   ANZ, EA 106/3/22, Part 5, Northcroft to former Chief Justice Myers, 18 May 1947.

93   Kay, *Documents II*, no. 707, Former Chief Justice (Myers) to the New Zealand Member, IMTFE, 24 April 1947, pp. 1667-68.

94   TNA, UK, FO 371 63820, F15007, Gascoigne to Foreign Office, 11 November 1947.

95   NZ Ministry of Foreign Affairs Archive, MFA 52/2/49, Pt. 3, Northcroft to Shanahan, 21 May 1948, cited in Trotter, 'New Zealanders and the IMT', 153.

and McDougall took control of its preparation.[96] Northcroft later defended what became the majority judgment as having

> conducted an historical inquiry into the actions of Japan, and ... traced the proximate causes. There is set upon its findings a seal of authority and, I trust, impartiality which cannot attend the work of any historian of recent events, for the Tribunal's decision was reached upon all the available evidence and after the fullest opportunity had been afforded for the presentation of opposing views.[97]

An exercise in formalism, the judgment takes the view that the Allies had a belligerent's right under international law to try war criminals including for crimes against peace.[98] However, it was the Charter that posited the law, and did not in Northcroft's view permit of an enquiry like that undertaken by Justice Pal into the state of the law.[99] Northcroft sustained his commitment to the Charter in his application of the death penalty (no longer available in New Zealand) because it was provided for in the Charter and he had agreed to sit on the tribunal.[100]

Northcroft did not, however, agree with Quilliam's argument that the Charter should have proclaimed that Japan's actions amounted to aggression, which in his opinion 'would have made plausible the popular criticism that such trials are acts of vengeance or retribution visited by victorious nations upon the vanquished'.[101] In the instant case, the defence had been given an ample opportunity to put the argument that Japan had acted in self-defence and this evidence had been refuted by a reasoned and objective enquiry.[102] Liability was individual and *tu quoque* arguments without purchase:

> The Tribunal did not attach a criminal liability to the Japanese nation, nor inflict punishment upon that nation. It found liable and ordered the punishment of certain individuals who knowingly used the resources of the Japanese nation to further a course of criminal conduct. It may be

---

96   ANZ, EA 106/3/22, Part 5, Northcroft to Myers, Wellington, 18 May 1947.

97   ANZ, EA 106/3/22, Part 9, Mr Justice EH Northcroft, *Memorandum for the Right Honourable the Prime Minister Upon the Tokyo Trials 1946-1948*, p. 3.

98   AWM, Papers of William Flood Webb, Series 1, Wallet 6 of 17, 3DRL/2481, *Jurisdiction: Opinion of Members for the United Kingdom, Canada and New Zealand*, no date, p. 20.

99   Northcroft, *Memorandum for the PM*, p. 3.

100   ANZ, EA 106/3/22, Part 9, Northcroft to PM Peter Fraser, 17 March 1949.

101   Northcroft, *Memorandum for the PM*, p. 14.

102   Ibid., p. 18.

alleged that other men at other times have acted similarly, and were not put on trial; but this allegation, even if it is well-founded, can furnish no moral or legal justification or excuse for the criminal conduct of those persons who were brought to justice.[103]

He agreed, however, that further Class A trials were undesirable, the substantial purpose of Nuremberg and Tokyo being to establish a code of international criminal law.[104] He tentatively cautioned that Tokyo's deterrent effect depended on its level of support and suggested New Zealand seek broader support through the establishment of a permanent international criminal court with jurisdiction over all major international crimes, including crimes against peace, before embarking on such an exercise again.[105] Northcroft's belated reward for staying, what became for him, an uncomfortable distance, was a knighthood, conferred in 1949.

The 'Devil' (an 'Industrious Person with Legal Qualifications'[106]): Quentin Quentin-Baxter

The burden on Northcroft of processing whether the evidence supported the mass of factual allegations made by the prosecution was in large part shouldered by Captain Quentin Quentin-Baxter, a young lawyer sent from New Zealand to help him. In June of 1946, Quilliam asked for someone to replace Northcroft's associate Evans so Evans could help Quilliam[107] and in July, Northcroft supported this request. Help did not arrive in the person of Quentin-Baxter until June 1947.[108] Quentin-Baxter worked a minor miracle, reading and summarizing all of the evidence relating to the principal charges of conspiracy to commit crimes against peace (a process that took nearly a year). Northcroft commented:

His work is so good that, unlike the contributions of others similarly employed, we are able to adopt his treatises on difficult and important

---

103   Ibid., p. 19.

104   ANZ, EA 106/3/22, Part 5, Northcroft to Foss Shanahan, NZ External Affairs, 20 April 1947.

105   Northcroft, *Memorandum for the PM*, pp. 22-23.

106   Trotter, 'Justice Northcroft', 85.

107   Kay, *Documents II*, no. 676, Associate Prosecutor for New Zealand, IMTFE, to Secretary for External Affairs 5 June 1946, p. 1593 at p. 1596, fn. 6.

108   Trotter, 'Justice Northcroft', 89.

aspects of Far Eastern historical developments in large measure with only slight alteration either in substance or expression.[109]

Although he worked in 'close association' with the judges and had taken a 'substantial part' in its preparation under their direction, Quentin-Baxter's summary forms a significant part of the majority judgment.[110] Alarmed, Webb complained ineffectually in mid-1948 that 'the joint judgment now being so well prepared in the first instance by Lt. Col. Hasting and Captain Baxter be abandoned' inter alia because it 'interposes new and unauthorised advocates between the parties and the Tribunal'.[111] Northcroft's confidence in Quentin-Baxter's analysis allayed some of Northcroft's apprehensions about the trial:

> The guilt or innocence of each individual depended not upon a single act or circumstance, but upon the cumulative effect of all evidence showing the membership of that individual in a conspiracy to wage an aggressive war or wars, his knowledge of the purposes of that conspiracy, and the part which he played in promoting it. It was only by studying the whole record of the individual concerned that his responsibility for crimes against peace could be assessed.[112]

Quentin-Baxter later admitted that he had neither experience nor knowledge of Japan and he consciously decided not to acquire it; he worked solely with the evidence before him.[113] Tellingly, his lecture on the IMTFE delivered to the 1949 New Zealand Law Conference discussed the events leading to war under the heading 'The Background of History'.[114] He claimed that the judgment 'establishes a chain of reasoning and a standard of objective enquiry which refutes the allegation that the nations which established this Tribunal have made improper use of their power....'.[115]

Nevertheless, the judgment's factual account is linear in that it denudes the story of complexity and contradiction, hegemonic in that it denudes the story

109   Letter from Northcroft to Dr Robert Hector Quentin-Baxter, 27 September 1948 cited by Trotter, 'Justice Northcroft', 89.

110   Trotter, 'New Zealanders and the IMT', 154.

111   AWM, Papers of Sir William Flood Webb, Series 4, Wallet 19, 3DRL/2481, Subject: Draft Judgment, Memorandum to: All Judges, Memorandum From: The President, 17 May 1948.

112   Northcroft, *Memorandum for the PM*, p. 11.

113   Trotter, 'New Zealanders and the IMT', 152.

114   Q. Quentin-Baxter, 'The Task of the International Military Tribunal at Tokyo', *New Zealand Law Journal*, 25 (1950), 133-35.

115   Quentin-Baxter, 'The Task of the International Military Tribunal', 138.

of all Allied responsibility, and highly subjective in that it seeks to ascribe blame to king-pins. Minear's criticism of the Tokyo judgment as representing the work of lawyers untutored in history[116] should not, however, be directed at Quentin-Baxter but rather at the methodological shortcomings of the prosecutorial analysis of history in international criminal trials generally. Participation in the Tokyo trial process, no matter how methodologically weak, did turn Quentin-Baxter into a believer in the validity of international criminal law as a response to the 'unscrupulous use of power'.[117] He went on to a stellar career in international law, arguing New Zealand's case in the nuclear test cases.[118]

The Observer: Harold Evans

Perhaps the most far-sighted New Zealand participant in the process was RAF Flight Lieutenant Harold Evans who, on behalf of the Department of External Affairs, accompanied Northcroft to Tokyo as his secretary and assisted Quilliam in developing the case for the prosecution. Evans, a lawyer recently appointed to the department,[119] wrote a series of articles describing the early phases of the trial in which he conceded that there had been criticism of its process.[120] In his communication with his superiors in Wellington he was more honest. He was scathingly critical of Keenan's cross examination of Tōjō, noting Keenan was 'entirely subject to his witness' and that Tōjō had put the self-defence rationale strongly.[121] After attending the Allied Council for Japan in 1948 he called it 'a debating society'.[122] Prior to Tokyo, Evans's political prospects had been good as he had been personal assistant to Prime Minister Peter Fraser, but in Tokyo he made the political error of marrying the daughter of the German Naval Attaché, Admiral Paul Wenneker. In his review of Tōjō's cross examination he cites

---

116   See R.H. Minear, *Victor's Justice: The Tokyo War Crimes Trial* (Princeton University Press, 1971), pp. 134-40.

117   Quentin-Baxter, 'The Task of the International Military Tribunal', 137.

118   He was a member of the International Law Commission and NZ's delegate to the Commission on Human Rights.

119   Trotter, 'New Zealanders and the IMT', 148.

120   H. Evans, 'The Trial of Major Japanese War Criminals', *New Zealand Law Journal*, 23 (1947), 8.

121   ANZ, EA 106/3/22, Part 6, Evans to AD McIntosh, Secretary of External Affairs, New Zealand, 9 January 1948.

122   Kay, *Documents II*, no. 513, Associate to the New Zealand Member, IMTFE, to Secretary for External Affairs, 9 January 1948, p. 1700 at p. 1701.

the opinion of one who has spent many years in Japan, who seems to know a good deal about the Japanese mentality, and for whose opinions I have formed a considerable respect over the last six months. He describes this unequal contest between Keenan and TOJO as 'the greatest blow the occupation has yet sustained'.[123]

One wonders whether he was relaying a German Admiral's view of the trial. Relegated to provincial Christchurch as a magistrate after the trial, the influence of Tokyo emerged in his post-retirement career as a major peace campaigner who helped engineer the International Court of Justice's advisory opinion on the legality of nuclear weapons.[124]

Wellington

The increasingly strenuous criticism of the trial coming from its own personnel in Tokyo soon rang alarm bells in Wellington. McIntosh had responded to Quilliam in early 1946 that '[i]n practice, of course, the Americans must dominate the scene but there is no reason why the international forms should not be preserved.'[125] In September 1946, Prime Minister Peter Fraser criticized the replacement of US judge Higgins by Cramer some way into the trial in a letter to the New Zealand ambassador in Washington.[126] It may be that Webb was recalled to Australia because Fraser had complained about him to the Australian prime minister at the Canberra Conference in 1947.[127] By 1948, New Zealand had limited its goal to the establishment of 'a code of international criminal law'.[128] It took a dim view of the US Supreme Court hearing an appeal

---

123   Kay, *Documents II*, no. 513, Associate to the New Zealand Member, IMTFE, to Department of External Affairs, 7 May 1948, p. 1701.

124   See Harold Evans, 'The *World Court Project* on Nuclear Weapons and International Law', *New Zealand Law Journal* (1993), 249-52.

125   Kay, *Documents II*, no. 676, Secretary of External Affairs to the New Zealand Associate Prosecutor, IMTFE, 21 May 1946, p. 1590 at p.1592.

126   ANZ, EA 106/3/22, Part 4, Fraser to NZ Minister in Washington, 20 September 1946.

127   Lord Patrick to Gascoigne, 9 October 1947, LC02 2992, Public Records Office, United Kingdom, cited in M. Harries and S. Harries, *Sheathing the Sword: The Demilitarisation of Japan* (New York: Macmillan, 1987), p. 167.

128   Kay, *Documents II*, External Affairs Wellington to First Secretary, New Zealand Embassy, Washington, 5 July 1948, referred to on p. 1717, fn. 7.

from an international tribunal[129] and of the parole of prisoners without agreement from the FEC,[130] and resisted US pressure for early release.[131] But it was unenthusiastic about participation in a further trial, warning the FEC that their duration presented a 'grave danger of their becoming farcical or at least open to serious criticism.'[132] A Soviet suggestion that Hirohito be tried together with those in charge of Japan's bio-warfare programme was decried by McIntosh as 'irresponsible' and politically unwise, even if there was substance to the allegations.[133]

Conclusion

New Zealand's narrow aim in joining the post-war reckonings in Paris and Tokyo was to achieve its traditional foreign policy objective; to show solidarity with its allies. It succeeded in doing so, although its experience raised doubts about how much they valued its solidarity. The broader aim of contributing to the emergence of international norms that might serve to maintain its own security by deterring powerful outliers was not attained because of the failure of the trial to secure that norm. New Zealand's involvement in these international enterprises tracks a repetitive descent from the utopian ideal of ensuring respect for the global rule of law to an apology for the brutal realism which emerged: the pursuit of the goal of tying down of political outliers like Germany and then Japan in principles of global justice was frustrated by a range of factors beyond its control. Justice Northcroft's wistful complaint to his prime minister about New Zealand's role at Tokyo sums up why:

> I suppose it is unlikely for a long time ... that there will be another invitation to send a New Zealand Judge on a similar errand. Were such a proposal to be made, however, I suggest it would require the gravest

129   Kay, *Documents II*, no.735, Minister of External Affairs to the New Zealand Ambassador, Washington, 17 December 1948, p. 1731.

130   ANZ, EA 106/3/22, Part 11, Memorandum from External Affairs to the NZ Ambassador, Washington 19 June 1950.

131   ANZ, EA W2619 106/3/22, Part 13, Aide Memoire attached to Memorandum from Office of NZ High Commissioner to Secretary of External Affairs, NZ, 9 June 1954.

132   Kay, *Documents II*, no. 729, Counsellor, New Zealand Legation, Washington, to Secretary of External Affairs, 29 July 1948, pp. 1719-21.

133   Kay, *Documents II*, no. 452, First Secretary, New Zealand Embassy Washington, to Secretary of External Affairs, 28 June 1950, and no. 453, Secretary of External Affairs to the First Secretary, New Zealand Embassy, Washington, 14 August 1950, pp. 1124-35.

consideration if, as with this Tribunal, it were to be substantially an American affair.[134]

What resulted was less a devastating critique of militarism than an apologia produced by men with the best intentions who might have been better off heeding the warnings of the dissenters at Versailles.[135] On a personal level, the relationship of New Zealanders to these trials shifted from a naïve enthusiasm to dismay. Politicians like Massey and technically competent lawyers like Quilliam were unable to cope with the transnational cultural politics of the institutions used to transact these post-war reckonings. The more politically astute, like Evans, were able to take a step out of the parochial into the global and develop a more nuanced view of what was at stake. What Paris and then Tokyo taught New Zealand as a state was that a multilateral process that institutionalized power more generally and evenly was a necessary condition for success in building an international criminal code constraining aggression; what it taught New Zealanders is that they would have to be highly adaptable to have any influence in that new multilateral environment.

Bibliography

Neil Boister and Robert Cryer, *The Tokyo International Military Tribunal: A Reappraisal* (Oxford University Press, 2008).

Gerald Chaudron, *New Zealand in the League of Nations: The Beginnings of an Independent Foreign Policy, 1919-1939* (London: McFarland & Co, 2012).

H.J. Constable, *From Ploughboy to Premier: A New Life of The Right Hon. William Ferguson Massey, PC* (London: John Marlowe Savage & Co Ltd, 1925).

Gordon Daniels, 'New Zealand and the Occupation of Japan' in Ian Nish (ed.), *The British Commonwealth and the Occupation of Japan, 1945-1952: Personal Encounters and Government Assessments* (Leiden: Brill, 2013).

Frederick Sherwood Dunn, *Peace-making and the Settlement with Japan* (Princeton University Press, 1963).

Harold Evans, 'The Trial of Major Japanese War Criminals', *New Zealand Law Journal*, 23 (1947) 8-10, 21-23, 37-38, 322-324.

Harold Evans, 'The World Court Project on Nuclear Weapons and International Law', *New Zealand Law Journal* (1993).

---

134   ANZ, 106/3/22, Part 8, Northcroft to O'Reilly, 13 September 1948.

135   Simpson, 'International Criminal Justice', 143.

Yee-Kuang Heng and Syed Mohammed Ad'ha Aljunied, 'Can Small States be more than Price Takers in Global Governance?' *Global Governance*, 21 (2015), 435-54.

Ian Hull, *A Scrap of Paper: Breaking and Making International Law during the Great War* (Ithaca: Cornell UP, 2014).

Robin Kay, 'Caging the Prussian Dragon: New Zealand and the Paris Peace Conference 1919' in John Crawford and Ian McGibbon (eds.), *New Zealand's Great War: New Zealand and the Allies and the First World War* (Auckland: Exisle, 2007).

Robin Kay (ed.), *Documents on New Zealand External Relations*, vol. 2, *The Surrender and Occupation of Japan* (Wellington: Government Printer, 1982).

Richard H. Minear, *Victor's Justice: The Tokyo War Crimes Trial* (Princeton University Press, 1971).

Walter Nash, *New Zealand: A Working Democracy* (New York: Duel, Sloan and Pearce, 1943).

Quentin Quentin-Baxter, 'The Task of the International Military Tribunal at Tokyo', *New Zealand Law Journal*, 25 (1950), 133-35.

G.A.R. Riddell, *Lord Riddell's Intimate Diary of the Peace Conference and After: 19-18-1923* (London: Gollancz, 1931).

William A. Schabas, 'Origins of Criminalization of Aggression: How Crimes Against Peace Became the "Supreme International Crime"', in Mauro Politi and Giuseppe Nesi (eds.), *The International Criminal Court and the Crime of Aggression* (Aldershot: Ashgate, 2004).

Guy H. Scholefield, *William Ferguson Massey MP PC Prime Minister of New Zealand, 1912-1925: A Personal Biography* (Wellington: Harry H. Thombs Ltd, 1925).

Kirsten Sellars, *Crimes against Peace and International Law* (Cambridge University Press, 2013).

Gerry Simpson, 'International Criminal Justice and the Past' in Gideon Boas, Wiliam Schabas and Michael Scharf (eds.), *International Criminal Justice: Legitimacy and Coherence* (Cheltenham: Edward Elgar, 2012).

Ann Trotter, 'New Zealanders and the International Military Tribunal for the Far East', *New Zealand Journal of History*, 23 (2) (1989).

Ann Trotter, 'Justice Northcroft' in Yuki Tanaka, Tim McCormack and Gerry Simpson (eds.), *Beyond Victor's Justice? The Tokyo War Crimes Trial Revisited* (Leiden and Boston: Nijhoff, 2011).

CHAPTER 9

Burdened by the 'Shadow of War': Justice Jaranilla and the Tokyo Trial

Hitoshi Nagai

In November 1948, Justice Delfin Jaranilla, the Philippines representative submitted his 'Concurring Opinion' to the court of the Tokyo war crimes trial.[1] This was the only separate opinion by the 'Majority' of judges who played a primary role in determining the Tokyo judgment. This chapter attempts to determine why Justice Jaranilla decided to write his 'Concurring Opinion' and analyses the essence of his argument. The Philippines, like India, was an emerging nation which became independent after the commencement of the Tokyo trial. Although the Philippines were not a signatory nation of the Japanese Instrument of Surrender in September 1945, it was asked to join this international tribunal. I attempt to analyse the reasoning behind the Philippine government's appointment of Justice Jaranilla as its representative and the perception of his role. This article makes use of Justice Jaranilla's private papers, interviews with his family members, the Philippine presidential papers and local newspapers.

An Elite Legal Professional in the American Colonial Period

Delfin Jaranilla was born to Antonio Jaranilla and Juana J. Jebucion on 24 December 1883, in La Paz, Iloilo Province of Panay Island, the Philippines.[2] Antonio was a farmer and owner of a fish farm, who also served as a judge. After Antonio passed away when Delfin was young, Juana had to struggle to raise her son by herself. From early childhood, Delfin was highly gifted and proved his exceptional abilities when he was admitted to the Seminario de Jaro, a prestigious school in Iloilo during the Spanish colonial period. In 1900,

---

1   This article is written based on the author's article in Japanese and subsequent research. See H. Nagai's 'Wasurerareta Tokyo saiban Firipin hanji: Delfin Jaranilla hanji no shogai' [The forgotten Filipino judge at the Tokyo trial: A biography of Justice Delfin Jaranilla] in K. Awaya (ed.), *Kingendai Nihon no senso to heiwa* [War and peace in modern Japanese history] (Tokyo: Gendai Shiryo Shuppan, 2010), pp. 303-66.

2   Delfin had a middle name (Jebucion) but seldom used it.

Filipino schools began teaching English after the country became an American colony as a result of the Spanish-American War (1898), and Delfin studied English intensely.[3]

In 1903, Delfin took the test for the 'Pensionado' scholarship programme, which was initiated that year to send young Filipinos to American universities. Among the applicants from Iloilo, he achieved the highest score and was dispatched to the United States in October 1903 as one of the first 104 students of the programme. After studying at Santa Ana High School in Orange County in California, he entered the State University of Tennessee in Knoxville in September 1904. In his second year, however, due to racial discrimination he was obliged to transfer to Georgetown University in Washington DC. While majoring in civil law, he thoroughly enjoyed campus life.[4]

In June 1907, he graduated from Georgetown University with a diploma in law and returned to the Philippines. After his four years in the US, naturally, his behaviour had become very much Americanized[5] and, furthermore, he had become pro-American in his views. What was possibly of even more importance for his career was that his diploma from a US university opened a door to various important posts during the American colonial period of the Philippines.

In May 1910 Jaranilla entered the civil service of the government and in October 1912 he passed the bar examination.[6] After serving as a law clerk of the Court of First Instance in Iloilo and Cagayan in northern Luzon, he became an attorney of the department of Mindanao and Sulu in July 1919. One year later, in July 1920, he took up a new post as an assistant attorney in the Department of Justice and moved to Manila. In May 1921, at the age of thirty-seven, he was appointed as an auxiliary judge for the first group of the judicial district and began his career as a judge. Subsequently, he was promoted to various important posts, including as a judge of the 22nd judicial district of Negros Occidental. These posts provided him with excellent opportunities to gain

---

3   'The Bench and Bar in News', *The Lawyers Journal*, 16, no. 2 (28 February 1951), pp. 103-4; Emma
    M. Jaranilla, interview by author, Mandaluyong, 16 March 2010.

4   A.C. Gonzaga, 'The Justice...', *Ang Tala: AFP Command Information Bulletin*, 11, no. 9, September
    1980, p. 25; Response given by Delfin S. Jaranilla, Jr., 6 June 1980, Cesar G. Hechanova Collection,
    Iloilo City, Philippines; R.P. Gumabong, 'The Many Sides of Justice Jaranilla', *Philippines Free
    Press*, 12 July 1958, 18.

5   B.V.A. Röling and A. Cassese, *The Tokyo Trial and Beyond: Reflections of a Peacemonger*
    (Cambridge: Polity Press, 1994), p. 28.

6   *Official Roster of Officers and Employees in the Civil Service of the Philippine Islands* (Manila:
    Bureau of Printing, 1912), p. 66; List of successful bar examinees, Supreme Court of the
    Philippines <http://sc.judiciary.gov.ph/baradmission/lawlist/j.php> (accessed 13 October
    2015).

deep practical experience. In September 1925, he was promoted to Attorney General and served various successive American Governor-Generals, including Leonard Wood and Henry L. Stimson. Thus Jaranilla developed his career as an elite legal professional during the American colonial period.[7]

His life continued smoothly until November 1926 (during the administration of Governor-General Wood), when he was involved in a power struggle concerning the abolition of the Board of Control. As the Attorney General, Jaranilla opposed Manuel L. Quezon, the president of the Philippine Senate, who was pressing to limit the power of the American Governor-Generals. Offended by Jaranilla's 'pro-American attitude', Quezon objected to the appointment of Jaranilla as a judge of the Supreme Court in 1931 by decreasing the court's membership.[8] Moreover, in December 1932, Quezon led a restructuring of governmental organizations and abolished the post of the Attorney General itself. In 1933, after having lost the position of Attorney General, Jaranilla was appointed as a judge of the Court of First Instance of Manila, which was, however, an inferior role. Humiliated by this demotion, Jaranilla resigned from public office in 1937.[9] Meanwhile, the US Congress passed the Philippine Independence Act, also known as the Tydings-McDuffie Act, in compliance with which the Philippine Commonwealth (a transitional administration in preparation for full independence) had been inaugurated in November 1935 with Quezon as the first president.

Jaranilla, on the other hand, remained a private citizen. He got married to Angela Salazar in 1914 and they had four children, but unfortunately Angela died in 1937. He opened his own law practice and taught at the University of the Philippines and the University of Manila.[10] Surprisingly, it was Quezon who requested Jaranilla resume public service. In 1940, President Quezon

---

7   'The Bench and Bar in news', p. 104; M.R. Cornejo (ed.), *Cornejo's Commonwealth Directory of the Philippines, 1939 Encyclopedic Edition* (Manila: Privately published, 1939), pp. 1822-23.

8   *Who's Who in the Philippines: A Biographical Dictionary of Notable Living Men of the Philippines*, vol. 2 (Manila: Philippines Ramon Roces, 1941), p. 90; Kensei-shiryoshitsu (Modern Japanese political history materials room), National Diet Library, Tokyo, Japan (hereafter NDLKS), Records of the Foreign Service Post of the Department of State, microfiche, FSP-225, John M. Allison to William J. Sebald, 16 September 1948. The original document is deposited at the National Archives at College Park, MD, USA (hereafter NARA).

9   NDLKS, Henry L. Stimson Papers (the original document is deposited at Yale University Library, New Haven, CT, USA), microfilm, Roll 120, Jaranilla to Stimson, 28 May 1948; D.S. Jaranilla, Jr., 'Autobiography of Col. Delfin S. Jaranilla, Jr.', unpublished manuscript, pp. 14-15, Mary Anne J. Ambrosio Collection, Manila.

10   Cornejo, *Cornejo's Commonwealth Directory*, p. 1823; 'The Bench and Bar in News', p. 104.

asked him to assume the post of the Judge Advocate General of the Philippine Army and to serve as the legal advisor to the president. Accepting this offer, in October 1940, Jaranilla became the Judge Advocate General and an actively serving officer with the rank of colonel.[11] At the age of fifty-six, he began serving in active duty for the first time in his life.[12] Shortly afterwards, the Pacific War broke out, which led him to fight against the Japanese Army under the leadership of General Douglas MacArthur, commander of United States Army Forces in the Far East (USAFFE).

In April 1942, following a fierce battle in the Bataan Peninsula and the defeat of American and Filipino troops by the Japanese Army, Jaranilla experienced the Bataan 'Death March'. He had expected that as an officer, the Japanese Army would treat him fairly and according to the Geneva Convention relative to the Treatment of Prisoners of War (1929); however, a Japanese soldier with a beard deprived him of his belongings, including shoes, and ordered him to join the march. When Jaranilla objected, he was severely beaten. He also saw the Japanese soldiers beat and kill other prisoners.[13] Before the war he had a close Japanese friend,[14] so such behaviour from the Japanese soldiers must have had been a shocking experience for him.

Jaranilla was forced to move to a distant internment camp, primarily on foot. Amid the severity of this march, with the death toll of Filipino and American prisoners of war (POWs) reaching at least 10,000, he continued walking using a bamboo cane, and assisted by his son, Lieutenant Delfin S. Jaranilla, Jr. During the march, the elder Jaranilla thought of escaping, but he had to give up the idea because he was unable to walk properly. Due to extreme fatigue and hunger, he occasionally fainted along the roadside.[15]

After the 'Death March', Jaranilla was interned in Camp O'Donnell in Capas in Tarlac. He nearly died in the POW camp from diarrhoea and malnutrition combined with extreme exhaustion from the march. After becoming extremely thin and frail (he had to go into hospital), he was relocated to Bilibid Prison in Manila, and then released from the prison in July 1942. When he returned to his

---

11   *Bulletin of the Judge Advocate General of the Armed Forces of the Philippines*, 1, no. 1 (July 1947), n.p.

12   E. Jaranilla, interview by author, Mandaluyong, 8 August 2010.

13   R.P. Gumabong, 'The "Hellish March": A Former Supreme Justice and a Former Chief of Staff Tell How They Survived the Infamous Death March', *Philippines Free Press*, 8 April 1961, 20.

14   For example, Jaranilla was a close friend with Eikichi Imamura, a Japanese businessman, and became a 'Compadre', a godfather of his son (E. Jaranilla, interview by author, Mandaluyong, 4 March 2009).

15   Gumabong, 'The "Hellish March"', 20-21.

home in Malate (Manila), his leg was still injured and he had lost more than fifty pounds.[16]

Because of ill-health, Jaranilla had to stay at home. In July 1942, just after his release, he got remarried to a relative, Sofia Hechanova, who was a head nurse at the General Hospital in Pampanga and had taken care of him when he was a prisoner. He declined offers of any public service on the grounds of ill-health, including offers to serve the Philippine Executive Commission, established in January 1942 as the governmental organization of the Philippines under the Japanese occupation; serving the Jose P. Laurel administration of the 'Republic of the Philippines'. In addition to poor health, he was also reluctant to serve in the 'pro-Japanese administration'.[17] During this period, because of his past career as an officer of USAFFE, the Japanese authorities occasionally suspected him of collaboration with the US and even searched his house.[18] In June 1943, Laurel was shot while playing golf in the suburbs of Manila and just after the incident, the *Kempeitai*, the Japanese military police, suspected Jaranilla was involved in the shooting because of his excellent marksmanship.[19] On the other hand, during the war his family became friends with a Japanese officer called 'Kawachi' who lived next to their house.[20] Throughout the period of the Japanese occupation, Jaranilla led a quiet life as a private citizen, in contrast to his brilliant and busy career during the pre-war period.[21] Like many other Filipino officials, Jaranilla was obliged to choose either cooperation with the Japanese or to resist them. His choice was to side with the resistance.

In February 1945, the Battle of Manila broke out, involving many citizens, including Jaranilla's family. On 9 February, the Japanese Army killed more than 400 civilians at St Paul's College, located close to Jaranilla's house. Naturally, this massacre filled his family with tremendous fear. Moreover, amid the intense gunfire between the Japanese and US forces, Jaranilla's house was bombed, and the family had to escape to Lepanto, in the vicinity of the Malacañang Palace, the official residence of the president of the Philippines.[22]

---

16   Jaranilla, 'Autobiography of Col. Delfin S. Jaranilla, Jr.', p. 37; *The Evening Star* (Washington DC), 12 March 1949.

17   *The Evening Star*, 12 March 1949; Gonzaga, 'The Justice', 26.

18   E. Jaranilla, interview by author, 16 March 2010.

19   Gumabong, 'The Many Sides', 18.

20   E. Jaranilla, interview by author, 4 March 2009.

21   Benita M. Santos, interview by author, Manila, 17 March 2010.

22   E. Jaranilla, interview by author, 4 March 2009.

Sadly, Jaranilla's first grandchild was killed in the battle. He also lost almost all of his property including his own house.[23] After surviving the calamity, however, he resumed service in the government. As a result of the reoccupation of the Philippines by the American forces, the Philippine Commonwealth was re-established on 27 February 1945. The new president of the Commonwealth, Sergio Osmeña, was one of Jaranilla's long-term friends. In setting up his cabinet, on 8 March Osmeña appointed Jaranilla as the Secretary of Justice.[24] When the press reported this news, they portrayed this new Secretary of Justice by describing his wartime experiences as a prisoner of war and his rejection of offers to serve Japan's authorities, in addition to his long pre-war career in public service.[25] On 6 June, Jaranilla also assumed the post of a judge of the Supreme Court, while maintaining his post as the Secretary of Justice. This was the moment he reached the peak of his career in the legal profession.[26]

Appointed as a Judge of the Tokyo Trial

On 3 June, President Manuel A. Roxas nominated Jaranilla as a judge for the International Military Tribunal for the Far East (IMTFE) and informed General MacArthur, the Supreme Commander for the Allied Powers (SCAP).[27] Since the trial had already commenced on 3 May 1946, Jaranilla was the last to be nominated among the judges selected from eleven countries.[28]

Upon the nomination, Jaranilla immediately left for Tokyo which begs the question: why did he leave in such haste? First and foremost, the participa-

---

23   Rose Mary Yenko, interview by author, Mandaluyong, 8 August 2010; E. Jaranilla, interview
      by author, 16 March 2010.
24   Jaranilla, 'Autobiography of Col. Delfin S. Jaranilla, Jr.', pp. 14, 54; National Library of the
      Philippines (hereafter NLP), Sergio Osmeña Papers, Box 12, Osmeña to Jaranilla, 27 Febru-
      ary 1945.
25   *Free Philippines*, 15 March 1945.
26   Osmeña to Jaranilla, 6 June 1945, Hechanova Collection. Jaranilla resigned as Associate
      Justice on 6 June 1946, the day before his appointment as justice of the Tokyo trial. See
      'Associate Justices', Supreme Court E-Library <http://elibrary.judiciary.gov.ph/supreme-
      courtjustices/associatejustice/55> (accessed 13 October 2015).
27   University Archives, University of the Philippines Diliman (hereafter UAUPD), Manuel A.
      Roxas Papers, General Correspondence, Subseries B, Box 8 (MacArthur, Douglas), Roxas
      to MacArthur, 3 June 1946; Box 10 (Romulo, Carlos P.), Roxas to Romulo, 3 June 1946.
28   Strictly speaking, the last appointment was American justice Myron C. Cramer, who took
      John P. Higgins' position in July 1946. See NDLKS, GHQ/SCAP Records (the original docu-
      ments are deposited at NARA), International Prosecution Section Papers, microfilm, IPS 7,
      Roll 7 (hereafter IPS 7/R7), General Orders no. 29, 22 July 1946.

tion of a judge from the Philippines was not included in the initial plan. The Charter of the IMTFE, issued by General MacArthur on 19 January 1946, stipulated that the tribunal should consist of nine members, appointed by the SCAP from the names submitted by the Signatories to the Instrument of Surrender (Article 2). India and the Philippines, which had not yet become independent at the time, did not have the right to nominate judges.[29] As a result, the Filipino judge was initially excluded from the tribunal, even though the participation of a Filipino prosecutor was admitted. As for the prosecutor, MacArthur and American prosecutors had specifically requested the inclusion of a Filipino, and also the US authorities concurred in recognizing the brutality of the crimes committed in the Philippines.[30]

In this situation, India, a member state of the Far Eastern Commission (FEC), the decision-making body regarding policy toward occupied Japan, strongly appealed for the participation of an Indian judge in the tribunal on the grounds of the country's contribution to the victory and sacrifices incurred in the battle against Japan. The British Commonwealth supported India and the United Kingdom argued that all members of the FEC (eleven countries, comprising the Signatories to the Instrument of Surrender plus India and the Philippines) should be allowed to nominate judges.[31] The United States supported the proposal by the UK on the condition that the participation of a Filipino judge should also be approved. This type of decision-making was of a political nature: opposing the participation of an Indian judge could worsen US-India relations, whereas supporting it would pave the way for the participation of the Philippines, an American colony and member state of the FEC; and the presence of India and the Philippines might help avoid criticism about the fairness of the tribunal in terms of racial balance (the US Department of State considered this increase was 'politically desirable to avoid being placed in the position of discriminating against Asiatic countries'). At that time, the Republic

---

29   Homudaijin kanbo shiho hosei chosabu [The judicial system research department, secretariat of the Ministry of Justice] (ed.), *Senso hanzai saiban kankeihoreishu* [Legal documents on war crimes trials], vol. 1 (Tokyo: 1963), p. 40.

30   NDLKS, IPS Papers, IPS 7/R13, Joseph B. Keenan to Richard J. Marshall, 27 December 1945; NARA, RG 59, Records of the Department of State, Central Decimal File, Box 3631, Paul P. Steintorf to the Secretary of State, 13 February 1946; Paul V. McNutt to Osmeña, 22 January 1946.

31   Y. Higurashi, *Tokyo saiban no kokusai kankei: Kokusai seiji ni okeru kenryoku to kihan* [The Tokyo trial and international relations: Power and norms in international politics] (Tokyo: Bokutakusha, 2002), pp. 219-27.

of China was the only Asian country scheduled to send a judge to the trial.[32] On 3 April 1946, the FEC decided to approve participation of an Indian and a Filipino judge.[33] On 24 April, the Secretariat of the IMTFE officially requested that the governments of the two countries nominate candidates for judges, and on 26 April, Article 2 of the Charter of the IMTFE was revised to stipulate the participation of the judges from the two countries.[34]

The Philippines had not yet achieved full independence and since the diplomatic affairs of the Philippines were theoretically under US control until its full independence pursuant to the Independence Act of 1934,[35] the participation in the tribunal was impractical without the support and engagement of the US, as in the cases of the Philippines' membership in the United Nations (UN) and the FEC. Despite this situation, the Filipino authorities accepted the offer from the Secretariat of the IMTFE and immediately began to select a candidate for nomination as a judge. The Filipino authorities probably wanted to seize the opportunity to enhance the national prestige in the international community in time for its independence, scheduled for July 1946.[36]

However, selection of an appropriate candidate judge did not progress as smoothly as expected. The fully-fledged selection process began upon the FEC's decision-making on 3 April 1946.[37] Jaranilla was not the primary candidate, as in the cases of the French and Indian judges. Instead, Francisco A. Delgado was singled out first. On 12 April, a week after the FEC's decision-making, it was reported in the Philippines that General MacArthur supported the nomination of Delgado. On 25 April, the staff dealing with the war crimes issue in Tokyo were informed by Washington that the Philippines had 'provisionally' designated Delgado as a judge for the IMTFE.[38] Delgado, who was sixty years

---

32   NARA, RG 59, Central Decimal File, Box 3631, Vincent to Acheson, 15 March 1946; NDLKS, IPS Papers, IPS 7/R13, WASHINGTON to CINCAFPAC, 16 March 1946.

33   'Far Eastern Commission policy decision FEC 007/3', 3 April 1946, United States, Department of State, *Foreign Relations of the United States* (hereafter *FRUS*), *1946*, vol. 8 (Washington DC: USGPO, 1971), p.424-27; *The Manila Chronicle*, 5 April 1946; *Nippon Times*, 5 April 1946.

34   NDLKS, IPS Papers, IPS 7/R15, PRO, GHQ, USAFPAC, Press Release, 24 April 1946; *Asahi Shimbun*, 25 April 1946; *Senso hanzai saiban kankeihoreishu*, vol. 1, pp. 57-58.

35   NLP, Osmeña Papers, Box 5, Herbert V. Evatt to Osmeña, 5 November 1945; Osmeña to Evatt, 7 November 1945.

36   NLP, Osmeña Papers, Box 8, Pedro Lopez to Romulo, 25 January 1946; UAUPD, Carlos P. Romulo Papers, Box 1.1, Romulo to Osmeña, 15 July 1945.

37   NDLKS, IPS Papers, IPS 2/R2, Teletype conference between Tokyo and Washington (hereafter Telecon), 4, 18 April 1946.

38   *The Manila Chronicle*, 12 April 1946; Telecon, 25 April 1946.

old at the time, was the president of the Philippine Bar Association, and, together with Jaranilla, among the first students of the 'Pensionado'. He received a master's degree in law from Yale University in 1909. After returning from the US, Delgado was employed with the Philippine government as a law clerk and later as chief of the law division of the Executive Bureau. Before the Pacific War, he served as a member of the Philippine Congress, Resident Commissioner of the Philippines to the United States, and a justice of the Court of Appeals. He remained in Manila during the war. After the liberation of Manila, he was appointed as the Philippine delegate to the United Nations Conference in San Francisco in April 1945, and participated in the preparation of the Statute of the International Court of Justice (ICJ). Immediately after the end of the war, he was nominated as one of the first ICJ judges.[39]

The selection process of the judge for the IMTFE did not proceed until late April 1946. In mid-May, the General Headquarters, the Supreme Commander for the Allied Powers (GHQ, SCAP) in Tokyo urged the Filipino authorities to finalize the nomination of Delgado. Concurrently, General MacArthur also requested Carlos P. Romulo, Resident Commissioner of the Philippines to the US (who was in Washington) to officially nominate Delgado.[40] However, Delgado declined the offer and assumed the post of member of the Philippine War Damage Commission on 23 May 1946.[41] The issue of the selection of the Filipino judge had to revert to the very beginning of the process. By that time, three weeks had already passed since the opening of the trial, and Radhabinod Pal, the Indian judge, had already been appointed on 16 May.[42]

At that time, a presidential election was also under way in the Philippines. On 23 April 1946, Roxas defeated the incumbent Osmeña. Given this result, the Filipino authorities announced that the nomination of a judge for the IMTFE would be suspended until the inauguration of the new president on 28 May.[43] In addition to the refusal by the original candidate, changes in the Filipino administration thus further delayed the nomination process.

---

39   NLP, Osmeña Papers, Box 2, Osmeña to Edward R. Stettinius Jr., 20 March 1945; Osmeña Papers, Box 8, Lopez to Romulo, 25 January 1946; *The Manila Chronicle*, 13, 25 January 1946; Telecon, 25 April 1946; *Philippines Free Press*, 10 November 1951. In the end, Delgado was not selected as an ICJ judge.

40   Telecon, 16 May 1946; NARA, RG153, Records of the Office of the Judge Advocate General (Army), Entry 145, Box 90, 'Memorandum of work done by Project K during current week', 17 May 1946.

41   *The Manila Chronicle*, 24 May 1946.

42   NDLKS, IPS Papers, IPS 7/R7, GHQ, SCAP, General Orders no. 23, 16 May 1946.

43   Telecon, 24 May 1946.

Urged on by the US authorities,[44] President Roxas strove to select a judge.[45] On 3 June 1946, a week after his inauguration, the new president nominated Jaranilla as the judge for the IMTFE. Although the reason for selecting Jaranilla is not known, Roxas probably did not select him simply because they were both from Panay. At that time, the Philippines still remained an American colony, and the tribunal was formed under the leadership of General MacArthur. Accordingly, in selecting the judicial candidate, Roxas had to consider the preferences of the US and MacArthur. In this situation, he was obliged to select an individual who had not obviously cooperated with Japan, and who would cooperate with the US. The candidate also needed sufficient legal knowledge to serve at a military tribunal and the experience of military service. We could say that the criteria for the nomination included a good relationship with the US (MacArthur), no evidence of collaboration with the Japanese during the war, legal qualifications and finally a distinguished public career. Although Jaranilla was sixty-two years old at the time, he was fluent in English, and had a wealth of experience as a pro-American legal professional. Moreover, during the war, he fought against the Japanese Army as the Judge Advocate General. His career as a legal professional was more than sufficient since he served as the Secretary of Justice and a judge of the Supreme Court.[46] Jaranilla accepted this unexpected offer by resigning his post as a judge of the Supreme Court,[47] probably because he considered it a great honour to be appointed by General MacArthur, whom he greatly respected, and was delighted to work under him.[48]

Days in Tokyo and the Judgment

On the early morning of 7 June 1946, only four days after his nomination, Jaranilla arrived in Japan. On the afternoon of that day, he visited General

---

44   Ibid.; UAUPD, Roxas Papers, General Correspondence, Subseries B, Box 8 (McNutt, Paul), SCAP to US Commissioner, 1 June 1946.

45   UAUPD, Romulo Papers, Box 5.20, Roxas to Romulo, [23 May 1946].

46   NDLKS, Douglas MacArthur Papers (the original documents are deposited at the MacArthur Memorial, Norfolk, VA, USA), microfilm, MMA 14, Roll 4 (hereafter MMA 14/R4), Roxas to MacArthur, 5 June 1946.

47   Jaranilla had already resigned as the Secretary of Justice on 31 December 1945.

48   E. Jaranilla, interview by author, 4 March 2009. Jaranilla became acquainted with General MacArthur before the war (NDLKS, MacArthur Papers, MMA 3/R60, Office Diary of General MacArthur, 1 March 1945). As for his great respect for MacArthur, NDLKS, MMA 14/R3, Jaranilla to MacArthur, 10 April, 18 August 1945.

MacArthur and was officially appointed as a judge of the IMTFE.[49] He was undoubtedly proud at having been selected for the service. Before long, however, his self-esteem was severely dented as the defendants' attorneys accused him of being unqualified as a judge of the tribunal.

On 9 June, two days after his arrival, Jaranilla attended a party, where he happened to meet David F. Smith, a graduate of the faculty of law at Georgetown University. Smith was an attorney for former prime minister Hirota Kōki. At the party, Smith learned that Jaranilla had survived the Bataan 'Death March' and had been a prisoner of war of the Japanese Army. On 11 June, together with Attorney Tadashi Hanai, Smith submitted a motion to eliminate Jaranilla from the judges for the tribunal, based on the belief that Jaranilla, who had been a victim of aggression by the Japanese Army, would have a 'personal bias' and therefore might not be impartial in his judgments. The next day (12 June), Justice William F. Webb, President of the IMTFE, dismissed the motion, stating that the judges could not cancel the appointments by the SCAP.[50]

Certainly, Jaranilla had never expected that his impartiality would be questioned so soon after his arrival in Tokyo. He had simply accepted the nomination by President Roxas, even though he had not expected the order and it was given to him with virtually no time for preparation. Moreover, he had had to resign as a judge of the Supreme Court to assume the new post. However, it would have been extremely difficult for President Roxas to find anyone 'completely neutral', since the majority of Filipinos, including those serving in the government, had been victims of Japanese aggression. At least in the Philippines, experiences of the Bataan 'Death March' and that of being a prisoner of war were regarded as 'heroic', whereas cooperating with Japan was severely criticized.[51] In Filipino society, non-cooperation with the Japanese was one of the conditions for employment in public service. Accordingly, Jaranilla's wartime experiences were never questioned in his country when he was nominated

49   NDLKS, IPS Papers, IPS 7/R16, PRO, GHQ, USAFPAC, Press Release, 7 June 1946; IPS 7/R7, GHQ, SCAP, General Orders no. 28, 7 June 1946; *Nippon Times*, 8 June 1946; NDLKS, MacArthur Papers, MMA 3/R60, Office Diary for SCAP, 7 June 1946; *Yomiuri Hochi*, 8 June 1946.

50   A.C. Brackman, *The Other Nuremberg: The Untold Story of the Tokyo War Crimes Trials* (New York: William Morrow and Company, 1987), pp. 116-17; T. Hanai and D.F. Smith, 'Motion Suggesting the Disqualification and Personal Bias of the Philippine Justice of the Tribunal' in Proceedings in chambers, 12 June 1946 in R.J. Pritchard and S.M. Zaide (eds.), *The Tokyo War Crimes Trial*, vol. 22 (New York and London: Garland Publishing Inc., 1981), pp. 20-27; *Mainichi Shimbun*, 12, 13 June 1946.

51   *The Manila Chronicle*, 30 November, 1 December 1945.

as a judge for the tribunal.[52] It was true that Jaranilla knew first-hand of the aggressions and atrocities committed by the Japanese Army – the main subjects to be dealt with at the Tokyo trial – and it was actually because of this first-hand experience that suspicions were raised about his qualifications as a judge. This development undoubtedly led Jaranilla to make even greater efforts than other judges of the tribunal to prove his impartiality throughout the trial.

On 13 June 1946, Jaranilla appeared in court and together with all other eleven judges assembled for the first time.[53] He was the eldest of the judges.[54] He commuted to the court from his room (110A) at the Imperial Hotel.[55] From January 1947, he had been allowed to bring his wife, Sofia, and eldest daughter, Emma, from the Philippines and they stayed in Tokyo until the end of trial.[56] Taking into account that many other judges were not permitted to bring their wives,[57] General MacArthur himself probably granted this privilege. Since there were no diplomatic missions of the Philippines in Japan at that time, he attended official ceremonies and delivered speeches on behalf of his country, thus playing the role of virtual ambassador.[58]

Jaranilla attended about 90 per cent of the proceedings. He absented himself for only thirty-eight days,[59] some of which coincided with the 'Philippine phase', when a Filipino prosecutor (Pedro Lopez) brought evidence of the Japanese atrocities to the court. Even though Jaranilla had attended the court until the day before, he began absenting himself from 10 December 1946, the first day of the 'Philippine phase' and returned to the Philippines.[60] He

---

52   *The Evening News*, 4 June 1946; *Manila Bulletin*, 5 June 1946; *The Manila Chronicle*, 5 June 1946.

53   *The New York Times*, 13 June 1946; *Asahi Shimbun, Mainichi Shimbun*, 14 June 1946.

54   Justice Cramer was born in November 1881 and he was 2 years older than Jaranilla.

55   UAUPD, Box 28, see the title of spine of the book binding of the proceedings of the trial owned by Jaranilla.

56   E. Jaranilla, interview by author, 4 March 2009.

57   H.Q. Röling (ed.), *Röling in Tokyo: Documenten 1946-1948* (Amsterdam: privately published, 2011), p. 66. Emma, a daughter of Justice Jaranilla, remembered that except for Jaranilla only Justice Webb accompanied his wife to Tokyo.

58   'Commencement address of Mr. Justice Delfin Jaranilla at the Panay College on April 14, 1953', Hechanova Collection; *Manila Bulletin*, 4 February 1947.

59   University of Maryland Libraries, MD, USA, Gordon W. Prange Collection, Owen Cunningham Papers, Box 4, Folder OC-039, [O. Cunningham] 'The trial of Tojo', unpublished manuscript, n.d.

60   NDLKS, Court Papers, journals, exhibits and judgments of the IMTFE (T918, NARA), microfilm, Roll 6, Court journal of IMTFE, 9, 10 December 1946.

explained that he left Tokyo in order to see his wife, who was ill.[61] On 29 November, Jaranilla visited MacArthur, 'after receiving an important telegraph from Manila'.[62] The contents of the telegraph are unknown, and so is the conversation that he had with MacArthur. However, we should pay close attention to the timing of said telegraph as it seems too coincidental that he suddenly absented himself on the day of the presentation of evidence by the Filipino prosecutor, even though he had been continually present in the court before the day of the 'Philippine phase'. It is true that he had to return to his country due to his wife's illness,[63] but at the same time, Jaranilla was a very proud and scrupulous person,[64] he most likely deliberately absented himself during the 'Philippine phase' to avoid any questions about his 'impartiality'.

More than two years later, on 4 November 1948, President Webb began reading the judgment. On 12 November, all twenty-five defendants were found guilty; seven of those were sentenced to death by hanging but none of the defendants were sentenced to capital punishment solely for 'crimes against peace'. Concerning the criminalization of 'crimes against peace', the attorneys had objected on the grounds that this would be an application of an ex-post facto law. As in the case of the Nuremberg judgment, all defendants sentenced to death were criminalized for Counts 54 or 55, in association with atrocities perpetrated. The critical factor for receiving the death penalty was therefore involvement in atrocities.[65] The judgment was written by the majority of judges, including Jaranilla. With assistance from private secretary Dominador N. Dizon, Jaranilla prepared to write the draft of the 'Individual Cases' for Akira Muto, Takazumi Oka and Naoki Hoshino.[66]

Submission of a 'Concurring Opinion'

In addition to the judgment, five judges submitted separate opinions. Of the five judges, only Jaranilla submitted a 'Concurring Opinion'. Moreover, among

---

61   *Pacific Stars and Stripes*, 12 December 1946; *Manila Bulletin*, 16 December 1946, 7 January 1947.
62   NDLKS, MacArthur Papers, MMA 3/R58, Daily Appointments of SCAP, 29 November 1946; NDLKS, MMA 3/R60, Office Diary for SCAP, 29 November 1946.
63   NDLKS, MacArthur Papers, MMA 3/R29, Jaranilla to Col. [Herbert B.] Wheeler, 22 December 1946.
64   Response given by Delfin S. Jaranilla, Jr.; E. Jaranilla, interview by author, 4 March 2009.
65   Higurashi, *Tokyo saiban no kokusai kankei*, pp. 458-65.
66   UAUPD, Delfin Jaranilla Papers, Box 46. These are the draft of individual case sent to the Darfting Committee of the majority judges. They might be one of the draft of the verdict.

the majority of judges who wrote the judgment, it was only Jaranilla who submitted a separate opinion. His 'Concurring Opinion', dated 1 November 1948, consists of eleven sections (including the conclusion) and comprises in total thirty-five pages in English.[67] In his opinion, Jaranilla wrote, 'We of the majority have written our decision in which I concur, but there being several points which, in my humble judgment, need further discussion and elucidation, I am constrained to write this concurring opinion'.[68]

While his opinion is highlighted by his interpretation of particular articles, it also includes arguments that reveal his lack of knowledge of international law.[69] Despite the title of 'Concurring Opinion', it includes questions concerning the interpretations adopted by the majority of judges (Sections 1-3). Since Jaranilla believed that the judges of the tribunal should fully abide by the Charter of the IMTFE, his argument was based on the Charter. He regarded the Charter as a given condition probably because he resorted to it as the backbone of his own qualification for being present. His bitter experience in which his qualification as a judge was questioned shortly after his arrival in Japan drove him to clarify his position as one of the 'eleven members from eleven different Allied nations, carefully chosen for their qualifications, fairness and impartiality' (Section 5). In any case, Jaranilla did not question the legitimacy of the tribunal, unlike Justice Pal.

In his 'Concurring Opinion', Jaranilla supported the legitimacy of the trial and evaluated their judgments thoroughly, believing that it would provide a precedent effective in deterring potential atrocities. This belief was reinforced by Resolution 95 (I) Affirmation of the Principles of International Law recognized by the Charter of the Nuremberg trial, which was adopted at the UN General Assembly and issued on 11 December 1946 (Section 7).[70] Based on this strong belief, Jaranilla responded with extraordinary sensitivity to the criticism of the defence counsels who argued that the tribunal represented 'victor's justice', that the accused were denied a fair and impartial trial, and that they were judged by ex-post facto laws, which were illegal. Jaranilla supported the legal legitimacy of the trial, since it was established by the SCAP on the basis of the Potsdam Declaration, which Japan accepted, along with the Instrument of

---

67 'Concurring opinion by the honorable Mr. Justice Delfin Jaranilla [,] member from the Republic of the Philippines' in Pritchard and Zaide (eds.), *The Tokyo War Crimes Trial*, vol. 21.

68 The Political Adviser in Japan to the Secretary of State, 23 November 1948, *FRUS, 1948*, vol. 6 (Washington DC: USGPO, 1974), pp. 905-6.

69 Hisakazu Fujita, interview by author, Kyoto, 24 July 2010.

70 N. Boister and R. Cryer, *The Tokyo International Military Tribunal: A Reappraisal* (Oxford University Press, 2008), p. 279.

Surrender (Section 5). Concerning the dispute about ex-post facto laws associated with new crimes, including 'crimes against peace', there was an argument that a new enactment may not apply to previous acts. Although Jaranilla admitted this 'as a general principle of law', he did not believe that the principle should be applied to this case. Instead, he believed that such a principle should be applied only to the national laws of a country, rather than to international law (Section 6).

Jaranilla strongly believed that trials of individuals who committed atrocities under international law would bring to an end the conventional practice of leaving offences and offenders unpunished. He also believed that the judgment would serve as a means of deterring the commitment of atrocities. He wrote, 'this war is the most hideous, hateful and destructive wherein such untold atrocities have been perpetrated and committed. Shall we overlook and let calmly the international criminal acts go unnoticed and unpunished?' (Section 6). His discussions, based on the perspectives of war victims, reveal his aspiration to reinforce legal means in order to prevent aggressions and atrocities. He also argued that individuals rather than a state should be responsible, stating that, 'The idea that a state or a corporation commits crimes may now be considered as fiction' (Section 7).

Driven by the strong aspiration to stop wartime aggressions and atrocities, Jaranilla must have been unable to overlook discussions concerning the legitimacy of the trial. He criticized Justice Pal and his 'Judgment' (dissenting opinion), by stating that Pal exceeded his authority as a judge of the tribunal, since the judges should abide by the Charter (Section 9). Pal undertook and completed his 'Judgment' from May to June 1948, and handed out copies to the other judges at the end of July.[71] Pal's dissenting opinion is included in the 'Delfin Jaranilla Papers', which is deposited at the University of the Philippines. Jaranilla's handwriting in the material indicates that he began studying Pal's opinion around August 1948.[72] Since his handwriting reveals his criticisms of Pal's views, he probably began writing his own opinion driven by his objections to Pal's view.

As noted above, Jaranilla was sensitive towards the feelings of victims of atrocities committed by the Japanese Army. On the other hand, his memories of the period of Japanese occupation sometimes interfered with his objective judgment, especially in relation to the issue of the atomic bombings. During the trials, the defence counsels brought up an issue related to the responsibility

---

71   N. Nakazato, *Paru hanji: Indo nashonarizumu to Tokyo saiban* [Justice Pal: Indian nationalism and the Tokyo trial] (Tokyo: Iwanami shoten, 2011), pp. 110-11.

72   UAUPD, Jaranilla Papers, Box 68.

for the atomic bombings. Jaranilla disagreed with the attorneys' approach since he believed that the attorneys were motivated by a desire to offset the atrocities of the Japanese Army and to mitigate the defendants' responsibility. He wrote, 'The purpose of the arguments, as I can see, was to minimize the responsibility of the defendants in this case for the atrocities and inhuman acts committed during the war'. From the viewpoint of those occupied by Japan, he justified the atomic bombings on the grounds that they led to the liberation of countries from the Japanese occupation (Section 8). At the time of the atomic bombings there were already attempts to restrict the use of weapons and materials that may give excessive pain to enemies, as well as to indiscriminate bombings. These attempts led to the preparation of The Hague Regulations concerning the Law and Customs of War on Land (1907) and the Draft Rules on Air Warfare (1923).[73] However, Jaranilla did not pay attention to these arguments and justified the atomic bombings by the United States by referring to the explanation of Henry Stimson,[74] former American Governor-General in the Philippines whom he had served and who was the US Secretary of War at the time of the bombings. Presumably his own experiences of the brutality of war during the Japanese occupation made him less sensitive to the cruelty of the indiscriminate bombing of civilians in Hiroshima and Nagasaki. Although the issue of the atomic bombings was not a fundamental point of the dispute and was not included in the indictment, Jaranilla dared to mention this particular issue in his 'Concurring Opinion', supposedly because he sought to defend the US. From the context of the 'Concurring Opinion', however, his priority was refuting the legitimization of atrocities by the Japanese Army by contrasting them with the atomic bombings.[75]

Jaranilla's 'Concurring Opinion' is best known for his argument for tougher sentences (Section 10). He wrote, 'I am constrained to differ on only a few of the penalties to be imposed by the Tribunal – the penalties are, in my judgment, too lenient, not exemplary and deterrent, and not commensurate with the gravity of the offense or offenses committed'. Jaranilla demanded tougher punishments for only a few defendants, however. Although he did not mention individual names, the interview he provided after the judgment implied that

---

73   H. Fujita, *International Regulation of the Use of Nuclear Weapons* (Osaka: Kansai University Press, 1988), pp. 101-49.

74   H.L. Stimson and M.H. Bundy, *On Active Service in Peace and War* (New York: Harper, 1948). Justice Jaranilla began to read the book from May 1948 (NDLKS, Stimson Papers, Roll 120, Jaranilla to Stimson, 28 May 1948).

75   About the arguments of the defence attorneys on atomic bombs, see the remarks of Ben Bruce Blakeney on 3 March 1947 and Floyd Mattice on 9 April 1948 in Pritchard and Zaide (eds.), *The Tokyo War Crimes Trial*, vol. 8, pp. 17657-9; vol. 19, p. 47226.

he was thinking of former Foreign Minister Mamoru Shigemitsu (who was sentenced to seven years' imprisonment) and a few of the other sixteen defendants who were sentenced to life imprisonment.[76] On the other hand, he stated in his opinion, 'As to the defendants who are afflicted with an incurable malady (names are not mentioned), I feel that they are entitled to such leniency as human conscience might permit' (Section 10). This suggestion, however, has seldom been discussed.

Conclusion

On 22 November 1948, ten days after the judgment, Jaranilla left Japan with his family. He travelled to America and Europe before returning to the Philippines in December 1949.[77] Subsequently, he retired from all public service. He passed away on 4 June 1980, in Manila, at the age of ninety-six.[78] In conclusion, I would like to discuss the historical significance of the presence of Justice Jaranilla at the trial, which was perhaps the climax of his long life.

Jaranilla attended almost the entire trial, listening to presentations of evidence by both prosecutors and defence counsels. As a judge belonging to the majority, he was involved in the preparation of the judgment, and he also submitted his own separate opinion. As suggested in his 'Concurring Opinion', Jaranilla expected that the judgment of the tribunal would present a precedent effective in deterring potential aggressions and atrocities.[79] In later years, he discussed the significance of the Tokyo trial as follows: rather than making an immediate decision, the tribunal spent 'two and a half long years to dispose of the case'. Both prosecutors and defence attorneys were provided ample opportunity 'to present all the evidence that they have'. In other words, both sides were treated equally, the 'same as in the trials of cases in the most democratic countries in the world'.[80] He likely emphasized that the legal procedures adopted at the IMTFE were appropriate because he wanted to present a striking contrast with the cases of the many Filipinos who were killed by the

---

76   *Manila Bulletin*, 13 November 1948; *San Francisco Examiner*, 14 January 1949.

77   *Mainichi Shimbun*, 13, 23 November 1948; E. Jaranilla, interview by author, 16 March 2010.

78   *Times Journal*, 5, 7 June 1980; *Bulletin Today*, 6, 7 June 1980; *Inquirer*, 7 January 2006.

79   *San Francisco Examiner*, 14 January 1949; *The Manila Times*, 7 March 1949.

80   'Commencement address'.

Japanese Army without being provided with any opportunity for trials or explanation.[81]

When Jaranilla came to Japan and took part in the tribunal, anti-Japanese sentiment was powerful in his country,[82] and Filipino people retained vivid memories of harsh wartime experiences. In consideration of the public sentiment in the Philippines and his own wartime experiences, of all the judges of the Tokyo trial, Jaranilla was probably the most susceptible to the influence of the war and acts of the Japanese Army. However, during the trial, he never expressed even to his own family, criticism toward the Japanese people. He did not comment on former prime minister Hideki Tōjō, or any other defendant.[83] There are virtually no records of his expressing his desire for revenge on Japan. It seems that Jaranilla tried to remain calm and unaffected by the anti-Japanese sentiment that dominated his own country. Such behaviour is clearly attributable to his own personality, as well as to his professionalism, which he fostered throughout his long career as a lawyer. Moreover, the suspicion concerning his qualification as a judge of the tribunal, which he experienced shortly after his arrival in Japan, would also have influenced his behaviour in Tokyo. In addition to these factors, he probably tried to moderate his own sentiments and maintain impartiality driven by his own sense of 'mission'. He believed it to be his duty to present new guidelines for international justice so as to prevent potential aggressions and atrocities in the future.[84] In conclusion, the presence of Jaranilla at the IMTFE contributed the perspective of Asian war victims to the international tribunal of war criminals, whose judges comprised legal professionals with diverse careers, perspectives and values.

Bibliography

Neil Boister and Robert Cryer, *The Tokyo International Military Tribunal: A Reappraisal* (Oxford University Press, 2008).

Arnold C. Brackman, *The Other Nuremberg: The Untold Story of the Tokyo War Crimes Trial* (New York: William Morrow and Company, Inc., 1987).

---

81   *The Washington Daily News*, 11 March 1949; 'They will hang the Japs', *Philippine Armed Forces Journal*, 1, no. 4 (February 1948), p. 10.

82   T.M. Locsin, 'Day of Reckoning', *Philippines Free Press*, 17 January 1948, 18; The Acting Secretary of State to the Acting Political Adviser in Japan, 2 November 1948, *FRUS, 1948*, vol. 6, p. 885; *Pacific Stars and Stripes*, 10 November 1948; *Manila Bulletin*, 8 December 1948.

83   E. Jaranilla, interview by author, 4 March 2009.

84   *Manila Bulletin*, 7 January 1947.

Miguel R. Cornejo (ed.), *Cornejo's Commonwealth Directory of the Philippines, 1939 Encyclopedic Edition* (Manila: Privately published, 1939).

Hisakazu Fujita, *International Regulation of the Use of Nuclear Weapons* (Osaka: Kansai University Press, 1988).

Rodolfo P. Gumabong, 'The Many Sides of Justice Jaranilla', *Philippines Free Press*, 12 July 1958.

Yoshinobu Higurashi, *Tokyo saiban no kokusai kankei: Kokusai seiji ni okeru kenryoku to kihan* [The Tokyo trial and international relations: Power and norms in international politics] (Tokyo: Bokutakusha, 2002).

Homudaijin kanbo shiho hosei chosabu [The judicial system research department, secretariat of the Ministry of Justice] (ed.), *Senso hanzai saiban kankeihoreishu* [Legal documents on war crimes trials], vol. 1 (Tokyo: 1963).

D.S. Jaranilla, Jr., 'Autobiography of Col. Delfin S. Jaranilla, Jr.', unpublished manuscript, Mary Anne J. Ambrosio Collection, Manila.

Hitoshi Nagai, 'Wasurerareta Tokyo saiban Firipin hanji: Delfin Jaranilla hanji no shogai' [The forgotten Filipino judge at the Tokyo trial: A biography of Justice Delfin Jaranilla] in K. Awaya (ed.), *Kingendai Nihon no senso to heiwa* [War and peace in modern Japanese history] (Tokyo: Gendai Shiryo Shuppan, 2010), pp. 303-66.

Nariaki Nakazato, *Paru hanji: Indo nashonarizumu to Tokyo saiban* [Justice Pal: Indian nationalism and the Tokyo trial] (Tokyo: Iwanami shoten, 2011).

R. John Pritchard and Sonia M. Zaide, eds., *The Tokyo War Crimes Trial*, vols. 8, 21, 22 (New York and London: Garland Publishing Inc., 1981).

B.V.A. Röling and Antonio Cassese, *The Tokyo Trial and Beyond: Reflections of a Peacemonger* (Cambridge: Polity Press, 1994).

H.L. Stimson and M.H. Bundy, *On Active Service in Peace and War* (New York: Harper, 1948).

United States, Department of State, *Foreign Relations of the United States, 1946*, vol. 8, *The Far East* (Washington DC: United States Government Printing Office (USGPO), 1971).

CHAPTER 10

Defending French National Interests? The Quai d'Orsay, Ambassador Zinovy Peshkoff, Justice Henri Bernard and the Tokyo Trial

Ann-Sophie Schoepfel

In recent years, numerous studies have shown that the foundations of the International Military Tribunal for the Far East (IMTFE) were weaker than those of the Nuremberg trial. Indeed, the historiography presents the Nuremberg trial as 'not only a precedent setting legal undertaking, but also a major, transformative trial in history',[1] according to the historian David M. Crowe, while research on the Tokyo trial argues that the justice performed in Tokyo was imperfect.[2] But no studies have emphasized the fact that the IMTFE established an open forum for international justice for the first time in the Far East. This aspect is particularly interesting since it represented a crucial change in international relations. This chapter analyses political discussions on justice through the prism of diplomacy.

This paper explores a case in which an Allied state involved at the Tokyo trial was pressing its representatives to follow the US-American strategy, while its representatives were denouncing the political foundations of the tribunal. The resistance of these officials contributed to the change of policy regarding the Japanese war criminals in 1949, introducing in Japan the movement for parole of war criminals after 1950. This chapter focuses on French participation at the Tokyo trial. It gives voice to a forgotten key actor in the Far East, Zinovy Peshkoff (1884-1966), the head of the French Military Mission in Japan from 1946 to 1949. Historical archives demonstrate that Peshkoff enjoyed an outstanding reputation in Asia: he was decorated in 1946 with the American

---

1   D.M. Crowe, *War Crimes, Genocide, and Justice: A Global History* (New York: Palgrave MacMillan, 2013), p. 193.

2   N. Boister, 'The Tokyo Military Tribunal: A Show Trial?', in M. Bergsmo, W.L. Cheah and P. Yi (eds.), *Historical Origins of International Criminal Law*, vol. 2 (Brussels: Torkel Opsahl, 2014), pp. 3-29; T. Maga, *Judgment at Tokyo* (Lexington: The University Press of Kentucky, 2001); R. Minear, *Victors' Justice: The Trials at Tokyo* (Princeton: Princeton University Press, 1971); Y. Totani, *The Tokyo War Crimes Trials: The Pursuit of Justice in the Wake of World War II* (Harvard: Harvard University Press, 2008).

© KONINKLIJKE BRILL NV, LEIDEN, 2018 | DOI 10.1163/9789004361058_013

Legion of Merit[3] and with Nationalist China's 'Grand Cordon of the Bright
Star'.[4] An analysis of his role in the Tokyo trial and his changing perception of
international justice highlights political disputes behind the scenes of the
Tokyo trial.

Peshkoff's position was important for three reasons. Firstly, the study of
Peshkoff's position deepens the research initiated by different scholars on
French war crimes trials policy in Asia. The historiography has demonstrated
that the Quai d'Orsay, the French Foreign Ministry, in organizing the war
crimes trial policy for Asia, faced a twofold challenge: the past collaboration
with Japan and the pressure of decolonization. On the one hand, the Vichy
Regime, which collaborated with Nazi Germany and Japan, survived longer in
Indochina than in the other French colonies. On the other hand, the French
pursuit of justice was entangled in the French effort to regain its colonial
empire in Indochina, 'one of the most mismanaged, most brutal and most con-
sequential transfers of power in the history of decolonization', according to the
historian Marc Frey.[5] War crimes helped France to be perceived as a victim of
Japanese militarism.

Secondly, Peshkoff's relationships with two other French figures at the
Tokyo trial reveal not only the learning process of the French delegation in a
transnational context, but also the formation of the French trial policy in post-
war Japan. These two men were the French prosecutor at the International
Prosecution Section (IPS), Robert Oneto, who was influenced by the Nuremberg
trial, and the French colonial judge Henri Bernard, who protested against the
legitimacy of the tribunal while in the international college of judges. Finally,
a close examination of the archives from the French Department of Foreign
Affairs helps us chart the development of Peshkoff's political, diplomatic and
legal position from 1946 to 1949. Through conversations and exchanges in
Japan, with the government in Paris, and with contacts in Germany, Indochina
and America, he developed a unique definition of justice and a new perspective on the Tokyo trial.[6] According to Kirsten Sellars, Peshkoff advocated 'a

3   AMAE-Nantes, 697PO/3/1, Legion of merit awarded to General Zinovi Peshkoff, 31 January 1946.
4   My translation. AMAE-Nantes, 697PO/3/1, Communication officielle de KAN Nai Kwang, 2
    August 1946.
5   M. Frey, 'War Revolution and Passage of Empire: France, the United States and Indochina,
    1945-c.1960', in Franz Knipping, Piyanart Bunnag and Vimolvan Phatharodom (eds.), *Europe
    and Southeast Asia in the Contemporary World: Mutual Influences and Comparisons* (Baden:
    Nomos Verlagsgesellschaft, 1999), p. 193.
6   Peshkoff's opinion of the Tokyo trial has been studied once before: Y. Miyashita, 'La France
    face au retour du Japon sur la scène internationale, 1945-1964', unpublished PhD thesis,
    Sciences Po Paris (2012), pp. 322-59.

compassionate approach – both for the sake of the protagonists and for the sake of mankind'.[7]

This chapter is divided into four parts. In the first it analyses the appointment of the French judge and prosecutor in Tokyo and the relationships between Zinovy Peshkoff, Robert Oneto and Justice Henri Bernard. Then, it examines the French colonial legacy at the Tokyo trial and the French trial strategy imposed from Paris. Finally, it investigates the dissenting opinion of the French representatives and its influence in Tokyo in the political discussions of Japanese war crimes.

The Appointment of the French Delegation in Tokyo

In September 1945, the Supreme Commander for the Allied Powers (SCAP), General Douglas MacArthur, ordered the arrest of major Japanese war crimes suspects. In November 1945, he invited China, Great Britain, the USSR, Australia, Canada, the Netherlands, New Zealand and France – the eight other signatories of the Japanese Instrument of Surrender – to designate representatives in preparation for an international military tribunal in the Far East.

It should be noted that the American position on French involvement in the prosecution of Japanese war criminals changed after August 1945. During World War II, the American president, Franklin D. Roosevelt, wanted to bring an end to French colonialism in Indochina and replace it with an international trusteeship.[8] In the summer of 1945, the United States was opposed to the French conducting trials of Japanese war criminals in Asia,[9] since it hoped to weaken the French position there.

The change in American policy can be explained by the fact that France had succeeded in imposing itself as a respected legal state with the opening of the Nuremberg trials in October 1945. The inclusion of France among other world powers in the prosecution of Japanese war criminals would contribute to the credibility of the trials.

The French diplomatic response to the American invitation demonstrates France's interest in participating in an international trial in the Far East. France

---

7   K. Sellars, *'Crimes Against Peace' and International Law* (Cambridge University Press, 2013), p. 255.

8   W. la Feber, 'Roosevelt, Churchill, and Indochina: 1942-1945', *The American Historical Review*, 80 (1975), 1279.

9   Archives Nationales (AN), BB30/1791, Note du Ministre des Affaires Etrangères au Ministre de la Justice, 27 September 1945.

was receptive to the American proposal, but the only thing they quibbled over was the fact that France wanted the authority to directly prosecute 'Japanese war criminals by virtue of the sovereign rights which France possesses in the territories in the [French] Union'.[10] This international recognition was central for France, which was convinced that the prosecution of Japanese war crimes was essential not only for the attainment of French 'prestige in the Far East',[11] but also for its 'beneficial effect' on the Indochinese population.[12] David Marr shows that France met with difficulties in reasserting its colonial sovereignty in Asia in 1945, since the struggle of decolonization had officially started in Indochina with the proclamation of the Vietnamese Declaration of Independence in August 1945.[13] The United States accepted French national claims. France, in turn, supported the basic principles for the creation of the Tokyo trial on 19 January 1946.

It should be emphasized that it was the Ministry of Foreign Affairs which was responsible for the conduct of the Tokyo trial, whereas the Ministry of Justice was responsible for the conduct of the Nuremberg trial. This distinction highlights the importance of the Tokyo trial for the French position in international relations. However, according to Yves Beidgeber, judging Japanese war criminals was perceived as relatively unimportant in devastated metropolitan France, since France had not played a significant role in the Pacific War. Unlike the Nuremberg trial, the Tokyo war crimes trial was not of direct concern to the French and remained far removed from Europe. Beidgeber argues that the French participation in the Tokyo trial could be explained by the forced collaboration of French Indochina with Japan in 1940 and 1941 and by the killings of French war prisoners by Japanese forces in 1945.[14] Philip Piccigallo has highlighted the fact that France was an active participant in Allied war crimes policy already during the war. For example, France was involved in the United Nations War Crime Commission, set up in Chungking in May 1944 to prosecute

---

10   My translation. AMAE-La Courneuve, Asie-Océanie/Japon, vol. 130, Note pour M. Gaucheron, Secrétariat des Conférences, 15 November 1945.

11   My translation. Archives Nationales d'Outre-Mer (ANOM), INF 1364, Rapport du Secrétaire général du Comité de l'Indochine, 30 October 1945.

12   My translation. AMAE-La Courneuve, Asie Dossiers Généraux, vol. 161, Rapport du Secrétariat des Conférences, 24 September 1945.

13   D.G. Marr, *Vietnam 1945: The Quest for Power* (Berkeley: University of California Press, 1995), pp. 347-540.

14   Y. Beigbeder, *Judging War Crimes and Torture: French Justice and International Criminal Tribunals and Commissions (1940-2005)* (Leiden/Boston: Martinus Nijhoff Publishers, 2006), p. 257.

Japanese war crimes.[15] The French government ensured continuity in the political commitment to prosecute Japanese war criminals.

France's participation in an international military tribunal raised some important questions, including who would represent France at the Tokyo trial. The government encountered difficulties in finding qualified staff. Many jurists who had not collaborated with Vichy France during the war were busy drafting the new constitution and taking part in constructing the foundations of the new French Fourth Republic. On 22 January 1946, the Quai d'Orsay requested that the Ministry of Justice and the Colonial Office provide names of eligible candidates for the positions of judge and prosecutor.[16]

The High Commissioner in Indochina, Admiral Thierry d'Argenlieu, suggested designating a professor of law as judge; in Nuremberg, the French judge had been a well-known law professor, Henri Donnedieu de Vabres.[17] France's first choice was Jean Escarra,[18] a French legal scholar known for having worked as a legal consultant for the Chinese government between 1921 and 1929. Escarra had provided advice on reforming the Chinese legal system and was a key participant in designing the Chinese Civil Code of 1929. With his extensive knowledge of Asia and his network of contacts, he would have been a good choice for the Tokyo trial. But Escarra refused the government's invitation. The Colonial Office then made two further proposals, first Henri Heimburger and then Jean Lambert. Heimburger could speak English and German and was an esteemed magistrate in France and the colonies, according to the Colonial Office.[19] Lambert, for his part, was considered a perfect choice for prosecutor. He was deputy public prosecutor in the Seine department and the Office Director of Ministry of Education. Like the French prosecutor in Nuremberg, François de Menthon,[20] Lambert had extensive political and legal experience.

---

15   P.R. Piccigallo, *The Japanese on Trial: Allied War Crimes Operations in the East, 1945-1951* (Austin/London: University of Texas Press, 1979), pp. 201-2.

16   AMAE-La Courneuve, Dossiers Généraux, vol. 162, Correspondance de Bidault à Teitgen, 22 January 1946.

17   A.-S. Schoepfel, 'La voix des juges français dans les procès de Nuremberg et de Tokyo. Défense d'une idée de justice universelle', *Presses Universitaires de France, Guerres mondiales et conflits contemporains*, 249 (2013), 104.

18   Ibid.

19   AMAE-La Courneuve, Dossiers Généraux, vol. 162, Correspondance de Jacques Soustelle à Bidault, 25 January 1946.

20   François de Menthon was a law professor and a politician. During the war, he was the founder of the first cell of the Liberté Resistance movement in Annecy in November 1940 and a second cell in Lyon shortly afterwards, as well as being the editor for the underground newspaper *Liberté*.

However, both Heimburger and Lambert withdrew from their appointments as judge and prosecutor respectively.

Their successive resignations embarrassed the Quai d'Orsay.[21] Jean Esmein explains that the Ministry of French Overseas Territories (founded on 26 January 1946) then lobbied for the appointment of a colonial judge.[22] Henri Bernard was a colonial magistrate who sided with the Free French in August 1940, when the French authorities joined de Gaulle's forces in French Equatorial Africa (Congo). A military tribunal convened under the Vichy regime had sentenced Bernard to death in absentia.[23] Bernard then became a judicial representative for de Gaulle's government in Beirut in 1944 and was later involved in the 1945 preparation of the prosecution of Nazi war criminals in Austria. According to Mickaël Ho Foui Sang, Justice Bernard can be distinguished from most of the judges at the Tokyo trial because of his independent and engaged character.[24] It is important to stress here that one should avoid misunderstandings: while Justice Henri Bernard had been involved in the French colonial administration, he did not share colonial values.

The Ministry of Justice then proposed Robert Oneto, prosecutor at the Court of First Instance in Versailles, for the open position of prosecutor.[25] According to Beatrice Trefalt, Robert Oneto's experience as an investigating judge in Occupied France was important in determining his role during the trial.[26] On 1 March 1946, the names of the French judge and prosecutor were publicly announced. Bernard and Oneto were delegated to the Quai d'Orsay by order of the Ministry of French Overseas Territories and the Ministry of Justice.[27] Since Bernard and Oneto were unable to understand the official languages – English and Japanese – used in the Tokyo trial, the Quai d'Orsay decided to send

---

21   AMAE-La Courneuve, Asie Océanie, Généralités 162, Lettre du Ministre des Affaires étrangères au Ministre de la France d'outre-mer, 1 March 1946.

22   J. Esmein, 'Le juge Henri Bernard au procès de Tokyô', *Vingtième siècle, revue d'histoire*, 59 (1998), 5-6.

23   *Dépôt central d'archives de la justice militaire (DCJAM)*, Minutes of the French Permanent Military Tribunal in Clermont, Judgment of Henri Bernard, 12 September 1941.

24   M. Ho Foui Sang, 'Justice Bernard', in Y. Tanaka, T. McCormack and G. Simpson (eds.), *Beyond Victor's Justice? The Tokyo War Crimes Trial Revisited* (Leiden/Boston: Martinus Nijhoff, 2011), p. 94.

25   AMAE-La Courneuve, Dossiers Généraux, vol. 162, Correspondance de Bidault à Marius Moutet, 28 February 1946.

26   B. Trefalt, 'The French Prosecution at the IMTFE: Robert Oneto, Indochina and the Rehabilitation of French Prestige', in Kerstin von Lingen (ed.), *War Crimes Trials in the Wake of Decolonization and Cold War* (Basingtoke: Palgrave MacMillan, 2016), p. 57.

27   AMAE-La Courneuve, Asie-Océanie/Japon, vol. 130, Note pour la direction du personnel et de la comptabilité, 1 March 1946.

Jacques Gouëlou, an associate professor of English in Paris, to assist them as secretary to the French delegation at the Tokyo trial.[28] The selection of the French representatives at the Tokyo trial reveals the intergovernmental importance accorded to war experience, legal expertise, and knowledge of the institutional framework of the French Colonial Empire.

The Diplomat, the Prosecutor and the Judge

According to Francis Huré, Zinovy Peshkoff was embarrassed whenever the French judge or the French prosecutor came to speak of the Tokyo trial, since the diplomat disagreed with the foundations of the trial.[29] However, this did not prevent the head of the French Military Mission in Tokyo from supporting them throughout the entire trial, according to its service mission as head of the French mission in Tokyo. According to Beatrice Trefalt, the Tokyo trial constituted an 'international arena for "cultural diplomacy"' for both the French prosecutor and the French representative, since France wanted to establish an official record of its victimhood.[30] The Tokyo trial can also be seen as playing a central role in the transitional process of French post-war self-definition. It helped create both a new post-war narrative and a memory of France as a nation. 'Nation' in this context has been described by Paul James as an imagined and abstract community whose members 'experience themselves as an integrated group of compatriots'.[31]

Robert Oneto was one of eight assistant prosecutors to the American prosecutor Joseph B. Keenan, a former assistant US attorney general and director of the Criminal Division of the Justice Department who worked at the prosecution agency in Tokyo. While prosecutors from Great Britain, the Netherlands, China, New Zealand, the Philippines and Canada arrived in early 1946, Robert Oneto only arrived on 4 April 1946. When he arrived in Tokyo, he received the indictment drafted in March 1946. The French prosecutor was shocked to discover that France was treated, like Germany and Italy, as a wartime ally of Japan due to the nature of relations between Vichy France and Japan in

---

28   AMAE-La Courneuve, Dossiers Généraux, vol. 162, Correspondance de Bidault à Marcel-Edmond Naelen, 8 March 1946.

29   Ibid, p. 334.

30   Trefalt, 'The French Prosecution at the IMTFE', p. 51.

31   P. James, *Nation Formation: Towards a Theory of Abstract Community* (London: Sage Publications, 1996), p. 34.

Indochina from 1940 to 1945.[32] Because Robert Oneto was representing Free France, the association with Vichy France was highly embarrassing.

The political importance accorded to the Tokyo trial became a problem for the head of the French Military Mission in Tokyo, Zinovy Peshkoff. While Peshkoff wanted to contribute to the restoration of France's image in the Far East, he disagreed with the French support of the Tokyo trial. Participation in the trial was part of a state-building process: France aimed to send a message to the rest of the world at the Tokyo trial that it had emerged from the war as a new republican power well-suited to protecting Indochina, thereby trying to erase its colonial past.[33]

'Like Justice BERNARD, I cannot subscribe to the verdict of the majority of the judges of the Tribunal and to the sentences which have been pronounced', wrote Zinovy Peshkoff on 22 November 1948.[34] The head of the French Military Mission in Tokyo sent a note to MacArthur to denounce the judgment reached at the Tokyo tribunal on 12 November 1948. Peshkoff called upon MacArthur's 'generosity' and requested commutation.[35]

Peshkoff's note represented a pressing diplomatic issue. The position of the French government was to accept the outcome of the trial,[36] but Peshkoff did not. Peshkoff supported the dissenting opinion of the French judge Henri Bernard, who raised substantive objections to the Tokyo tribunal's foundations.[37] Indeed, recent research indicates that the French strategy in the Far East was to give support to Allied war crimes trials policy to consolidate its power in the international decision-making process.[38] This chapter argues

---

32   AMAE-La Courneuve, Secrétariat des Conférences, Nations Unies et Organisations Internationales, 372Q099, Correspondance de Robert Oneto au Ministre des Affaires Etrangères, 22 October 1946.

33   A.-S. Schoepfel, 'The War Court as a Form of State Building: The French Prosecution of Japanese War Crimes at the Saigon and Tokyo Trials' in M. Bergsmo, W.L. Cheah and P. Yi (eds.), *Historical Origins of International Criminal Law*, vol. 2 (Brussels: Torkel Opsahl, 2014), pp. 119-42.

34   Archives du Ministère des Affaires Etrangères (from here on: AMAE) Nantes, 697PO/3/8, Statement of Zinovi Peshkoff to MacArthur, 22 November 1948.

35   Ibid.

36   AMAE-La Courneuve, Asie Dossiers Généraux, vol. 167, Télégramme du sécrétariat des Conférences, 20 November 1948.

37   Bibliothèque de documentation internationale contemporaraine (BDIC), F delta rès 874/10, Dissenting Opinion of Justice Bernard, 12 November 1948.

38   C. Namba, 'La France face aux procès de Saigon et de Tokyo', *Outre-mers, Revue d'histoire*, 380-381 (2013), at 313-31; Schoepfel, 'The War Court as a Form of State Building', 119-42; B. Trefalt, 'Japanese War Crimes in Indochina and the French Pursuit of Justice: Local and International Constraints', *Journal of Contemporary History*, 49 (4) (2014), 727-42.

that Zinovy Peshkoff's position exposed the political foundations of the Tokyo trial's judgment which superseded moral and ethical considerations.

The French Ministry of Foreign Affairs appointed Zinovy Peshkoff as head of the French Military Mission to the SCAP in May 1946. The diplomatic representation in SCAP from 1945 to 1951 represented a significant opportunity for the organization to assert its national position in the Far East. In August 1945, Japan had been placed under the control of SCAP. According to John Dower, American military occupation forced Japan to democratize and demilitarize.[39] Tokyo, as SCAP's capital, became the centre of important geopolitical issues in the aftermath of the Pacific War. In this context, decisions regarding the punishment of major Japanese war criminals took place in Tokyo. The appointment of the head of the French Military Mission in Tokyo was therefore very important for the Quai d'Orsay.

In 1946, the Quai d'Orsay believed that Zinovy Peshkoff could best protect French national interests in Tokyo. His biography supported this idea. He embodied the fundamental values of the new French government emerging from World War II.[40] Firstly, Peshkoff, the adopted son of Maxim Gorky, had decided to embrace French values when, in 1914, he volunteered for the French Army. As a successful officer in the French Foreign Legion, he obtained French citizenship and was decorated with the Légion d'honneur in 1917. During World War II, he joined Free France, the government-in-exile of General Charles de Gaulle. His military career shows that he was a defender of the principles of democracy in the service of the state. Secondly, Peshkoff had gained extensive knowledge and experience in Asia. After World War I, the Quai d'Orsay sent him to East Asia. In January 1944, Free France designated him as the head of the military mission in Chungking, the provisional capital of Nationalist China.

Moreover, when he arrived in Tokyo, Peshkoff earned the trust and respect of General MacArthur. Yuichiro Miyashita shows that William Macmahon Ball, the British Commonwealth's representative at SCAP, considered Peshkoff the most remarkable spokesman among the foreign representatives.[41] Historical archives prove that Peshkoff enjoyed an outstanding reputation in Asia. The French ambassador was also much respected by the United States and China, the two major powers there after 1945. In January 1946, he was decorated with the American Legion of Merit 'for exceptionally meritorious conduct in the

---

39   J.W. Dower, *Embracing Defeat: Japan in the Wake of World War II* (New York: W.W. Norton & Company, 2000), p. 23.

40   The biographical information of General Peshkoff is provided in the book of the French diplomat Francis Huré, *Portraits de Pechkoff* (Paris: De Fallois, 2006).

41   Miyashita, 'La France face au retour du Japon', p. 18.

performance of outstanding services to the Government of the United States',
providing 'skilled technical assistance' in intelligence services in the 'setting
up' of 'weather reporting stations, radio facilities and a courier service on the
French Indo China Coast'.[42] In August 1946, Nationalist China bestowed on
him the title 'Grand Cordon of the Bright Star' in appreciation of his services in
China.[43]

But how is it possible to explain Peshkoff's official rejection of the outcome
of the Tokyo trial? To find answers to this question, one must look closely at
political issues that were raised while the prosecution of Japanese war criminals was being prepared.

French Trial Strategy and the Colonial Legacy

France's legacy in Asia was contested. Indeed, during World War II, the
Indochinese population had witnessed various contradictions within imperial
policies. One aspect, as Chizuru Namba underlines, was the Japanese occupation of the French colony Indochina, which had weakened French colonial
foundations.[44] While Vichy France ruled Indochina from 1940 to March 1945,
the Japanese Imperial army had troops stationed there and tried to monopolize Indochina's economic output. Eric Jennings has demonstrated how Jean
Decoux, the Governor-General of French Indochina, led a National Revolution
in Indochina that was characterized by its anti-parliamentarism and the rejection of the constitutional separation of powers, personality cult, the promotion
of traditional values and the rejection of modernity.[45] On 9 March 1945, the
Japanese coup d'état, Operation Mei-go, overthrew the French colonial administration.[46] Japan pressed Vietnam, Laos and Cambodia to declare their
independence. When Japanese troops surrendered in August 1945, Indochina

---

42   AMAE-Nantes, 697PO/3/1, Legion of merit awarded to General Zinovi Peshkoff, 31 January
      1946.

43   My translation. AMAE-Nantes, 697PO/3/1, Communication officielle de KAN Nai Kwang, 2
      August 1946.

44   C. Namba, *Français et Japonais en Indochine (1940-1945): Colonisation propagande et
      rivalité culturelle* (Paris: Karthala, 2012).

45   J. Cantier and E.T. Jennings, *L'Empire colonial sous Vichy* (Paris: Editions Odile Jacob,
      2004), p. 14.

46   K. Kurusu Nitz, 'Japanese Military Policy Towards French Indochina during the Second
      World War: The Road to the Meigo Sakusen (9 March 1945)', *Journal of Southeast Asian
      Studies*, 14 (1983), 328-53.

was in disarray due to a power vacuum.[47] Although it was decided at the Potsdam Conference that Indochina would be divided in two – at the 16th parallel, between the Chinese in the North and the British in the South – it took time for the Allied troops to gain control of Indochinese territory.

De Gaulle's government attempted to reassert its sovereignty over Indochina with the creation of a French Indochinese Union on 27 October 1946.[48] It is clear that discrepancies between imperial projects led to the reinforcement of the struggle for decolonization and the outbreak of the first Indochina war on 19 December 1946 between French forces and their Viet Minh opponents.

The Quay d'Orsay defined the mission of the French representative to General MacArthur as the 'defence of the French political, economical and cultural position'.[49] Zinovy Peshkoff's position was particularly tricky in postwar Japan since he supported the independence movement in Indochina. But, as Yuichiro Miyashita demonstrates, he remained faithful to the French government's policy on the defence of the French political mission in Japan by following the recommendations of the Quai d'Orsay.[50]

The head of the French Military Mission in Tokyo disagreed with the American policy of occupation in Japan, putting him at odds with the basis of the Tokyo trial.[51] The French diplomat Francis Huré in his memoirs explained that Peshkoff regretted the Allied indictment against Japan since 'on the core concepts of human conduct and its responsibility, the American Western World and the Japanese Far East were not meeting. The debate, aiming at easing consciences, opened the abyss that divided them.'[52] Hence, one can see here that Peshkoff was caught in an ethical dilemma: while the Quai d'Orsay demanded national representation in Japan and support for the Tokyo trial, Peshkoff wished to express his strong disagreement with the political foundations of the trial.

In early April 1946, there was only a little time before the filing of charges on 29 April 1946. For reasons of time, Robert Oneto was unable to consult the Quai d'Orsay for complete instructions. He took the risk of defending the French

---

47   A.-S. Schoepfel, 'Dynamics of justice in Indochina (1944-1946): France's Commitment to the Rule of Law and the Punishment of Japanese War Crimes' in P. Tolliday, M. Palme and D. Choon Kim (eds.), *Societies in Transition: Asia-Pacific between Conflict and Reconciliation* (Göttingen: xx Verlag, 2016), p. 107.

48   F. Turpin, *De Gaulle, les gaullistes et l'Indochine: 1940-1956* (Paris: Les Indes Savantes, 2005).

49   My translation. AMAE-Nantes, 697PO/3/1, Instructions du Ministre des Affaires Etrangères, 24 March 1950.

50   Miyashita, 'La France face au retour du Japon', p. 111.

51   Ibid., p. 335.

52   My translation. Huré, *Portraits de Pechkoff*, p. 134.

position in the International Prosecution Section. Without the support of Paris and without providing strong evidence, Robert Oneto presented the idea that Free France was very active in the Pacific War.[53] He highlighted the point that Free France provided strong support for the rallying of New Caledonia, which became an important American naval base, and he disavowed the policy of Vichy France's occupation in Indochina during the war.[54] Oneto's intervention resulted in France's removal from the list of Japanese wartime allies and to changes in the indictment.[55]

Zinovy Peshkoff's arrival in May 1946 reinforced the argument that France had not been a Japanese collaborator in World War II, since the head of the French Military Mission in Tokyo was the symbol of the French resistance in Asia.[56] In mid-May 1946, Peshkoff met with General MacArthur and informed him that he was offended by the suspicions about France at the Tokyo trial and its collaboration with Japan in Indochina. At the meeting, MacArthur had a sympathetic attitude and showed his support toward the French delegation.[57]

Despite difficulties in compiling evidence,[58] prosecutor Robert Oneto managed to strengthen the French position at the Tokyo trial. On 22 September 1946, a few days prior to the introduction of the French case before the trial, Oneto presented his strategy to the French government: he wanted to present the Japanese objective of invading Indochina, to prove how 'Japan took advantage of Indochina's weakness, of its isolation, and of France's military setbacks' to engage in a policy of aggression and expansion. Interestingly, Oneto avoided speaking about the Japanese support for the independence movement in Indochina and the American anti-colonial position. 'If I stress this point, that is unquestionably contrary to the Hague Convention, I would give the defence a certain part of public opinion in the Far East as a pretext for extensive debates, which seem to be inappropriate right now.'[59]

Robert Oneto and his assistant, Roger Depo, introduced their evidence about the relations between Japan and France from 30 September 1946 to 7 October 1946. On 30 September, Oneto refused to read the indictment aloud in English, one of the two official languages of the tribunal (along with Japanese),

---

53   Miyashita, 'La France face au retour du Japon', p. 331.

54   Ibid.

55   BDIC, F delta res 0874/01, Indictment Act, Offence 33 'Waging aggressive war against French Indochina after 22 September 1940', 29 April 1946.

56   Miyashita, 'La France face au retour du Japon', p. 145.

57   ANOM, HCI 132/382, Correspondance de Peshkoff à Président Gouin, 21 May 1946.

58   My translation. AMAE-La Courneuve, Asie-Océanie/Japon, vol. 130, Télégramme de Robert Oneto, 16 Mai 1946.

59   My translation. ANOM, FM/INDO/NF/1364, Télégramme de Peshkoff, 22 September 1946.

instead reading it in French. The court requested that Oneto express himself in English. But in the face of the French prosecutor's refusal, a debate about the issue of language ensued at the trial. Peshkoff supported the French prosecutor's wish to read the indictment act in French. Keenan agreed to allow Oneto to speak in French. But on 1 October, when Oneto took the floor again, the court president, Justice William Webb, forbade him to speak in French, and Oneto withdrew in protest from the court. At this time, Keenan and the English prosecutor Arthur Comyns-Carr intervened to defend the French position. The court finally recognized Oneto's right to speak in French.[60] This 'language crisis' was, according to Kayoko Takeda, the most famous incident of linguistic and cultural competition at the trials.[61] For the French delegation, it contributed to the strengthening of the French position.[62] The Quai d'Orsay asked Zinovy Peshkoff to convey the Ministry of Foreign Affairs' satisfaction with the outcome to Oneto.[63]

It is necessary and important here to put the French trial strategy in Tokyo into perspective. The Japanese did not perceive the accusations in the same way as the French did. In January 1947, the unique witness of the French accusation gave his evidence to the tribunal.[64] Initially, Oneto wanted to present two witnesses.[65] But, due to the return of the witnesses from Indochina to France, Oneto questioned only one witness, Captain Fernand Gabrillagues, a member of the War Crimes Unit in Saigon.[66] Fernand Gabrillagues presented affidavits on war crimes committed by the Japanese forces in Indochina.

William Logan, an American attorney defending the Japanese war criminals, attacked Gabrillagues for being neither a victim nor a real witness of Japanese war crimes committed in Indochina. Logan succeeded in embarrassing Gabrillagues, who refused to answer questions about the collaboration between Vichy France and Japan. The cross-examination revealed that Fernand

---

60 AMAE-La Courneuve, Asie-Océanie/Japon, vol. 130, Télégramme de Peshkoff (de la part d'Oneto), 11 October 1946.

61 Kayoko Takeda, *Interpreting the War Crimes Trials: A Socio-political Analysis* (University of Ottawa Press, 2010), pp. 22-26.

62 AMAE-La Courneuve, Asie-Océanie/Japon, vol. 130, Télégramme de Peshkoff (de la part d'Oneto), 11 October 1946.

63 AMAE-Nantes, 697PO/3/8, Correspondance signée Diplomatie, 4 October 1946.

64 AMAE-La Courneuve, Asie Dossiers généraux, vol. 164, Télégramme de Peshkoff (de la part d'Oneto), 13 January 1947.

65 AMAE-La Courneuve, Asie Dossiers généraux, vol. 164, Télégramme de Peshkoff (de la part d'Oneto), 10 December 1946.

66 AMAE-La Courneuve, Asie Dossiers généraux, vol. 164, Télégramme de Peshkoff (de la part d'Oneto), 13 January 1947.

Gabrillagues was not even in Indochina during the war but served under the Vichy Regime in Africa.[67] Yuichiro Miyashita highlights that the Japanese defendants were not convinced by the accusation presented by the French.[68]

Robert Oneto complained of a lack of freedom of expression at the IPS. According to the French prosecutor, the British and the American members were imposing their own vision and the 'accusation signed by the representatives of eleven Allied nations was mainly the work of the Americans and the British'.[69]

Zinovy Peshkoff supported the position of the French prosecutor at the IPS in affirming the positive French role during World War II. He played a pivotal part in the interactions between the Quai d'Orsay and Robert Oneto. He issued the necessary instructions from the Quai d'Orsay and transmitted Oneto's reports. In the short term, this collaboration helped reassert French power in Tokyo. It should also be highlighted that the French prosecution served primarily American interests, as Robert Oneto participated in writing an indictment against major Japanese war criminals.

Dissenting Opinion

The position of Justice Bernard is very important, as he wanted to provide recommendations to posterity on the use of international law concepts and on the procedure for making international criminal law practicable for the future.[70] According to him, the right to establish the Tokyo trial was based on natural and universal law. Furthermore, the Allies' respect for procedural justice and the fundamental rights of the accused should have enhanced the legitimacy of the trial.[71]

Nonetheless, Justice Bernard disapproved of the way in which investigations were conducted in Tokyo and the use of new international law concepts such as conspiracy and crimes against peace. Bernard believed that the right of the accused to a proper defence was not being respected.[72] Furthermore, he regretted that the prosecution was conducted ad personam, as the failure to

---

67   AN, BB35/776, Record of Proceedings of the International Military Tribunal for the Far East, vol. 68, pp. 15455-66, 17 January 1947.

68   Miyashita, 'La France face au retour du Japon', pp. 333-34.

69   My translation. AMAE-Nantes, 697PO/3/8, Correspondance de Robert Oneto à Bidault, 2 March 1948.

70   Ho Foui Sang, 'Justice Bernard', 97.

71   Bernard, 'Dissenting Opinion', p. 2.

72   Ibid., p. 18.

indict Emperor Hirohito served as a clear illustration of the selective approach of the tribunal. According to him, the Japanese emperor was the head of state during Japan's imperial expansion, militarization and involvement in World War II, and he should have been prosecuted by the American government for war crimes. He believed that Japan's declaration of war 'had a principal author who escaped all prosecution and of whom in any case the present Defendants could only be considered as accomplices'.[73]

Bernard informed the president of the trial of his strong disagreement with the proceedings before the final position of the tribunal was decided. He also sent many memorandums to his colleagues, but none of them had been taken into consideration. When the final judgment was published, he decided to make his disapproval known in his dissenting opinion on 12 November 1948 in which he stated: 'A verdict reached by a Tribunal after a defective procedure cannot be a valid one'.[74] Bernard's dissenting opinion drew attention to the significance of the application of justice, fairness and equality in the procedure.

During the trial, Zinovy Peshkoff supported the French judge. Political ethics led Peshkoff to make key decisions for his political career, since he decided to formulate a moral judgment about the political foundations of the tribunal. This shows how Peshkoff's moral problems had been augmented by the need for political compromise and real justice when the Tokyo trial's judgment was revealed on 12 November 1948. While political realists argue that personal ethics have no place in politics,[75] and that ambassadors should have protected national interests, this chapter shows the political action of a pragmatic ambassador.

From the start to the end of the Tokyo trial, the correspondence of the head of the French Military Mission in Tokyo with the Quai d'Orsay makes clear that Zinovy Peshkoff strongly disagreed with the political foundations of the Tokyo trial. However, Peshkoff had already started to form independent and critical thoughts on the trial by 1946.[76] While Peshkoff did not demonstrate strong interest in the trial, he was really concerned with the confrontation between Hideki Tōjō, the most important individual accused at the Tokyo trial, and the American prosecutor Keenan. For this reason, he was invited to the cross-examination between Tōjō and Keenan from 31 December 1947 to 6 January 1948.

---

73   Ibid., p. 8.

74   Ibid.

75   R. Ned Lebow, *The Tragic Vision of Politics: Ethics, Interests and Orders* (Cambridge University Press, 2003).

76   Miyashita, 'La France face au retour du Japon', p. 335.

Peshkoff disliked the atmosphere at the tribunal, stating 'there is, in the atmosphere of this tribunal and of this trial in general, a malaise, a hard embarrassment'.[77] In addition, he believed that the weakness of the court would contribute to reanimating the Japanese ultranationalism demonstrated during the Pacific War, and create a legend around Tōjō, who had been the general of the Imperial Japanese Army and Japanese prime minister during most of World War II. In a telegram addressed to the French government, Peshkoff described the American prosecutor as a 'man of little education' without 'any subtle dialectic'.[78] Conversely, Tōjō not only had 'superior intelligence' but was also 'prestigious'.[79] Although Peshkoff strongly disapproved of the arguments about Tōjō, he was aware of the danger Tōjō represented for the future of Japan.

Only when the judgment was reached on 12 November 1948 did Peshkoff start to make his critical stance in view of the trial publicly known. According to Yuichiro Miyashita, the head of the French Military Mission in Tokyo shared Justice Henri Bernard's view on the Tokyo trial.[80] Unlike Peshkoff, the French judge had contested the legal foundations of the trial since 1946.

On 15 November 1948, Zinovy Peshkoff sent a note to the Quai d'Orsay to request the authority to express his opposition to the Tokyo trial's judgment at a meeting organized by MacArthur. He wanted to request commutation,[81] and highlighted that he strongly supported Bernard's dissenting opinion. Peshkoff openly criticized the political foundations of the tribunal: 'there is some inconsistency to condemning the leaders of ancient Japan who are seeking prominence for their country in Asia, while the present leaders are still trying to get it but this time under the auspices of the Americans'.[82] Moreover, he contested the legal grounds of the accusations and the application of the concept of crimes against peace.[83] According to him, this notion was too abstract and elastic.[84]

---

77   My Translation. AMAE-La Courneuve, Asie/Japon, vol. 41, Correspondance de Peshkoff, January 1948.

78   AMAE-La Courneuve, Asie Dossiers Généraux, vol. 165, Correspondance de Peshkoff à Bidault, 7 January 1948.

79   Ibid.

80   Miyashita, 'La France face au retour du Japon', p. 343.

81   AMAE-La Courneuve, Asie Dossiers Généraux, vol. 167, Correspondance de Peshkoff, 15 November 1948.

82   Ibid.

83   Ibid.

84   Ibid.

But the Quai d'Orsay disagreed with Bernard and Peshkoff's point of view. On 17 November, it sent a note to Peshkoff asking him to clearly present the legal grounds for Henri Bernard's dissenting opinion.[85] In Tokyo, Peshkoff met Bernard to formulate a solid answer. On 19 November, Peshkoff explained that, according to Henri Bernard, the lack of investigation was prejudicial to the accused. He noted that Justice Bernard insisted that Japanese history was very different from that of the Germans. For the judge, the role played by each Japanese individual accused was episodic. None of them could have played a role comparable to the role of Hitler, or the leaders of Nazi Germany, and it had not been proven that the final consequences of their acts were premeditated. Therefore, it was difficult for the accused to make a connection between their behaviour and a penal rule condemning the aggressive war, which international lawyers could not define clearly. Peshkoff explained that, as a consequence, Bernard believed that it was not clearly proven that the accused were aware of the criminal aspect of their acts during the period in question.[86]

On 20 November 1948, the Quai d'Orsay sent its answer to the head of the French Military Mission in Tokyo, to the President of the Republic, and to the Council Presidency. The Quai d'Orsay gave a negative answer to the request for commutation. It asked Peshkoff to 'adopt an attitude of reserve', although 'equity considerations could advocate for commutation of sentence'.[87] The Quai d'Orsay wanted to cause problems for MacArthur. Peshkoff's attitude was seen to be an embarrassment for France on the world stage.

At the consultative meeting organized by MacArthur on 22 November 1948, the representatives from the United States, Great Britain, New Zealand, China and the Philippines agreed with the Tokyo trial's judgment. Representatives from Canada and Australia raised the question of commutation. The Dutch representative asked for a reduction of sentences. The Indian representative stated that India was against the death penalty.[88] Peshkoff adopted an attitude of reserve during the meeting but submitted a note in English to MacArthur criticizing the foundations of the Tokyo trial and requesting commutation.[89]

---

85   AMAE-La Courneuve, Asie Dossiers Généraux, vol. 167, Télégramme du Secrétariat des Conférences, 17 November 1948.

86   AMAE-La Courneuve, Asie Dossiers Généraux, vol. 167, Télégramme de Peshkoff, 19 November 1948.

87   My translation.AMAE-La Courneuve, Asie Dossiers Généraux, vol. 167, Télégramme du Secrétariat des Conférences, 20 November 1948.

88   AMAE-La Courneuve, vol. 167, Télégramme de Peshkoff, 23 November 1948: Asie Volumes Généraux,.

89   AMAE-Nantes, 697PO/3/8, Statement of Zinovy Peshkoff, 22 November 1948.

Peshkoff had followed the instructions of the Quai d'Orsay, writing that 'the statement which I would like to make does not in any way engage my government. It is my personal sentiment which I believe to be my moral duty to express to the Supreme Commander of the Allied Powers.'[90] First, Peshkoff questioned legal aspects of the trial, such as the accusation of conspiracy and crimes against peace.[91] Second, he asked MacArthur to think about 'the horrors unchained by all of us during the last war, during the years 1939 to 1945'.[92] Third, he called for generosity and the abolishment of the death penalty: 'Generosity is always a paying proportion. The results may not be instant, it may not be acknowledged immediately but it goes deep into one's heart, it remains in the sacred corners of our soul, it imprints deeply on our memory; be it of an individual or a nation … I wish that capital punishment should be abolished from the codes of justice.'[93]

On 24 November 1948, Peshkoff asked the French Foreign Minister Robert Schuman to be relieved of his duties and to leave Japan as soon as possible, to show his disapproval of the prosecution of Japanese war criminals in Tokyo.[94] But Robert Schuman did not accept Peshkoff's resignation.[95] He sent a note to the Quai d'Orsay, in which he stressed that 'despite the majority judgment, the grievance of conspiracy was not grounded…. Under these conditions, doubt, instead of leading to severity, should have engaged clemency.'[96] Peshkoff's opinion did not have a strong influence. On 23 December 1948, seven of the accused were executed. In May 1949, Peshkoff finally left Japan. His departure demonstrated his disapproval of the political foundations of the Tokyo trial and, more broadly, the manner of the American occupation of Japan. But his position introduced the new trial policy after 1949, characterized by clemency for war criminals.

---

90   Ibid.

91   Ibid.

92   Ibid.

93   Ibid.

94   AMAE-La Courneuve, Asie Volumes Généraux, vol. 167, Télégramme de Peshkoff à Schuman, 24 November 1948.

95   AMAE-La Courneuve, Asie Volumes Généraux, vol. 167, Télégramme de Schuman à Peshkoff, 27 November 1948.

96   My Translation. AMAE-La Courneuve, Asie Volumes Généraux, vol. 167, Télégramme de Peshkoff à Schuman, 2 December 1948.

Conclusion

In Tokyo, the French delegation played a minor role during the trial. The two main actors remained isolated because they could not speak English. However, the chapter has offered a new perspective on the Tokyo trial and on the role the head of the French Military Mission in Tokyo played behind the scenes during the tribunal. While scholars have until now focused on the fact that the French involvement at the Tokyo trial was linked to the question of the recolonization of Indochina, this chapter shows that this was only a small consideration. First and foremost, both the French prosecutor Oneto and the French ambassador Peshkoff were aware of the political foundations of the trial and used it to prove that France had been among the victims of Japanese aggression. Secondly, the positions of Justice Henri Bernard and Zinovy Peshkoff demonstrated the ambivalence of the position of the Quai d'Orsay. While the Quai d'Orsay knew that the accusations were not solid enough to condemn the twenty-eight major war criminals indicted at the Tokyo trial to death, it did not support the positions of the French judge and the French ambassador. Thus it requested the head of the French Military Mission in Tokyo to take a passive attitude in order to avoid political trouble with MacArthur. However, Zinovy Peshkoff was too concerned with his moral duty and decided to make his dissenting opinion known by drafting a note to MacArthur and eventually leaving Japan a few months after the Tokyo judgment had been reached.

Bibliography

Yves Beigbeder, *Judging War Crimes and Torture: French Justice and International Criminal Tribunals and Commissions (1940-2005)* (Leiden/Boston: Martinus Nijhoff Publishers, 2006).

Neil Boister, 'The Tokyo Military Tribunal: A Show Trial?', in Morten Bergsmo, Cheah Wui Ling and Yi Ping (eds.), *Historical Origins of International Criminal Law*, vol. 2 (Brussels: Torkel Opsahl, 2014), pp. 3-29.

Jacques Cantier and Eric T. Jennings, *L'Empire colonial sous Vichy* (Paris: Editions Odile Jacob, 2004).

David M. Crowe, *War Crimes, Genocide, and Justice: A Global History* (New York: Palgrave MacMillan, 2013).

John W. Dower, *Embracing Defeat: Japan in the Wake of World War II* (New York: W.W. Norton & Company, 2000).

Jean Esmein, 'Le juge Henri Bernard au procès de Tokyô', *Vingtième siècle, revue d'histoire*, 59 (1998), 3-14.

Marc Frey, 'War Revolution and Passage of Empire: France, the United States and Indochina, 1945-c.1960', in Franz Knipping, Piyanart Bunnag and Vimolvan Phatharodom (eds.), *Europe and Southeast Asia in the Contemporary World: Mutual Influences and Comparisons* (Baden: Nomos Verlagsgesellschaft, 1999).

Mickael Ho Foui Sang, 'Justice Bernard', in Yuki Tanaka, Tim McCormack and Gerry Simpson (eds.), *Beyond Victor's Justice? The Tokyo War Crimes Trial Revisited* (Leiden: Brill, 2011).

Francis Huré, *Portraits de Pechkoff* (Paris: De Fallois, 2006).

Paul W. James, *Nation Formation: Towards a Theory of Abstract Community* (London: Sage Publications, 1996).

Kiyoko Kurusu Nitz, 'Japanese Military Policy Towards French Indochina during the Second World War: The Road to the Meigo Sakusen (9 March 1945)', *Journal of Southeast Asian Studies*, 14 (1983), 328-53.

Walter La Feber, 'Roosevelt, Churchill, and Indochina: 1942-1945', *The American Historical Review*, 80 (1975), 741-51.

Richard Ned Lebow, *The Tragic Vision of Politics: Ethics, Interests and Orders* (Cambridge University Press, 2003).

Tim Maga, *Judgment at Tokyo* (Lexington: The University Press of Kentucky, 2001).

David G. Marr, *Vietnam 1945: The Quest for Power* (Berkeley: University of California Press, 1995).

Richard Minear, *Victors' Justice: The Trials at Tokyo* (Princeton University Press, 1971).

Yuichiro Miyashita, 'La France face au retour du Japon sur la scène internationale, 1945-1964', unpublished PhD thesis, Sciences Po Paris (2012).

Chizuru Namba, *Français et Japonais en Indochine (1940-1945). Colonisation propagande et rivalité culturelle* (Paris: Karthala, 2012).

Chizuru Namba, 'La France face aux procès de Saigon et de Tokyo', *Outre-mers, Revue d'histoire*, 380-381 (2013), 313-31.

Philip. R. Piccigallo, *The Japanese on Trial: Allied War Crimes Operations in the East, 1945-1951* (Austin/London: University of Texas Press, 1979).

Kirsten Sellars, *'Crimes Against Peace' and International Law* (Cambridge University Press, 2013).

Ann-Sophie Schoepfel, 'La voix des juges français dans les procès de Nuremberg et de Tokyo. Défense d'une idée de justice universelle', *Presses Universitaires de France, Guerres mondiales et conflits contemporains*, 249 (2013), 101-14.

Ann-Sophie Schoepfel, 'The War Court as a Form of State Building: The French Prosecution of Japanese War Crimes at the Saigon and Tokyo Trials' in Morten Bergsmo, Cheah Wui Ling and Yi Ping (eds.), *Historical Origins of International Criminal Law*, vol. 2 (Brussels: Torkel Opsahl, 2014), pp. 119-42.

Ann-Sophie Schoepfel, 'Dynamics of Justice in Indochina (1944-1946): France's Commitment to the Rule of Law and the Punishment of Japanese War Crimes' in

Philip Tolliday, Maria Palme and Dong Choon Kim (eds.), *Societies in Transition: Asia-Pacific between Conflict and Reconciliation* (Göttingen: Vandenhoeck & Ruprecht, 2016), pp. 103-24.

Kayoko Takeda, *Interpreting the War Crimes Trials: A Socio-Political Analysis* (University of Ottawa Press, 2010).

Frédéric Turpin, *De Gaulle, les gaullistes et l'Indochine: 1940-1956* (Paris: Les Indes Savantes, 2005).

Yuma Totani, *The Tokyo War Crimes Trials: The Pursuit of Justice in the Wake of World War II* (Harvard University Press, 2008).

Beatrice Trefalt, 'Japanese War Crimes in Indochina and the French Pursuit of Justice: Local and International Constraints', *Journal of Contemporary History*, 49 (4) (2014), 727-42.

Beatrice Trefalt, 'The French Prosecution at the IMTFE: Robert Oneto, Indochina and the Rehabilitation of French Prestige', in Kerstin von Lingen (ed.), *War Crimes Trials in the Wake of Decolonization and Cold War* (Basingtoke: Palgrave MacMillan, 2016), pp. 51-68.

CHAPTER 11

In the Footsteps of Grotius: The Netherlands and Its Representation at the International Military Tribunal for the Far East, 1945-1948

Lisette Schouten

As a judge I feel sole responsibility for my own conscience, but I am also aware of the fact that I, as a representative of the Netherlands, am also more or less acting on behalf of my country. A strange position, in which even abstaining from adjudication doesn't seem to be a reasonable solution to the conflict. For now, I am convinced that it would be desirable if I would voice my dissent. It seems to me that I, the representative of the country of Grotius, would be keeping in line with our history when I express supremacy of law over power and the aversion of power disguised as justice.[1]

∴

This quotation from Professor B.V.A. Röling, the Dutch judge at the International Military Tribunal for the Far East (IMTFE), epitomizes how individual and national norms and ideals of justice can be jeopardized when they are to be applied in an international framework. While contemplating disregarding the Chamber's agreement to secrecy – a tradition deeply entrenched in the Dutch legal system – Röling was well aware that his growing reservations against the law of the tribunal's Charter and a possible dissent could imperil the Netherlands' international position and cause unwanted political consequences. Yet, while acknowledging his government's concerns, he was not willing to leave the law or himself in the hands of power politics and chose to let the development of international law prevail.

International trials, and the Tokyo tribunal in particular, have often been portrayed as contested encounters between legal, national and transnational

---

1 B.V.A. Röling to Van Eysinga, 3 January 1947 (original in Dutch, translated by author) quoted in L. van Poelgeest, *Nederland en het Tribunaal van Tokio. Volkenrechtelijke polemiek en internationale politiek rond de berechting en gratiëring van de Japanse oorlogsmisdadigers* (Arnhem: Gouda Quint, 1989), pp. 74-75.

forces. In reality, complex external factors, including post-war idealism, colonialism and Cold War politics, were coupled with more internal dynamics. As shown by James Sedgwick's dissertation 'The Trial Within'[2], justice emerged from several intricate concurrent processes wherein the 'human element' had profound consequences on the trial's proceedings and outcomes.

While scholarship on the Netherlands' contribution at the IMTFE is limited, it has generally had a strong focus on individual agents, acknowledging the importance of participant experiences.[3] Additionally, most literature has been devoted to Röling, whose career in Tokyo 'exemplifies the complex and contested production of international justice', as his dissent eventually made him one of the most renowned Dutch international jurists but also caused him to clash with his government back home.[4]

It is therefore the aim of this chapter to shed light on a lesser-known group of representatives: the Netherlands Prosecution Section. A small but effective division headed by W.G.F. Borgerhoff-Mulder, it was able to provide a valuable contribution to the IMTFE's proceedings, irrespective of and perhaps even due to the lack of interest and guidance from its government.

A Japanese Nuremberg?[5]

In October 1945, Supreme Commander of the Allied Powers (SCAP) General D. MacArthur was tasked with setting up an international tribunal for the adjudication of Japanese war criminals. The US State Department subsequently called on The Netherlands to nominate a judge, substitute judge and assistant

---

2   J.B. Sedgwick, 'The Trial Within: Negotiating Justice at the International Military Tribunal for the Far East, 1946-1948', unpublished PhD thesis, the University of British Columbia (2012).

3   Poelgeest, *Tribunaal*; H. Röling, *De rechter die geen ontzag had. Bert Röling en het Tokiotribunaal* (Amsterdam: Wereldbibliotheek, 2014); B.V.A. Röling and A. Cassese, *The Tokyo Trial and Beyond: Reflections of a Peacemonger* (Cambridge: Polity Press, 1994); R. Cryer, 'Justice Röling (The Netherlands)' in Y. Tanaka, T. McCormack and G. Simpson (eds.), *Beyond Victor's Justice? The Tokyo War Crimes Trial Revisited* (Leiden/Boston: Martinus Nijhoff Publishers, 2011), pp. 109-26. K. Ushimura, *Beyond the 'Judgment of Civilization': The Intellectual Legacy of the Japanese War Crimes Trials, 1946-1949*, translated by S.J. Ericson, LTCB International Library Selection no. 14, first English edition (Tokyo: The International House of Japan, 2003).

4   Sedgwick, 'The Trial Within', p. 311; Poelgeest, *Tribunaal*, pp. 78-96; K. Sellars, 'William Patrick and "Crimes against Peace" at the Tokyo Tribunal, 1946-1948', *The Edinburgh Law Review*, 15 (2011), 166-96, at 180.

5   'Het Japansche Neurenberg. Een onderhoud met mr. Borgerhoff-Mulder', *Het Dagblad* no. 158, 3 May 1946, front page.

prosecutor by 5 January 1946.[6] When J. Loudon, the Dutch ambassador in Washington, forwarded the request to the Ministerie van Buitenlandse Zaken (Dutch Ministry of Foreign Affairs (MFA) it was received with scepticism and reservations. The MFA was preoccupied with internal reforms, shifting international relations and a de facto colonial war in the Netherlands East Indies (NEI). The adjudication of foreign war criminals, especially those in the 'Far East', was by no means a priority.[7] The prevailing feelings towards the trial were aptly expressed by MFA jurist E. Star Busmann, who proclaimed:

> As far as Europe is concerned, one can say that according to Western standards unthinkable things have indeed occurred that require action. In the Far East, however, very different views on what is and is not allowed dominate. What happened there, one cannot judge by Western standards, nor treat according to Western methods.[8]

The same official subsequently considered Dutch participation in the tribunal 'unrealistic and not in our interest' in light of the more recent political developments in Indonesia and pointed out that it could well be possible that the Netherlands, when suppressing the Indonesian independence fighters, would use methods that other countries might regard as war crimes.[9] Considering the later developments, his comments prove remarkably prophetic and mirror the different perception of punishable crimes in Europe and Asia, as well as the 'double standards' applied by the old colonial powers in Asia with regard to

---

6   The first unamended IMTFE Charter provided for only nine judges to be selected. Only in late April 1946 were judges from India and the Philippines appointed. N. Boister and R. Cryer, *The Tokyo International Military Tribunal: A Reappraisal* (Oxford: Oxford University Press, 2008), p. 27, 80.

7   It is important to note that the Dutch representation at the Nuremberg Trial was – much to their disapproval – limited to S.J. Baron van Tuyll van Serooskerken, who assisted the (French) prosecution section of the International Military Tribunal. The invitation for the IMTFE extended to the Netherlands therefore entailed a first; for the first time, the Netherlands could actually contribute to the adjudication of major war criminals at an international level. Nationaal Archief, The Hague (NL-HaNA), 2.09.09, 'Ministerie van Justitie: Centraal Archief van de Bijzondere Rechtspleging (CABR) 1945-1952 (1983)', inventory number (inv. no.) 462, letter from Directeur-Generaal voor Bijzondere Rechtspleging to Secretaris-Generaal Kabinet, 22 February 1949. NL-HaNA, 2.09.61, 'Ministerie van Justitie: Commissies tot Opsporing van Oorlogsmisdadigers [COOM], (1942) 1944-1949 (1984)', inv. no. 28, letter Mouton to Woltjer, 20 October 1945 and letter Woltjer to Mouton, 2 October 1945.

8   (Original in Dutch, translated by author) Poelgeest, *Tribunaal*, p. 26.

9   NL-HaNA, 2.05.117, 'Ministerie van Buitenlandse Zaken: Code-archief 1945-1954', inv. no. 6671, Nota Star Busmann, October 1945.

their former colonies. Nonetheless, Minister of Foreign Affairs E.N. van Kleffens realized that the Netherlands could no longer hold on to its pre-war neutrality policy and should fulfil its Allied 'duty'. Furthermore, participation in an international tribunal fitted well with the long-standing Dutch tradition of the promotion of an international legal system and, according to Kleffens, one should also take the publicity that would be given to these trials into consideration. Thus, although the Netherlands saw little merit in joining an international war crimes tribunal, national interests, the chance to regain recognition and a commitment to international law prevailed; it was decided that the Netherlands would partake.[10]

Choosing Grotius's Representatives

The lack of enthusiasm within the ministry was reflected in the search for suitable candidates; finding agreeable legal staff presented a serious challenge. The MFA initially requested the Ministerie van Overzeese Gebiedsdelen (Ministry of Overseas Territories, MOT) to provide jurists from the judiciary or colonial administration in the Netherlands East Indies.[11] However, due to their wartime experiences, many of the qualifying men were in no state to return to work – most of the European population had spent years in Japanese internment camps and/or had performed hard labour. In addition, priority was given to staffing the local NEI temporary courts martial. Both Ambassador Loudon and the MOT came up with lists of proposed candidates, but with the exception of J.K. van Onnen – former president of the Supreme Court of the Netherlands Indies, who had to decline due to health issues – none of the candidates met with the approval of the Foreign Office.[12] Meanwhile, as MacArthur's deadline of 5 January 1946 rapidly approached, Loudon kept pressing the MFA for results.[13] He pointed out that

> In recent years, we have made démarches to the American government on a number of occasions to state that we were not or not sufficiently

---

10   Poelgeest, *Tribunaal*, pp. 25-26.

11   NIOD Institute for War, Holocaust and Genocide Studies (NIOD), 'Collection 400, Indische Collectie', inv. no. 5190, Minister of Foreign Affairs to Minister of Overseas Territories, 27 October 1945.

12   Poelgeest, *Tribunaal*, pp. 27-28.

13   NL-HaNA, 2.05.75, 'Ministerie van Buitenlandse Zaken: Gezantschap, later Ambassade, in de Verenigde Staten van Amerika te Washington DC, (1912) 1940-1954', inv. no. 2752, Telegram Loudon to The Hague, 29 December 1945.

recognized in certain matters. For our part we therefore need to show our willingness to cooperate fully in those cases in which the American government appears to be willing to substantially take our position into consideration, so that we cannot be accused of appearing to be unprepared to partake, or at least not in a timely manner, in international agreements etc.[14]

As the US and UK attached 'extremely great significance' to 'a prompt and fullest possible punishment of war criminals', it was of 'great national importance' that the Netherlands actively participate and assert itself as a 'Pacific power'.[15]

When it became clear that no suitable jurists could be found in the NEI, the MFA turned to the Ministry of Justice. However, their quest for representatives did not proceed much better; mostly due to the long list of requirements – jurists had to be of a certain standing, uncompromised by the war, and able to understand and speak English – and the fact that most of the suitable Dutch jurists were already otherwise engaged.[16] The Ministry of Justice eventually submitted various names for approval, but for reasons unknown, none of the candidates were appointed.[17] Nevertheless, on 12 January 1946, after the Ministry received another pressing telegram from Loudon, Van Kleffens finally notified Washington to assure them of the Netherlands' participation in the tribunal.[18] Some days later, Prof. Mr B.V.A. Röling, who held a chair in criminal law and criminal procedural law of the Netherlands East Indies at the University of Utrecht, accepted the offer to become the Dutch representative on the bench.[19]

A Dutch prosecutor, however, was still to be found. In early January, the Ministry of Foreign Affairs once more turned to the Ministry of Overseas Territories, who subsequently passed the request on to Lieutenant Governor-General (Lt GG) H.J. van Mook. When a timely answer from the Indies did not arrive, the MFA, Röling and representatives of the MOT held a meeting in which

---

14   (original in Dutch, translated by author) NIOD, 400, inv. no. 5190, Minister of Foreign Affairs to Minister of Overseas Territories, 28 November 1945.

15   NL-HaNA, 2.05.75, inv. no. 2752, Telegram Loudon to Ministry of Foreign Affairs, 24 November 1945; Loudon to Minister of Foreign Affairs, 10 December 1945; Loudon to Ministry of Foreign Affairs, 22 January 1946.

16   Poelgeest, *Tribunaal*, pp. 27-29.

17   Some of the candidates were deemed ineligible by the Ministry while others politely declined the offer. Ibid., pp. 28-29.

18   Ibid., p. 29.

19   Röling was proposed by his colleague J. Ph. Suyling, the dean of the Law Faculty in Utrecht who had earlier declined the ministry's offer of the same position. Ibid.

Jhr. L.H.K. C van Asch van Wijk was proposed. Van Asch van Wijk declined the offer but suggested Mr W.G.F. Borgerhoff-Mulder instead. Borgerhoff-Mulder, a graduate from Leiden University, who had been a barrister in Batavia and now sat on the bench of the District Court in The Hague, accepted on certain conditions.[20] Yet before the MFA made Borgerhoff-Mulder's nomination final, it awaited a definitive answer from Batavia, tellingly asking Loudon to notify its American ally that in these circumstances it would be difficult to find a 'truly excellent representative'.[21] Immediately after it became clear that no suitable candidates were to be found in the Indies, Borgerhoff-Mulder left for Tokyo where he arrived on 19 March 1946.[22]

   In Japan, Borgerhoff-Mulder was joined by two assistants: Mr August Th. Laverge and Mrs Coomee R. Strooker-Dantra. Laverge (born 1920), another graduate from Leiden University, had managed to escape the Netherlands during the war, and found refuge in the United Kingdom where he worked as a lawyer in the Dutch maritime court. After the war, he had been employed by the Directorate General for Extraordinary Justice, which coordinated the post-war investigation and prosecution policy of collaboration and war crimes cases in the Netherlands.[23] Strooker (born 1905), a Parsi originating from Rangoon, had studied law in Cambridge and later opened her own law firm in Rangoon. After marrying a Dutchman in 1932, she moved to the Netherlands where she worked as a translator. Mrs Strooker was the only female member on the Dutch prosecution team and was among only three women who served as assistant prosecution counsel and appeared before the tribunal.[24]

---

20   Like Röling, Borgerhoff-Mulder wanted to visit Nuremberg and bring his wife with him to Tokyo. He also asked for all possible assistance in the gathering of evidence in the Netherlands and the Netherlands Indies, as well as a small staff who could assist him in Tokyo. Poelgeest, *Tribunaal*, p. 30.

21   Ibid.

22   Poelgeest (*Tribunaal*, p. 31) mentions March 9. NL-HaNA, 2.05.75, inv. no. 2752, travel details Borgerhoff-Mulder. Sedgwick, 'The Trial Within', p. 4.

23   A. Smit, *Nederlandse maritieme rechtspraak op het grondgebied van Groot-Brittannië gedurende de Tweede Wereldoorlog* (Arnhem: Gouda Quint, 1989), p. 139.

24   Poelgeest, *Tribunaal*, p. 31. Female attorneys Virginia Bowman, Lucille Brunner, Eleanor Jackson, Helen Grigware Lambert, Grace Kanode Llewellyn and Bettie Renner (all from the US) worked on various phases of the prosecution's case. In addition to Mrs Strooker-Dantra, Grace Kanode Llewellyn and Helen Grigware Lambert were also listed as assistant prosecution counsel and presented to the court. IMTFE-transcript p. 2270, p. 40925. See also 'Women's Involvement' at *The Tokyo War Crimes Trial. A Digital Exhibition* via lib.law.virginia.edu/imtfe/exhibit/womens-involvement (last accessed 2 November 2015).

The Indictment and the Scramble for Evidence

Upon the arrival of the members of the Netherlands Prosecution Section (NPS) in Japan, they realized that a great part of the International Prosecution Section's (IPS) preparatory work had already been completed. The defendants for the trial had been selected and available evidence had been collected. Most of the associate prosecutors (with the exception of France, Russia and India) had arrived before the Dutch and had, together with the Chief of Counsel and his staff, drawn up the indictment.[25] The arrival of the NPS in Tokyo had, however, been eagerly awaited, as the IPS expected Borgerhoff-Mulder to bring along great amounts of evidence. The arrival of Borgerhoff-Mulder on 19 March must therefore have been a disappointment to his new-found international colleagues; he did not bring any evidence to substantiate the prosecution's case or to expand the charges in the indictment as expected.[26] The NPS was generally ill-prepared for their undertaking; Borgerhoff-Mulder, Laverge and Strooker had neither personal experience nor much knowledge of the wartime situation in the Netherlands Indies. Moreover, none of them was versed in international criminal law nor, with the exception of Mrs Strooker, familiar with the Anglo-Saxon legal system.[27] No written instructions for Borgerhoff-Mulder have been found with regard to the indictment, but it seems that the Dutch government did urge the NPS to place emphasis on Japan's expansionist and occupational policies in the NEI.[28] However, in the existing draft indictment, no separate charges as to Japanese activities and atrocities in the Netherlands East Indies

---

25   The selection of defendants, preparation of the indictment and formulation of all basic policy decision for the trial had been in the hands of the prosecutor's Executive Committee (which was composed of all Associate Counsel and several senior members of the US staff, chaired by Arthur Comyns-Carr). The indictment was eventually drafted by a sub-committee of the Executive Committee, also chaired by Comyns-Carr. A.C. Brackman, *The Other Nuremberg: The Untold Story of the Tokyo War Crime Trials* (London: Collins, 1989), p. 85; S. Horwitz, *The Tokyo Trial*, International Conciliation 465 (New York: Carnegie Endowment for International Peace, 1950), pp. 490-501; Boister and Cryer, *The Tokyo International Military Tribunal*, pp. 50-54 and NIOD, 'Archief (402) van het International Military Tribunal for the Far East: papers from the International Prosecution Section, Netherlands Division, and judge B.V.A. Röling', inv. no. 20, Minutes of Meeting of the Executive Committee, 4 March 1946.

26   NIOD, 402, inv. no. 37, Minister of Overseas Territories to Lieutenant Governor General, 3 April 1946.

27   Poelgeest, *Tribunaal*, p. 31. 'Mrs C.R. Strooker-Dantra Papers', private collection (SDP), Travel Diary, 9, 10, 11, 12, 18 April 1946.

28   Poelgeest, *Tribunaal*, p. 32. NIOD, 402, inv. no. 37, Borgerhoff-Mulder to Attorney General NEI, 12 July 1946. NIOD, 402, inv. no. 21, Borgerhoff-Mulder to Keenan, 9 April 1946; J.S. Sin-

had been included. Because no facts and evidence relating to Japan's activities in the Netherlands East Indies were available in Tokyo, the charges had been left out altogether.[29] Due to their late arrival, the NPS was not in a position to insist on postponing the presentation of the indictment to the tribunal, which made the addition of charges unlikely. With the support of the French, Philippine and Chinese associate counsel, Borgerhoff-Mulder and Laverge did manage to include a general charge of ill-treatment of civilians and pillage, plunder and exploitation of the occupied territories into the indictment (sections eleven and twelve of Appendix D), but were unable to include a separate charge concerning the Japanese political machinations in the NEI or a general Japanese annexationist policy as they would have preferred.[30]

In order to be able to prove the charges that related to the Netherlands, both on the planning and preparing of a war of aggression and on the war crimes committed by the Japanese in the Netherlands East Indies, more substantial evidence than that already available to the IPS needed to be obtained by the NPS. Pressured by Borgerhoff-Mulder, the Ministry of Foreign Affairs tried its best to gather useful documentation during the months of March and April, but as many of the necessary archives had been destroyed, their efforts were fruitless.[31] An alarmed NPS reported: 'If further difficulties and delays are encountered, our position will become extremely difficult, and it is not impossible that the Netherlands' charges will have to be dropped altogether'.[32] Soon the NPS realized that the main body of evidence would have to be supplied by the NEI authorities.[33] In a desperate bid for evidence and data, Borgerhoff-Mulder – accompanied by Comdr. McMullin, NPS's American liaison – left for the Netherlands Indies, while Laverge and Strooker stayed behind in Tokyo.[34]

---

ninghe Damsté, *Advocaat-Soldaat. Oorlogsherinneringen* (Amsterdam: Van Soeren &Co, 1999), p. 227.

29 NL-HaNA, 2.05.75, inv. no. 2752, Report Laverge, 25 April 1946.

30 Poelgeest, *Tribunaal*, pp. 31-32: NL-HaNA, 2.05.75, inv. no. 2752, Report Laverge, 25 April 1946 and Report Borgerhoff-Mulder, 29 May 1946: NIOD, 402, inv. no. 21, Borgerhoff-Mulder to Keenan, 15 April 1946. The Chinese, Dutch, Philippine and French associate prosecutors were generally dissatisfied with regards to the matter and form of the indictment. NIOD, 402, inv. no. 21, Tavenner to Keenan, 14 April 1946 and Memorandum Borgerhoff-Mulder to Keenan, 12 April 1946.

31 Poelgeest, *Tribunaal*, pp. 31-32.

32 NL-HaNA, 2.05.75, inv. no. 2752, Report Laverge, 25 April 1946.

33 Ibid.

34 To provide the NPS with necessary legal assistance during the trial, the Americans had assigned liaison officers. Firstly Commander B.M. McMullin who, after a conflict with Keenan, was sent back to the USA. He was succeeded by Mr A. Williams and later Mr

In Batavia, where they arrived on 30 April, the group met several high government and army officials. They also made the acquaintance of Mr J.S. Sinninghe Damsté.[35] Sinninghe Damsté, a barrister from Surabaya who had spent the war in POW camps on Java, Sumatra and the Moluccas, had been appointed as a second assistant to the NPS in mid-March to cover the charges concerning the Netherlands Indies.[36] Before his departure, Sinninghe Damsté was commissioned to compile a general survey of the crimes committed by the Japanese in the Netherlands Indies, 'including the Japanese aggression and the so called Japanization of that area'.[37] When Borgerhoff-Mulder and his team arrived in Batavia, Mr Sinninghe Damsté had just closed his investigations and had completed a substantial overview in which he had conveniently listed the atrocities that had been committed on the different islands.[38] Sinninghe Damsté's report provided quite a comprehensive view of the crimes that the Japanese had committed in the NEI and enabled the NPS to consider which sections had to be brought forward in the trial brief. But Sinninghe Damsté had not been given sufficient time to secure the evidence in the form that was expected in court. It was therefore left to K.A. de Weerd, who was to be appointed as Sinninghe Damsté's assistant, to assemble the documents proving the collected facts.[39]

O.G. Hyde. NL-HaNA, 2.05.75, inv. no. 2752, Report Laverge, 25 April 1946, Report Borgerhoff-Mulder, 31 October 1946.

35   NL-HaNA, 2.05.75, inv. no. 2752, Report Borgerhoff-Mulder, 29 May 1946.

36   Poelgeest, *Tribunaal*, pp. 33-34.

37   NL-HaNA, 2.05.75, inv. no. 2752, Report Borgerhoff-Mulder, 29 May 1946; Sinninghe Damsté, *Advocaat-Soldaat*, pp. 200-201. Both of the official government agencies responsible for the investigation of war crime, NEFIS and the Regeringsbureau tot Nasporing van Oorlogsmisdrijven (The Governmental Office for Investigation of War Crimes), were severely understaffed and not in a position to help with an investigation into Japanese warfare and occupation measures.

38   Sinninghe Damsté, *Advocaat-Soldaat*, pp. 200-210; NL-HaNA, 2.05.75, inv. no. 2752, Report Borgerhoff-Mulder, 29 May 1946.

39   NL-HaNA, 2.05.75, inv. no. 2752, Report Borgerhoff-Mulder, 29 May 1946. Like Borgerhoff-Mulder and Laverge, Sinninghe Damsté and De Weerd were also law graduates from Leiden University. De Weerd, a barrister at Medan, had been confined in several POW camps on Java, where he acted as camp translator of newspapers in the Malay language. This work allowed him to keep abreast of developments in the Indies and during the war he had already started to collect and index data about the political and economic measures of the Japanese occupation authorities. After the war, he continued his research when he was assigned to the political section of the Netherlands Indies Civil Administration (NICA) and later to the Netherlands Forces Intelligence Service (NEFIS). His work for the NPS was supervised by the Attorney General of the NEI.K.A. de Weerd, *Prepared*

Convinced that he had secured the cooperation of the authorities at Batavia and that the necessary evidentiary documentation would follow soon, Borgerhoff-Mulder, accompanied by Sinninghe Damsté, returned to Japan with peace of mind.[40] Nonetheless, the work of the NPS was once more impeded as 'administrative obstruction' delayed the official appointment of De Weerd for weeks.[41] An infuriated Borgerhoff-Mulder reported back to the Minister of War: 'My staff and I feel utterly disappointed that our government is not able to provide at the very moment before the whole world the full truth about the most serious crimes ever committed against its subjects'.[42] In addition, Borgerhoff-Mulder emphasized that not only was the NPS's work in a precarious position but that, as a result of the (non-)actions of their government, there was also a 'spectacular Netherlands interest' at stake. With a flair for drama he continued: 'Of all areas concerned, the NEI probably have been the worst treated by the Japanese. If provided properly with the evidence available, our division would have been in a rather prominent position in this trial'.[43]

Fortunately, this unfavourable situation did not last long; De Weerd was officially appointed at the end of May and the first documental evidence was sent from Batavia to Tokyo soon after.[44] In the end, due to the slower than expected progression of the trial, there was enough time and even more importantly, enough evidence at hand to prepare the Dutch phase of the prosecution.[45]

Statement of K.A. de Weerd (Tokyo: International Prosecution Section, Netherlands Division, 1946), pp. 1-3. NL-HaNA, 2.05.75, inv. no. 2752, Report Borgerhoff-Mulder, 29 May 1946, Borgerhoff-Mulder to Minister of General Warfare (Minister President), 5 June 1946, Report Borgerhoff-Mulder, 31 October 1946 and Attorney General NEI to Van Mook, 9 April 1946.

40   NL-HaNA, 2.05.75, inv. no. 2752, Report Borgerhoff-Mulder, 29 May 1946.

41   NIOD, 402, inv. no. 37, De Weerd to P. Eijssen, 24 May 1946; Poelgeest, *Tribunaal*, p. 35.

42   NL-HaNA, 2.05.75, inv. no. 2752, Borgerhoff-Mulder to Minister of General Warfare (Minister President), 5 June 1946.

43   Ibid.

44   Poelgeest, *Tribunaal*, p. 35.

45   NL-HaNA, 2.05.75, inv. no. 2752, Report Borgerhoff-Mulder, 30 June 1946.

The NPS: 'A True 4-Star General, a Nice Darling, a Real Lawyer, a
Competent Young Man and a Middle-Aged Woman'[46]

Although the Dutch delegation was small, it was fairly homogeneous. Its members, with the exception of Mrs Strooker, all shared the same educational
background and had been born and raised in the Netherlands. Indonesian rep-
resentation in the IPS was limited to Mr Soewanto and Mr Oemarjadi.[47] Raden
Soewanto, a former student of Batavia's Law College and former official at the
NEI's Department of Transport and Public Works, had been recruited by the
Japanese during the war and was sent to Tokyo for further study. He was now a
member of IPS's Translation Section. Mr Oemarjadi worked for the American
Headquarters in Tokyo and assisted Soewanto with the translation of the *Kan
Po* (official newspaper of Japan during the occupation of Java) and Japanese
propaganda movies.[48] Borgerhoff-Mulder contemplated including Soewanto
in the NPS but eventually decided not to do so, quoting 'political consider-
ations'.[49] Besides the two Indonesian assistants, Cosmo Torisawa, a young
Dutch-Japanese man who had been raised in the Netherlands, also assisted the
NPS.[50]

Quite apart from all the difficulties that the NPS experienced with regard to
organizational matters and the gathering of evidence, they also faced the challenge of working in a foreign country, surrounded by people they were
unacquainted with. For most of the delegates, Japan was a fascinating place
that at the same time evoked feelings of cultural disconnection and 'other-
worldliness'.[51] Mrs Strooker writes: 'I live in a completely different world and

---

46   In her letter of 16 May 1946, Strooker described the NPS as follows: 'BM [Borgerhoff-Mul-
     der] true 4 star general, so full of importance. The Commander [McMullin] a nice darling,
     half deaf; Damsté a real lawyer, quite nice; but not exactly attractive; Laverge, all there [?]
     and competent, a young man who is quite sure of himself, and inclined to be aggressive;
     lastly, the undersigned middle-aged women, who gets flustered, tries to please everybody
     has a great deal of conscience'.

47   NL-HaNA, 2.05.75, inv. no. 2752, Report Borgerhoff-Mulder, 30 June 1946.

48   NL-HaNA, 2.05.75, inv. no. 2752, Report Borgerhoff-Mulder, 31 October 1946.

49   During his time in Japan, Soewanto functioned as a leader for the Indonesians in Japan.
     After the first Dutch 'police action', he gave a speech during a Sarekat Islam meeting in
     which he criticized the Dutch military aggression. L. van Poelgeest, *Japanse Besognes.
     Nederland en Japan 1945-1975* (Den Haag: SDU uitgevers, 1999), p. 132; NL-HaNA, 2.05.75, inv.
     no. 2752, Report Borgerhoff-Mulder, 30 June 1946.

50   SDP, Sinninghe Damsté to Strooker, 1 January 1947; Laverge to Strooker, 28 June 1947,
     10 December 1947 (in 22 October 1947), 3 February 1947.

51   J. Sedgwick, 'A People's Court: Emotion, Participant Experiences, and the Shaping of Post-
     War Justice at the International Military Tribunal for the Far East, 1946-1948', *Diplomacy &*

my only link with the world I've come from is through your letters'.[52] These
feelings were amplified by the language barriers; 'the Japanese are really very
charming – if only I could make myself understood and could understand
them, I'd get along fine with them'.[53] The juxtaposition of destruction and luxury that they were confronted with was unsettling as well; 'there's the extreme
contrast of living in occupied Holland compared with the luxury of this trip'.[54]
While the Dutch prosecutors generally enjoyed their new 'glamorous' lifestyle
provided by the American army, they weren't blind to the situation of the
Japanese people: 'It hurt eating their food, even tho' it was so excellent and
plentiful in appearance, 'cos behind the screen I know they are hungry, like we
were in Holland'.[55] Issues on a more personal level also had profound consequences for the working of and relations within the NPS. Strooker describes
how she believed Laverge held prejudices against her due to the colour of her
skin and how people's egos impacted cooperation; 'people are not really working as a team here, but all trying to show off'.[56] However, while initial tensions
existed between both Mrs Strooker and Laverge and Laverge and Sinninghe
Damsté, it seems that after a couple of months the three assistant prosecutors
had developed a steady working relationship.[57] Their relationship with Borgerhoff-Mulder and later also De Weerd – who according to Laverge 'would drive
even a Saint into a temper'[58] – seems, however, to have been a more complicated one. Letters from Strooker, Laverge and Röling give us a peek behind the
scenes and show us that, as the work progressed, Borgerhoff-Mulder's presence
became more 'symbolical and undefinable'[59], while he left the real work for his
assistants. 'To be frank, he is somewhat of a big zero, who does nothing, lets his
subordinates do the work and just struts around in his general's outfit'.[60] Mrs

---

Statecraft, 22 (2011), 480-99, at 482-83.

52   SDP, Strooker, 22 June 1946. Feelings of disconnection also existed with regard to the
      Dutch authorities: 'People in The Hague and in Washington have no real idea of the state
      of affairs here'. SDP, Strooker, 9 May 1946.

53   SDP, Strooker, 19 April 1946,

54   J. Sedgwick, 'A People's Court', 484; SDP, travel diary Strooker-Dantra, 8 April 1946.

55   SDP, Strooker, 28 August 1946; Sinninghe Damsté, *Advocaat-Soldaat*, p. 214, pp. 232-34.

56   SDP, Strooker, 12 June 1946, 27 April 1946, 29 October 1946.

57   SDP, Strooker, 1 September 1946 and 19 November 1946: Laverge to Strooker, 3 February
      1947.

58   SDP, Laverge to Strooker, 28 June 1947.

59   SDP, Jongejans to Strooker, 25 May 1947 and Strooker, 23 May 1946.

60   (Original in Dutch, translated by author) Röling, *Rechter*, p. 207. After Borgerhoff-Mulder
      had proposed to make Röling prosecutor and himself the judge, Röling's and Borgerhoff-
      Mulder relationship remained strained.

Strooker describes how Borgerhoff-Mulder's attachment to titles confused and startled people and how he at one point became the laughing stock of the division:

> The first day I was here, he asked me to stop people calling him 'Dr. Mulder', & see that the authorities knew he was Mr. Justice Borgerhoff-Mulder. I went to the head of the administrative dept. & the nice Col. in charge made his stenographer take down a note to be sent to all depts. concerned, to take note of the fact in future. Now after a 3 weeks 'absence in Batavia', the gentleman has returned as 'Maj. General' with 4 stars. McArthur & Eisenhower being the only 2 with 5 stars and as far as I know there being only 1 other general in Tokyo with 4 stars! (Gen. Eichelberger) I don't like making all these reports to Headquarters on the rapid promotion of my boss & hate the thought of tomorrow's stenographic note!! He wants the record of the Court proceedings corrected from A-Z wherever his name appears!! No light matter, & everyone is laughing at him, which is not a nice thing to have done to one's boss.[61]

Borgerhoff-Mulder's behaviour could have been a way to cope with personal insecurities. His language skills were not up to par with those of his subordinates who – with the exception of De Weerd – were fluent in English and this might have made it more difficult for him to connect with his foreign colleagues.[62] In general, however, the NPS, both as a division and as a group of individuals, was in close contact with many of the other prosecution divisions.[63] Exchange of evidence and documents took place between the NPS and the Australian, British and American prosecution sections while two British officers served as witnesses during the presentation of the Dutch B and C phas-

---

61   SDP, Strooker, 16 May 1946.

62   Poelgeest, *Tribunaal*, p. 39. Both Laverge and Röling also mention an incident where Borgerhoff-Mulder, heavily intoxicated, fell from the stairs at a cocktail party, resulting in such a black eye that he had to stay in bed for a week. Röling, *Rechter*, p. 210; SDP, Laverge to Strooker, 3 February 1947.

63   According to Sinninghe Damsté, all prosecution sections entered each other's offices freely, expect those of the Russian division who had blocked their workplace with iron doors. Sinninghe Damsté, *Advocaat-Soldaat*, p. 220, pp. 232-33. See also, C. Williams 'The Tokyo War Crimes Trial before the International Military Tribunal for the Far East', in J. Carey, W. Dunlap and R. Pritchard (eds.), *International Humanitarian Law: Origins* (Ardsley, NY: Transnational, 2003), pp. 105-59, at pp. 116-17.

es.[64] Sinninghe Damsté, together with the American naval captain Robinson, established an international study group to discuss questions of international criminal law, which was attended by other prosecutors.[65] Mrs Strooker had dinner parties with fellow prosecutors Mr Menon, Mr Comyns-Carr and Comdr McMullin, made several trips to Mount Fuji with American attorney Renner and Chinese assistant prosecutor Liu (with whom she also studied the legal aspects of the trial) and frequently met other prosecutors and legal staff during her numerous social engagements.[66] And, even though MacArthur disapproved of personal 'fraternization' with the Japanese population, it did not stop the Dutch delegates from socializing with the Japanese.[67] As is shown in the next paragraph, the warm relations that existed between the NPS and other legal staff would eventually have a lasting impact on the tribunal's proceedings.

The Dutch Contribution to the Prosecution

While certain aspects of the indictment that related to the Netherlands had been dealt with in earlier phases of the trial, the NPS started their 'Dutch' phase on 3 December 1946 with the opening statement of Borgerhoff-Mulder.[68] His statement was the first of the three parts into which the Dutch phase had been more or less divided; the first two parts formed the twelfth phase (Aggression

---

64   SDP, Sinninghe Damsté to Strooker, 1 January 1947; NL-HaNA, 2.05.75, inv. no. 2752, Report
      Borgerhoff-Mulder, 30 June 1946.
65   Sinninghe Damsté, *Advocaat-Soldaat*, pp. 228-29.
66   SDP, Strooker, 7 and 12 June 1946. In her letters Strooker mentions amongst others: Man-
      ning, Professor Dr Brown (law expert to the prosecution), Mr Ballentyn (most probably
      Ballentine, political advisor to the prosecution), Virginia Bowen (American attorney),
      Prof. Rousseau (art expert and lecturer at Harvard University), Mr Esposito (lawyer, artist,
      philosopher), Dr Jain (economic advisor to the Allied Council), Lt. Evans (associate to
      Judge Northcroft), Japanese couple the Nomura's and a Japanese professor in Shintoism.
67   Mrs Strooker, for example, gave a presentation about the German occupation of the Neth-
      erlands before a Japanese women's group who held an interest in international affairs,
      'The United Nations Study Group', visited the Nomura's together with Judge Röling,
      attended lectures of Japanese professors, visited the home of a Japanese vice-admiral,
      dined with Japanese friends and got acquainted with several well-known Japanese, such
      as Shigeichi Kure, with whom she kept up a correspondence even after her return to the
      Netherlands.
68   As no instructions had been received from the Netherlands or Netherlands Indies govern-
      ment, Borgerhoff-Mulder and his team were responsible for the selection and presenta-
      tion of the evidence. Poelgeest, *Tribunaal*, p. 42.

against the Netherlands) of the 'A' section of the prosecution's phase, while the third was part of the IPS's larger phase which dealt with atrocities against civilians and against prisoners of war.[69]

The first part, the opening statement, had largely been written by Laverge and was intended to paint a complete picture of the Japanese aggression against the Netherlands and discuss and summarize the evidence that would be admitted. Laverge aligned the statement with the approach taken by the American and British and made many references to documents previously submitted by other parties, thus ensuring that the statement fitted well within the general framework of the indictment.[70] Before Borgerhoff-Mulder could start, however, American defence counsel Cunningham challenged the presence of the Dutch at the tribunal, claiming that the Netherlands government had not been a party to the Potsdam Agreement and was therefore not a proper party to the trial proceedings.[71] While C. Higgins, the American liaison officer to the Dutch prosecutors immediately got up to refute the statements, the Dutch prosecution was 'saved' by President Webb who, to their surprise, briskly overruled the stated objections.[72] As further interruptions by Logan and Cunningham were also rejected by Webb, Borgerhoff-Mulder and his colleagues were able to finish the first Dutch part without much further trouble.[73] Mrs Strooker even received a personal compliment from President Webb when she finished presenting her part of the supporting evidence: 'Mrs. Strooker, my colleagues and I who have heard you assure you that we regard you as a distinct acquisition to the Bar of this Tribunal'.[74] These small and seemingly unimportant gestures helped the Dutch to make their case, or as BM put it: 'it might have been incidental, it nevertheless enormously helped to keep the attention of the Court and to create and keep a benevolent mood'.[75]

The 'second' part of the Dutch phase, started on 6 December and concerned the sworn witness statement of K.A. de Weerd on the occupation and so-called Japanization of the NEI. As the NPS had not been able to include the violation

---

69   The prosecution's case was delivered in fifteen separate phases.

70   Poelgeest, *Tribunaal*, pp. 41-43.

71   NL-HaNA, 2.09.61 inv. no 76, Report Borgerhoff-Mulder, 31 December 1946.

72   Poelgeest, *Tribunaal*, p. 43.

73   IMTFE-transcript, pp. 11784-85, pp. 11942-43, pp. 12065-66 and p. 12127. Also Poelgeest, *Tribunaal*, pp. 44-45. Other members of the defence counsel objected with regard to more procedural issues. See, for example, IMTFE-transcript, p. 11904, p. 12009 and p. 12060.

74   IMTFE- transcript, p. 11757.

75   NL-HaNA, 2.09.61 inv. no. 76, Provisional Report Borgerhoff-Mulder, 10 December 1946; NIOD, Collection 402, inv. no. 34, Letter Pennink to Minister of Foreign Affairs, 13 December 1946.

of the 'Regulations concerning the Laws and Customs of War on Land' in the indictment, Borgerhoff-Mulder decided to present it as a 'sequel of the aggression charge; as a result of "aggression"'.[76] This part was the most controversial one; it described Japan's occupation policy in the NEI, implicitly accusing Japan of political, social and economic imperialism at a moment when Indonesians accused the Netherlands of the same. In addition, it intended to show the ways Japan had 'attempted to hold on to the fruits of their aggression' by stimulating the nationalistic feelings of the Indonesians and by influencing the proclamation of Indonesian independence.[77]

It is therefore not surprising that this part received special attention from the Minister of Foreign Affairs, who approached Borgerhoff-Mulder in August 1946, curious to know how he would prove the Japanese influence on the indigenous population and the Japanese role in the establishment of the Indonesian Republic after the capitulation.[78] Borgerhoff-Mulder eventually informed his government that the NPS would not address events that had taken place after the Indonesian declaration of independence as their connection to the defendants could not be proven.[79] Yet, notwithstanding the debatable nature of their claim, the NPS did want to show that by promoting the Indonesian independence movement, Japan had tried to establish a permanent hegemony over the NEI.[80] However, as it proved impossible to procure enough evidence to document this particular charge, the NPS decided that the available evidence would be presented by De Weerd in a so-called 'prepared statement', which provided an extensive overview of Japan's occupation policy.[81] During the presentation of De Weerd's prepared statement it became clear once more that partiality

---

76 NL-HaNA, 2.05.75, inv. no. 2752, Report Borgerhoff-Mulder, 30 September 1946. Poelgeest, *Tribunaal*, p. 45.

77 IMTFE-transcript, pp. 11666-68. Van Poelgeest, *Tribunaal*, p. 45.

78 It was only after the reading of the opening statement and the prepared statement that the NPS received the Minister of Foreign Affairs' recommendations. NIOD, 402, inv. no. 33, Minister of Foreign Affairs to Borgerhoff-Mulder, 8 November 1946; NIOD, 400, inv. no. 5190, Letter Borgerhoff-Mulder to Minister of Foreign Affairs, 9 January 1947.

79 NIOD, 402, inv. no. 36, Code telegram Minister of Foreign Affairs to Borgerhoff-Mulder, 19 August 1946. NIOD, 402, inv. no. 33, Borgerhoff-Mulder to Minister of Foreign Affairs, 21 August 1946 (scan no. 37)

80 NIOD, 402, inv. no. 33, Borgerhoff-Mulder to Minister of Foreign Affairs, 21 August 1946; NIOD, 402, inv. no. 31, Laverge to Borgerhoff-Mulder, 11 April 1946.

81 Poelgeest, *Tribunaal*, pp. 45-46. NIOD, 402, inv. no. 38, Borgerhoff-Mulder to Attorney General NEI, 16 August 1946. Although the defence counsel objected to the NPS's proposed 'prepared statement', President Webb reluctantly agreed to the NPS plan – mainly because it was in the interests of time – on the condition that De Weerd would significantly shorten his statement, which Webb even offered to do himself. De Weerd's initial state-

played a part at the IMTFE, as the NPS was yet again 'protected' by President Webb who overruled most objections by the defence and prohibited the most difficult questions posed to De Weerd during his cross-examination.[82]

After the conclusion of the 'A' phase it was Sinninghe Damsté's turn to present the prosecution's case concerning Japanese conventional war crimes and crimes against humanities committed in the Netherlands East Indies. Damsté took the stand on 20 December 1946. His intentions, apart from showing the sheer scale and brutality of the atrocities, were twofold: firstly, to prove that conditions in each occupied area were similar arguing that mistreatment was part of a general policy of the Japanese government; and secondly, and perhaps more importantly, to substantiate that the accused could be held accountable for the ill-treatment.

After his introductory remarks, Sinninghe Damsté provided synopses for five of the seven areas into which the Netherlands Indies, for the convenience of the trial, had been divided: Dutch Borneo, Java, Sumatra, Timor and Lesser Sunda Islands and Celebes.[83] As Totani has concluded, by attributing equal importance to each type of victim (POWs, interned civilians and non-interned civilians) and clustering the cases and evidence according to various categories of offences, Damsté managed to establish common patterns of atrocity across the Japanese-occupied Dutch East Indies.[84] The charges were strengthened by three witnesses who provided testimony on the wartime situation in Sumatra. The choice of witnesses was both a pragmatic and strategic one.[85] While all three witnesses were knowledgeable, they also resided in Tokyo, reducing transportation costs.[86]

---

ment counted 129 pages, but with support of the American jurists was brought down to a mere 56. NL-HaNA, 2.05.75, inv. no. 2752, Report Borgerhoff-Mulder, 30 November 1946.

82   Poelgeest, *Tribunaal*, pp. 46-47.

83   IMTFE-transcripts, p. 13478. The Australian prosecution section presented the synopses for Ambon and New Guinea. During the B and C phase, synopses of the evidence were presented to the tribunal; as a result it was no longer necessary to read exhibits in court, thus saving time.

84   Y. Totani, *The Tokyo War Crimes Trial: The Pursuit of Justice in the Wake of World War II* (Cambridge, Mass.: Harvard University Press, 2008), pp. 173-74.

85   Although many of the crimes mentioned were committed against the Indonesian population, no Indonesians were asked to stand witness for the NPS due to the 'particular difficulties when hearing Indonesian villagers'. NL-HaNA, 2.05.75, inv. no. 2752, Report Borgerhoff-Mulder, 30 June 1946.

86   More witnesses had been planned for, but due to unavailability and the fact that Keenan wanted to limit the length of the B and C phase, their number was brought down to three. NL-HaNA, 2.05.75, inv. no. 2752, Borgerhoff-Mulder to Prime Minister, 31 October 1946 and Report Borgerhoff-Mulder, 30 September 1946.

Although the synopsis system caused some issues and Sinninghe Damsté encountered problems with his exhibits due to hasty preparations,[87] he got away with it: 'the defence was courteous, because I had shown the same attitude towards them, as Blewett told me'.[88] Sinninghe Damsté closed his presentation with a film screening; 'I succeeded in showing the film "Nippon presents", and it was a success, although some of the judges were doubtful about its probative value, as I understand.... When Sir William tried to prevent the show, our general (Borgerhoff-Mulder) twice advised me to withdraw but I didn't want to give in (Hij is zoo goed met Sir W.[89])'.[90] Sinninghe Damsté concluded the Dutch contribution to the prosecution on 30 December 1946.

In the end, Borgerhoff-Mulder's anxiety – he had expressed fear that the Netherlands phase would be overpowered by the US phase which was held prior to the Dutch – proved to be unfounded, as the NPS received praise from both prosecution and judiciary.[91] Lord Patrick mentioned to Röling that 'I had expected to see the whole trial handled in this way and I am sorry to say that it was well done for the first time', while Sinninghe Damsté remarked after the conclusion of the Dutch phase: 'Mansfield and Higgins are very satisfied and so our general [Borgerhoff-Mulder] looks like a peacock. Cdr. Carr and Ashton told us that the Dutch division gave the least trouble to them'.[92] The NPS was relieved; although less powerful than many of the other contributors to the trial and without much support from its government, the Netherlands prosecution was of the opinion that it had managed to assert its own agenda and had given a relatively decent performance in court.[93]

---

87   SDP, Laverge to Strooker, 3 February 1947.

88   SDP, Sinninghe Damsté to Strooker, 1 January 1947. In his memoirs Sinninghe Damsté attributes this sentence to Logan. Sinninghe Damsté, *Advocaat-Soldaat*, p. 228.

89   Only this part of the letter is in Dutch 'Hij is zoo goed met Sir W'. Translation by author: 'He is so friendly with Sir W.'

90   SDP, Sinninghe Damsté to Strooker, 1 January 1947.

91   NL-HaNA, 2.05.75, inv. no. 2752, Report Borgerhoff-Mulder, 30 November 1946; NL-HaNA, 2.09.61 inv. no 76, Report Borgerhoff-Mulder, 31 December 1946.

92   SDP, Sinninghe Damsté to Strooker, 1 January 1947. Laverge later wrote to Strooker; 'all in all we came out comparatively well, although the glowing terms in which the B & C phase was described in the report to Holland was to my mind rather exaggerated'. SDP, Laverge to Strooker, 3 February 1947.

93   In the Netherlands, reactions were less enthusiastic as the Dutch press showed no interest in the Trial whatsoever. The Dutch authorities only started to show real interest when confronted with the fact that Röling was planning to give a dissenting opinion. Brackman, *The Other Nuremberg*, p. 248; NL-HaNA, 2.05.75, inv. no. 2752, Report Borgerhoff-Mulder, 31 October 1946. NIOD, 402, inv. no. 39, Laverge to De Weerd, 28 February 1947.

The IPS rested its case on 24 January 1947 and, after recess was granted for preparatory purposes, the defence delivered their opening address on 24 February. While Strooker and Sinnighe Damsté left Tokyo respectively in mid-December 1946 and mid-January 1947, Borgerhoff-Mulder and Laverge stayed behind for rebuttal.[94] However, as the Dutch charges were not challenged by the defence, there was not much to be done. Borgerhoff-Mulder kept writing his monthly reports home and engaged himself in social activities, while Laverge made himself useful by assisting the IPS by researching Chinese history, writing part of the Pacific War summation and preparing the cross-examination[95] of and summation on Togo.[96] It would take almost a year and a half, until early November 1948 when the eleven Allied judges were able to give their judgment and Röling presented his dissenting opinion, before the Dutch representation at the IMTFE once more stood in the limelight.

Bibliography

Neil Boister and Robert Cryer, *The Tokyo International Military Tribunal: A Reappraisal* (Oxford University Press, 2008).

Arnold C. Brackman, *The Other Nuremberg: The Untold Story of the Tokyo War Crimes Trial* (New York: William Morrow and Company, Inc., 1987).

Robert Cryer, 'Justice Röling (The Netherlands)' in Yuki Tanaka, Tim McCormack and Gerry Simpson (eds.), *Beyond Victor's Justice? The Tokyo War Crimes Trial Revisited* (Leiden: Martinus Nijhoff Publishers, 2011).

Solis Horwitz, *The Tokyo Trial*, International Conciliation no. 465 (New York: Carnegie Endowment for International Peace, 1950).

Bart van Poelgeest, *Nederland en het Tribunaal van Tokio: volkenrechtelijke polemiek en internationale politiek rond de berechting en gratiëring van de Japanse oorlogsmisdadigers* (Arnhem: Gouda Quint, 1989).

---

94   Soewanto left the NPS in mid-December 1946 while De Weerd returned to the NEI in early January 1947. NL-HaNA, 2.09.61 inv. no. 76, Report Borgerhoff-Mulder to MP, 6 January 1947.

95   To the disappointment of Laverge, Togo's cross-examination in court was done by Keenan who had a special interest in this defendant, but was ill-prepared for the task. This was a recurring problem, as during the cross-examination of Tōjō, Keenan had also stepped in at the last minute, leading to a rather disastrous cross-examination. SDP, Laverge to Strooker, 10 December 1947. Brackman, *The Other Nuremberg*, pp. 391-96.

96   SDP, Laverge to Strooker, 25 June 1947 and Laverge to Strooker, 10 December 1947. Laverge left Tokyo only in the beginning of February 1948, while Borgerhoff-Mulder left mid-March. SDP, Laverge to Strooker, 4 February 1948.

B.V.A. Röling and Antonio Cassese, *The Tokyo Trial and Beyond: Reflections of a Peacemonger* (Cambridge: Polity Press, 1994).

Hugo Röling, *De rechter die geen ontzag had. Bert Röling en het Tokiotribunaal* (Amsterdam: Wereldbibliotheek, 2014).

James Sedgwick, 'A People's Court: Emotion, Participant Experiences, and the Shaping of Postwar Justice at the International Military Tribunal for the Far East, 1946-1948', *Diplomacy & Statecraft*, 22 (2011), 480-99.

James Sedgwick, 'The Trial Within: Negotiating Justice at the International Military Tribunal for the Far East, 1946-1948', unpublished PhD thesis, The University of British Columbia (2012).

Kirsten Sellars, 'William Patrick and "Crimes against Peace" at the Tokyo Tribunal, 1946-1948', *The Edinburgh Law Review*, 15 (2011), 166-96.

J.S. Sinninghe Damsté, *Advocaat-Soldaat. Oorlogsherinneringen* (Amsterdam: Van Soeren & Co, 1999).

Anna Smit, *Nederlandse maritieme rechtspraak op het grondgebied van Groot-Brittannië gedurende de Tweede Wereldoorlog* (Arnhem: Gouda Quint, 1989).

Yuma Totani, *The Tokyo War Crimes Trial: The Pursuit of Justice in the Wake of World War II* (Cambridge, Mass.: Harvard University Press, 2008).

Kei Ushimura, *Beyond the 'Judgment of Civilization': The Intellectual Legacy of the Japanese War Crimes Trials, 1946-1949*, translated by S.J. Ericson, LTCB International Library Selection no. 14, first English edition (Tokyo: The International House of Japan, 2003).

Carrington Williams, 'The Tokyo War Crimes Trial before the International Military Tribunal for the Far East', in J. Carey, W. Dunlap and R. Pritchard (eds.), *International Humanitarian Law: Origins* (Ardsley, NY: Transnational 2003).

CHAPTER 12

India's 'Subaltern Elites' and the Tokyo Trial

Milinda Banerjee

Indian involvement in the Tokyo trial (1946-48) was marked by a remarkable diversity of voices. Given India's transitional political status, from colony to independent state, during the trial (India achieved independence from British rule on 15 August 1947), there was little scope for developing a national strategy towards the trial in the manner of some of the other participant countries. However, the very ambiguity of India's decolonizing status allowed for certain actors to leave a dominant, and individualized, influence, from enabling the country's very (late) entry into the trial (through a maelstrom of race-inflected debate) to challenging the fundamental premises of the trial itself, including in relation to the vital questions of colonialism and state sovereignty. It might even be said that in the case of no other participating country at Tokyo was the individualized nature of intervention so striking and the lack of any effective 'national' policy so obvious. A biographical approach is therefore especially fruitful in analysing Indian contributions to the trial. I focus in particular on two key actors: Girja Shankar Bajpai (1891-1954), the Agent General for India in Washington, who was instrumental in ensuring the entry of an Indian judge into the trial; and Radhabinod Pal (1886-1967), the Indian judge himself.

Historians of international law, working from a bird's eye perspective of macro-history, have often presented diffusionist models of the spread of international law, accounting for the globalization of modern Western legal norms and practices in terms of the transfer of institutions, standards and personnel from (European) cores to (extra-European) peripheries. From this viewpoint, even decolonization comes to be visualized as a fulfilment and expansion of a (juridically) 'hyperreal Europe'.[1] Non-European colonial societies are seen as translating European legal frameworks even as they throw off the mantle of formal colonial rule; they are assumed to increasingly approximate some constructed idea of Europe, thereby resulting in 'the proliferation of formal resemblances around the world'.[2] Such accounts have, however, come under

---

1 On 'hyperreal Europe', see D. Chakrabarty, *Provincializing Europe: Postcolonial Thought and Historical Difference* (Delhi: Oxford University Press, 2001), pp. 27-46.
2 K. Manjapra, 'Transnational Approaches to Global History: A View from the Study of German-Indian Entanglement', *German History*, 32 (2014), 275.

sustained criticism in recent years. This chapter adds to these critical voices by showing how an attention to micro-scales, including the scale of individual biography, substantially complicates narratives of unidirectional diffusion and translation. It emphasizes alternative models of transnationally-entangled contestation and competition,[3] foregrounds zones of intellectual ambivalence, and points to radically transformative conceptual apertures opened up in international forums by non-European actors. In line with trends in recent scholarship on transnational and global history, this essay situates the Indian actors within 'cosmopolitan thought zones',[4] and highlights the processes of hybridization[5] through which they related 'Indian' and 'Western' legal, political and philosophical concepts.

Legal records offer particularly good sources for tracing transnational Asian actors.[6] Some of the most exciting work in recent legal history has been pre-occupied with recovering the contributions of non-European actors in the emergence of modern norms and practices of law.[7] With respect to colo-nial India, scholars working through transnationally-inflected biographical approaches (whether they label it as such or not) have shown in a detailed manner the extent to which Indian experiences shaped the juristic interven-tions and thinking of metropolitan British legal actors,[8] as well as the ways in which Western legal training shaped the attitudes towards rule of law among celebrated Indian politicians and legal figures.[9] This essay draws meth-

3   This point is made strongly by S. Moyn, 'On the Nonglobalization of Ideas' in S. Moyn and A. Sartori (eds.), *Global Intellectual History* (New York: Columbia University Press, 2013), pp. 187-204.

4   K. Manjapra, 'Introduction' in S. Bose and K. Manjapra (eds.), *Cosmopolitan Thought Zones: South Asia and the Global Circulation of Ideas* (New York: Palgrave Macmillan, 2010), pp. 1-19.

5   C.A. Bayly, *Recovering Liberties: Indian Thought in the Age of Liberalism and Empire* (Cam-bridge: Cambridge University Press, 2012), p. 5.

6   T. Harper and S. Amrith, 'Introduction' in T. Harper and S. Amrith (eds.), *Sites of Asian Interaction: Ideas, Networks and Mobility* (Delhi: Cambridge University Press, 2014), pp. 6-7.

7   E.g. A.B. Lorca, *Mestizo International Law: A Global Intellectual History, 1842-1933* (Cam-bridge: Cambridge University Press, 2014).

8   E.g. K.J.M. Smith, *James Fitzjames Stephen: Portrait of a Victorian Rationalist* (Cambridge: Cambridge University Press, 1988); K. Mantena, *Alibis of Empire: Henry Maine and the Ends of Liberal Imperialism* (Princeton: Princeton University Press, 2010); M.J. Franklin, *Orientalist Jones: Sir William Jones, Poet, Lawyer, and Linguist, 1746-1794* (New York: Oxford University Press, 2011).

9   E.g. S. Gooptu, *Cornelia Sorabji, India's Pioneer Woman Lawyer: A Biography* (Delhi: Oxford University Press, 2006); S. Banerjee, *Becoming Imperial Citizens: Indians in the Late-*

odological inspiration from such writings, even as it takes a cue from Partha Chatterjee's concept of 'subaltern elite',[10] in order to interpret the polyvalent strategies through which colonized actors negotiated between their enforced position of colonial subjection and their (relatively and in a differentiated degree) elite location within dominant classes in indigenous society. I relate this biographical bivalence (being simultaneously subaltern and elite) to an intellectual bivalence, in terms of the ways in which Bajpai and Pal both appropriated and disrupted Western-dominated spaces of international law, and made possible novel legal imaginings of 'the world'.

Law and Equality: Girja Shankar Bajpai, Debates in the United States, and India's Entry into the Tokyo Trial

An Allahabad-born and Oxford-trained Brahmin, Sir Girja Shankar Bajpai joined the Indian Civil Service, served as a Secretary to the Government of India (1932-40), and rose to be a Member of the Executive Council of the Viceroy of India (1940). He was appointed the first Agent General for India in Washington in 1941. Bajpai's appointment manifested the growing political autonomy of India (even in diplomatic affairs) within the British Empire, especially in view of India's manpower and financial contribution to the Second World War. Through the 1940s and into the 1950s, including later in his crucial role as the first Secretary General of the Ministry of External Affairs of independent India (1947-52), Bajpai championed a pro-Western orientation for Indian foreign policy. He had hopes for the continuing importance of the British Commonwealth, with independent India as a significant constituent. However, he aspired for this Commonwealth to be adequately multiracial in composition and objective.[11]

Victorian Empire (Durham: Duke University Press, 2010); M. Mukherjee, *India in the Shadows of Empire: A Legal and Political History, 1774-1950* (Delhi: Oxford University Press, 2010); M. Sharafi, 'Two Lives in Law: The Reminiscences of A.J.C. Mistry and Sir Norman Macleod, 1884-1926', University of Wisconsin Law School Legal Studies Research Paper Series Paper No. 1252 <http://papers.ssrn.com/sol3/papers.cfm?abstract_id=2408064>, accessed 24 October 2015.

10   P. Chatterjee, 'A Religion of Urban Domesticity: Sri Ramakrishna and the Calcutta Middle Class' in P. Chatterjee and G. Pandey (eds.), *Subaltern Studies VII: Writings on South Asian History and Society* (Delhi: Oxford University Press, 1999 [1992]), pp. 40-68.

11   *The Hindu*, 6 December 1954, <http://www.thehindu.com/2004/12/06/stories/2004120600 270901.htm, accessed 29 October 2015; R.J. McMahon, *The Cold War on the Periphery: The United States, India, and Pakistan* (New York: Columbia University Press, 1994), pp. 34, 44,

When first appointed to Washington, Bajpai worried about facing trouble in the United States 'because of any prejudice as to color', and had to be reassured by Thomas M. Wilson, his American counterpart in India, that he was 'light in color' and would not be mistaken for an African.[12] Lord Halifax (1881-1959; Viceroy of India as Lord Irwin, 1926-31) of the British Foreign Office also felt that the Indian representative should have such an appearance that 'he would be easily recognised as Indian and not mistaken as an ordinary coloured man.'[13] This racial ambiguity as an Indian representative of a colonial government permeated Bajpai's diplomatic career. While in the United States, he gradually moved towards a sympathetic stand on India's freedom from British rule.[14] He was supportive towards Vijaya Lakshmi Pandit, a famous Indian politician, who toured America, rallying support for Indian independence in 1944-45. In 1946, Bajpai urged her to head the Indian delegation to the United Nations.[15] Bajpai emblematizes the biographical complexities of subaltern elitehood: a British-educated Brahmin elite administrator, who was also anxious about his subaltern race status; someone aligned to the Anglo-American West, and yet aspiring for Indian freedom.

Bajpai's sustained pressure ultimately enabled India's entry into the Tokyo trial. At the request of Britain, and with American agreement, India had entered the Far Eastern Commission in October 1945; Bajpai was the Indian representative.[16] Initially, the United States wanted India (and the Philippines)

47; K.J. Clymer, *Quest for Freedom: The United States and India's Independence* (New York: Columbia University Press, 1995), pp. 32-34; A. Weigold, *Churchill, Roosevelt and India: Propaganda during World War II* (New York: Routledge, 2008), pp. 33, 47, 70, 73-75, 82-84, 113-14, 138-39, 153; Commonwealth Oral Histories, 'Interview with K. Shankar Bajpai', <http://www.commonwealthoralhistories.org/2015/interview-with-k-shankar-bajpai>, accessed 29 October 2015. For brief discussions on Bajpai's role in relation to the Tokyo trial, see Y. Takatori, 'America's War Crimes Trial? Commonwealth Leadership at the International Military Tribunal for the Far East, 1946-48', *The Journal of Imperial and Commonwealth History*, 35 (2007), 557; and J.B. Sedgwick, 'The Trial Within: Negotiating Justice at the International Military Tribunal for the Far East, 1946-1948', unpublished PhD thesis, The University of British Columbia (2012), pp. 268-69.

12   G. Horne, *The End of Empires: African Americans and India* (Philadelphia: Temple University Press, 2008), 137.

13   Clymer, *Quest,* p. 33.

14   Weigold, *Churchill.*

15   M. Bhagavan, *India and the Quest for One World: The Peacemakers* (Basingstoke: Palgrave Macmillan, 2013), p. 50.

16   'Statement on the Establishment of a Far Eastern Commission to Formulate Policies for the Carrying Out of the Japanese Surrender Terms', issued in London by James F. Byrnes, US Secretary of State on 29 September 1945, and released to the press on 1 October 1945, in

to send only an associate prosecutor to the trial, not a judge. Only those nations – the USA, China, UK, USSR, Australia, Canada, France, Netherlands and New Zealand – which had been signatories to the Japanese surrender were allowed to send a judge.[17] In response, Bajpai framed the issue as one of 'equality'. His letter (January 1946) to the US Secretary of State is worth quoting:

> The Government of India desire to urge in the strongest possible terms their claim to nominate at least one Indian judge to serve on the tribunal. Indian nationals, whether prisoners of war or civilians, resident in territories in Southeast Asia and Burma which were invaded by Japanese forces, were the victims of Japanese brutalities. Indian armed forces played a major part in the defeat of Japan in Burma. India can, therefore, legitimately claim participation in the trial of Japanese war criminals on a footing of equality with the other powers who participated in the war against Japan. Besides a Federal Court, India has eight High Courts of Judicature, and a distinguished Bar whose members have had training and experience in Western principles of jurisprudence. Should her claim to nominate a judge to the tribunal be conceded, as she confidently hopes it will be, the appointing authority can rest assured that a person of recognised eminence in law will be nominated to serve on the court.[18]

Bajpai's vocabulary reflects a basic acceptance of the hegemonic status of the West. Indians could claim 'a footing of equality' because they had training in 'Western' law and because they had allied with the Western powers in defeating Japan; shared victimhood while confronting Japanese aggression was also important.

Bajpai's agenda for India's entry into Tokyo stemmed from an older political commitment about an autonomous India that resisted racial militarism globally. In an article published in an American journal in 1942, he had hoped

---

       United States The Department of State Bulletin, 1945, vol. 13, 545; 'Appointment of Indian Representative', 29 October 1945, in ibid., 728.

17   National Archives at College Park, College Park, MD (hereafter NARA), General Records of the Department of State, RG 59, File No. 740.00116 PW/1-446 CS/LE, Box 3631, Decimal File, 1945-49, Letter from the Acting Secretary of State to the Agent General for India, 23 January 1946.

18   Letter from the Agent General for India to the Secretary of State, 4 January 1946, in ibid. Bajpai also related India's entry into the Tokyo trial as following 'logically' from its membership in the Far Eastern Commission. See NARA, General Records of the Department of State, RG 59, Department of State, File No. 740.00116 PW/1-346 CS/D, Box 3631, Memorandum of Conversation, Office of Far Eastern Affairs, 3 January 1946.

that 'India can, after the war, realize her ambition, her legitimate hope of and natural desire for complete self-government'. He underlined that this autonomous India would take full part in future international mechanisms (including 'an international police force') to control aggression of the sort that Germany and Japan were perpetrating.[19] He admitted that many Indians had looked to Japan as a symbol of 'an Asiatic Renaissance', especially after the Japanese victory in the Russo-Japanese War of 1904-5, but had grown disenchanted as they saw Japan's imperial aggression against China from 1932 onwards, juxtaposed with the Italian invasion of Abyssinia and German attacks against Czechoslovakia and Poland. Bajpai affirmed that most Indians opposed those states like Germany and Japan which aimed 'to establish throughout the world and over the world the supremacy ... of one master race', whether an 'Aryan' or a 'Japanese' one.[20] For Bajpai, 'the world' was a fundamental sphere of action: it had to be protected from race domination, and in the effort to bring the race aggressors down and create a new 'world order', 'India will take her share according to her own modest parts, firmly convinced that only in such international association lies the hope of lasting and stable world peace.'[21] This was a vision of the world[22] that was forged under and against the sign of racial violence.

Though Bajpai did not explicitly invoke the question of race with respect to the Tokyo trial, nevertheless, within the US Department of State, the matter was soon enough seen in racial terms. General MacArthur, the Supreme Commander for the Allied Powers and in charge of the Allied occupation of Japan, as well as Dean Acheson, Under-Secretary of the Department of State (and often the Acting Secretary), had opposed India sending a judge.[23] However Loy W. Henderson, then head of the Near Eastern Bureau in the Department of State, raised the stakes by suggesting to the US Secretary of State in March 1946 that 'the virtually all-white character of the proposed Tribunal' was 'looked upon most unfavorably by Indians'; the inclusion of 'only one Asiatic country, China' to judge another Asiatic country would not go down well. Henderson feared that it would be 'harmful to this country's [United States'] relations with

---

19   G.S. Bajpai, 'An Indian Looks at the War', *The Annals of the American Academy of Political and Social Science*, 222 (1942), 38-41; quotes from 41.

20   Ibid., 38-39.

21   Ibid., 41.

22   On 'the world' as an increasingly significant twentieth-century conceptual category, see D. Bell, 'Making and Taking Worlds' in S. Moyn and A. Sartori (eds.), *Global Intellectual History* (New York: Columbia University Press, 2013), pp. 254-82.

23   NARA, General Records of the Department of State, RG 59, File No. 740.00116 PW/1-1846 CS/D, Box 3631, Decimal File, 1945-49, Telegram, 18 January 1946.

India' if the Americans continued to oppose India's entry to the trial. He also felt 'Since this is a judicial matter, the question as to whether or not India is completely independent is irrelevant.'[24] Britain (in December 1945, after ascertaining the views of the Government of India)[25] and New Zealand (in January 1946)[26] had meanwhile also lent their voice to India's bid for a judge. In this context, J.C. Vincent, the director of the Office of Far Eastern Affairs, suggested that the US should not oppose the entry of an Indian judge; further, a Filipino judge could also be appointed if the Philippine Commonwealth government so desired. Secretary of State James F. Byrnes agreed.[27]

The debate's racial framing is visible in a letter sent by Vincent to Acheson in March 1946 about the importance of adding an Indian as well as a Filipino judge, since the Department felt that 'it was considered politically desirable to avoid being placed in the position of discriminating against Asiatic countries'.[28] The perceived need not to alienate India, the formation of transnational support for India, and the feared loss of political-juridical legitimacy if the Tokyo tribunal was seen as being discriminatory towards Asians, thus led the Department of State to support the inclusion of an Indian judge. The Charter of the International Military Tribunal for the Far East was accordingly amended on 25 April 1946.[29] On 29 April, Bajpai wrote to the US Secretary of State that

---

24   NARA, General Records of the Department of State, RG 59, File No. 740.00116 PW/3-146 CS/A, Box 3631, Decimal File, 1945-49, Office Memorandum from Mr Henderson, NEA, to Mr Secretary, 1 March 1946.

25   The National Archives, United Kingdom, LCO 2/2983 and FO 371/57422; The British Embassy in Washington DC, to the Department of State, 2407/41/45, 12 December 1945, in United States Department of State, Foreign Relations of the United States: Diplomatic Papers, 1945, vol. 6, 983, available at <http://uwdc.library.wisc.edu/collections/FRUS> (accessed 13 October 2014); Sedgwick, 'The Trial', pp. 266-69.

26   NARA, General Records of the Department of State, RG 59, File No. 740.00116 PW/1-3146 CS/LE, Box 3631, Decimal File, 1945-49, Letter from the Chargé d'Affaires ad interim of New Zealand to the Secretary of State, 31 January 1946.

27   NARA, General Records of the Department of State, RG 59, File No. 740.00116 PW/3-146 CS/A, Box 3631, Decimal File, 1945-49, Office Memorandum from Mr. Vincent, FE, to Mr Secretary, 2 March 1946; NARA, General Records of the Department of State, RG 59, File No. 740.00116 PW/3-446 CS/D, Box 3631, Decimal File, 1945-49, Office Memorandum from Mr Vincent, FE, to Mr Henderson, NEA, 4 March 1946.

28   NARA, General Records of the Department of State, RG 59, File No. 740.00116 PW/3-1546 CS/A, Box 3631, Decimal File, 1945-49, Office Memorandum from Mr Vincent, FE, to Mr Acheson, U, 15 March 1946.

29   International Military Tribunal for the Far East Charter, available at <http://www.jus.uio. no/english/services/library/treaties/04/4-06/military-tribunal-far-east.xml> (accessed 13 October 2014); NARA, General Records of the Department of state, RG 59, File No.

Radhabinod Pal, 'formerly Judge of the Calcutta High Court', had been selected as the Indian representative to the IMTFE.[30]

Eventually, as James Sedgwick has noted, the Indian contingent at Tokyo consisted of '[t]wo prosecutors, Govinda Menon and Krishna Menon, one judge, Radhabinod Pal, and one judicial assistant, Radha S. Sinha'.[31] Sedgwick has shown in detail two things. First, the Indian presence in Tokyo was enabled through the emergence of significant intra-Commonwealth solidarity (Britain, crucially, rallying to India's support). Sedgwick's broader argument, that the trial 'took on historical and symbolic valence as a groundbreaking postcolonial institution by including Indian, Burmese, and Filipino representatives before their respective countries achieved full independence from colonial rule', is provocative, though perhaps more debatable.[32] Second, he shows – and this is related to the broader ambiguity of India's political status – that none of the appointees were first choices. The British initially wished to appoint a British associate prosecutor to represent India, and only after failing (twice) to find someone suitable and willing, made their Indian choice. In terms of a judge too, their initial preference was for someone British; only later, through communication between the British and the Indian governments, did the tide turn in favour of an Indian appointment. The clinching factor here was the desire to mollify Indian political opinion;[33] we have observed Bajpai's critical role in this. Nariaki Nakazato's detailed and pioneering research has revealed that the specific appointment of Pal was, however, somewhat fortuitous. For the British, the initial Indian choices were a certain Wadia, a former judge of the Bombay High Court (who declined) and (subsequently) a Varma, a judge of the Allahabad High Court (who did not respond). In Nakazato's narration, the colonial War Department then requested the Chief Justices of the High Courts of Calcutta, Bombay, Madras and Lahore to ask their puisne judges; on 24 April, Pal became the first (but not the only, or even the best qualified, one) to respond, and was hence selected.[34] Unlike the Menons, who pleased (the American) Chief Prosecutor Joseph B. Keenan and the British Associate

---

740.00116 PW/4-2246 CS/A, Box 3631, Decimal File, 1945-49, Telegram Sent, Department of State, 22 April 1946.

30 NARA, General Records of the Department of State, RG 59, File No. 740.00116PW/4-2946 CS/A, Box 3631, Decimal File, 1945-49, Letter from the Agent General for India to the Secretary of State, 29 April 1946.

31 Sedgwick, 'The Trial', p. 261.

32 Ibid.

33 Ibid., pp. 266-69.

34 N. Nakazato, *Neonationalist Mythology in Postwar Japan: Pal's Dissenting Judgment at the Tokyo War Crimes Tribunal* (Lanham: Lexington Books, 2016), pp. 7-9.

Prosecutor Arthur Comyns-Carr with their work,[35] Pal was to raise storms in Tokyo.

Sovereignty and Natural Law: Radhabinod Pal in Tokyo and Beyond

Unlike Bajpai, Pal was not a Brahmin; he came from a poor 'lower caste' (potter community) family of the Bengal countryside. He completed his doctoral dissertation from the University of Calcutta on Hindu law; the dissertation was the product of scholarly networks that were reinterpreting precolonial South Asian ideas in the light of modern Western concepts and ideologies. His lectures on the philosophy and history of Hindu law at the University of Calcutta were brilliantly original works that drew transverse lines across Indian and European history in order to create a fundamental binary between 'sovereignty' and 'natural law', and thereby to simultaneously criticize Indian forms of social oppression as well as the violence embedded in European formats of state sovereignty and racism. In structuring this comparativism, Pal's involvement with European-global legal networks was of significance. In 1937, Pal became a member of the International Law Association. He served as a rapporteur of the Legal Philosophy section in the 1937 Congress of Comparative Law held at the Hague, and was elected one of the Presidents of the Congress. Pal's writings are strewn with references to some of the legal thinkers whom he met here.[36]

By adopting a transnational biographical approach, I wish to elaborate on certain existing assumptions about Pal. One dominant trend has been to identify him as the representative of an almost timeless mythic-religious Indian vision which eschews Western-Christian principles of a good-evil binary, and thereby also rejects the principles of international criminal justice which

---

35   Sedgwick, 'The Trial', p. 263.

36   Ministre des Affaires Etrangères, La Courneuve, Nations Unies et Organisations Interna-
      tionales (NUOI) 372, Box 100, Crimes de Guerre Extrême-Orient, Tribunal Militaire Inter-
      national de Tokio, Le Procureur Français près le Tribunal Militaire International des
      Crimes de Guerre en Extrême-Orient a Son Excellence Monsieur le Ministre des Affaires
      Etrangères (Secrétariat des Conférences), 27 February 1947, Biographie sommaire des
      Membres du Tribunal Militaire International des Crimes de Guerre en Extrême-Orient,
      'Le Juge Pal: Représentant de l'Inde', 6; *Questions Inscrites au Programme du Deuxième
      Congrès International de Droit Comparé, La Haye, 4-11 Aout 1937: Rapporteurs Généraux et
      Rapporteurs Spéciaux*, 16 ; A. Nandy, 'The Other Within: The Strange Case of Radhabinod
      Pal's Judgment on Culpability', *New Literary History*, 23 (1992), 45-67.

underpinned the Tokyo trial.[37] A second trend is to see him as a positivist defender of the idea of state sovereignty, and therefore also an antagonist to the naturalist-inflected moral claims put forward by the prosecution and some of the judges in Tokyo. The positivist Pal is either championed as a herald of future postcolonial/Third World approaches to international law,[38] or denigrated as an opponent of the universalistic anti-sovereignty demands of international criminal law.[39] A third way equates Pal with Keenan in terms of following comparable (if also antithetical) naturalism-inflected ideas of just war.[40] The problem I see with each of these positions is that they do not con-

---

37   The *locus classicus* for this view is Nandy, 'The Other Within'. T. Nakajima, 'Justice Pal
      (India)' in Y. Tanaka, T. McCormack and G. Simpson (eds.), *Beyond Victor's Justice? The
      Tokyo War Crimes Trial Revisited* (Leiden: Martinus Nijhoff, 2011), p. 140, similarly writes
      that 'Pal was a believer of humanism based on the philosophy of "dharma" from ancient
      India.' A recent, though more nuanced, iteration can be found in B. Hill, 'Reason and Love-
      lessness: Tagore, War Crimes, and Justice Pal', *Postcolonial Studies*, 18 (2015), 145-160. While
      I agree with Hill in noting that Pal drew on ancient Indian texts to critique legal dogma-
      tism and modern state authority (we seemingly arrived at this conclusion near simultane-
      ously and from parallel routes), I find Hill's uncritical placing of Pal within a timeless
      trajectory of Indian *dharma* to be very problematic. Nandy's view is accepted as quasi-
      authoritative by R. Cryer and N. Boister, *The Tokyo International Military Tribunal:
      A Reappraisal* (Oxford: Oxford University Press, 2008), pp. 289-91, by Y. Totani, *The Tokyo
      War Crimes Trial: The Pursuit of Justice in the Wake of World War II* (Cambridge, MA: Har-
      vard University Press, 2009), pp. 222-23, and by Hill, 'Reason'.
38   J.N. Shklar, *Legalism: An Essay on Law, Morals and Politics* (Cambridge, MA: Harvard Uni-
      versity Press, 1964), pp. 181-90; R. Minear, *Victors' Justice: The Tokyo War Crimes Trial*
      (Princeton: Princeton University Press, 1971); E.S. Kopelman, 'Ideology and International
      Law: The Dissent of the Indian Justice at the Tokyo War Crimes Trial', *New York University
      Journal of International Law and Politics*, 23 (1990/91), 373-444; K. Sellars, '*Crimes against
      Peace' and International Law* (Cambridge: Cambridge University Press, 2013); L. Varadara-
      jan, 'The Trials of Imperialism: Radhabinod Pal's Dissent at the Tokyo Tribunal', *European
      Journal of International Relations*, 2014, 1-23.
39   Totani, *Tokyo*, pp. 218-62; Nakazato, *Neonationalist*.
40   A naturalist tone in Pal is noticed by R. Cryer, 'The Doctrinal Foundations of International
      Criminalization' in M.C. Bassiouni (ed.), *International Criminal Law*, vol. 1, *Sources, Sub-
      jects and Contents* (Leiden: Martinus Nijhoff, 2008), p. 112; R. Cryer, 'The Philosophy of
      International Criminal Law', in A. Orakhelashvili (ed.), *Research Handbook on the Theory
      and History of International Law* (Cheltenham: Edward Elgar, 2011), pp. 242-43; Cryer and
      Boister, *Tokyo*, pp. 285-91; and K. Sellars, 'Imperfect Justice at Nuremberg and Tokyo', *The
      European Journal of International Law*, 21 (2011), 1096. These writings neglect Pal's natural-
      ist reflections on Hindu law, leading to interpretative problems. Sellars thus asserts that
      Pal framed Japanese actions against Western powers in terms of 'just war' theory, 'in the
      process stepping onto the same naturalist terrain as Keenan.... Instead of reframing the

sider Pal's intellectual formation in its totality, by, for example, looking, with adequate empirical density and theoretical rigour, at the parallels and intersections between his writings on Hindu law, on international law in general, and his Tokyo dissent. Many scholars foreground the dissent while analysing Pal, without contextualizing it within Pal's broader intellectual life and career. This creates a research vacuum, which this essay addresses. I build on arguments set at length in two other essays authored by me,[41] while reframing the issues involved through a novel biographical analytical focus. I am indebted to previous generations of scholarship on Pal (as some of the empirical contents of this essay shows), but shed a new theoretical light on his dissent, through a fresh reading of the sources.

I would argue that Pal's triple subalternity (in terms of race, caste, and, initially, class location) left a significant impact on his ideological stance. In his 1958 volume on the history of Hindu law, he elaborately compared caste discrimination with race discrimination, condemning both for violently entrenching the hereditary power of ruling classes over subjugated peoples.[42] The transnational orientation of his comparativist thinking is evident, for example, from the way he castigated the German philosopher Friedrich Nietzsche (1844-1900) for invoking ancient Indian ideas of caste hierarchy (as expressed by the mytho-historical seer Manu) to justify the alleged need for a modern master people.[43] Such comparativist thinking dated at least to the 1920s when, in lectures on the philosophy and history of Hindu law, Pal outlined two different ways of conceptualizing the relation between sovereignty and law. One way would be to privilege the ethical ideals of natural law over the dictates of state authority (he identified such notions in Vedic texts, and

---

debate, he found himself trapped within it.' In contrast, I think that Pal's naturalism differed radically from Keenan's. One has to read Pal's dissent in conjunction with his Hindu law writings, to appreciate his anxiety about sovereignty (whether exerted by single states, by inter-state coalitions like the Allied Powers, or even by religious communities) as well as his quest for supra-sovereign natural justice.

41   M. Banerjee, 'Does International Criminal Justice Require a Sovereign? Historicising Radhabinod Pal's Tokyo Judgment in Light of his "Indian" Legal Philosophy' in M. Bergsmo, W.L. Cheah and P. Yi (eds.), *Historical Origins of International Criminal Law*, vol. 2 (Brussels: Torkel Opsahl, 2014), pp. 67-118; M. Banerjee, 'Decolonization and Subaltern Sovereignty: India and the Tokyo Trial' in K. von Lingen (ed.), *War Crimes Trials in the Wake of Decolonization and Cold War in Asia, 1945-1956: Justice in Time of Turmoil* (Cham: Palgrave, 2016), pp. 69-91.

42   Banerjee, 'International Criminal Justice', 73-80.

43   R. Pal, *The History of Hindu Law in the Vedic Age and in Post-Vedic Times down to the Institutes of Manu* (Calcutta: University of Calcutta, 1958), p. 13, pp. 226-69.

especially in the Rgvedic concept of *rta*, as well as in European-Christian principles of natural law); and the other would be to subordinate law to the dictate of some sovereign authority, be it that of a state or of a theological body (he found such tendencies in Manu as well as in vast stretches of premodern and modern European history).[44]

Appreciating this transnational inflection in Pal (even before his entrance into Tokyo) puts us in a better position to broaden our reading of the judgment as well. Historians have noted how it was clear, almost from the very beginning, that Pal would develop his dissenting stance.[45] As Pal's final dissenting judgment makes clear, he was uncomfortable with the idea that a trial could ever represent the legal-political perspective of victorious powers (one outlined by the IMTFE Charter); his dissent expressed this impulse to articulate (what he considered to be) a sensibility of 'justice' against a sensibility of 'power':

> The clear intention is that we are to be 'a judicial tribunal' and not 'a manifestation of power' .... The so-called trial held according to the definition of crime *now* given by the victors obliterates the centuries of civilization which stretch between us and the summary slaying of the defeated in a war. A trial with law thus prescribed will only be a sham employment of legal process for the satisfaction of a thirst for revenge. It does not correspond to any idea of justice. Such a trial may justly create the feeling that the setting up of a tribunal like the present is much more a political than a legal affair, an essentially political objective having thus been cloaked by a juridical appearance.[46]

Such a contrary perspective provoked concern, especially in British governmental circles, in April-May 1947. Thanks to information flows between Tokyo (the British judge Lord Patrick and the United Kingdom Liaison Mission in Japan) and London (the Lord Chancellor, the Attorney General, the Dominions Office, and the Foreign Office), news spread in Britain about Pal's oppositional stance, and it was feared that his 'backslaps' would be directed especially at

---

44   Banerjee, 'International Criminal Justice', 73-86, 115-17. In addition to the 1958 book (cited above), see also R. Pal, *The Hindu Philosophy of Law in the Vedic and Post-Vedic Times Prior to the Institutes of Manu* (Calcutta: Biswabhandar Press, 1927?); R. Pal, *The History of Hindu Law in the Vedic Age and in Post-Vedic Times down to the Institutes of Manu* (Calcutta: Biswabhandar Press, 1929?). The dating of these books is approximate.

45   Sellars, *Crimes*, pp. 234-35; Sedgwick, 'The Trial Within', p. 83.

46   IMTFE Transcripts, *United States of America et al. v. Araki Sadao et al.,* Judgment of The Hon'ble Mr. Justice Pal, Member from India ('Pal Judgment') (https://www.legal-tools.org/en/go-to-database/ltfolder/0_29521/#results), pp. 36-37. Emphasis in original.

Britain.[47] Pal's friendship with the Dutch judge B.V.A. Röling caused concern, as that friendship certainly influenced, in part, Röling's critical stand towards the imperialist underpinnings at Tokyo.[48] Compelled by this, along with the conflicts caused by Keenan and the (Australian) President Judge William Webb, the British official circles felt a clear need to consolidate a strong majority judgment. The British Foreign Secretary Ernest Bevin seems to have feared 'a shattering blow to European prestige' if the trial failed.[49] Pressure was put on Röling; in the candour of a British Foreign Office note: 'If the Indian is unsupported he may in the end toe the line.'[50] (Röling ultimately toned down his dissent.) As late as September 1947, the British hoped, using a strikingly paternalist and pastoral imagery in an age of decolonization, to return Pal 'into Nuremberg fold.'[51]

There were complex intellectual reasons behind Pal's recalcitrance. We can identify throughout his Tokyo dissent two parallel voices. Pal's first voice supported the idea of an 'International Court of Criminal Justice', cited with approval the wish for such a court expressed after the end of the First World War by an Advisory Committee of Jurists which met at the Hague in 1920, and invoked the jurist Hersch Lauterpacht (1897-1960) in maintaining that 'international law should recognize the individual as its ultimate subject and maintenance of his rights as its ultimate end'. Pal insisted, in part by quoting the jurist Hans Kelsen (1881-1973), that this future international criminal court, however, had to be a truly neutral one, to which both victor and vanquished nations would submit, rather than a tribunal composed only of the victor nations as was the case with the Tokyo trial; it was to be empowered to try members from both victor and defeated nations who had committed war crimes.[52] As with Bajpai, Pal's vision of the global, of 'the world' as a theatre of action, was constituted through the negation of racial divides. He underlined in his dissent: 'I doubt not that the need of the world is the formation of an international community under the reign of law, or correctly, the formation of

---

47   The National Archives, United Kingdom (hereafter TNA), FO 371/66552, From United Kingdom Liaison Mission in Japan to Foreign Office, 25 April 1947. See also, e.g., TNA, LCO 2/2992, FO 371/63820, FO 371/66552, FO 371/66553.

48   On Röling, see L. Schouten, 'From Tokyo to the United Nations: B.V.A. Röling, International Criminal Jurisdiction and the Debate on Establishing an International Criminal Court, 1949-1957', in Bergsmo et al. (eds.), *Historical Origins*, 184-92.

49   TNA, FO 371/66553, U 666/1/73, Foreign Office, 22 May 1947.

50   TNA, FO 371/66553, Foreign Office Note, 23 May 1947.

51   TNA, FO 371/63820, From United Kingdom Liaison Mission in Japan to Foreign Office, 21 September 1947.

52   IMTFE Transcripts, Pal Judgment, 10-15, 145 (source of quote).

a world community under the reign of law, in which nationality or race should find no place.'[53]

Pal's second voice was more critical towards the possibility of instituting, either in Tokyo or in the immediate future, such a neutral international criminal court. He criticized the idea that natural law norms could be used to create a line of distinction between the good Allied Powers and an evil Japan, and to punish the top political-military leadership of Japan even in the absence of positive law frameworks (and thereby to overcome the problem posed by the principle of *nullum crimen nulla poena sine lege*). Pal's criticism of natural law stemmed from the way in which Christianity-inflected naturalist ideas were deployed by the (American) chief prosecutor Joseph B. Keenan and the (Australian) president Judge William Webb against the Japanese accused. Pal saw here, and more generally in the Tokyo tribunal's dealings with the Japanese, a tone of legal sanctimoniousness which could not mask the desire of the dominant Allied Powers to justify their imperial goals, whether as evident in their occupation of Japan or, more generally, in their colonial interests in Asia.[54] Pal felt that there was no moral justification for the Allied attempt to maintain their hegemony in Asia and elsewhere in the colonial world through a scaffolding of legally-policed 'peace': 'Certainly, dominated nations of the present day *status quo* cannot be made to submit to eternal domination only in the name of peace... To them the present age is faced with not only the menace of totalitarianism but also the *actual plague* of imperialism.'[55]

The sovereignty versus natural law binary thus became incredibly complex in the context of Tokyo. It is true that Pal wished to defend the sovereignty of the defeated power, Japan, from Allied domination; but this was only in reaction to his fear that the dominant Allied Powers were claiming a sort of super-sovereignty over Japan on the basis of winning a 'just war'. He saw the Tokyo tribunal as instituting a new kind of imperial sovereignty, maintained by a coalition of powerful states, and legitimating itself in part through the use of natural law arguments (the super-sovereign codifying natural law into positive law, and thereby punishing Japan: a stance starkly visible in Keenan and Webb), and in part through the simple fact of victory (emblematized by the hegemonic claims of the IMTFE Charter which were accepted by the majority of the judges as the basis of their juridical authority).[56] Hence Pal remarked in his dissenting judgment that the Allied Powers could not claim to be the 'sovereign of the

---

53 Ibid., 146.
54 Banerjee, 'International Criminal Justice', 92-108.
55 IMTFE Transcripts, Pal Judgment, 239.
56 Banerjee, 'International Criminal Justice', 92-108.

international community. It is not the sovereign of that much desired super-state', nor could the powers 'claim to be the custodian of "the common good"'. Pal's defence of Japanese sovereignty was thus, in a sense, only a strategic move to obviate the construction of a more dangerous Allied sovereignty (particu-larly in Asia, through the return and/or reconsolidation of the Western powers in their colonies and occupied territories) justifying itself through a language of legal-moral universalism. He became an apologist for non-European sover-eignty only because he saw no alternative: he was 'not in love with this national sovereignty', but nevertheless recognized that 'even in the postwar organiza-tions after this Second World War *national sovereignty still figures very largely*.'[57]

This structural bivalence (being both anti-sovereignty and pro-sovereignty, as the context demanded) helps us explain why Pal could simultaneously con-demn Japanese war crimes as 'devilish and fiendish'[58], while also arguing that these were committed by lower level personnel, and that the top Japanese political-military leadership needed to be exonerated of the charge of any direct responsibility in committing these crimes; moreover, whatever they had done, they had only done as part of a broader governmental machinery. (This was, he felt, unlike the case of the Nazi crimes or the American atomic bomb-ing of Hiroshima and Nagasaki, or with Kaiser Wilhelm II's role in the First World War, where there was much more direct individuated responsibility of the leaders in the actual crimes.) In a similar manner, Pal condemned the hor-rors of the Second World War, while suggesting that Japan alone could not be blamed. Rather, the war was another, albeit gruesome, episode in the modern trajectory of totalitarian wars (dating at least to the American Civil War), which resulted from a combination of large-scale industrialization and mass mobilization of peoples in an age of nationalist democracy. If anything, it was Western imperialism and racism, as manifested clearly in Asia, which had overdetermined Japanese aggressive militarism.[59]

Pal thus suggested that the Japanese accused in the Tokyo trial could neither be charged with direct responsibility for war crimes nor for having been unilat-erally responsible for provoking the war. In conclusion, he exculpated them from all the charges of conventional war crimes, crimes against humanity, and crimes against peace: 'each and everyone of the accused must be found not guilty of each and every one of the charges in the indictment and should be acquitted of all those charges'.[60] In trying to protect Japanese sovereignty, Pal

---

57   IMTFE Transcripts, Pal Judgment, 55, 151, 186.
58   Ibid., 1070, 1089.
59   Ibid., e.g. 9, 70, 136-38, 485-87, 558, 570-80, 735-36, 761-68, 1227-28.
60   Ibid., 1226.

seemingly defended (albeit in roundabout ways, and with many qualifications) the most brutal manifestations of Japanese imperialism and sovereign violence. Arguably, he minimized the guilt of the Japanese leadership by presenting it as only a by-product of Western colonialism.

By the time Pal was delivering his judgment, India had become an independent nation-state. Yet the postcolonial state remained in a complex relation of intellectual-political dependence on the former colonial master when it came to the issue of the Tokyo trial. V.K. Krishna Menon, a close aide of Prime Minister Jawaharlal Nehru and then the High Commissioner for India to the United Kingdom, communicated with the British Secretary of State for Commonwealth Relations, Philip Noel-Baker, in August 1948, about 'whether the Indian Government should issue a statement dissociating themselves from the opinions published by Justice Pal'. Noel-Baker initially 'mildly encouraged' Menon, but also sought the opinion of other British authorities.[61] The issue of 'backslap' continued to haunt British government quarters.[62] But in the end, the Foreign Office,[63] the United Kingdom Liaison Mission in Japan, and Lord Patrick,[64] all agreed that it was best if India did not make an official statement, since that would only give unwanted publicity to the dissent; further, the matter was thought to be sub judice. Noel-Baker presented this opinion to Menon.[65]

Though the Government of India thus ultimately did not give any official statement of dissociation from the Pal dissent, Nehru himself, in semi-official communication with Indian political figures in November-December 1948, distanced himself from, and indeed castigated, the dissent. Simultaneously, however, he criticized the death sentences passed in Tokyo.[66] His government, through its representative in a Far Eastern Commission meeting, had requested that the death sentences be commuted to life imprisonment; however, the proposal was shot down by General MacArthur.[67] Thus Nehru and his government, no less than Pal, demonstrated remarkable ambiguities in their attitudes

---

61   TNA, DO 35/2938, Record of Conversation between the Secretary of State and the High Commissioner for India, 3 August 1948.

62   TNA, DO 35/2938, F. 3151/17, 5 August 1948.

63   TNA, DO 35/2938, F 10950/48/G, Letter from F.S. Tomlinson, Foreign Office, to J.M.C. James, Commonwealth Relations Office, 20 August 1948.

64   TNA, DO 35/2938, Telegram from United Kingdom Liaison Mission in Japan to Foreign Office, 7 September 1948.

65   TNA, DO 35/2938, Letter from Philip Noel-Baker to V.K. Krishna Menon, 2 October 1948.

66   J. Nehru, *Selected Works of Jawaharlal Nehru*, vol. 8 (Delhi: Jawaharlal Nehru Memorial Fund, 1989), p. 415; J. Nehru, *Letters to Chief Ministers (1947-1964)*, vol. 1 (Delhi: Jawaharlal Nehru Memorial Fund, 1985), pp. 234-35.

67   TNA, FO 371/69833, Telegram from Tokyo to Foreign Office, 22 November 1948.

towards the Tokyo trial and the Japanese accused. These ambiguities (which have also been empirically noticed by other scholars), while they did not reflect any consistent Indian 'national' position, certainly mirrored many of the schizophrenias of a postcolonial ruling class in its attitudes to international justice, non-European sovereignty, and Western-hegemonic rule of law.

Looking at Pal after Tokyo helps us appreciate the continuing ambiguities. On the one hand, he abstained from voting on a draft code on international criminal law at the sixth Session of the International Law Commission held in Paris in 1954. In a 1955 book, he elaborated his rationale, arguing that the hypocrisy of the Allied Powers had been evident in the way that the Dutch and the French sought (with British, American and Soviet complicity) to legitimate their reconsolidation of power in Indonesia and Indochina (in part by using anti-Japanese rhetoric), brutally suppressing local anti-colonial nationalists, and in the way in which the Americans and the Soviets fought over Korea and devastated it. Pal thought that any top-down codification and imposition of international criminal justice would only support such hegemonic power projects on the part of the Western powers.[68] Simultaneously, in his capacity as a member of the International Law Commission (1952-66; twice elected Chairman of the Commission, in 1958 and 1962) as well as a public intellectual, he repeatedly endorsed the ideal of a new order of global law and peace. Decolonizing states, such as in Asia and Africa, would have to play the leading role in bringing about this international cooperation, expressing thereby 'the popular will of the world', which was instigated by a 'sense of injustice ... universally felt', and moved people to 'weld their souls and spirits in one flaming effort', forging new 'legal provisions' which would be 'the instruments of the conscience of the community'.[69]

---

68   Official Records of the UN General Assembly, Ninth Session, Supplement No. 9, Report of the International Law Commission Covering the Work of its Sixth Session, 3, 28 July 1954, and Summary Record of the 276th Meeting of the International Law Commission, Document No. A/CN.4/SR.276, in International Law Commission database <http://legal.un.org/ilc/index.html> (accessed 8 March 2015); R. Pal, *Crimes in International Relations* (Calcutta: University of Calcutta, 1955), especially pp. iii-ix, 44-52.

69   Report on the Fifth Session of the Asian-African Legal Consultative Committee (Rangoon, January 1962) by Mr. Radhabinod Pal, Observer for the Commission, 153-54, in International Legal Commission database (accessed 8 March 2015). See also Pal, *History*, 1958; R. Pal, *Lectures on Universal Declaration of Human Rights* (Calcutta: Federation Hall Society, 1965); R. Pal, *World Peace Through World Law* (Tokyo: United World Federalists of Japan, 1967).

Conclusion

Samuel Moyn has perceptively referred to Pal's dissenting judgment as offering 'a subaltern critique of Western international law'.[70] This is not to imply that the 'subaltern' necessarily offers a pure emancipatory moment. The overture to resist alleged external Others may intensify various forms of authoritarian violence, especially when the (racial) 'subaltern' is (in most other social markers) a member of an elite group with aspiration to rule, with the ultimate aim of constituting a new order of sovereignty. While theorizing about subaltern elite-hood, Partha Chatterjee has shown how high-caste Hindu Bengali men sought to overcome the stigma of subalternity in white-dominated public places by attempting to reconstitute their private selves and households as realms of 'spiritual' sovereignty and interiority, thereby reproducing hegemonic control over women (and the indigenous lower classes).[71] In the international context I underline here, I identify different sorts of binaries in the way that the 'subaltern elite' project of overcoming Western racial dominance was complicit with the internal constitution of non-European sovereignty, by translating and appropriating Western-origin conceptions of legality and statehood as well as producing apologetics for state violence.

Faced with the 'contagion of sovereignty',[72] what resulted was often not a stable inner/outer, private/public, divide, but a bifurcation of interiority, as the anti-colonial self manifested tensions between the political yearning for state sovereignty and the ethical pathos for universal justice and natural law. Acknowledging these complexities can help us to appreciate better the torn selves of many Indian actors – including Bajpai and Pal – who, in their divergent ways, had to negotiate between playing a Western-dominated, imperially-overdetermined, game of legality and an anxiety to change the rules of the game; and in a related manner, between vernacularizing Western formats of law and sovereignty, and transforming these formats in revolutionary ways in the name of a higher order of justice. They made complex choices that defy easy (Western versus non-Western; colonial versus anti-colonial; elite versus subaltern) binaries. Often these choices were constitutively transversal, simultaneously splitting and joining divergent locations of power. Thereby such players transformed the field of international law, giving new valences to the category of the global in the realm of juridicality and politics which had not

---

70   S. Moyn, 'Judith Shklar versus the International Criminal Court', *Humanity*, 4 (2013), 485.

71   Chatterjee, 'Religion'.

72   D. Armitage, *The Declaration of Independence: A Global History* (Cambridge, MA: Harvard University Press, 2007).

existed before. Through its biographical focus, this essay has ultimately underlined how a transnational approach can help us trace the formation of such
complex mental geographies at the interstices of equally multi-layered legal
geographies of power. It hopes to have probed into the passions that impelled
many twentieth-century Indians to think about building 'one world',[73] and the
anxieties that made them simultaneously reluctant to achieve such a reality.

Bibliography

David Armitage, *The Declaration of Independence: A Global History* (Cambridge, MA:
Harvard University Press, 2007).

Girja Shankar Bajpai, 'An Indian Looks at the War', *The Annals of the American Academy
of Political and Social Science*, 222 (1942), pp. 38-41.

Milinda Banerjee, 'Decolonization and Subaltern Sovereignty: India and the Tokyo Trial'
in K. von Lingen (ed.), *War Crimes Trials in the Wake of Decolonization and Cold War
in Asia, 1945-1956: Justice in Time of Turmoil* (Cham: Palgrave, 2016), pp. 69-91.

Milinda Banerjee, 'Does International Criminal Justice Require a Sovereign? Historicising
Radhabinod Pal's Tokyo Judgment in Light of his "Indian" Legal Philosophy' in Morten
Bergsmo, Cheah Wui Ling, and Yi Ping (eds.), *Historical Origins of International
Criminal Law*, vol. 2 (Brussels: Torkel Opsahl, 2014), pp. 67-118.

Sukanya Banerjee, *Becoming Imperial Citizens: Indians in the Late-Victorian Empire*
(Durham: Duke University Press, 2010).

C.A. Bayly, *Recovering Liberties: Indian Thought in the Age of Liberalism and Empire*
(Cambridge: Cambridge University Press, 2012).

Duncan Bell, 'Making and Taking Worlds' in Samuel Moyn and Andrew Sartori (eds.),
Global Intellectual History (New York: Columbia University Press, 2013), pp. 254-82.

Manu Bhagavan, *India and the Quest for One World: The Peacemakers* (Basingstoke:
Palgrave Macmillan, 2013).

Dipesh Chakrabarty, *Provincializing Europe: Postcolonial Thought and Historical
Difference* (Delhi: Oxford University Press, 2001).

Partha Chatterjee, 'A Religion of Urban Domesticity: Sri Ramakrishna and the Calcutta
Middle Class' in Partha Chatterjee and Gyanendra Pandey (eds.), *Subaltern Studies
VII: Writings on South Asian History and Society* (Delhi: Oxford University Press, 1999
[1992]), pp. 40-68.

Kenton J. Clymer, *Quest for Freedom: The United States and India's Independence* (New
York: Columbia University Press, 1995).

---

73   Bhagavan, *The Peacemakers*, offers a recent and wide-ranging overview of these efforts.

Robert Cryer, 'The Doctrinal Foundations of International Criminalization' in M. Cherif Bassiouni (ed.), *International Criminal Law*, vol. 1, *Sources, Subjects and Contents* (Leiden: Martinus Nijhoff, 2008), pp. 107-128.

Robert Cryer, 'The Philosophy of International Criminal Law', in A. Orakhelashvili (ed.), *Research Handbook on the Theory and History of International Law* (Cheltenham: Edward Elgar, 2011), pp. 232-267.

Robert Cryer and Neil Boister, *The Tokyo International Military Tribunal: A Reappraisal* (Oxford: Oxford University Press, 2008).

Michael J. Franklin, *Orientalist Jones: Sir William Jones, Poet, Lawyer, and Linguist, 1746-1794* (New York: Oxford University Press, 2011).

Suparna Gooptu, *Cornelia Sorabji, India's Pioneer Woman Lawyer: A Biography* (Delhi: Oxford University Press, 2006).

Tim Harper and Sunil Amrith, 'Introduction' in Harper and Amrith (eds.), *Sites of Asian Interaction: Ideas, Networks and Mobility* (Delhi: Cambridge University Press, 2014), pp. 1-9.

Barry Hill, 'Reason and Lovelessness: Tagore, War Crimes, and Justice Pal', *Postcolonial Studies*, 18 (2015), pp. 145-60.

Gerald Horne, *The End of Empires: African Americans and India* (Philadelphia: Temple University Press, 2008).

Elizabeth S. Kopelman, 'Ideology and International Law: The Dissent of the Indian Justice at the Tokyo War Crimes Trial', *New York University Journal of International Law and Politics*, 23 (1990/91), pp. 373-444.

Arnulf Becker Lorca, *Mestizo International Law: A Global Intellectual History, 1842-1933* (Cambridge: Cambridge University Press, 2014).

Kris Manjapra, 'Introduction' in Sugata Bose and Kris Manjapra (eds.), *Cosmopolitan Thought Zones: South Asia and the Global Circulation of Ideas* (New York: Palgrave Macmillan, 2010), pp. 1-19.

Kris Manjapra, 'Transnational Approaches to Global History: A View from the Study of German-Indian Entanglement', *German History*, 32 (2014), pp. 274-293.

Karuna Mantena, *Alibis of Empire: Henry Maine and the Ends of Liberal Imperialism* (Princeton: Princeton University Press, 2010).

Robert J. McMahon, *The Cold War on the Periphery: The United States, India, and Pakistan* (New York: Columbia University Press, 1994).

Richard Minear, *Victors' Justice: The Tokyo War Crimes Trial* (Princeton: Princeton University Press, 1971).

Samuel Moyn, 'On the Nonglobalization of Ideas' in Samuel Moyn and Andrew Sartori (eds.), *Global Intellectual History* (New York: Columbia University Press, 2013), pp. 187-204.

Samuel Moyn, 'Judith Shklar versus the International Criminal Court', *Humanity*, 4 (2013), pp. 473-500.

Mithi Mukherjee, *India in the Shadows of Empire: A Legal and Political History, 1774-1950* (Delhi: Oxford University Press, 2010).

Takeshi Nakajima, 'Justice Pal (India)' in Yuki Tanaka, Tim McCormack and Gerry Simpson (eds.), *Beyond Victor's Justice? The Tokyo War Crimes Trial Revisited* (Leiden: Martinus Nijhoff, 2011), pp. 127-144.

Nariaki Nakazato, *Neonationalist Mythology in Postwar Japan: Pal's Dissenting Judgment at the Tokyo War Crimes Tribunal* (Lanham: Lexington Books, 2016).

Ashis Nandy, 'The Other Within: The Strange Case of Radhabinod Pal's Judgment on Culpability', *New Literary History*, 23 (1992), pp. 45-67.

Jawaharlal Nehru, *Selected Works of Jawaharlal Nehru*, vol. 8 (Delhi: Jawaharlal Nehru Memorial Fund, 1989).

Jawaharlal Nehru, *Letters to Chief Ministers (1947-1964)*, vol. 1 (Delhi: Jawaharlal Nehru Memorial Fund, 1985).

Radhabinod Pal, *Crimes in International Relations* (Calcutta: University of Calcutta, 1955).

Radhabinod Pal, *The History of Hindu Law in the Vedic Age and in Post-Vedic Times down to the Institutes of Manu* (Calcutta: University of Calcutta, 1958).

Radhabinod Pal, *Lectures on Universal Declaration of Human Rights* (Calcutta: Federation Hall Society, 1965).

Radhabinod Pal, *World Peace Through World Law* (Tokyo: United World Federalists of Japan, 1967).

Lisette Schouten, 'From Tokyo to the United Nations: B.V.A. Röling, International Criminal Jurisdiction and the Debate on Establishing an International Criminal Court, 1949-1957' in Morten Bergsmo, Cheah Wui Ling, and Yi Ping (eds.), *Historical Origins of International Criminal Law*, vol. 2 (Brussels: Torkel Opsahl, 2014), pp. 184-92.

James Burnham Sedgwick, 'The Trial Within: Negotiating Justice at the International Military Tribunal for the Far East, 1946-1948', unpublished PhD thesis, University of British Columbia (2012).

Kirsten Sellars, *'Crimes against Peace' and International Law* (Cambridge: Cambridge University Press, 2013).

Kirsten Sellars, 'Imperfect Justice at Nuremberg and Tokyo', *The European Journal of International Law*, 21 (2011), pp. 1085-1102.

Mitra Sharafi, 'Two Lives in Law: The Reminiscences of A.J.C. Mistry and Sir Norman Macleod, 1884-1926', University of Wisconsin Law School Legal Studies Research Paper Series Paper No. 1252 <http://papers.ssrn.com/sol3/papers.cfm?abstract_id=2408064>, accessed 24 October 2015.

Judith N. Shklar, *Legalism: An Essay on Law, Morals and Politics* (Cambridge: Cambridge, MA: Harvard University Press, 1964).

K.J.M. Smith, *James Fitzjames Stephen: Portrait of a Victorian Rationalist* (Cambridge: Cambridge University Press, 1988).

Yuki Takatori, 'America's War Crimes Trial? Commonwealth Leadership at the International Military Tribunal for the Far East, 1946-48', *The Journal of Imperial and Commonwealth History*, 35 (2007), pp. 549-568.

Yuma Totani, *The Tokyo War Crimes Trial: The Pursuit of Justice in the Wake of World War II* (Cambridge, MA: Harvard University Press, 2009).

Latha Varadarajan, 'The Trials of Imperialism: Radhabinod Pal's Dissent at the Tokyo Tribunal', *European Journal of International Relations*, 2014, 1-23.

Auriol Weigold, *Churchill, Roosevelt and India: Propaganda during World War II* (New York: Routledge, 2008).

CHAPTER 13

Loser's Justice: The Tokyo Trial from the Perspective of the Japanese Defence Counsels and the Legal Community

Urs Matthias Zachmann

The Japanese defence counsels and the legal community were the groups most marginal to the actual proceedings of the Tokyo trial. Yet, considering the long afterlife of the trial in the Japanese debate about historical responsibility, their positions are arguably at the centre of it, their relevance even increasing over time. This in spite of the fact that the trial has otherwise sunk into popular, and probably well-deserved, oblivion.

Judgments about the Tokyo trial, however, always seem somewhat unbalanced. In 1947, a young Texan jurist who had just come back from a brief stint as 'Associate Counsel for the United States, Prosecution, International Tribunal For The Far East' observed on the importance of his experience: 'International press has classed the Tokyo War Crimes Trial as one of the great trials in the recorded history of man. It is placed after the trial of Jesus and with the Nuremberg trial.'[1] And yet, barely three years after this grandiloquent statement, another commentator observed a strange disinterest in the Far Eastern version of the Nuremberg trial: 'In this respect it differs substantially from its European counterpart. The Nuremberg trials received much publicity and relatively widespread newspaper coverage throughout the proceedings. Scant attention was paid by the American press to the Tokyo trials.'[2]

Little has changed today. Whereas in the literature on international criminal justice, the Nuremberg trial often appears as the iconic starting point of the discipline and its 'legacy' as manifest in the Rome Statute of 1998 and the founding of the International Criminal Court in 2002, the Tokyo trial has been called the 'forgotten trial'.[3] In comparison with its European counterpart, it is

---

1 E.M. Hyder, 'The Tokyo Trial', *Texas Bar Journal*, 10.4 (1947), 136.

2 S. Horwitz, 'The Tokyo Trial', *International Conciliation*, 465 (Nov. 1950), 475.

3 M. Futamura, *War Crimes Tribunals and Transitional Justice* (London: Routledge, 2008), pp. 8-11.

at best remembered as an embarrassing hiccup on the trajectory towards international justice, an unfortunate event better not talked about.[4]

Reasons for the uneven assessment of the European and Far Eastern trials are numerous: a certain Eurocentrism, which directed popular attention away from the Tokyo trial, was arguably one factor (as it may be today). However, as we shall see presently, this may have even worked in favour of Japan. On the other hand, professional negligence and a somewhat cavalier attitude towards fair procedure constitute a persistent motif in the discussion of the trial, and it is for this reason that a detailed study of its conduct concludes that, '[w]hile the trial was formally fair in terms of the rights and obligations of the Charter and Rules, it was not substantively fair in terms of the application of those rules. In this sense, it really was victor's justice.'[5]

'Victor's justice', therefore, is the phrase most commonly associated with the Tokyo trial, either in an affirmative or a more differentiating way.[6] The image is particularly strong in Japan itself, and the polemical attitude towards it still 'raw' if compared with the relatively settled acceptance of the Nuremberg trial in Germany.[7] The purport of the phrase is, as it is well known, that the victorious reserve the prerogative to declare their war as 'just' and purely defensive, and condemn the vanquished as 'criminals' and 'aggressors' *ex post facto*. In a way, it is argued, the trial and its underlying outlawry of war are but the continuation of the flawed medieval concept of *bellum iustum*, the 'just war' in which God was always on the side of the victorious (like in an *ordal*).[8] On a

---

4   See, for example, the historical chapter in R. Cryer, H. Friman, D. Robinson and E. Wilmshurst (eds.), *Introduction to International Criminal Law* (Cambridge University Press, 2007), pp. 91-101 (on the Tokyo trial pp. 96-100).

5   N. Boister and R. Cryer, *The Tokyo International Military Tribunal: A Reappraisal* (Oxford University Press, 2008), p. 114.

6   See, *inter alia*, R. Minear, *Victor's Justice: The Tokyo War Crimes Trial* (Princeton University Press, 1971); K. Ushimura, *Beyond the 'Judgment of Civilization': The Intellectual Legacy of the Japanese War Crimes Trial, 1946-49* (Tokyo: International House of Japan, 2003); Y. Tanaka, T. McCormack and G. Simpson (eds.), *Beyond Victor's Justice? The Tokyo War Crimes Trial Revisited* (Leiden: Martinus Nijhoff Publishers, 2011).

7   B. Simma, 'The Impact of Nuremberg and Tokyo: Attempts at a Comparison', in N. Ando (ed.), *Japan and International Law: Past, Present and Future* (The Hague Kluwer Law International, 1999), p. 82; for a historical overview of the Japanese perception of the Tokyo trial, see Futamura, *War Crimes Tribunals*, pp. 68-86; also M. Futamura, 'Japanese Societal Attitude towards the Tokyo Trial: From a Contemporary Perspective', in Tanaka, McCormack and Simpson, *Beyond Victor's Justice?*, pp. 35-54; for a discussion of the contemporary perspective, see Y. Ōnuma, *Tōkyō saiban, sensō sekinin, sengo sekinin* (Tokyo: Tōshindō, 2007).

8   See K. Takayanagi, *Kyokutō saiban to kokusaihō / The Tokyo Trials and International Law* (Tokyo: Yūhikaku, 1948), p. 28.

more secular level, the phrase represents a variation on the popular saying that 'might is right' and that politics trumps justice.

The polemics against the Tokyo trial may well rest on a somewhat unreflecting understanding of the relationship between politics and justice in war crimes trials.[9] However, rather than discussing the rights or wrongs of the accusation itself, this chapter proposes to trace its origin back to the defence strategy of the Japanese counsels, and how it was actually understood in the legal community at the time. The topos of 'victor's justice' is often attributed to Judge Pal's dissenting opinion. However, before that, it was already the mainstay of the Japanese defence, particularly of Takayanagi Kenzō (1887-1967), a leading member of the Japanese defence team who presented the main arguments against the prosecution's case. As the chapter will show, Takayanagi's strategy was in part shaped by his allegiance to the 'civil' faction in the defence team. Moreover, a contextual interpretation of Takayanagi's defence published in Japanese and English under the parallel titles *Kyokutō saiban to kokusaihō* / *The Tokio* [sic] *Trials and International Law* (1948) reveals the rather impossible position from which the Japanese side had to argue, considering the intellectual tradition in which its counsels stood. Thus Japanese pre-war thought in general took an ultra-realist politicized approach towards international law which would have forced the Japanese defence team to acknowledge 'victor's justice', albeit not in a polemic, but in an affirmative way as legitimate. This made it almost impossible to launch an effective defence and may also account for the observation that the Japanese defence seemed so lacklustre and doctrinaire, or, as a polemic account would have it, merely seemed 'to put flowers gracefully on [their clients'] grave'.[10]

The tortuousness of the Japanese defence becomes all the more apparent compared with opinions in the legal community outside of the court. Here, the affirmation of a realist and relativist interpretation of international law and politics demonstrated an unbroken continuity with pre-war thought, although adapted to the new circumstances of a *Pax Americana*. The pull of the political is especially reflected in the position of the most influential international lawyer of the post-war period, Yokota Kisaburō (1896-1993). Yokota had been one of the few critics of Japanese military expansion in the 1930s and in 1947 pub-

---

9   For a discussion of this nexus, see G. Simpson, *Law, War and Crime: War Crimes Trials and the Reinvention of International Law* (Malden, Mass.: Polity Press, 2007), pp. 11-29.

10   See G. Ireland, 'Uncommon Law in Martial Tokyo', *The Yearbook of World Affairs*, 4 (1950), 71; the phrase is quoted again by Judge Röling in B.V.A. Röling and A. Cassese, *The Tokyo Trial and Beyond: Reflections of a Peacemonger* (Cambridge: Polity Press, 1993), p. 38.

lished the treatise *Sensō hanzai ron* [On war crimes],[11] which was seen by the public (correctly) as a semi-official apology for the Tokyo trial. However, in a closer reading of the text in comparison with Takayanagi's treatise – in fact, Takayanagi's was a conscious response to Yokota's intervention[12] – we can observe a similar tendency towards realism that undermines the very core of Yokota's inherently idealistic argument.

The study of the Japanese perspective at the time of the Tokyo trial thus demonstrates the two following points: firstly, that the very tradition of Japanese thought on international law and politics shaped early perceptions of the Tokyo trial as 'victor's justice', although it was initially seen as legitimate in principle (the Japanese defence's arguments notwithstanding). It was only later, through more nationalist interpretations, that the concept was turned to the negative and polemic itself. However, this too, throws a bright light on the history debates today, and on a recurring topic in the critique of international criminal justice in general.

The Composition and Strategies of the Tokyo Trial Defence Team

According to Article 9 (c) and (d) of the Charter of the International Military Tribunal for the Far East, in order to ensure fair trial, each accused was granted 'the right to be represented by a counsel of his own selection, subject to the disapproval of such counsel at any time by the Tribunal' and 'to conduct his defense, including the right to examine any witness, subject to such reasonable restrictions as the Tribunal may determine'. To this end, the Japanese government started preparations from quite early on.[13] Thus, already in October 1945, it drafted a 'Strategy for the Defence of so-called war criminals (political criminals)' (*Iwayuru sensō hanzaijin (seiji hannin) bengo hoshin*) which set down the principal arguments for the Japanese defence later on: the illegitimacy of punishing war criminals under international law; the legitimacy of Japan's war; and the general dismissal of any charges of war crimes against the defendants.[14] However, the Japanese side was at first completely in the dark as to what form the trial would take; it was only by the end of 1945 that this became somewhat

---

11   K. Yokota, *Sensō hanzai ron* (Tokyo: Yūhikaku, 1947).

12   Y. Totani, *The Tokyo War Crimes Trial: The Pursuit of Justice in the Wake of World War II* (Harvard University Asia Center, 2008), p. 211.

13   Y. Higurashi, 'Tōkyō saiban no bengo-gawa: Nihon-jin bengo-dan no seiritsu to Amerika-jin bengonin', *Kagoshima daigaku shakai kagaku zasshi*, 16 (Sept. 1993), 32.

14   Ibid., 32.

clearer. Subsequently, the government formed a task force which coordinated the collection of documents in support of the Japanese defence. Likewise, diverse ministries set up their own committees for the study of problems associated with the Japanese defence in which some future counsels, such as Takayanagi Kenzō, already participated.[15]

Since, according to the interpretation of the Potsdam Declaration, the government was banned from directly involving itself in the defence, the organization of a Japanese defence was coordinated by the Association of Japanese Lawyers (Dai-Nihon bengoshi rengōkai). By March 1946, a first list of counsels was drawn up. However, it was only very late, in May 1946, after the trial had already begun, that the final list of counsels was officially approved by the tribunal.[16] The defence team was formally led by Uzawa Sōmei (1872-1955) and Kiyose Ichirō (1884-1967), two experienced forensic lawyers; another prominent member was Takayanagi Kenzō, professor of Anglo-American law and legal philosophy at Tokyo Imperial University.[17]

From the beginning, the Japanese defence was beset by a number of problems. These ranged from the very mundane and practical to the inherently structural and strategic. The living and working conditions of the counsels in bombed-out Tokyo were difficult, and the funding of the operation was limited and precarious. Kiyose Ichirō, for example, had been made homeless by the air raids and had to live in a shelter. To pay for research assistants and material costs, he went knocking on the doors of companies, begging for donations.[18] SCAP and the Japanese government also contributed.[19] They were given access to the defendants only a week prior to the indictment.[20] Moreover, there was the problem of the imbalance of resources between the prosecution and the defence, particularly in terms of research and translation assistance.[21] Thus when the trial began, the prosecution had 102 translators at its disposal, the defence only three.[22] The transcripts of the trial were available in English on the day, the Japanese translation, however, regularly took twenty to thirty

---

15   Ibid., 33-36.

16   Ibid., 38.

17   Ibid., 38; Boister and Cryer, *Tokyo International Military Tribunal*, p. 79.

18   K. Kobori, *Tōkyō saiban Nihon no benmei* (Tokyo: Kōdansha, 1995), pp. 38-41.

19   Boister and Cryer, *Tokyo International Military Tribunal*, p. 79; Higurashi, 'Tōkyō saiban', 36; Röling and Cassese, *Tokyo Trial*, p. 37.

20   Ireland, 'Uncommon Law', 69.

21   However, Horwitz ('Tokyo Trial', 493) indicates that the defence could use the facilities of the prosecution 'upon completion of the prosecution case'.

22   J. Dower, *Embracing Defeat: Japan in the Wake of World War II* (New York: W.W. Norton, 1999), p. 467 with further references.

days.[23] Only a few Japanese lawyers spoke English and they appeared 'clumsy', and 'uncomfortable' with the proceedings.[24] Finally, despite the quite non-technical nature of the Charter, the Tokyo IMT – which consisted of judges who came mostly from common law countries – began to import more and more common law rules into the proceedings. Besides the fact that the introduction 'made an already hybrid structure even more indeterminate' and open to abuse,[25] most Japanese lawyers were unfamiliar with the practical details of common law procedure.

This handicap has led to a rather mixed assessment of the quality of the Japanese counsels by contemporary observers. Whereas one source praised them as 'extremely able' and noted that they 'readily adapted themselves to the novel situation of an international trial',[26] others denounced their inexperience in 'cross-examination and the other elements of practical presentation of a case under the concepts of the Anglo-Americans'.[27] Another complaint was that the counsels tended to deliver 'long rhetorical abstract, often political or propagandist speeches for their clients, but did not know what it meant to make a real common law technical defense'.[28]

The accusation of inexperience was unfounded, as both Uzawa and Kiyose had been active as defence counsels in many, often high-profile, cases before, only Japanese criminal procedure followed (and follows) the Continental, inquisitorial system. However, the Japanese side, too, soon realized its linguistic and technical handicap and therefore asked SCAP to provide foreign lawyers familiar with the Anglo-American system. This eventually led to the appointment of twenty-eight American lawyers, mostly from various departments in Washington, whose mission was to assist the Japanese lawyers.[29] Again, opinion on their quality differs, ranging from conscientious and extremely hard-working[30] to 'political hacks' who had been made redundant in Washington and were of dubious professional and moral integrity.[31] Be that as it may, despite

---

23   Higurashi, 'Tōkyō saiban', 50.

24   Röling and Cassese, *Tokyo Trial*, pp. 36f.

25   Boister and Cryer, *Tokyo International Military Tribunal*, p. 115.

26   Horwitz, 'Tokyo Trial', 491.

27   Hyder, 'Tokyo Trial', 166.

28   Ireland, 'Uncommon Law', 71.

29   Boister and Cryer, *Tokyo International Military Tribunal*, p. 79; Ireland, 'Uncommon Law', 72; Horwitz, 'Tokyo Trial', 491-93; R.J. Pritchard, 'An Overview of the Historical Importance of the Tokyo Trial', in C. Hosoya, N. Andō, Y. Ōnuma and R. Minear (eds.), *The Tokyo War Crimes Trial* (Tokyo: Kōdansha International, 1986), p. 93.

30   Pritchard, 'Overview', pp. 91ff.

31   Ireland, 'Uncommon Law', 72.

their initial role as mere helpers, they soon came to dominate the proceedings due to their linguistic and technical expertise, whereas the Japanese counsels rarely spoke up.[32]

The most intractable and, for the argument of this chapter, most relevant problem was the factionalism and incoherence of interests and strategies in the defence team as a whole. Thus Western observers often defined the general objectives of the Japanese defence to prove the legality of Japan's actions as a whole and thereby 'to protect the honour of the country, of the emperor and Japan, and not worry too much about the individual fate of the accused man'.[33] However, the situation was much more differentiated, as the Japanese team was notoriously factionalist and pursued different strategies, which could be roughly divided into two;[34] they agreed on only one thing, namely keeping the emperor out of the trial. Otherwise, the military faction (in itself again divided, into the army and the navy faction) pursued a 'country-before-individual' strategy that sought to demonstrate the legitimacy of Japan's wars themselves. The Gaimushō (Ministry of Foreign Affairs) or civil faction, however, disagreed and pursued an 'individuals-first' defence strategy that sought individual acquittals, especially of the civil leaders among the defendants. The military faction therefore accused them of a 'traitorous attitude', i.e. pointing fingers at the military and the ultra-right as the real culprits of the war and thereby trying to absolve the civil leadership and the population of any war guilt.[35] Moreover, the civil faction also emphasized the argument that the tribunal had no right to judge the defendants under international law in the first place.

The internal divisions in the defence team were further increased by the group of American counsels, which was equally incoherent and pursued yet another strategy;[36] the American lawyers, not altogether convinced by any of the Japanese strategies, sought to achieve an acquittal or review of the trial on technical grounds. For this, they were called by SCAP 'American shysters' and frequently blamed for drawing out the trial.[37] However, a recent study of the conduct of the trial argues that this was more due to the prosecution over-

---

32   Pritchard, 'Overview', p. 93.

33   Boister and Cryer, *Tokyo International Military Tribunal*, p. 80; Röling and Cassese, *Tokyo Trial*, p. 37.

34   Higurashi, 'Tōkyō saiban', pp. 37-38.

35   Ibid., p. 37.

36   Boister and Cryer, *Tokyo International Military Tribunal*, p. 80; Higurashi, 'Tōkyō saiban', 39-49; Röling and Cassese, *Tokyo Trial*, p. 37.

37   Boister and Cryer, *Tokyo International Military Tribunal*, p. 80.

reaching itself in its indictments and the laxness of the bench.[38] The Japanese lawyers appeared to have their own reservations about the American strategy,[39] but acquiesced. None of the factions communicated well with each other, nor did the ministries whose interests they represented.

In conclusion, the factionalism of the defence team throws a somewhat more differentiated light on the relative success of their strategies. Neither the 'American' strategy of technical defence nor the 'military' strategy of justifying Japan's wars as legitimate found any strong supporters among the judges (at best, Judge Pal defended Japan's wars in the light of Western colonial expansion). However, the 'civil faction' gained most traction with its strategy, namely casting doubt on the culpability of the civil leadership (as witnessed by Judge Röling's dissenting opinion)[40] and in general supporting the so-called 'Tokyo trial historical perspective' (*Tokyo saiban shikan*) which saw the real culprits in a militant minority that had hijacked the reins of the state and led a docile and deceived majority into destruction.[41] However, it was less successful in the real mainstay of its defence, namely that international law did not allow *ex post facto* punishment at all. As the following section will demonstrate in a contextual interpretation of Takayanagi Kenzō's defence, this was because the argument was already unconvincing from the Japanese perspective itself.

Takayanagi Kenzō, the Tokyo Trial and International Law

Takayanagi Kenzō was the chief counsel for Shigemitsu Mamoru and Suzuki Teiichi and, by the personal request of Foreign Minister Yoshida Shigeru and Justice Minister Iwata Chūzō, a central figure in the preparation of the Japanese defence.[42] As such, he belonged to the 'civil' faction of counsels in the defence team.

Takayanagi is often introduced as a professor of international law at Tokyo University[43] yet, based on his publication record, his real expertise lay in Anglo-American law (and some legal philosophy and history). Before the Tokyo trial, Takayanagi had produced no publications in the field of international law, but a large number of studies on English commercial law, the Anglo-American

---

38   Ibid. pp. 97ff.
39   Röling and Cassese, *Tokyo Trial*, p. 37.
40   Ibid. p. 38.
41   Ōnuma, *Tōkyō saiban*, p. 128.
42   Higurashi, 'Tōkyō saiban', 37.
43   E.g. Boister and Cryer, *Tokyo International Military Tribunal*, p. 79.

legal system, and even a translation of Roscoe Pound's *Law and Morals* (1924).[44] Thus it is quite clear that Takayanagi had not been invited to join the defence for his expertise in international law, but for his familiarity with the Anglo-American legal system and his linguistic abilities.

It was quite common that law professors (mostly from Tokyo Imperial University) would act as advisors or counsels for the Japanese government, particularly in the pre-war period.[45] Therefore, Takayanagi arguably also acted in a semi-official function when he delivered a lecture at Chatham House on 10 November 1938 entitled 'A Japanese View of the Struggle in the Far East'.[46] Although Takayanagi professed to speak solely in an academic and private function, the following discussion (also recorded) clearly indicates that the audience readily understood his role as unofficial diplomat, justifying Japan's war with China (in fact, sending high-ranking intellectuals abroad to sway adverse foreign opinion during a war was already an established practice of the Japanese government[47]). In his address, Takayanagi explained that Japan's actions in China were solely the product of circumstance, blaming the pressure of capitalism brought to Japan by the Western powers, and the lack of resources that forced Japan to (peacefully) advance into North-east Asia, as all other parts of the world had been already occupied by Western powers. However, the Kuomintang had blocked access to Chinese markets and also incited the population against the Japanese. These were the roots of the present war in China. Takayanagi thus effectively blamed the Western powers for Japan's conundrum in East Asia. Moreover, he showed himself particularly disappointed in the League of Nations, whose failure he attributed to a premature and misguidedly idealistic internationalism:

> The majority of the people of various nations are in reality not yet in a mood to accept a vague loyalty to a world authority at the cost of the destiny of their own countries which actually protect their life and property.... The League of Nations made its appearance all of a sudden, swayed

---

44   Roscoe Pound, *Hō to dōtoku*, transl. Takayanagi Kenzō and Iwata Arata (Tokyo: Iwanami, 1929).

45   Y. Ōnuma, '"Japanese International Law" in the Prewar Period – Perspectives on the Teaching and Research of International Law in Prewar Japan', *The Japanese Annual of International Law*, 29 (1986), 33. This role, however, gradually became lost in the post-war period.

46   Published in *International Affairs* (Royal Institute of International Affairs), vol. 18, no. 1 (1939), 29-55.

47   See R.B. Valliant, 'The Selling of Japan: Japanese Manipulation of Western Opinion, 1900-1905', *Monumenta Nipponica*, vol. 29, no. 4 (1974), 415-38.

by elevated sentiment created by the World War, but without necessary psychological preparations.... Whether we like it or not, we must for the present endeavour to build up international peace based upon a different organisation of force.[48]

To this end, Takayanagi proposed 'the establishment of a system somewhat along the lines of the British Commonwealth of Nations. The Commonwealth of East-Asian Nations may be visualised.'[49] Currying favour with the British audience, this was at the same time a transparent justification of the 'New Order in East Asia' declared exactly one week earlier (on 3 November 1938) by the Konoe Cabinet in Tokyo.[50] Takayanagi's lecture – assuming it also reflected his personal opinion – thus places him firmly in the tradition of mainstream Japanese thought on international order and international law at the time, which was characterized by a strong realism and a strategic scepticism towards any form of multilateralism or supranationalism, including international adjudication of crimes.[51] This perspective would also shape his defence at the trial.

Ten years later, in March 1948, Takayanagi delivered the Japanese response to the Chief Prosecutor's argument at the IMTFE, which he published the same year in Japanese and English under the parallel title *Kyokutō saiban to kokusaihō / The Tokio* [sic] *Trials and International Law*. It was the sum and centrepiece of Takayanagi's defence and, at the same time, of the Japanese defence in general. However, as such, it was strangely ineffective and lacklustre, almost as if Takayanagi did not believe in his own arguments.

Reading the treatise, one is struck by the almost monomaniacal obsessiveness with which Takayanagi focuses on one single argument throughout, namely the principle of *nullum crimen nulla poena sine lege*, i.e. the principle of legality which prohibits the retroactive criminalization and sanctioning of actions *ex post facto*. This was, as we have seen, the core strategy of the 'civil' faction which, rather than arguing for the legitimacy of Japan's wars, sought to cut the prosecution off at the knees by insisting on the illegitimacy of the charges themselves.

---

48   Takayanagi, 'A Japanese View of the Struggle', 30-31.

49   Ibid., 42.

50   See R. Brown, 'The Konoe Cabinet's 'Declaration of a New Order in East Asia. 1938', in S. Saaler and C. Szpilman (eds.), *Pan-Asianism: A Documentary History* (Lanham: Rowman and Littlefield, 2011), vol. 2, pp. 167-73.

51   For this, see U.M. Zachmann, 'Does Europe Include Japan? – European Normativity in Japanese Attitudes towards International Law, 1854-1945', *Rechtsgeschichte – Legal History* 22 (Sept. 2014), 228-43; Zachmann, *Völkerrechtsdenken und Außenpolitik in Japan, 1919-1960* (Baden-Baden: Nomos, 2013).

Already the opening line, 'Law is a common consciousness of obligation' (foreword, p. 1), addresses this argument, and the whole treatise is an explication of it, namely that, neither in Japan nor among the Allied powers, had there existed before the trials a 'common consciousness' (thus invoking again his 1938 argument against the League of Nations) that war, even illegal war, should be criminalized and that individual persons should be penalized for it. This, however, was the prerequisite for law, whether codified or customary, and therefore the trials had no legal grounds. Although Takayanagi in the following sections addresses the arguments of the Chief Prosecutor's indictments point by point, this is the red line that runs throughout his argumentation.

The argument, as it is well known, has remained the pillar of opposition against the verdict even today, bolstered by Judge Pal's dissenting opinion in which he equally rested his rejection on this contention. However, as intuitive and convincing the argument seems at first sight, from the perspective of international law it is misleading and beside the point. It is highly doubtful that the principle of legality was binding in international law at the time of the Tokyo trials.[52] The Nuremberg judges discussed this and, in a somewhat contorted way of saying so, rejected the idea that the principle was legally binding under all circumstances:

> [T]he maxim 'nullum crimen sine lege' is not a limitation of sovereignty but is in general a principle of justice. To assert that it is unjust to punish those who in defiance of treaties and assurances have attacked neighbouring states without warning is obviously untrue for in such circumstances the attacker must know that he is doing wrong, and so far from it being unjust to punish him, it would be unjust if his wrong were allowed to go unpunished (Nuremberg Judgment 217).

Strictly speaking, the principle *nullum crimen* has been binding in court cases of international criminal justice only since 2002, with the entering into force of the Rome Statute, which clearly codifies the applicable customary law in statutory definitions (Articles 6-8 Rome Statute) and precludes their retroactive application (Articles 11 and 24 Rome Statute).[53]

---

52   On the principle and its development, see C. Kreß, 'Nulla poena nullum crimen sine lege', in Rüdiger Wolfrum (ed.), *Max Planck Encyclopedia of Public International Law* (Oxford University Press, online edition, article last updated February 2010).

53   Kreß, 'Nullum crimen', no. 18.

Thus, Takayanagi's whole argument (as well as that of Pal and his acolytes) rested on a misunderstanding. The source of this is given by himself in a rather telling passage:

> The principle which the Chief Counsel invokes, viz: 'a principle that follows the needs of civilization and is a clear expression of the public conscience' ... may appear to untutored eyes as 'deserving of penalty according to the fundamental conceptions of a penal law and sound popular feeling.' As a matter of fact, such a vague principle when it actually operates in the administration of criminal justice is just as cruel and as oppressive as the penal doctrine which characterized the Third Reich.... The sentiment that punishment by ex post facto legislation is *sheer lynch law* in the guise of justice is not a product of the so-called Era of Enlightenment in Europe, but represents the universal conception of justice, ancient and modern, East and West ...[54]

Takayanagi here not only manages to insult his judges indirectly as 'Nazi judges', he also betrays the source of misunderstanding about the application of *nullum crimen* in the phrase 'sheer lynch law'. The stigma of 'lynching' only makes sense in a domestic context, where there is a monopoly of power and violence. However, international society, with its typically flat, horizontal structure, characteristically has no such monopoly of power, no state-like guarantor of security established on the basis of a social contract that obliges individuals to relinquish their arms. Takayanagi's use of the phrase 'lynch law' thus hints at a fundamental misunderstanding, assuming an analogous structure of the municipal and the international legal order. The fundamental difference of both legal spheres is also the reason why the principle of legality, although doubtless applicable to the municipal sphere, is not automatically applicable in the international order: it is exactly *because* there is no monopoly of power, including legislative power, that there is no law and wherefore it is nonsensical to absolutely demand a law before the fact that constitutes a crime.

Yet, even from Takayanagi's perspective, the insistence on a rather formalistic application of a principle of municipal law to international adjudication seems somewhat surprising and rings hollow, considering that the Japanese discourse on international law was imbued with a strong anti-formalist tendency towards arguments of natural and politicized law from the late nineteenth century onwards.[55] An early case of such a cavalier attitude towards

---

54   Takayanagi, *Kyokutō saiban*, English text, pp. 11-12 (emphasis added by author).
55   See Zachmann, 'Does Europe Include Japan?', 233ff.

the letter of international law would be, for example, Uchimura Kanzō's notorious justification of the Sino-Japanese War (1894-95):

> [W]e *have* a right to interfere, and it is our duty to interfere, when they are dying of hunger, when they are attacked by robbers, when our plain common-sense shows us that they are rapidly going toward the brink of destruction. *Laissez-faire* is a vicious principle if it means total indifference to all human souls... As we have said, legalities are manufacturable, and as such we attach but little value to them as justifiers of our cause; but considering what International Law demands, we believe we have been consistent with all its requirements.[56]

Equally, and more importantly, this anti-formalism culminated in the 1930s in a conscious politicization and historicization of international law that aimed at 'overcoming' the status quo of allegedly Western-centric positivism.[57] One of the main pillars of attack against Western-centric positivism was the rejection of municipal law as a model for international order and the insistence on the fundamental difference of the latter. The international lawyer Taoka Ryōichi in 1943 most famously argued against this facile analogy:

> Of course, international relations are a matter distant to us and their true appearance is hard to guess. Therefore, we are easily tempted to apply the phenomena of the domestic society in which we live and which is familiar to international relations and by way of analogy imagine the norms of the latter somehow to conform to the former.... Those scholars who claim the analogy of international law and national law, who are unconcerned about the social and political conditions of norms and do not pay much attention to the fundamental differences of the national and international society are much like gardeners who do not understand the difference of the quality of earth and think that if trees grow in one area, they can easily transplant them to another.[58]

---

56 K. Uchimura, 'Justification for [sic] the Korean War', in *Uchimura Kanzō zenshū* (Tokyo: Iwanami shoten, 1980-84), vol. 3, pp. 42-43 (emphasis as in the original).

57 On this, see T. Sakai, *Kindai Nihon no chitsujo-ron* (Tokyo: Iwanami, 2007); Zachmann, *Völkerrechtsdenken*, pp. 205-78.

58 R. Taoka, *Kokusaihō-gaku taikō*, vol. 1, 2nd ed. (Tokyo: Gensōdō, 1943), pp. 2, 4. All translations, if not otherwise indicated, are those of the author.

Thus Taoka argued for understanding more precisely the specific characteristics of international law through the analysis of its relation to the social and political context which produced the norms. This became the dominant mode of Japanese legal thought henceforth and also strongly shaped legal studies in post-war Japan. Taoka famously used this method in dissecting the Kellogg-Briand Pact of 1928 and declaring it 'void'.[59]

As we have seen in his 1938 speech, Takayanagi clearly shared the distaste of his colleague Taoka Ryōichi for the 1920s idealistic positivism of the 'Geneva sentiment with its supra-state ideologies'.[60] He even agreed with his pre-war colleagues in rejecting the facile state-international order analogy in quoting John Bassett Moore who denounced

> Genevan international law ... proceeding as they did on the facile assumption that there was a close analogy between the law within a State and the international system ... as a 'bedlam theory', destructive of sound international law.[61]

However, for obvious reasons, Takayanagi could not make the logical and consistent step, namely rejecting on these grounds the principle of *nullum crimen* as well, as this would have left him eventually defenceless during the trial. It would have rendered Japan in the same position in which Takayanagi in fact saw Germany, namely under the absolute jurisdictive powers of the Allies:

> They could, if they liked, behave as an absolute monarch like Louis XIV. They could, if they were so minded, set up a Tribunal to punish those persons they disfavoured by laying down an *ex-post-facto* law, the rule of abstention from such legislation being a principle of justice not absolutely binding on their sovereign authority.... The discussion of international law in the Nuremberg decision is, therefore, a sort of *obiter dictum*, a display of learning which was not strictly necessary for the judgment itself.[62]

Arguing from this politicized perspective, it was patently impossible to maintain a credible defence solely based on the formalistic, and ultimately

---

59 See U.M. Zachmann, 'TAOKA Ryoichi's Contribution to International Legal Studies in Pre-War Japan: With Special Reference to Questions of the Law of War', *Japanese Yearbook of International Law*, 57 (2014), 134-162.

60 Takayanagi, *Kyokutō saiban*, English text, p. 26.

61 Ibid., p. 26.

62 Ibid., pp. 1ff.

unsuitable, notion of *nullum crimen*. Eventually, Takayanagi in his own defence speech gave the best arguments why adjudication in the Tokyo trial, despite reservations from a domestic positivist point of view, was legitimate from an international perspective. This legitimacy, moreover, was completely in tune with the traditional pre-war Japanese perspective on international law and order as intrinsically realist and politicized. Therefore, if Takayanagi protested against the unfairness of 'victor's justice' at the Tokyo trial, this was ultimately against his and his colleagues' own long-held convictions. It is probably this conflicted mindset which Judge Röling claimed to have observed during the trial:

> Someone described the attitude of the Japanese lawyers as 'putting flowers gracefully upon the grave of their client'.[63] There is some truth in that. They seemed to have given up. They had lost the war, and they realized that their actions would be condemned. They just wanted to prove to the world that what they did, from a certain point of view, could be understood and perhaps justified.[64]

In this sense, the Tokyo trial really was a 'show trial', even from the Japanese perspective, as it seemed merely an opportunity to present an alternative interpretation of the facts.[65] The legal argument was never meant to convince.

The Perspective of the Japanese Legal Community

The speciousness of the Japanese counsels' arguments in the Tokyo trial stand out even more clearly when compared with the comments of their peers and public opinion.

The Japanese legal community remained largely intact and weathered defeat and occupation rather well. Despite the fact that most law professors had supported the war actively in some way or another, only a few of them were purged from their offices after the war. This applied to the legal community in general, as all professions in the legal field, such as judges and public prosecutors, were not subject to the 'Removal and Exclusion of Undesirable

---

63   The phrase is also quoted in Ireland, 'Uncommon Law', 71.

64   Röling and Cassese, *Tokyo Trial*, p. 38.

65   On the Tokyo trial as 'show trial', see N. Boister, 'The Tokyo Military Tribunal: A Show Trial?', in M. Bergsmo, W.L. Cheah and P. Yi (eds.), *Historical Origins of International Law* (Brussels: Torkel Opsahl, 2014), vol. 2, pp. 3-30.

Personnel from Office' as ordered by SCAP.[66] However, what changed was that, whereas before the war lawyers had worked for the government and behind the closed doors of ministries, in the immediate post-war period, many of them turned public intellectuals and often voiced their opinion against the government.[67] This coincided with a general and rather sudden shift in public discourse from strong nationalist support of wartime goals to ardent support of 'peace and democracy' as the new mantra immediately after surrender.[68] Thus many academics and lawyers conveniently forgot their past and, in the process, rather ingeniously translated their pre-war thought into the conditions of post-war democracy.[69]

In this spirit, the Japanese public accepted the trial quite readily, albeit for transparent reasons: not for the prosecution of 'crimes against peace', but because their leaders had led them into war and untold hardship and therefore deserved punishment.[70] Moreover, the 'Tokyo trial narrative', as we have seen, exculpated the common people as being deceived by a military minority. Political parties, too, used the trial rather strategically to attack their opponents for their past misdeeds and present themselves as the champions of the new democracy.[71]

The Japanese legal community was no exception to this and demonstrated a similar flexibility under new circumstances.[72] As could be expected, most

---

66   K. Obata, 'Historical Functions of Monism with Primacy of International Law – A View Based on the Japanese Experience during the Early Period of the Allied Occupation', *The Japanese Annual of International Law*, 49 (2006), 13.

67   Zachmann, *Völkerrechtsdenken*, pp. 293-95; Y. Ōnuma, '"Japanese International Law" in the Postwar Period – Perspectives on the Teaching and Research of International Law in Prewar Japan', *The Japanese Annual of International Law*, 33 (1990), 48; on the role of experts as 'public intellectuals' in the early post-war period, see J.V. Koschmann, 'Intellectuals and Politics', in Andrew Gordon (ed.), *Postwar Japan as History* (Berkeley: University of California Press, 1993), pp. 395ff.

68   On this shift, see J. Dower, 'Peace and Democracy in Two Systems: External Policy and Internal Conflict', in Gordon, *Postwar Japan as History*, pp. 3-6.

69   On this, see U.M. Zachmann, 'Sublimating the Empire: How Japanese Experts of International Law Translated "Greater East Asia" into the Postwar Period', in B. Kushner and S. Muminov (eds.), *The End of Empire and Japan's Search for Legitimacy* (London: Routledge, 2017), pp. 167-81.

70   On the popular perception of Japan, see Ōnuma, *Tōkyō saiban*, pp. 126ff.; Futamura, *War Crimes Tribunals*, pp. 69-71.

71   Ōnuma, *Tōkyō saiban*, pp. 136ff.

72   On the reaction of legal experts, see Totani, *Tokyo War Crimes Trial*, pp. 189-217; Futamura, *War Crimes Tribunals*, pp. 71ff.; P. Osten, *Der Tokioter Kriegsverbrecherprozeß und die japanische Rechtswissenschaft* (Berliner Wissenschaftsverlag, 2003), pp. 130-61.

public statements on the Tokyo trial came from experts in criminal and international law. The overwhelming majority of legal experts saw the war crimes trial as a necessary reckoning with the 'feudalistic' past of Japan and a demonstration of the new values of democracy and human rights in legal practice. Thus the Japanese civil law expert Kainō Michitaka (1908-75) published in April 1948 a comment in which he fully endorsed the trial, as Japan clearly had fought an 'aggressive war' that was also clearly criminal. Kainō argued that invoking the *nullum crimen* principle in this case would contradict the general principle of justice: considering its origin, the principle was supposed to protect individuals from oppressive rulers, not such states from their own wrongdoings.[73] This statement is all the more remarkable when considering that Kainō at the same time acted as Associate Counsel for Suzuki Teiichi in the IMTFE and thus worked under none other than Takayanagi Kenzō (who was Suzuki's Chief Counsel).

However, Kainō reconfirmed his assessment of the trial in another article in 1953 in which he declared it a 'revolutionary trial' (*kakumei saiban*) that could not apply the *nullum crimen* principle by necessity:

> A revolutionary trial always applies ex post facto law, and it always rejects the norm or the principle that no punishment can be meted out without pre-existing law.... This kind of switchover in political ethics may appear to be loathsome confusion for those who love orderliness. However, the matter at issue is that no revolution can ever take place if revolutionaries do not possess the right to punish those who suppress revolution.... In this respect, revolution does not know law.[74]

This politicized natural-law approach was most common among Japanese lawyers commenting on the Tokyo trial at the time. It was particularly remarkable and conspicuous in the cases of lawyers who, until the end of the war, had been steadfast legal positivists and thus opposed the majority of their colleagues who had wanted to 'overcome' the allegedly Western-oriented legal status quo in favour of an 'East Asian law'. Yet, facing the Tokyo trial, they were forced to overcome their own positivism and assume the politicized approach they previously opposed in order to defend the trial. There are a number of such cases as, for example, the criminal law expert Dandō Shigemitsu (1913-2012) who

---

73   Kainō, 'Sensō saiban no hōritsu riron' [The legal theory of war crimes trials], *Rekishi hyōron*, April 1948, as summarized in Totani, *Tokyo War Crimes Trial*, pp. 197ff.

74   Kainō, 'Kyokutō saiban: sono go' [The Tokyo Trial: afterwards], 1953, as translated in Totani, *Tokyo War Crimes Trial*, p. 214.

published one of the first positive comments on the Tokyo trial in June 1946.[75] During the war, Dandō had pursued an emphatically positivist position and thus managed to keep out of politics.[76] However, in 1946, he clearly came out in favour of the trial and declared the *nullum crimen* principle inapplicable, for much the same reasons as Kainō did.

Arguably the most remarkable volte face in terms of legal philosophy, if not conviction, could be seen in the case of the leading international law expert Yokota Kisaburō who, in 1947, published a long study entitled *Sensō hanzai ron* [On war crimes]. The work is considered, even today, a benchmark study of the subject in Japan.[77] Yokota was well qualified to speak on the subject with academic and moral authority. As a professor of international law at Tokyo Imperial University, he had been one of the very few who had openly criticized the actions of the Kwantung Army in Manchuria in 1931 as obviously 'excessive' and therefore, as a matter of course, subject to the scrutiny of the League of Nations. For this, he was harshly criticized and even threatened with murder by ultranationalists.[78] However, in the early post-war period, the same position functioned, as it were, as a moral carte blanche and made Yokota an authority on the subject in the public's eyes. Yokota made good use of this opportunity and in a whirlwind of writing and lecturing all across the country sought to spread his utopian ideals of international adjudication and global governance.[79] His study of 'war crimes' belongs to this phase.

From pre-war times, Yokota had been a staunch supporter of international institutions and jurisdiction. Therefore, it is quite understandable that Yokota took a very positive perspective of the Tokyo trial and was a passionate supporter of it. His verdict was clear:

> In hindsight, since the Manchurian Incident and for fifteen years, Japan, driven by the military and the bureaucracy, has waged an extremely aggressive war and has executed one imperialist attack after another on the principle of the survival of the fittest [*jakuniku kyōshoku*]. It ignored treaties, scorned justice and has committed horrendous atrocities. It is obvious to everyone today that this was wrong.[80]

---

75   See Totani, *Tokyo War Crimes Trial*, pp. 190-95; Osten, *Tokioter Kriegsverbrecherprozeß*, pp. 139-42.

76   Osten, *Tokioter Kriegsverbrecherprozeß*, p. 135.

77   Ibid., p. 153.

78   Zachmann, *Völkerrechtsdenken*, pp. 114-16, 191-95.

79   Ibid., pp. 304-15.

80   Yokota, *Sensō hanzai ron*, p. 6.

Considering this, Yokota followed the Chief Prosecutor (and the Nuremberg judges) in arguing that the technicality of *nullum crimen* should give way to consideration of the gravity of the crimes:

> The most important thing, however, is the substance [*jisshitsu*], i.e. whether in substance a crime has been committed and whether therefore there is reason to punish it or not. If in substance there is sufficient reason, one should not go against one's better knowledge and feel constricted by merely petty formalistic considerations. It cannot be that just because of a mere formal requirement, a simple legal technicality, we ignore the substance of the matter.[81]

Thus, despite formal concerns, Yokota justified his impassioned support for the Tokyo trial as a matter of substantive justice. In light of the tradition of anti-formalism pointed out above, this recourse to the natural law idea of a 'transcending justice' should not surprise us. In fact, Yokota's line of argument was but the continuation of Takayanagi's reservations against 1920s positivism and its formalistic argumentation, and in line with the majority opinion. However, Yokota's 'switchover' to the majority met with criticism from his peers.

One reason for this criticism was that Yokota's intervention did not seem disinterested. In fact, one year before Japan had surrendered, Yokota had already begun to study the implications of an international post-war order under American leadership. Once occupation started, Yokota set up a 'study group' which researched the legal implications of occupation, and became a close advisor of SCAP, also in the preparation of the Tokyo trial. Once the judgment had been handed down, he and other colleagues helped SCAP to prepare the official translation of it. Therefore, some of his colleagues saw Yokota as a spokesperson, as it were, of the American occupation and saw this as an intervention ex parte which lacked objectivity.[82]

However, at an even more fundamental level, Yokota's argumentation lacked credibility in that it went against the grain of the position which he had held in pre-war times. In fact, Yokota had been the most influential proponent of the 'Geneva sentiment with its supra-state ideologies' (Takayanagi) in the 1920s and 1930s. Moreover, if Taoka Ryōichi rebelled against '[t]hose scholars who claim the analogy of international law and national law', this was an invective predominantly directed against his colleague Yokota Kisaburō. Yokota was

---

81   Ibid., p. 5.
82   Zachmann, *Völkerrechtsdenken*, pp. 337ff.

famous for publishing a textbook in 1933 in which he developed an international law fully modelled on the structures of municipal law, with a division of powers, a central executive body, an administrative law, and war as 'crime' or 'tort', just as in (Continental) civil law.[83] Yokota himself admitted at the time that the current level of codification and institution-building did not support such a structure in reality, but considered the state analogy as the best way to advance international law towards this goal of 'world government'.

From such a perspective, Yokota's post-war cavalier treatment of the principle of legality as a core tenet of municipal law was a rather bold and somewhat implausible deviation from his former position. It undermined his position to credibly support the Tokyo trial in the way he did. This, if anything, illustrates the strong 'pull' which a realist, politicized interpretation of international law, i.e. an affirmative view of 'victor's justice' exerted on the Japanese legal community at the time.

Conclusion

As the above cases illustrate, the Tokyo trial put Japanese lawyers in a quandary. No matter on which side they stood regarding the trial, Japanese lawyers had to argue from a position which they, given different circumstances and different cases (such as, for example, Germany's) would or should have rejected on the basis of their previously held opinions. This is most apparent in the case of Takayanagi Kenzō, one of the leaders of the Japanese defence in the trial. Ostensibly, Takayanagi had to reject the legitimacy of the trial on the grounds of the *nullum crimen* principle. However, this clearly went against the Japanese pre-war tradition of a highly politicized interpretation of international law, an interpretation which Takayanagi shared. Thus, his own arguments inadvertently supported the Chief Prosecutor's case. Moreover, as other voices outside the courtroom show, the pre-war tradition was still very much alive among his peers and the general public, who openly supported the trial. This is most apparent in the positions of legal experts (like Yokota Kisaburō) who had steadfastly clung to legal positivism as a shield against the politicization of the law in pre-war times but saw themselves forced to abandon this position in the post-war period in order to justify the trial, which they considered just from their *political* beliefs.

Contextualizing the Japanese defence and the opinion of the legal community in the tradition of a realist, politicized view of international law therefore

---

83   Ibid., pp. 116-19.

helps to explain two things: firstly, the strangely unconvincing and lacklustre strategy of the Japanese defence; and secondly, the ingrained nature of the concept of 'victor's justice' in this tradition which, at first, led to an affirmative view of the trial, only to be repositioned again, in later decades, to fit a more polemic, nationalist agenda.[84] In each case, one should be aware that the assertion of 'victor's justice' is but the mirror of the speaker's own underlying assumptions about the nature of law and politics.

Bibliography

Neil Boister, 'The Tokyo Military Tribunal: A Show Trial?', in Morten Bergsmo, Cheah Wui Ling and Yi Ping (eds.), *Historical Origins of International Law*, vol. 2 (Brussels: Torkel Opsahl, 2014), pp. 3-30.

Neil Boister and Robert Cryer, *The Tokyo International Military Tribunal: A Reappraisal* (Oxford University Press, 2008).

Neil Boister and Robert Cryer (eds.), 'Introduction', in *Documents on the Tokyo International Military Tribunal: Charter, Indictment and Judgments* (Oxford University Press, 2008).

Roger Brown, 'The Konoe Cabinet's "Declaration of a New Order in East Asia". 1938', in Sven Saaler and Christopher Szpilman (eds.), *Pan-Asianism: A Documentary History* (Lanham: Rowman and Littlefield, 2011), vol. 2, pp. 167-73.

Robert Cryer, Håkan Friman, Darryl Robinson and Elizabeth Wilmshurst, *Introduction to International Criminal Law* (Cambridge University Press, 2007).

John Dower, 'Peace and Democracy in Two Systems: External Policy and Internal Conflict', in Andrew Gordon (ed.), *Postwar Japan as History* (Berkeley: University of California Press, 1993).

John Dower, *Embracing Defeat: Japan in the Wake of World War II* (New York: W.W. Norton, 1999).

Madoka Futamura, *War Crimes Tribunals and Transitional Justice* (London: Routledge, 2008).

Madoka Futamura, 'Japanese Societal Attitude towards the Tokyo Trial: From a Contemporary Perspective', in Yuki Tanaka, Tim L.H. McCormack and Gerry J. Simpson (eds.), *Beyond Victor's Justice? The Tokyo War Crimes Trial Revisited* (Leiden: Martinus Nijhoff Publishers, 2011), pp. 35-54.

---

84   For this negative development of opinion, see Totani, *Tokyo War Crimes Trial*, pp. 219ff; Futamura, *War Crimes Tribunals*, pp. 72-85.

Yoshinobu Higurashi, 'Tōkyō saiban no bengo-gawa: Nihon-jin bengo-dan no seiritsu to Amerika-jin bengonin', *Kagoshima daigaku shakai kagaku zasshi*, 16 (Sept. 1993), 29-57.

Solis Horwitz, 'The Tokyo Trial', *International Conciliation*, 465 (Nov. 1950), 475-584.

E.M. Hyder, 'The Tokyo Trial', *Texas Bar Journal*, 10.4 (1947).

Gordon Ireland, 'Uncommon Law in Martial Tokyo', *The Yearbook of World Affairs*, 4 (1950), 54-104.

Keiichirō Kobori, *Tōkyō saiban: Nihon no benmei* (Tokyo: Kōdansha, 1995).

J. Victor Koschmann, 'Intellectuals and Politics', in Andrew Gordon (ed.), *Postwar Japan as History* (Berkeley: University of California Press, 1993), pp. 395-423.

Claus Kreß, 'Nulla poena nullum crimen sine lege', in Rüdiger Wolfrum (ed.), *Max Planck Encyclopedia of Public International Law* (Oxford University Press, online edition, article last updated February 2010).

Richard Minear, *Victors' Justice: The Tokyo War Crimes Trial* (Princeton University Press, 1971).

Kaoru Obata 'Historical Functions of Monism with Primacy of International Law – A View Based on the Japanese Experience during the Early Period of the Allied Occupation', *The Japanese Annual of International Law*, 49 (2006), 1-35.

Yasuaki Ōnuma, *Tōkyō saiban, sensō sekinin, sengo sekinin* (Tokyo: Tōshindō, 2007).

Yasuaki Ōnuma, 'Japanese International Law' in the Prewar Period – Perspectives on the Teaching and Research of International Law in Prewar Japan', *The Japanese Annual of International Law*, 29 (1986), 23-47.

Yasuaki Ōnuma, '"Japanese International Law" in the Postwar period – Perspectives on the Teaching and Research of International Law in Prewar Japan', *The Japanese Annual of International Law*, 33 (1990), 25-53.

Philipp Osten, *Der Tokioter Kriegsverbrecherprozeß und die japanische Rechtswissenschaft* (Berliner Wissenschaftsverlag, 2003).

R. John Pritchard, 'An Overview of the Historical Importance of the Tokyo Trial', in Chihiro Hosoya, Nisuke Andō, Yasuaki Ōnuma and Richard Minear (eds.), *The Tokyo War Crimes Trial* (Tokyo: Kōdansha International, 1986), pp. 89-97.

B.V.A. Röling and Antonio Cassese, *The Tokyo Trial and Beyond: Reflections of a Peace-monger* (Cambridge: Polity Press, 1993).

Tetsuya Sakai, *Kindai Nihon no chitsujo-ron* (Tokyo: Iwanami, 2007).

Bruno Simma, 'The Impact of Nuremberg and Tokyo: Attempts at a Comparison', in Nisuke Ando (ed.), *Japan and International Law: Past, Present and Future* (The Hague Kluwer Law International, 1999), pp. 59-84.

Gerry J. Simpson, *Law, War and Crime: War Crimes Trials and the Reinvention of International Law* (Malden, Mass.: Polity Press, 2007).

Ryōichi Taoka, *Kokusaihō-gaku taikō*, vol. 1, 2nd ed. (Tokyo: Gensōdō, 1943).

Kenzō Takayanagi, 'A Japanese View of the Struggle in the Far East', *International Affairs* (Royal Institute of International Affairs), vol. 18, no. 1 (1939), 29-55.

Kenzō Takayanagi, *Kyokutō saiban to kokusaihō* / *The Tokio Trials and International Law* (Tokyo: Yūhikaku, 1948).

Yuki Tanaka, Tim L.H. McCormack and Gerry J. Simpson (eds.), *Beyond Victor's Justice? The Tokyo War Crimes Trial Revisited* (Leiden: Martinus Nijhoff Publishers, 2011).

Yuma Totani, *The Tokyo War Crimes Trial: The Pursuit of Justice in the Wake of World War II* (Cambridge, Mass.: Harvard University Asia Center, 2008).

Robert B. Valliant, 'The Selling of Japan: Japanese Manipulation of Western Opinion, 1900-1905', *Monumenta Nipponica*, vol. 29, no. 4 (1974), 415-38.

Kanzo Uchimura, 'Justification for [sic] the Korean War', in *Uchimura Kanzō zenshū* (Tokyo: Iwanami shoten: 1980-84), vol. 3, pp. 38-48.

Kei Ushimura, *Beyond the 'Judgment of Civilization': The Intellectual Legacy of the Japanese War Crimes Trial, 1946-49* (Tokyo: International House of Japan, 2003).

Kisaburo Yokota, *Sensō hanzai ron* (Tokyo: Yūhikaku, 1947).

Urs Matthias Zachmann, 'Does Europe Include Japan? – European Normativity in Japanese Attitudes towards International Law, 1854-1945', *Rechtsgeschichte – Legal History*, 22 (Sept. 2014), 228-43.

Urs Matthias Zachmann, 'Sublimating the Empire: How Japanese Experts of International Law Translated "Greater East Asia" into the Postwar Period', in B. Kushner and S. Muminov (eds.), *The End of Empire and Japan's Search for Legitimacy* (London: Routledge, 2017), pp. 167-81.

Urs Matthias Zachmann, 'TAOKA Ryoichi's Contribution to International Legal Studies in Pre-War Japan: With Special Reference to Questions of the Law of War', *Japanese Yearbook of International Law*, 57 (2014), 134-62.

Urs Matthias Zachmann, *Völkerrechtsdenken und Außenpolitik in Japan, 1919-1960* (Baden-Baden: Nomos, 2013).

The Composition of the Court at Tokyo[*]

Judges

The President: Sir William Webb, Australia, Justice of the High Court of Australia
Mei Ru'ao, Republic of China, Member of the Legislative Yuan
Edward Stuart McDougall, Canada, Former Judge, King's Bench Appeal Side
Henri Bernard, France, Chief Prosecutor, First Military Tribunal in Paris
Radhabinod Pal, India, Lecturer, University of Calcutta Law College
B.V.A. Röling, Netherlands, Professor of Law, Utrecht University
Harvey Northcroft, New Zealand, Judge Advocate General of New Zealand
Delfin Jaranilla, Philippines, Attorney General, Supreme Court Member
Lord Patrick, U.K., Judge, Senator of the College of Justice
John P. Higgins, U.S., Chief Justice, Massachusetts State Superior Court
Myron C. Cramer, U.S., replaced Judge Higgins in July 1946
I.M. Zarayanov, U.S.S.R, Member, Military Collegium of the Supreme Court

Prosecution

Chief of Counsel
Joseph. B. Keenan, U.S.
Alan Mansfield, Australia
Henry Nolan, Canada
Xiang Zhejun, Republic of China
Robert L. Oneto, France
P. Govinda Menon, India
W.G. Frederick Borgerhoff-Mulder, Netherlands
Ronald Quilliam, New Zealand
Pedro Lopez, Philippines
Arthur Comyns-Carr, U.K.
S.A. Golunsky, U.S.S.R.

Defence Counsel

Chief of Defence Counsel: Beverly M. Coleman
Chief of the Japanese Defence Section: Sōmei Uzawa
Associate Chief of the Japanese Defence Section: Ichirō Kiyose

---

[*] Pritchard, *Tokyo Trial* (1981), vol 1, part v, List of Judges and Defense Counsel.

Index